Accounting for Carbon

The ability to accurately monitor, report and verify greenhouse gas emissions is the cornerstone of any effective policy to mitigate climate change. *Accounting for Carbon* provides the first authoritative overview of the monitoring, reporting and verification (MRV) of emissions from the industrial site, project and company level to the regional and national level. It describes the MRV procedures in place in more than 15 of the most important policy frameworks – such as emissions trading systems in Europe, Australia, California and China, and the United Nations Framework Convention on Climate Change – and compares them along key criteria such as scope, cost, uncertainty and flexibility. This book draws on the work of engineers and economists to provide a practical guide to help government and non-governmental policy makers and key stakeholders in industry to better understand different MRV requirements, the key trade-offs faced by regulators and the choices made by up-and-running carbon pricing initiatives.

VALENTIN BELLASSEN is a researcher at Institut National pour la Recherche Agronomique (INRA) where he focuses on the economics of agro-ecology. He is also an accredited UNFCCC reviewer for national greenhouse gas inventories. For four years, he worked at CDC Climat where he managed the research unit on MRV, agriculture and forestry.

NICOLAS STEPHAN is an investment officer at CDC Climat where he is in charge of voluntary carbon offsetting as well as participations in innovative carbon investment vehicles. He worked for five years in the research department of CDC Climat on various topics related to carbon and energy markets.

Accounting for Carbon

Monitoring, Reporting and Verifying
Emissions in the Climate Economy

Edited by

VALENTIN BELLASSEN AND
NICOLAS STEPHAN

CAMBRIDGE
UNIVERSITY PRESS

CAMBRIDGE
UNIVERSITY PRESS

University Printing House, Cambridge CB2 8BS, United Kingdom

One Liberty Plaza, 20th Floor, New York, NY 10006, USA

477 Williamstown Road, Port Melbourne, VIC 3207, Australia

314-321, 3rd Floor, Plot 3, Splendor Forum, Jasola District Centre, New Delhi - 110025, India

103 Penang Road, #05-06/07, Visioncrest Commercial, Singapore 238467

Cambridge University Press is part of the University of Cambridge.

It furthers the University's mission by disseminating knowledge in the pursuit of education, learning and research at the highest international levels of excellence.

www.cambridge.org
Information on this title: www.cambridge.org/9781009243216

© Cambridge University Press 2015

First published 2015
First paperback edition 2022

A catalogue record for this publication is available from the British Library

Library of Congress Cataloging in Publication data
Accounting for carbon : monitoring, reporting and verifying emissions
in the climate economy / edited by Valentin Bellassen and Nicolas Stephan.
    pages   cm
Includes bibliographical references and index.
ISBN 978-1-107-09848-0 (hardback)
1. Greenhouse gases–Measurement.   2. Environmental monitoring.
3. Pollutants–Reporting.   4. Greenhouse gases–Government
policy.   5. Emissions trading.   6. Climatic changes–Economic
aspects.   I. Bellassen, Valentin, 1985–   II. Stephan, Nicolas.
TD885.5.G73A28   2015
363.738´7463–dc23
2014043078

ISBN   978-1-107-09848-0   Hardback
ISBN   978-1-009-24321-6   Paperback

Contents

v

Figures and map

Tables

Boxes

Contributors

Valentin Bellassen has worked as a researcher for the Environmental Defense Fund and as an international negotiator on forests at the UNFCCC, in the delegation of Papua New Guinea. For four years, he worked at CDC Climat where he managed the research unit on carbon offsets, agriculture and forestry. He is currently a researcher at INRA where he focuses on the economics of agro-ecology. He is also an accredited UNFCCC reviewer for national greenhouse gas inventories. Valentin graduated from École Normale Supérieure (Ulm) and holds a PhD in Environmental Sciences.

Nicolas Stephan worked for five years in the research department of CDC Climat on various topics related to carbon and energy markets. He was editor in chief of *Tendances Carbone*, a monthly publication which focuses on CO_2 prices. He is currently working in the investment department of CDC Climat, in charge of voluntary carbon offsetting as well as participations in innovative carbon investment vehicles. He holds a Master's in Economics and Business Management from Pantheon-Sorbonne University and a Master's in International Business from Paris-Dauphine University.

Marion Afriat works at CDC Climat and she focuses her research on the development of carbon markets in the world and on recent developments made in national carbon and energy efficiency policies among twenty countries. Marion has a Master's degree in International Relations from Paris II Assas University and Paris IV Sorbonne University.

Emilie Alberola is a research unit manager – European climate policy at CDC Climat. Her research work deals mostly with an analysis of the development of the European Union Emissions Trading Scheme and its carbon prices. She teaches carbon market economics in the 'Energy, Finance and Carbon' Master's program at Paris-Dauphine University and the 'Energy and Finance' Certificate at the HEC Paris business school. Emilie has a PhD in Economics from Pantheon-Sorbonne University and a Master's degree in Sustainable Development Management from HEC.

Alexandra Barker is a research scientist at NPL and holds an MSc in Environmental Protection and Management from the University of Edinburgh and a BSc in Geography from the University of Southampton. She has extensive experience in remote environmental sensing techniques for carbon measurement and is also involved in research projects investigating metrology improvements in carbon offsetting programs. Alexandra is also working in close collaboration with NPL's Centre for Carbon Measurement investigating forest carbon accounting.

Jean-Pierre Chang focuses on the coordination of national French emission inventories, greenhouse gases (for UNFCCC and Kyoto) and air pollutants (for UNECE). He was one of the architects of the European project "CORINAIR" which set the basis of the national air emission inventory systems for the Member States. He has a Postgraduate Diploma (DEA) in Chemistry–Physics from Paris VI – Pierre et Marie Curie University.

Caspar Chiquet is Head of Implementation for the Advisory Unit and manages the MRV practice of South Pole Carbon. He is responsible for monitoring and certifying emission reductions for 100+ installations throughout Greater China and providing consulting services in the field of monitoring, reporting and verification. He is an expert on IT questions and holds an MA from the University of Zürich in Chinese Studies and International Law and is business-fluent in Chinese.

Ian Cochran coordinates CDC Climat's research on the integration of climate change and the low-carbon energy transition into investment and finance decision-making. Focusing on the financial flows and instruments contributing to reducing greenhouse gas emissions, this work analyzes the methods and metrics to redirect capital towards the development of a low-carbon society. Ian holds a PhD degree in Economics from Université Paris-Dauphine. He also holds a Master of Public Affairs (MPA) from Sciences-Po Paris and a Bachelor's degree in Policy Studies from the Maxwell School-Syracuse University.

Mariana Deheza is a research fellow at CDC Climat. Mariana's fields of expertise include project mechanisms, in particular those linked to voluntary offsets and forestry projects. Before working for CDC Climat, Mariana worked for two years at the Bolivian Ministry of Development Planning on problems linked to the environment and the forestry industry. Mariana has a degree in Industrial Engineering from the Catholic University of La Paz in Bolivia, and an MSc in Environmental Economics from AgroParisTech-Ecole Polytechnique in Paris.

Chris Dimopoulos is a Higher Research Scientist at NPL and Team Leader in the Stack Emissions Environmental Measurement team. In addition to his role at NPL, Chris is a member of the CEN Committee for Air Quality TC 264. Chris holds an MSc in Environmental Engineering and Project Management from the University of Leeds and has over seven years of experience in all aspects of stack emission measurements including research and development of monitoring techniques. Chris is also involved in research investigating metrology improvements in GHG measurement.

Claudine Foucherot is a research fellow at CDC Climat and focuses her research on economic and political instruments to mitigate climate change in the agricultural sector. She is also in charge of the Climate and Agriculture Club, whose aim is to promote and share knowledge on technical and economic tools which can be used for climate change mitigation and adaptation in the agricultural sector. Trained as an agronomical engineer at AgroParisTech, Claudine has a Master's degree in the economics of sustainable development, energy and environment.

Guillaume Jacquier is a technical project manager at CITEPA. He is in charge of projects about the European Union Emissions Trading Scheme and gives training sessions on this subject. He also undertakes studies on air pollution in general, and emission inventories for the Ministry of Environment, subnational authorities or companies. Guillaume has a Master's degree in Energy, Combustion and Environment from the University of Orleans.

Romain Morel is a project manager at CDC Climat Research. He is in charge of analyzing policies and tools dedicated to the mobilization of public and private climate finance, including the monitoring of its impact and its efficiency. His research also focuses on international climate negotiations. He holds an MSc in Engineering from ISAE-SUPAERO and an MSc in Energy Economics from the IFP School.

Roderick Robinson is Principal Research Scientist with over 20 years' experience at NPL. He is scientific lead for emissions monitoring at NPL including fugitive emissions measurement using DIAL (Differential Absorption Lidar). In addition to his role at NPL, Rod is Vice Chairman of the CEN Committee for Air Quality TC 264.

Igor Shishlov works at CDC Climat and his research focuses on carbon offset projects as well as on monitoring, verification and reporting (MRV) of greenhouse gas emissions. Igor has also been a PhD student at AgroParisTech since September 2012. His thesis focuses on the economics of monitoring ecosystem services on the example of carbon offset projects. Igor holds an MSc in Sustainable Development from HEC Paris and a Diploma in International Business from St. Petersburg State University.

Acknowledgements

First and foremost, we would like to thank the sponsors of the MRV project, without whom this book would never have been written:

- Agence Française de Développement;
- EIT Climate-KIC;
- Ministère français de l'Agriculture, de l'Agroalimentaire et de la Forêt;
- Ministère français de l'Ecologie, du Développement Durable et de l'Energie;
- Union des Industries de la Fertilisation.

We are also grateful to Marco Loprieno (European Commission) and Massamba Thioye (UNFCCC) who accepted the invitation to discuss our findings at our MRV conference in June 2014. We also thank Xueman Wang and Pierre Guigon (Partnership for Market Readiness, The World Bank) for the useful connection provided with new carbon pricing mechanisms being developed in emerging economies.

Many more people contributed to this book through interviews, comments or reviews. Their contribution is acknowledged in the relevant chapters.

1 | Introduction: key notions and trade-offs involved in MRVing emissions

VALENTIN BELLASSEN AND IAN COCHRAN

1.1 Purpose and audience for this book

This book focuses on the monitoring, reporting and verification (MRV) of greenhouse gas emissions as it is practiced in the climate economy, that is in operational carbon pricing mechanisms as well as in the quantification of operational and territorial emissions for management purposes. It provides a description of the MRV procedures in place in the fifteen most important policy frameworks – national greenhouse gas inventories supervised by the United Nations, the European Emissions Trading System, the Australian carbon tax, the Clean Development Mechanism supervised by the United Nations, etc. – and compares them along key criteria such as scope, cost, uncertainty and flexibility. As such, this book does not consider other types of MRV than that of greenhouse gas emissions, such as the MRV of climate finance or the monitoring of the efficiency of climate policies, although they also have their place in climate economics.

This book leans heavily towards the practical problems and solutions employed by those involved in the MRV of existing frameworks. In other words, it describes how MRV is currently practiced by economic agents much more than how greenhouse gas emissions could or should be monitored, reported and verified based on the most recent developments in climate sciences or the deepest rooted economics theory. As such, this book does not consider the MRV of future frameworks for which there is no set of identifiable rules and practices such as the elusive and multiform Nationally Appropriate Mitigation Actions (NAMAs) for which plans are being communicated by various countries to the United Nations.

The audience for this book are those who wish to understand the key stakes attached to monitoring, reporting and verifying emissions, and the choices made by up-and-running carbon pricing initiatives

1

regarding these stakes. This book is written by engineers and economists active in this field, but for a general audience who may not be
proficient in climate economics or MRV procedures. This audience
includes:

- businesses involved in carbon pricing and willing to grasp what
  underpins the intangible commodity they buy or sell;
- regulators of existing or upcoming carbon pricing and management
  mechanisms who seek to benchmark their regulation against similar
  programs;
- technology and service providers looking to assess the added value
  they can bring to existing practices in terms of cost-effectiveness;
- academics, in particular those working on the transaction costs
  associated with monitoring.

1.2 Climate economics at work

Carbon pricing mechanisms are incentives for a set of economic stakeholders to reduce their greenhouse gas emissions. The incentive is
often a hard economic one (e.g., a carbon tax), but it can take softer
forms, such as reputational incentives attached to meeting an emissions reduction pledge for a country, local government or a company,
or branding incentives derived from environmental labeling (e.g.,
carbon footprint of products). The first explicit economic incentive
to reduce greenhouse gas emissions was created by a bilateral contract between two private actors – an electricity producer and a forest
owner – in 1989 (Bellassen and Leguet, 2009). However, carbon pricing mechanisms only started to bloom in the 1990s. This occurred
first in the form of carbon taxes in a few countries such as Sweden
and Denmark, and then, in the early 2000s, as cap-and-trade system
and offset mechanisms which create a supply and a demand for greenhouse gas emissions reductions among nations and businesses.

In 2013, implemented and scheduled emissions trading schemes and
carbon taxes put an explicit carbon price on at least 7 percent of the
world's emissions (World Bank, 2013). They are being implemented
in all countries of the European Union, in some American States and
Canadian Provinces and in Asia (Japan, South Korea, some Chinese
provinces). The largest listed companies made their carbon footprint
part of their reputation through the Carbon Disclosure Project (2,132

reporting companies in 2011). The same goes for industrialized countries through the United Nations Framework Convention on Climate Change (UNFCCC) and, to a lesser extent, to local governments and economic actors through national reporting requirements. In a nutshell, carbon is now an important asset for many public and private stakeholders. It is nevertheless quite a peculiar asset, as it is intangible, invisible and odorless. These characteristics make the MRV of greenhouse gas emissions all the more crucial, as the only concrete link between the physical world and these large but intangible markets and mandates.

Climate economics are currently undergoing far-reaching changes. The European Union Emissions Trading System and the Clean Development Mechanism, which together made up 99 percent of carbon markets in 2011 value, are imperiled: as of June 2013, carbon allowances in the European Emissions Trading Scheme plummeted by 70 percent to around €5/tCO$_2$e in two years' time while carbon credits issued by the Clean Development Mechanism are not worth more than 50 euro cents (Bellassen et al., 2012; World Bank, 2013). This stupendous fall raises questions on the very relevance and effectiveness of cap-and-trade mechanisms and has revived discussion of alternative solutions such as carbon taxes in Europe. At the same time, new local cap-and-trade schemes are being enacted in other parts of the world such as the US and China.

International agreements on climate change do not look healthier than European carbon markets. The clout of the Kyoto Protocol is also fading: it will at most cap 14 percent of global emissions between 2013 and 2020 (Morel et al., 2013) following the withdrawal of Canada, Russia and Japan. Yet, its successor due by the end of 2015 is far from having disentangled the thorny question of effort sharing between signatory parties.

MRV procedures stand through this storm as one of the few solid pillars of climate action. Indeed, the need for MRV is a common feature of all the possible future carbon pricing mechanisms, be they carbon taxes, cap-and-trade systems, environmental labeling or carbon footprint disclosure. Moreover, while national governments have historically been reluctant to commit to emissions caps in an international agreement, they all stand to gain in common methods and procedures to quantify emissions occurring elsewhere – whether internationally or subnationally. This is probably why MRV is one of the fastest-moving topics in international climate negotiations, and one of the most likely to succeed (Dupont et al., 2013). This is why we believe that a reference book on MRV in climate economics is timely and that its relevance will not be decreased as the details of upcoming carbon pricing mechanisms unfold.

1.3 Scale, scope, uncertainty and related trade-offs: key definitions and stakes of MRV in climate economics

Before MRV gets its entry in all English dictionaries with its corresponding grammar, MRVed, MRVing, etc., it is worth distinguishing what exactly is covered by each of the three terms.

- **Monitoring** covers the *scientific* part of the process. It involves getting a number for each variable part of the equation which results in the emissions estimate. This ranges from direct measurement of gas concentration using gas meters to the recording of proxies such as fuel consumption based on the bills of a given entity. The use of proxies is common practice, through the general equation:

  Activity data × Emission factor = Greenhouse gas emissions

  where activity data is the proxy (e.g., fuel consumption, heads of cattle) and emission factor is the conversion factor (e.g., tons of CO_2 per liter of burnt fuel, tons of CO_2e per animal per year). Both activity data and emission factor change over time and hence need to be monitored. Activity data nevertheless tends to vary more frequently than emission factors.
- **Reporting** covers the *administrative* part of the process. It involves aggregating and recording the numbers, explaining how you came up with them in the requested format, and communicating the results to the relevant authority, such as the regulator or the top management of the company.
- **Verification** covers the *police* part of the process. It is usually conducted by a party not involved in monitoring and reporting who checks that these two steps were conducted in compliance with the relevant guidelines. Its purpose is to detect errors, be they innocent mistakes or frauds.

Although not plentiful, the existing literature on MRV in climate economics agrees on three possible scales which greatly influence how

MRV can be conducted: territory, entity and project (Cochran, 2010; IGES, 2012; Ninomiya, 2012).

- The **territorial scale** includes all emissions occurring within a given geographic area such as a country or an administrative region. All activities and entities operating within the area are considered. Examples include national greenhouse gas inventories supervised by the United Nations, regions or cities which have committed to a voluntary or statutory cap on emissions, and jurisdictions engaged in programs for Reducing Emissions from Deforestation, forest Degradation and other changes in forest carbon stocks (REDD+). Although the last example is restricted to forest-related emissions, it still includes all those occurring within the jurisdiction, no matter the activity or entity responsible for them.
- The **entity scale** includes emissions related to the operations of a given public or private entity. In a few cases, all the emissions of the entity are included, such as businesses participating in the Carbon Disclosure Project or entities subject to the "Grenelle 2" French environmental law enacted in 2010. Most often, however, only part of the emissions corresponding to a restricted set of operations is included. This is the case of mechanisms putting an explicit price on carbon such as the European Union Emissions Trading System, the Australian carbon tax or the Californian Emissions Trading Scheme. In those cases, the MRV occurs at the scale of individual facilities.
- The **project scale** includes emissions stemming from specific emissions reduction projects. These projects are often focused on a given activity, such as destroying an industrial gas or spreading efficient cookstoves. The number of entities and the geographic area considered is then adapted *ad hoc* to the considered activity. The main example is offset projects, be they certified by the dominant Clean Development Mechanism of the United Nations, or by other standards such as the Verified Carbon Standard or the Gold Standard. As opposed to the two other scales, the MRV of greenhouse gas emissions always comes together with the MRV of greenhouse gas emissions reduction at the project scale: both the project emissions and its counter-factual – or baseline – emissions are monitored, reported and verified at the same time, and along the same rules.

No matter the scale, the first question that comes to mind when quantifying greenhouse gas emissions is: which type of emissions shall be taken into account? Answering this question means choosing the gas – CO_2, CH_4, N_2O, etc., the activities – combustion, manufacturing processes, agricultural practice, the size threshold and more technically, the **scope**. The scope broadly defines how far the responsibility of a territory, entity or project extends in terms of emissions. The three scopes defined by the World Resource Institute and the World Business Council on Sustainable Development's *Greenhouse Gas Protocol* (WRI/WBCSD, 2004) are currently the reference in this regard.

- **Scope 1** includes only the direct emissions from a project, entity or territory. For a restaurant offering delivery services, Scope 1 emissions would likely be limited to fuel consumption during the delivery.
- **Scope 2** includes the direct and indirect emissions produced elsewhere linked to electricity, steam, heating and cooling used by the project, entity or territory in question. For our restaurant, this would include its electricity and heat consumption, even if both are likely produced elsewhere by a separate entity.
- **Scope 3** corresponds to direct, indirect and up-stream and embodied emissions of goods and services either consumed in the project, by an entity or within a territory (carbon footprint approach). For our restaurant, Scope 3 would include many activities such as the emissions embedded in the food it processes, in the journey of its employees and customers, in the manufacturing of the motorcycle used for delivery, etc.

A similar concept closely linked to the idea of responsibility for emissions and commonly encountered is the gradient from *production-based approach* to *consumption-based approach*. Scope 1 corresponds to an entirely *production-based approach* while Scope 3 corresponds to a pure *consumption-based approach*.

The last concept which is mobilized throughout the book is the **uncertainty** associated with the MRV of emissions. This concept involves a flurry of terms which are not always understood in the same manner. In this book, we adopt the terminology of the Intergovernmental Panel on Climate Change (IPCC): uncertainty corresponds to the difference between the estimate and the actual value. Hence, it covers all potential sources of error. Two types of errors are commonly distinguished

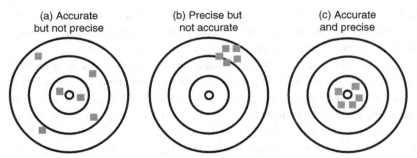

Figure 1.1 Uncertainty: accuracy and precision
Assuming the objective is to sample the bulls eye in the center of the
target: (a) the average of all sampling points would be close to the center and
so would have low bias, but the points are widely spaced and therefore have
low precision; (b) all points are closely grouped indicating precision but they
are far from the center and so are biased and inaccurate; (c) all points are
close to the center and closely grouped, so they are precise and accurate. The
uncertainty is then minimal.
Source: Adapted from IPCC (2006).

(Figure 1.1): systematic errors or bias which decrease the **accuracy** of
the estimate (e.g., miscalibrated gas meter, unit error in the reporting)
and random errors which decrease the **precision** of the estimate (e.g.,
sampling error, errors of copy in the reporting). In monitoring, lack of
precision and accuracy can both lead to uncertain estimates but only
the first can be dealt with by increasing the number of samples. Bias
can only be reduced by monitoring and reporting the same source of
emissions with a change in the method. In reporting, both types of
errors can be reduced through quality control and verification.

Scale, scope and uncertainty lead to the two necessary trade-offs
in the MRV of greenhouse gas emissions, as explained by Cochran
(2010): cost vs. uncertainty and information relevance vs. comparability. The trade-off between **cost and uncertainty** is one of the key
threads of this book. For each carbon pricing mechanism considered,
this book identifies whether flexibility provisions are in place to adapt
uncertainty requirements to the cost incurred by stakeholders. These
provisions may take the form of *de minimis* **thresholds,** that is, threshold levels of emissions under which monitoring and reporting are not
required, or **materiality thresholds,** that is, threshold levels of errors
under which errors are tolerated during verification. They can also

take a more continuous form, for example by increasing the cost of compliance or discounting the benefits from carbon credits in proportion to the uncertainty of monitoring.

The second trade-off between **information relevance and comparability** comes from the difference in information needs from case to case. A country with only a few trees such as Monaco will see the quantification of emissions from its forestry sector as a complete waste of resources when it comes to designing climate mitigation policies. But Canada or Brazil may not see it that way. However, letting each country choose the sources it monitors, the method it uses to report them and the format under which all this is reported would greatly hamper the comparison of emission levels between countries. The same goes for cities, companies and offset projects depending on their specific context and needs. As this book focuses on carbon pricing and reporting mechanisms for which dominant guidelines exist, in most cases issued by a regulator who has the ability to enforce them, this second trade-off is somewhat less relevant. It nevertheless comes up here and there (e.g., Chapter 3 on subnational inventories and Chapter 9 on company-level carbon footprint).

In a nutshell, five cross-cutting questions are asked in each chapter on the schemes being presented:

- What are the MRV requirements?
- What are the costs for entities to meet these requirements?
- Is a flexible trade-off between requirements and costs allowed?
- Is requirements stringency adapted to the amount of emissions at stake (materiality)?
- What is the balance between comparability and information relevance?

1.4 Outline, editorial choices and comparison tools between chapters

This book contains the description and analysis of fifteen of the MRV approaches practiced in carbon pricing and management mechanisms of various forms: cap-and-trade, tax, offsets, environmental labeling, etc. In choosing these mechanisms, we gave the priority to compliance schemes, that is schemes designed by a regulator who issues clear and mandatory guidelines and who has some means of enforcing the guidelines. These schemes are more relevant than voluntary schemes for two reasons: first, they are far more important in terms of amount of emissions concerned or in terms of amount of money at stake when they exist. Second, the practice of MRV in compliance schemes is necessarily unique as it follows a unique set of guidelines published by the regulator. In other words, it is not up to each entity to choose how it proceeds in terms of MRVing its emissions. This allows us to state what are the existing MRV requirements rather than describe how some entities proceed in terms of MRV within a flurry of different approaches. This explains why there is no chapter on the carbon footprint of products, for example. Although it has voluntarily been monitored and reported in some cases, it is not yet widely practiced. There is no mandatory or consensual set of guidelines, and hence, no verification by a third party that guidelines have been correctly implemented. No ex-post analysis is therefore possible in such a case.

To allow the comparison between the different systems treated in distinct chapters written by different authors, an *MRV ID Table* compiles the answers to 41 MRV-related questions in each chapter. These tables provide a clear and concise basis for comparison to readers. They were also instrumental in compiling the general lessons drawn in Chapter 15 on the uncertainty requirements of the different systems, the costs incurred by stakeholders and the provisions that help in striking a good balance between cost and uncertainty in monitoring, in reporting and in verification. A glossary for each of the 41 items of this MRV ID Table is provided in the appendix to this chapter.

This book contains three main parts. Each one is dedicated to one of the three scales of MRV described earlier: territory, entity and project. Each part begins with a chapter on the system we identified as the *trendsetter* for this scale. Criteria for qualifying as a *trendsetter* include number of entities concerned, amount of emissions concerned, longevity of the scheme, amount of money at stake, etc. The other chapters of the part consist of a shorter description and analysis of other examples of MRV – or *variants* – at the same scale. To select these *variants*, we used the same criteria as for the *trendsetter*, but we also valued their originality compared to the *trendsetter*.

Part I addresses MRV at territorial scale. National GHG inventories supervised by the United Nations set the trend in this category: they have been compiled on a yearly basis since 2003 by about 40 parties to the United Nations Framework Convention on Climate Change

(UNFCCC). Almost all these countries have strong incentives to comply: countries whose inventories are assessed as inadequate during the verification by international experts may be disconnected from the flexibility mechanisms for the Kyoto Protocol. Being disconnected often entails millions of euros of losses for businesses within this country in addition to the reputational losses for the country itself. Chapter 2 addresses this *trendsetter* in detail. Two smaller *variants* are discussed for comparison: Chapter 3 discusses the MRV of emissions conducted by subnational governments – whether cities or regions – over their territorial jurisdiction. While the regulatory incentives and guidelines are still in their infancy and are often non-binding at this scale, three similar sets of guidelines can be considered as forming the norm: the Global Protocol for Community-Scale Greenhouse Gas Emissions at the international level, the European Commission's Covenant of Mayors at the EU level and the Bilan Carbone Territorial at the French national level. The second *variant* addressed in Chapter 4 addresses the MRV of forest emissions at jurisdictional scale. Although still in its infancy as well, REDD+ has touted several jurisdictions to implement an MRV framework for their forests in order to benefit from existing and upcoming incentives tied to the reduction of forest emissions at jurisdictional level. The guidelines published by the Verified Carbon Standard – the dominant standard for voluntary offsetting – provide MRV requirements which are starting to set the norm in this field. They are compared to the more recent UNFCCC MRV guidelines for REDD+, agreed upon at COP19 in November 2013.

Part II addresses MRV at the entity scale. The European Union Emissions Trading System (EU ETS) caps the emissions of 11,000 industrial sites and generates exchanges worth between €50 and €80 billion per year (Kossoy and Guigon, 2012). In operation since 2005, it was the first large-scale cap-and-trade system to be set up for greenhouse gas emissions. Failing to comply with the scheme is fined at the heavy rate of €100 per tCO_2e. At the entity scale, it therefore sets the trends for other burgeoning carbon pricing mechanisms worldwide. Chapter 5 addresses this *trendsetter* in detail. Five smaller *variants* are presented for comparison: Chapter 6 describes the Australian carbon tax. Very similar to the EU ETS as it is also based on Scope 1 emissions from industrial sites, this carbon pricing mechanism covers the waste sector which is not subject to the EU ETS. The Californian emissions trading scheme which started in 2013 brings an additional MRV

complexity as it accounts for the emissions from electricity importers. This entails MRVing emissions which do not occur within the
Californian jurisdiction. It is in some way the first carbon border tax
adjustment implemented. Chapter 7 presents the system and how it
deals with this thorny issue. On the other side of the Pacific, 2013 also
saw the start of seven pilot cap-and-trade systems in China at the provincial or municipal level. Chapter 8 focuses on the Shenzhen carbon
pricing mechanism which caps emissions from both electricity production and consumption, MRVing twice the same emission. Another
originality of this scheme is the consolidation of reporting at company
rather than site level. Finally, Chapter 9 moves away from explicit
carbon pricing to the reputation stakes associated with the MRV of
the carbon footprint of an entire company reporting to the Carbon
Disclosure Project (CDP). This chapter pays particular attention to
the overlap between the CDP and the mandatory reporting schemes
in place in France. In addition to these five *variants*, Chapter 10 discusses the uncertainty that is actually achieved by industrial sites subject to the EU ETS, and how a direct measurement approach may
replace the traditional *activity data × emission factor* approach in a
cost-effective way.

Part III addresses MRV at the project scale. Although most MRV
requirements for offset projects are common within a given standard, those regarding monitoring accuracy and monitoring costs
largely depend on the project type. The structure of this part therefore
slightly differs from the two previous ones. The Clean Development
Mechanism sets the trend in this category: since 2001, it has registered
more than 7,000 projects which reduced more than 1.4 billion tons
of CO_2e and attracted more than €200 billion of private investment
which makes it the largest offset standard without contest (Shishlov
and Bellassen, 2012). Chapter 11 therefore describes the generic MRV
requirements of this *trendsetter* in detail. But it also contains a short
analysis of the differences brought by other more minor offset standards such as the Verified Carbon Standard and the Climate Action
Reserve in these generic requirements. Accordingly, the rest of the part
does not deal with *variants*, but goes into more detail on monitoring requirements pertaining to a set of subsectors, and the associated
costs. Chapter 12 discusses the methodological requirements specific
to offset projects which reduce N_2O emissions from croplands in agriculture across standards. The case of forestry offset projects – other

than jurisdictional REDD+ which belong to the territorial scale – are addressed in Chapter 13. Finally, Chapter 14 addresses offset projects aiming at reducing fugitive methane emissions in refineries.

Chapter 15 wraps up the book, discussing the overall findings and drawing lessons from the comparison of the MRV practiced in the different carbon pricing and management mechanisms.

Appendix

Table 1.1 *MRV ID table*

Context	
Regulator	The regulator is the entity which sets the MRV rules and/or guidelines. In most cases, the entity also sets the rules of the system in general. There can be several regulators for the same system (e.g., UNFCCC COP and IPCC for national greenhouse gas inventories).
Type and level of incentive to comply	The type and severity of the punishments when non-compliance is detected (e.g., inability to use the Kyoto flexibility mechanisms for national greenhouse inventories).
Entities concerned	Type of entity, number of entities, related market value.
Sectors concerned	List of sectors
Gases concerned	List of gases
Overall MRV costs	Cost estimates
Monitoring	
Rules	References of the official documents setting the monitoring rules for the system.
Other reference documents	Document references (i.e., ISO, GHG protocol, etc.).
Uncertainty requirements	Precision of monitoring required under the system, if applicable, expressed in % or tCO_2e. In most cases, it will be a range of values varying with sectors, gases or categories.

Table 1.1 (*cont.*)

Achieved uncertainty range	Precision of monitoring achieved under the system, if applicable, expressed in % or tCO_2e. In most cases, it will be a range of values varying with sectors, gases or categories.
Cost range	Estimate of current costs of monitoring, expressed in €/country or site or company or project or tCO_2e.
Scope	Scope of the emissions monitored. Three elements are specified: A. Scope 1, 2 or 3 according to the definition of the GHG protocol (1 = direct emissions, 2 = direct emissions and emissions related to electricity consumption, 3 = direct and indirect emissions). B. Territorial/jurisdictional vs. patrimonial/operational. (Territorial emissions are the emissions occurring on the territory of a given jurisdiction, no matter who is responsible for these emissions (e.g., emissions of an administrative region), whereas operational emissions correspond to the emissions of the entity itself (e.g., buildings, staff and activities of a regional council). C. Site vs. entity: are the emissions from a type of site monitored or rather emissions from a type of entity?
Frequency	Frequency of monitoring (daily, monthly, yearly, etc.).
Source for activity data	The primary sources of information for activity data.
Uncertainty range for activity data	Precision of monitoring required under the system, if applicable, expressed in % or tCO_2e. In most cases, it will be a range of values varying with sectors, gases or categories.

Table 1.1 (*cont.*)

Source for emission factors	The primary sources of information for emission factors.
Uncertainty range for emission factors	Precision of monitoring required under the system, if applicable, expressed in % or tCO_2e. In most cases, it will be a range of values varying with sectors, gases or categories.
Direct measurement	Direct measurement is the measurement of the gas itself with a sensor (often optical), possibly integrated in an intelligent data assimilation system. Is direct measurement allowed or mandatory in the system? Under what conditions? Is it used or not used in practice?
Incentives to reduce uncertainty	Is there an incentive to improve monitoring precision built in the rules (e.g., a conservativeness principle increasing carbon debits in proportion to monitoring uncertainty)?
Is requirements stringency adapted to the amount of emissions at stake (materiality)?	It makes good economic sense to be most stringent on the largest and most concentrated sources of emissions as the cost of monitoring tends to decrease with the concentration of emissions (economies of scale). Is this reflected in the rules/guidelines (e.g., decreasing precision demand with decreasing installation size)?
Reporting	
Rules	References of the official documents setting the reporting rules for the system.
Other reference documents	Document references (i.e., ISO, GHG protocol, etc.).
Format	Description of the common reporting format if relevant.

Table 1.1 (*cont.*)

Level of source disaggregation	Quantitative explanation (number of sites, production units, spatial resolution/ aggregation, etc.). There may be a difference between the required reporting level of disaggregation and the published level of aggregation.
Frequency	E.g., monthly, quarterly, yearly, etc.
Timeline	Key dates with regard to reporting (e.g., reporting deadline for year XX).
Language	Possible languages for reporting.
Is requirements stringency adapted to the amount of emissions at stake (materiality)?	It may make good economic sense to be most stringent on the largest and most concentrated sources of emissions as the cost of reporting tends to decrease with the concentration of emissions (economies of scale). Is this reflected in the rules/guidelines (e.g., decreasing reporting frequency with decreasing installation size)?
Cost range	Estimate of current costs of reporting, expressed in €/country or site or company or project or tCO_2e.
Verification	
Rules	References of the official documents setting the verification rules for the system.
Other reference documents	Document references.
Format	Description of the common verification format if relevant.
Frequency	Eg., monthly, quarterly, yearly, etc.
Timeline	Key dates with regard to verification (e.g., verification deadline for year XX).
Language	Possible languages for verification.

Table 1.1 (*cont.*)

Accredited entities for verification	Description of the procedure and key criteria for obtaining accreditation (if relevant). Examples of accredited entities.
Control of accredited entities	Description of the procedure and key criteria for maintaining accreditation (if relevant). Examples of reason for suspension (if relevant).
Cost of accreditation	Cost estimates of obtaining and maintaining the accreditation (€ per year).
Support of accredited entities	Description of the type of support that accredited entities receive, and from whom they receive it (if relevant).
Is requirements stringency adapted to the amount of emissions at stake (materiality)?	It may make good economic sense to be most stringent on the largest and most concentrated sources of emissions as the cost of verification tends to decrease with the concentration of emissions (economies of scale). Is this reflected in the rules/guidelines (e.g., materiality/*de minimis* rules)?
Cost range	Estimate of current costs of verification, expressed in €/country or site or company or project or tCO_2e.

Bibliography

Bellassen, V. and Leguet, B., 2009. *Comprendre la compensation carbone.* Pearson Education France, Paris.

Bellassen, V., Stephan, N. and Leguet, B., 2012. Will there still be a market price for CERs and ERUs in two years time? (No. 13), Climate Brief. CDC Climat Research, Paris.

Cochran, I., 2010. A use-based analysis of local-scale GHG inventories (No. 2010–7), Working paper. CDC Climat Research, Paris.

Dupont, M., Morel, R., Bellassen, V. and Deheza, M., 2013. International Climate Negotiations – COP 19: do not underestimate the MRV break-through (No. 33), Climate Brief. CDC Climat Research, Paris.

IGES, 2012. Measurement, reporting and verification (MRV) for low carbon development: learning from experience in Asia (No. 2012-03), IGES Policy Report. IGES, Kanagawa, Japan.

IPCC, 2006. *2006 IPCC Guidelines for National Greenhouse Gas Inventories*. IGES, Hayama, Japan.

Kossoy, A. and Guigon, P., 2012. *State and Trends of the Carbon Market 2012*. World Bank, Washington, DC.

Morel, R., Leguet, B. and Bellassen, V., 2013. International climate negotiations at COP 18: the art of the Doha-ble (No. 24), Climate Brief. CDC Climat Research, Paris.

Ninomiya, Y., 2012. Classification of MRV of GHG emissions/reductions: for the discussions on NAMAs and MRV (No. 25), Policy Brief. IGES, Hayama, Japan.

Shishlov, I. and Bellassen, V., 2012. 10 lessons from 10 years of the CDM (No. 37), Climate Report. CDC Climat Research, Paris.

World Bank, 2013. *Mapping Carbon Pricing Initiatives – Developments and Prospects*. World Bank, Washington, DC.

WRI/WBCSD, 2004. The Greenhouse Gas Protocol – A Corporate Accounting and Reporting Standard.

PART I

MRV of territorial/jurisdictional emissions

2 | *Trendsetter for territorial schemes: national GHG inventories under the UNFCCC*

JEAN-PIERRE CHANG AND VALENTIN
BELLASSEN

2.1 Context

The MRV of territorial/jurisdictional emissions, especially in the frame of the United Nations Framework Convention on Climate Change (UNFCCC) and its Kyoto Protocol, is the longest-lasting implementation of monitoring, reporting and verifying of GHG emissions. The concept of MRV was developed progressively in the frame of the UNFCCC and Kyoto Protocol through negotiation and scientific inputs from the Intergovernmental Panel on Climate Change (IPCC).[1] The UNFCCC created an actual dynamic in this field, bringing together scientists, politicians, technicians and economists to build international consensus on how to track GHG emissions and their trends, in order to demonstrate compliance with emissions reduction targets. This MRV process has been applied for several years on a national scale: the related experience and feedback are also useful for application to other scales.

The United Nations Framework Convention on Climate Change (UNFCCC) was adopted at the "Rio Earth Summit" in 1992. Initially signed by 154 nations, it has 195 parties to date (end of 2014). The ultimate objective of this Convention is "to stabilise greenhouse gas concentrations in the atmosphere at a level that would prevent dangerous anthropogenic interference with the climate system" (Article 2 of the Convention). The scope of this Convention was to monitor all greenhouse gases not controlled by the Montreal Protocol. The countries which signed the Convention (so-called Parties) meet annually

---

[1] The IPCC comprises an extensive panel of scientists. Its main task is to produce an assessment on climate science, mitigation potential and climate economics every five years. The panel also produces more specific reports ("special reports") focused on a given topic or purpose such as the Guidelines for national GHG inventories.

to assess progress in combating climate change and possible changes in the framework of the Convention. This is called the Conferences of the Parties (COP). Thus, common rules on MRV, among other topics, have been decided at the COPs. In particular, the 9th COP in 2003 decided that Parties have to use the Intergovernmental Panel on Climate Change (IPCC) guidelines as a reference of good practice for the national GHG emissions inventories.

The Convention divides countries into two sets of Parties. Annex I Parties are the industrialized countries which were members of the Organisation for Economic Co-operation and Development (OECD) in 1992 as well as countries with Economies In Transition (EITs), i.e., the former communist bloc. Non-Annex I Parties are all other countries that were so-called "developing" countries in 1992. Concerning green-house gas (GHG) emissions inventories, article 4 of the Convention states that the Parties in the Convention should "develop, period-ically update, publish and make available to the Conference of the Parties, ... national inventories of anthropogenic emissions by sources and removals by sinks of all greenhouse gases not controlled by the Montreal Protocol, using comparable methodologies to be agreed upon by the Conference of the Parties."

National GHG emissions inventories are the basis on which com-pliance with the Kyoto Protocol – which established legally binding emissions reduction targets for Annex I Parties to reduce their GHG emissions in the commitment period 2008–2012 – is assessed.

For the first Kyoto commitment period (2008–2012), the IPCC ref-erences for national GHG emissions inventories in the framework of the Convention are:

- IPCC Revised 1996 Guidelines for National GHG Inventories;
- IPCC Good Practice Guidance and Uncertainty Management in National Greenhouse Gas Inventories, 2000;
- IPCC Good Practice Guidance for LULUCF, 2003.

These three IPCC documents represent complementary guidelines and good practice guidance on how National GHG Inventories have to be prepared, in other words how to monitor GHG emissions. The IPCC 1996 Guidelines provided the basis of sector-specific methods for esti-mating GHG emissions. The IPCC GPG 2000 completed the methodo-logical guidelines and added different cross-cutting issues concerning monitoring: organization and resources (concept of national system), documentation, archiving, quality assurance & quality control, uncertainty assessment, key category sources and methodological choice (the different tier 1, 2, 3 approaches), etc. Finally, with a three-year delay compared to other sectors, the IPCC Good Practice Guidance for land-use, land-use change and forestry (LULUCF) was finalized in 2003.

In the frame of the Kyoto Protocol and its second commitment period, these three IPCC documents are replaced by the IPCC 2006 Guidelines for National GHG Inventories which builds on ten years of inventory developments by the IPCC and experience acquired using the previous IPCC guidance.

Figure 2.1 illustrates the main milestones of UNFCCC and IPCC history. This history is driven by the COP. Indeed, during each COP, the countries which ratified the Convention can revise the rules and requirements with regards to the national inventories of GHG emissions. Changes can occur every year, often in the form of the formalization, completion, refining or reinforcing of certain points related to the requirements of the Parties. For instance, following the Nairobi Conference of the Parties (2006), the UNFCCC reporting Guidelines on annual inventories were updated to include new decisions on LULUCF. In most cases, such changes require retrospective updating of national inventories which is quite time consuming for Parties. However, significant changes to the rules and requirements with regards to national inventories are not so common. Convention/ Protocol signing, changes of commitment periods or reinforcement of commitments are the only cases where important changes of rules and requirements usually occur. For example, the second commitment period of the Kyoto Protocol, which covers the years from 2013 to 2020, was adopted at the 18th COP in Doha in 2012, with the aim of reducing emissions of Annex B Parties[2] by 18 percent compared to 1990 by the year 2020 (Figure 2.1). On the inventory side, changes include the replacement of the three aforementioned IPCC guidelines by the 2006 IPCC Guidelines and some supplementary guidelines for LULUCF for Kyoto Protocol Parties.

Developed countries and developing countries are not subject to the same rules for their national GHG emissions inventories (Figure 2.1). Initially, the only requirement of non-Annex I countries under the

---

[2] Annex B Parties are "industrialized" countries. The list is almost the same as the Annex I of the UNFCCC (see above).

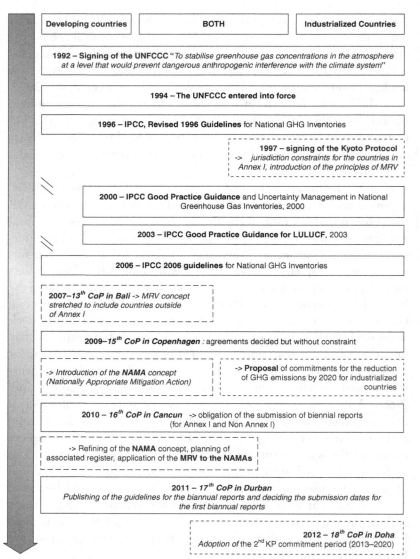

Figure 2.1 Main and latest steps under the UNFCCC regarding MRV and reduction target

UNFCCC was to provide an initial national communication including a rough estimate of national GHG emissions.

MRV requirements for non-Annex I countries will likely be reinforced for the specific case of national emissions reduction programs – the so-called Nationally Appropriate Mitigation Actions (NAMAs) – introduced in 2009 at the 15th COP in Copenhagen (Figure 2.1): "Nationally Appropriate Mitigation Actions by developing country Parties in the context of sustainable development, supported and enabled by technology, financing and capacity-building, in a measurable, reportable and verifiable manner" (decisions 1/CP.13). More specific requirements were agreed at the 19th COP in Warsaw in 2013: they remain much less precise and demanding than IPCC guidelines, except for the forestry sector. Indeed, in the frame of Reducing Emissions from Deforestation, forest Degradation and enhancing forest carbon sequestration (REDD+), the 19th COP adopted a set of MRV decisions for developing countries seeking international funding for REDD+ which are almost as demanding as the MRV rules for the forestry part of the national inventories of Annex I Parties (Dupont et al., 2013).

Furthermore, in addition to National Communications, since 2014, both Annex I and non-Annex I Parties will have to submit a biennial report which includes estimates of their national emissions and a description of steps taken or envisaged to implement the Convention and any other related information.

Because MRV constraints on GHG emissions inventories currently target Annex I Parties more than non-Annex I Parties, the focus will be put on Annex I Parties in the rest of this section.

Especially, the Kyoto Protocol introduced the additional following MRV requirements:

- **Monitoring:** Article 5 of the Kyoto Protocol states that a national system shall be established which estimates national GHG emissions. It also states that the methodologies used shall be approved by the IPCC and the COP.
- **Reporting:** Article 7 states the reporting requirements in the framework of the Kyoto Protocol (national GHG inventory and other specific KP information, according to guidelines that can be periodically reviewed by the COP).

- **Verification:** Article 8 states that the elements of "reporting," in the Kyoto Protocol framework (national GHG inventory and additional specific KP information), shall be verified by review teams (managed by the UNFCCC Secretariat) who in turn prepare review reports assessing the compliance of the Parties and their progress towards achieving their goals, as well as any potential problems.

The rules relating to the different aspects of Monitoring, Reporting and Verification have been revised by different COPs since the adoption of the Kyoto Protocol in 1997. At the end of the 1st Kyoto period (2008–2012), the main current references complementing the texts of the Convention and the Kyoto Protocol are:

- **Regarding monitoring**
  - 1996–2003: the 1996 IPCC guidelines, along with the IPCC "Good Practice Guidelines and Uncertainty Management in National Greenhouse Gas Inventories" from 2000, and the IPCC "Good Practice Guidance for LULUCF" from 2003. These guidelines apply to all national inventories submitted before 2015.
  - 2006: "Updated UNFCCC reporting guidelines on annual inventories following incorporation of the provisions of decision 14/CP.11," FCCC/SBSTA/2006/9, 18 August 2006, for the part concerning monitoring: concerning the requested qualities of the GHG inventories and methodology issues (use of the different IPCC tier methods, IPCC default emission factors versus national emission factors, time consistency and recalculations, etc.).
  - 2006: IPCC 2006 Guidelines for National GHG Inventories, for national GHG inventories submitted after 2014.

- **Regarding reporting**
  - "Updated UNFCCC reporting guidelines on annual inventories following incorporation of the provisions of decision 14/CP.11," FCCC/SBSTA/2006/9, 18 August 2006. These guidelines provide updated requirements relating to the "Common Reporting Format" (CRF) for the reporting of GHG emissions, and the requirements for the structure and content of the "National Inventory Report" (NIR) submitted along with the annual GHG national inventory.

- FCCC/KP/CMP/2005/8/Add.3, 30 March 2006, following the COP in Montreal, parts relating to requirements concerning LULUCF in the framework of the Kyoto Protocol.
- FCCC/SBSTA/2006/9, "Annotated outline of the National Inventory Report including reporting elements under the Kyoto Protocol," for the additional information related to the Kyoto Protocol to be included in the national inventory report by Annex I Parties.

- **Regarding verification**
  - The quality assurance and quality control (QA/QC) chapters in the IPCC GPG 2000 and its annex 2 on verification.
  - FCCC/CP/2002/8, 28 March 2003, part on "Guidelines for the technical review of GHG inventories from Parties included in annex I to the Convention." This document set the basis of the UNFCCC review process for Annex I Parties.
  - FCCC/KP/CMP/2005/8/Add.3, Decision 22/CMP.1, "Guidelines for the review under Article 8 of the Kyoto Protocol." This document deals with the different issues of: national inventories, national systems, national registers, etc.

This Decision 22/CMP.1 introduces additional constraints in terms of verification for Annex I Parties which have ratified the Kyoto Protocol: in particular, expert review teams (ERTs) can adjust – that is conservatively recalculate – emissions when the monitoring or reporting is deemed uncompliant. Kyoto Protocol reporting notably differs from Convention reporting for the LULUCF sector. Accordingly, countries which did not ratify or withdrew from the Kyoto Protocol, such as the USA or Canada, do not face exactly the same MRV requirements as other Annex I countries.

2.2 Objectives, national inventory system and challenges

Following the different aforementioned rules and requirements designed in the framework of the UNFCCC and the Kyoto Protocol, the main overall objective concerning National GHG Inventories for Annex I Parties is to build a National Inventory System which can respond to all these requirements relating to the monitoring, reporting and verification of national GHG emissions. The national systems have to take on board the required specifications of the GHG inventories in the framework of UNFCCC and the good practice guidance from IPCC concerning the management of the national GHG inventories.

Specifications of UNFCCC national GHG inventories

The different gases
Under the UNFCCC and Kyoto Protocol (first commitment period), the different gases that have to be monitored are:

- six direct GHGs: carbon dioxide (CO_2), methane (CH_4), nitrous oxide (N_2O), perfluorocarbons (PFCs), hydrofluorocarbons (HFCs) and sulfur hexafluoride (SF_6).
- four indirect GHGs: carbon monoxide (CO), nitrogen oxides (NOX) and non-methane volatile organic compounds (NMVOCs) and sulfur oxides (SOX).

Starting from Annex I Party submissions in 2015, one additional direct GHG is monitored, namely nitrogen trifluoride (NF_3). Other direct GHGs are covered by the IPCC 2006 Guidelines: trifluoromethyl sulfur pentafluoride (SF_5CF_3), halogenated ethers, and other halocarbons not covered by the Montreal Protocol, but these additional gases are not required by the UNFCCC for now.

Other greenhouse gases exist such as water vapor, ozone (O_3) and CFCs. These GHGs are not monitored within the UNFCCC and Kyoto Protocol.

- **Water vapor:** the UNFCCC and Kyoto Protocol only focus on anthropogenic GHG emission/removal sources. Water vapor in the atmosphere is considered not significantly affected by human activities (except possibly at local scale).
- **Ozone:** generally this substance is not directly emitted by human activities, but results mainly from photo oxidation from precursors (NOx, CO, NMVOCs) in the presence of sunlight.
- **CFCs:** they are already reported and regulated under the Montreal Protocol.

Black carbon, which is not a GHG, however, has a significant warming effect on the atmosphere as a short-lived climate forcer. This substance is not monitored under the UNFCCC, but monitoring started in May 2012 on a voluntary basis in the framework of the amended multi-pollutants/multi-effects Gothenburg Protocol.

Commitment scope
The "GHG Protocol" defines three scopes according to direct and indirect GHG emissions:

- **Scope 1:** all direct GHG emissions (emissions directly generated by the considered entity or territory).
- **Scope 2:** indirect GHG emissions from consumption of purchased electricity, heat or steam (emissions related to the consumption of electricity, heat or steam, not directly generated by the considered entity or territory).
- **Scope 3:** other indirect emissions (other emissions related to the consumption of products and services, not directly generated by the considered entity or territory...).

Both under the Convention and Kyoto Protocol, the emission scope corresponds to a "production-based" approach on the national territory, i.e., Scope 1, instead of a "consumption-based" approach, i.e., Scope 3.

Under the Convention, the geographic scope of the national GHG inventory is the entire country (including all the territories under the sovereignty of the country). In the case of the Kyoto Protocol, the Parties may have negotiated and signed the Protocol for a geographical scope that could exclude a part of the national territory. This is the case for the Member States of the European Union which have overseas territories that do not belong to the EU (some of these territories are excluded from the Kyoto scope).

The temporal scope
In the frame of the UNFCCC and Kyoto Protocol, the temporal scope covers the reference years up to the last available year. The reference year is generally 1990 (exceptionally, a more recent year may be chosen for specific GHGs such as F-gases or for Parties involved more recently). The frequency of the national GHG inventory is annual for Annex I Parties of the Convention.

Required qualities of national inventory systems

"Good practices" in inventory management must produce an inventory which is, according to IPCC GPG 2000:

- accurate, i.e., without systematic over- or underestimates so far as can be judged (a monitoring issue);
- transparent, i.e., understandable and documented, with explicit reference to the original sources of data or emission factors (a monitoring and reporting issue);
- consistent over time, i.e., using the same methods for all inventory years (a monitoring issue);
- complete, i.e., estimating all anthropogenic sources of emissions (a monitoring issue);
- comparable, i.e., following the common UNFCCC reporting format (a reporting issue);
- subject to QA/QC (quality assurance and quality control, a verification issue);
- and in which uncertainties are gradually reduced as better information becomes available (a monitoring and reporting issue).

Concerning the organization, it is also "good practice" to establish an inventory agency (see IPCC GPG 2000, 8.4 Inventory Agency) in charge of managing the national inventory.

Parties to the Convention which have signed the Kyoto Protocol must establish a National Inventory System (see FCCC/KP/CMP/2005/8/Add.3, Decision 19/CMP.1, Annex on National system guidelines) with the following characteristics:

- The National Inventory System includes all institutional, legal and procedural arrangements for estimating anthropogenic emissions by sources and removals by sinks in the frame of the requirements under the UNFCCC and Kyoto Protocol.
- It ensures and improves the quality of their inventories.
- It facilitates the UNFCCC review.
- It should be designed and operated to ensure the transparency, consistency, comparability, completeness and accuracy of inventories.
- Its inventory activities include collecting activity data, selecting methods and emission factors appropriately, estimating anthropogenic GHG emissions according to IPCC guidelines and IPCC Good Practice Guidance.

- It implements uncertainty assessment and quality assurance/quality control (QA/QC) activities and other verifications at national level (see "Verification" section).

National information system

The National Inventory System has to manage the different institutional, legal and procedural arrangements for estimating the national GHG emissions. One important basis of this system is the national information system.

The national information system corresponds to the system that the national authority has established to respond to the different needs and requirements concerning the communication of information for national and international purposes, e.g., the need to produce and communicate different statistics on energy consumption. Most of the time, when new requirements are established, such as the need to monitor and to report national GHG emissions in the frame of the UNFCCC, Parties do not set up an entirely new and specific environmental information system from scratch. Rather, they tend to base their monitoring and reporting on existing information systems such as those generally set up for the production of economics statistics. Then possible adaptations/changes or extensions of the existing national information system may occur. In any case, the national information system should be able to provide data sources (activity data and/or national emission register) to the emission inventory compilers for preparing the national GHG inventories.

Generally these national statistics provide activity data concerning:

- energy fuel consumption statistics;
- transport statistics;
- industrial statistics;
- agriculture statistics;
- forest statistics;
- waste statistics.

Another important possible component of the national information system used for the national GHG inventory is the national emissions registry of individual industrial plants under annual reporting. Especially in case of EU Member States, national emissions registries are implemented for the EU emission requirements both for:

- EU-ETS EU Directive 2003/87/EC, establishing a scheme for greenhouse gas emission allowance trading within the European Union;
- E-PRTR EU Regulation (EC) n° 166/2006 of 18 January 2006, concerning the establishment of a European Pollutant Release and Transfer Register;
- LCP Directive 2001/80/EC of 23 October 2001, on the limitation of emissions of certain pollutants into the air from Large Combustion Plants.

The European Commission recommends the different EU requirements (national GHG inventories, national air pollutant inventories, EU-ETS emissions, E-PRTR Register, LCP Directive) be managed at national level within a streamlined national system (see also related issue in the reporting section).

Challenges and incentives

For Parties to the Kyoto Protocol, the "good practices" for inventory management described by IPCC become "requirements" with different degrees of severity. Under the Convention, the only incentive to comply with good practices is of a "name and shame" nature, namely the risk of receiving a review report which contains much criticism on the quality of the inventory.

Under the Kyoto Protocol, incentives to comply with the requirements are stronger:

- possible re-submissions of the national GHG inventories in the same year when necessary;
- possible adjustment of the national inventories in the event of underestimations of emissions;
- and most importantly, the loss of eligibility to the Kyoto flexibility mechanisms (especially emissions trading) in the event of unsolved compliance problems (see "Verification" section). This loss of eligibility, even when only temporary, causes significant economic losses as the country and its businesses are thus forced to stop trading carbon units. Between 2007 and 2014, six countries were temporarily suspended, usually as a result of failure in the national system.

Beside these severe requirements leading to possible sanctions, there is room for annual improvements through recommendations made by UNFCCC reviewers (without related immediate sanctions, see "Verification" section).

2.3 Monitoring

Sources of GHG emissions to be monitored

Generally speaking, the scope of emission sources and removals under the UNFCCC and the Kyoto Protocol can be presented as the emission sources or removals linked to all human activities. Concerning the monitoring of emissions sources, completeness is indeed one of the required characteristics of national GHG inventories from Annex I Parties. The UNFCCC defines the completeness as follows (in document "FCCC/SBSTA/2006/9"):

Completeness means that an inventory covers all sources and sinks, as well as all gases, included in the IPCC Guidelines as well as other existing relevant source/sink categories which are specific to individual Annex I Parties and, therefore, may not be included in the IPCC Guidelines. Completeness also means full geographic coverage of sources and sinks of an Annex I Party.

The limit between anthropogenic and natural emissions and removals can be narrow. Enteric fermentation from wild animals producing methane is considered as a natural process, but the enteric fermentation from agricultural livestock is considered as an anthropogenic source of emissions. Emission sources or removals from managed forests are taken into account as a LULUCF (Land Use, Land Use Change and Forest) source and/or removal, whereas natural forests are excluded from the scope. Natural wetlands are excluded, whereas managed or human-induced wetlands (e.g., hydroelectric dams) are included in the scope of sources/removals.

Concerning emission sources relating to combustion activities, the sources to be monitored are those related to the use and production of energy, waste incineration and open fires:

- electricity and heat production installations;
- heating in the residential and commercial sectors, cooking;
- industrial energy equipment;
- transport (air, road, railway, navigation);

- waste incineration plants (with or without energy recovery);
- open fires (residential, agriculture, forest fires, etc.);
- etc.

Concerning emission sources relating to non-combustion activities, further sources of emissions must be monitored:

- leakage of gas from oil or gas refineries, coal mining, etc., called fugitive emissions;
- industrial chemical or physical processes such as in cement production emitting CO_2, adipic and nitric acid productions emitting N_2O;
- fugitive emissions of fluorinated gases (HFC, PFC and SF_6) emitted from industrial and refrigeration activities;
- farming activities and practices generating non-combustion emissions, mainly N_2O emissions resulting from the application of organic and mineral fertilizers, CH_4 emissions from enteric fermentation and rice cultivation, CH_4 and N_2O emissions from manure management, CO_2 from agriculture soils and biomass;
- forest activities (wood harvest, forest growth, etc.) especially on deforested areas and on managed forest lands, contributing to the large fluxes of CO_2 in these areas, etc.;
- waste treatment/management, such as waste disposal sites emitting CH_4 due to the anaerobic decomposition of organic waste, the handling of domestic and industrial wastewater producing CH_4 under anaerobic conditions;
- etc.

Methodology

Bottom-up vs. top-down approaches

There are different types of methodologies for estimating emissions or removals of GHGs according to the sources and the available data/dedicated resources.

A bottom-up approach involves aggregating or extrapolating information available with a finer resolution than needed for the final estimate. The resolution may be finer for:

- the sectoral definition of sources (estimates made at detailed subsector level and possibly by type of technology before aggregation of results);

- the geographical resolution (estimates made at the level of territorial units before aggregation of results at national level);
- possibly the time resolution (estimates made at the level of hours, days, months or seasons, before aggregation of results for annual emissions), e.g., in the case of emission models depending on weather conditions.

A top-down approach refers to estimates that are calculated directly at a high level of aggregation and then possibly split down into more detailed levels. For the energy sector for example, the "reference approach" is a typical top-down approach. It involves tracking all fuels imported to or produced in a country, and then applying fuel type emission factors, irrespective of the subsector/engine in which the fuel is actually burnt (e.g., transport, heating, etc.). Annex I Parties have to use this Tier 1 "reference" energy approach for comparison with the more bottom-up sectoral energy approach which is used for the national total emissions, taking into account the fact that the sectoral approach may be implemented at different degrees of disaggregation: estimation by energy sectors but without engine/technology split (Tier 1 sectoral approach), estimation by energy sectors and engine/technology split (Tier 2 sectoral approach) and estimation summing all the emissions from each combustion plant by sector (Tier 3 sectoral approach).

Generally speaking, bottom-up approaches are considered more specific and less uncertain (if reliable information at detailed level is used) and top-down approaches are generally based on average emission factors.

Use of emission factors vs. measurements
According to the implemented methodologies and the category sources (see the next item on methodology), emissions estimates can be derived from calculations based on activity data and emission factors (EF), or from specific measurements of emissions or associated parameters.

The calculation approach summarized as "activity data × EF" may in fact be a very simple formula with only two terms, or a formula with many parameters (some of them possibly resulting from measurements), even a complex emission model (with detailed and complex relations).

Specific site measurements of emissions or measurement of relevant parameters are generally available in the case of important industrial plants under specific regulation requiring continuous or periodical measurements. For instance, European regulation mandates direct measurements of the carbon content in fuels to be carried out in large plants in order to obtain plant-specific CO_2 emission factors, whereas default or average national emission factors are allowed for the smaller ETS plants. N_2O emissions must be directly measured with metering devices in adipic acid and nitric acid production plants. In the iron and steel industry, to estimate CO_2 emissions, the mass balance of carbon between input and output is generally used to assess the emissions resulting from industrial processes.

Generally, emissions based on measurements (when reliable) are less uncertain than those estimated using activity data and average EF (international EF or even national EF). But emissions based on direct measurements are more resource demanding, difficult to integrate within a National Inventory System and therefore cannot be generalized to all source categories.

Tier approaches of methodologies and key category sources

Some sources of emissions – categories – are identified as "key" and should therefore, according to IPCC guidance, be monitored with more detailed approaches. The IPCC good practice guidance defines how to identify key categories (see IPCC GPG 2000 chap. 7):

- either the category is a major contributor to the overall level of emissions (it belongs to the most important categories which, when added up, make up 95 percent of the national GHG total emissions);
- or the category is a major contributor to the trend of the national GHG emissions over time (it belongs to the most contributing categories which, when added up, make up 95 percent of the total emissions trend).

The objective of identifying key category sources is to prioritize efforts and resources: in particular, it is "good practice" to use more elaborated methodologies, so-called Tier 2 or Tier 3, rather than the simpler Tier 1 method (see below).

The methodological choice relating to the different IPCC tier approaches are indeed defined as follows:

- Tier 1 generally corresponds to the less demanding IPCC approach using default IPCC emission factors.

- Tier 2 generally corresponds to the implementation of an IPCC equation taking into account country-specific conditions. For certain subcategories, it may involve more or less advanced calculation processes described in IPCC GPG (e.g., a possible more information-demanding equation in terms of variables and parameters). In all cases, the equation and its components remain explicitly described in the IPCC GPG.
- Tier 3 generally follows a complex set of equations which are not necessarily included in the IPCC GPG. A typical example of a Tier 3 approach is to use a complex peer-reviewed and most often country-specific model of a given sector. Tier 3 for some source sectors may also consist of using bottom-up plant emissions to obtain the total emissions of a given sector (e.g., for some industrial sectors where all plants are monitored and their emissions registered).

National statistics and inventory methodology

Activity data for the energy sector (combustion) are usually the amount and type of fuel combusted or delivered. These data are generally available from national energy statistics agencies which collect them directly from the operators or from suppliers of fuels who record the quantities delivered relating to the economic activity code of their customers. This collection of fuel consumption data may occur through periodic surveys of a sample of operators, or, in the case of important combustion plants, through reports made to the national energy statistics agency or under emission control regulations.

The compilers of national energy data will have to reconcile different sources of data (import and export fuel supply statistics, industry figures, etc.) to establish their national energy balance per sector of activity.

Because the fuels used have different carbon contents, energy statistics per fuel type are needed to estimate CO_2 emissions.

Since the formation of some GHGs (e.g., CH_4 and mainly N_2O) is technology-specific, detailed fuel combustion technology data are needed in order to provide rigorous emissions estimates. To disaggregate the fuel consumption into the share used by major technology types, bottom-up surveys of fuel consumption and combustion technology, or top-down allocations and statistical sampling will be needed. Specialized statistical offices or ministerial departments are generally in charge of regular data collection and handling. Inclusion of representatives from these departments in the inventory process therefore facilitates the acquisition of appropriate activity data.

The "reference" approach for the energy sector is directly based on the global energy balance: energy production + energy importation − energy exportation +/− stock changes (it is used by Annex I countries for consistency check with the sectoral approach).

The sectoral energy approach requires energy balance data per fuel and subsector.

The structure and the definition of activity sectors between energy statistics and the GHG inventories may be different. This is for instance the case for auto-production of electricity in industrial plants: in national energy statistics the fuel consumptions for this activity are generally included in the sector "production of electricity," whereas in GHG emissions inventories, this fuel consumption is allocated into the industrial combustion sector.

Furthermore, when preparing an emissions inventory, it is important to avoid both double counting and omission of activities and emissions when combining data from multiple sources. Identifying double counting is not always easy. Raw materials in certain processes may give rise to by-products used as fuels elsewhere in the plant or sold for fuel use to third parties (e.g., blast furnace gas derived from coke and other carbon inputs to blast furnaces). These by-products may not appear in the energy balance, especially when they are auto-consumed in plants. Other possible products used as fuel (such as waste tires in the cement manufacturing industry, solvents in the chemical industry, etc.) may not be included in energy statistics but need to be included in the sectoral approach.

It is also necessary to consider the issue of non-energy uses of fuels. Generally national energy statistics include them but their estimation or separation from energy uses is often challenging (e.g., natural gas use in ammonia production, solid fuel used in the steel industry, etc.).

Another source of differences between energy statistics and GHG inventories is the possible use of different conversion factors (such as net calorific values) to convert physical data into energy data. In such a case, that may result in apparent inconsistencies when cross-checking the reference approach for energy and the sectoral approach.

Consultations between emission inventory compilers and the national energy statistics agency are useful to specify how the energy statistics may be used without double counting, omission or misallocation.

Activity data and emission factors

Generally speaking, it should be noted that activity data are implicitly country-specific. The main challenge with activity data is to obtain available activity data which are the most appropriate for calculating emissions, i.e., the best proxy relating to what is expected relative to the emission factors. The other challenge with activity data is to obtain it in the most disaggregated format possible in terms of technologies/operating conditions when using Tier 2 or 3 methods. Concerning emission factors, when using default international IPCC emission factors, because of constant factors over the years, the national inventory for the given activity could be blind to possible changes in the country actually reducing the emissions (technology or operating condition changes over time, emissions reductions projects, see chapter on reduction projects, etc.). Conversely, national specific emission factors may reflect parameters taking into account national situations and their changes: in such case the national reduction measures or specific reduction projects may be visible in the national GHG inventories. If it is still not the case, a national specific inventory method may be developed/enhanced to solve this consistency issue.

Within the energy sector and concerning fuel combustion activities, the main activity data are the amount of fuel consumed in the different thermal equipment per fuel type for each subsector. These activity data are resulting either from a bottom-up approach (e.g., plant activity data) or from a top-down approach (e.g., from energy balance). For fugitive emissions in energy production, the activity data may be the production data or the amount of fuel transported. These data are generally included in energy statistics.

For industrial processes, activity data used to estimate GHG emissions are either production data or the consumption of the different materials entering the process (e.g., carbonate in mineral industry, natural gas for ammonia production, coke in steel industry, fluorinated gases for refrigeration activities, etc.).

For agriculture, the main activity data are the livestock population per animal categories for husbandry (with enteric fermentation and manure management), the amount of mineral fertilizer (nitrogen) spread on the agricultural soil, the crop productions (per main species of cereals, pulses, tubers and roots) and the percentage of crop area burnt. When using Tier 2, other parameters are necessary, such as the share between the different manure management systems for husbandry, the amount of gross energy ingested per animal and per year, etc.

Concerning the waste sector, the relevant activity data are the amounts of waste treated per type of waste treatment (landfill, incineration, biological treatment). These activity data may result from periodic surveys. Emission factors for waste incineration may be based on a bottom-up plant approach when this activity is monitored within the national regulations and emissions registry. For landfill, IPCC Tier 2 methodology proposes a first-order decay equation taking into account the kinetic effect over years (the waste deposited in a given year continues to emit CH_4 many years after) and possible recovery processes. Concerning biological treatment (composting, biogas production), emission factors may be based on IPCC default values, or when possible based on national studies.

The LULUCF sector is strongly dependent on land-use data because a large proportion of emissions and removals estimated under LULUCF is related to land-use changes. Data sources are very heterogeneous among countries because the collection of data can be implemented in different ways: land-uses can be monitored by remote sensing, statistical surveys, declarations or transactions of land users reported in the cadastre. Furthermore forest areas are both carbon sinks (through plant growth) and forest emission sources (through harvest). These fluxes can be estimated thanks to different datasets such as forest inventory data on gross production, wood harvest and forest disturbances. Yet part of this information can also be obtained thanks to indirect indicators such as wood sales or wood consumption data.

Data and process management

Annex I Parties need to monitor GHG emissions each year. In practice this is a good incentive to enable continuous expertise and permanent inventory teams. In Annex I countries, generally, the activity data/statistics for the inventoried year n are available during the year n+1. The last quarter of the year n+1 is generally an intensive period to calculate the GHG emissions for the year n.

Archiving the different processes of the monitoring

To ensure the traceability of the inventory process, and to facilitate its annual updates and its improvements, it is important to have clear procedures to archive all the information used to prepare the GHG emission inventory. This starts with the recording and the archiving of all input data (statistics, activity data, emission factors, etc.) and reference information (international requirements/specifications, guidelines, good practices, scientific publications, etc.). Maintaining documentation explaining the processes and the methodologies implemented is also essential. These are also archived together with calculation files and/or databases or specific model applications. All these archives of previous inventory submissions are used to explain recalculations of time series according to IPCC good practices, in a transparent manner, when the method is changed.

How to manage confidential data

Among the various input data for GHG inventories, some of them may be confidential, most often commercially sensitive information provided by individual sites.

The confidentiality of data is a complex issue where possible international regulations/rules have to be managed versus possible national and private regulations/agreements (e.g., the INSPIRE Directive on the infrastructures for spatial information of EU Member States takes into account the case of confidentiality of commercial, industrial or private data. In summary, two typical types of situation may be highlighted:

- data covered by legal restrictions;
- data covered by specific ad-hoc agreements.

Specific agreement on confidentiality issues may deal with nominated persons or with the inventory agency as a whole. In both cases, data management must be designed to guarantee that the confidential data will not be communicated to unauthorized people.

To manage this issue of confidentiality, when preparing the national emission inventories, one practice involves aggregating confidential data into non-confidential data. For example, the French national statistics rules state that aggregating more than three sites is enough, if no single site represents more than 85 percent of the total, to ensure that the resulting aggregation is no longer confidential.

Generally, activity data or other parameters might be considered as confidential but not air emissions. Nevertheless, possible cases may happen with confidentiality even on emissions, e.g., F gas emission from one plant which generates 100 percent of the F gas consumption. The possible solution will be to aggregate the emissions of this plant with other confidential data, or to aggregate these emissions within another sector.

Monitoring accuracy and uncertainties

In the frame of the UNFCCC and Kyoto Protocol, there are two main general requirements concerning accuracy and uncertainties: absence of systematic bias ("accuracy criterion") and the objective to gradually reduce the uncertainty of the GHG inventory.

There is no quantitative objective or threshold for uncertainty in the UNFCCC and Kyoto framework. Nevertheless, there is a qualitative requirement to use advanced methodologies (Tier 2 or 3 methods) for the main sources (key category sources), thus ensuring more reliable emissions estimates. This requirement is subject to "national circumstances," i.e., among others the resources that a country can reasonably be expected to put into the improvement of its GHG inventory.

Uncertainty assessment and inventory improvements
In the objective to gradually reduce uncertainty, it is good practice to monitor the continuous improvement of the national GHG inventories, to regularly assess the use of appropriate tier methods according to the changes in available data and studies. This improvement process can be managed by a national monitoring group (inventory committee or consultative group, etc.) following and periodically revising an inventory improvement plan. It includes a prioritization of the different improvements to be implemented with most emphasis put on key category sources not yet estimated with Tier 2 or 3 methods. The inventory agency is then responsible for implementing the improvement plan. It is then up to the inventory monitoring group to assess the relevance of the upgraded methods. This activity is part of the quality assurance task at national level (see Section 2.5, subsection on national verification).

The uncertainties of the GHG inventories are regularly assessed. The IPCC GPG 2000 provides guidance to calculate the uncertainty of national GHG inventories based on the uncertainties on activity data and emission factors. This background information may be collected from statistical analyses, measurements, literature, studies, guidebooks, expert opinions, etc. The IPCC GPG 2000 provides two methods to combine the uncertainties for estimating the uncertainty of the national inventory:

Tier 1 approach, with simple equations of propagation of uncertainties for addition and multiplication operations.

Tier 2 approach, with the implementation of a Monte Carlo analysis (computer stochastic simulation using the probability density function of the parameters of the emission calculation).

The Tier 1 approach for uncertainty assessment is generally sufficient, but as far as possible, the Tier 2 Monte Carlo approach is recommended especially to be able to take into account correlations between data/parameters.

From the UNFCCC submissions in 2013, here are the results of a benchmark of 35 countries reporting their uncertainties:

- Concerning uncertainties in level for the year 2011 of national GHG total emissions:
  - With LULUCF uncertainties in level are within [2%–53%] according to the countries, with an average uncertainty of 16% and a standard deviation of 13 points.
  - Without LULUCF uncertainties in level are within [2%–25%] according to the countries, with an average uncertainty of 9% and a standard deviation of 7 points.
- Concerning uncertainties in trend of national GHG inventories:
  - With LULUCF uncertainties in trend are within [2%–36%] according to the countries, with an average uncertainty of 7% and a standard deviation of 8 points.
  - Without LULUCF uncertainties in trend are within [1%–19%] according to the countries, with an average uncertainty of 4% and a standard deviation of 4 points.

From these reported uncertainty assessments, LULUCF can be identified as a sector with larger than average uncertainty. The reported uncertainty tend to be as high, if not higher, in other sectors, such as agriculture, or categories such as fugitives, some industrial processes, etc. (Pacala et al., 2010).

The overall uncertainty is however dominated by the energy sector, and is therefore quite low. Furthermore, the uncertainties in trend are even lower. In other words, the uncertainties of national emission reductions (or increases) over time are less uncertain than the national GHG emissions of a given year especially due to the correlation effects of national inventories over time.

Incentives to reduce uncertainty

Incentives to reduce uncertainty are rather low under the UNFCCC and mainly involve "name and shame." The Kyoto Protocol adds a few incentives, but they are not much stronger.

Positive incentives ("carrots") to reduce uncertainty are:

- competition between countries to try to be part of the "good pupils of the classroom";
- the possibility that improvements result in lower emission estimates, thus easing the constraint of the Kyoto Protocol or freeing carbon allowances for international trade (Kyoto Parties only);
- making inventories more sensitive to specific emissions reduction projects, thus facilitating their reward through offset credits (Kyoto Parties only).

Negative incentives ("sticks"):

As there are no quantitative uncertainty requirements, there are no negative incentives ("sticks") to reduce uncertainty.

Illustration of improvements driven by specific studies with technical and research centers

A French example concerning the agriculture sector: direct and indirect N_2O emissions on cultivated soils (due to nitrogen fertilizer and manure spreading on the field, N-fixing crops and crop residues) represent respectively 4.4 and 3.7 percent of total French GHG emissions for the year 2011. For direct emissions due to nitrogen and manure spreading, France currently uses Tier 1 which consists in applying a default emission factor of 1.25 percent kg $N-N_2O/kgN$ to the amount of nitrogen spread on fields (IPCC GPG 2000). Developing the methodology to move to higher tiers has been prioritized in the inventory improvement plan. CITEPA, Agricultural Technical Institutes (CETIOM, Arvalis-Institut du Végétal, InVivo and ITB) and INRA (Agriculture Research Institutes) are currently working on the development of a country-specific methodology to improve direct N_2O emissions estimation from cultivated soils (for the future GHG French inventories, possibly the 2015 submission). As of 2013, only a very few countries implemented methodologies taking into account national practices and conditions for direct N_2O soil emissions (e.g., Canada). In France, CH_4 emissions due to enteric fermentation accounted for 5.8 percent of total GHG emissions in 2011. In the 2013 inventory submission, the methodology for cattle was improved to Tier 2.

2.4 Reporting

Reporting requirements

The reporting requirements for national GHG inventories under the UNFCCC and Kyoto Protocol are listed in the UNFCCC reporting guidelines on annual inventories ("FCCC/SBSTA/2006/9").

The national GHG inventories have to be reported annually to the Conference of the Parties through the UNFCCC Secretariat. In addition to the direct GHGs already mentioned, indirect GHG emissions also have to be reported (CO, NOx, NMVOCs and SOx).

For Annex I Parties, the annual national GHG inventory submission comprises more than 60 Excel sheets for a given inventory year containing the inventory data (emissions, activity data, implied emission factors and other background parameters), i.e., the so-called Common Reporting Format or CRF tables, and a National Inventory Report (NIR). To illustrate the extensive amount of reported data, for the UNFCCC submissions on 2013, the national inventories included the years 1990–2011, so more than 1,260 CRF sheets (21 years × 60 sheets) of data. In the case of France, this meant about 94,000 input figures into the CRF Reporter.[3] For some Parties for which the geographic scopes for UNFCCC and Kyoto Protocol reporting are not the same, two sets of CRF tables must be provided, resulting in twice the amount of reported data.

---

[3] The CRF Reporter is the software provided by the UNFCCC to help countries filling in the CRF tables.

GHG emissions and removals are reported on a gas-by-gas basis in mass unit, per IPCC categories, separating sources from removals by sinks. Some reported summary tables present aggregated emissions as CO_2 equivalent for the different GHGs using IPCC Global Warming Potentials over a 100-year time horizon for the different GHGs in tCO_2e (see example of Table 2.1).

As illustrated in Table 2.1, some specific anthropogenic activities are reported as "memo items" and excluded from the national GHG total emissions:

- international bunkers (international aviation and international maritime transport, i.e., transports between one national airport/ port with one foreign airport/port); and
- multilateral operations (IPCC 2006, chap. 8: emissions from fuel sold to any air or marine vessel engaged in multilateral operations pursuant to the Charter of the United Nations should be excluded from the totals and subtotals of the military transport, and should be reported separately).

CO_2 emissions from biomass are included in the national total but already reported in the LULUCF sector. This is why it appears as a memo item in the Energy sector (Table 2.1). Emissions and removals should be reported at the most disaggregated level of the IPCC source/ sink category (taking into account possible need for aggregation in case of confidential data or military information).

The most disaggregated reporting level of reporting corresponds to subcategories to those displayed in Table 2.1 (see Table 2.2 for the example of the energy sector).

The emissions have to be reported per disaggregated category, but also per fuel type for combustion activities.

In addition to emissions, other background data are requested for the reporting to the UNFCCC and Kyoto Protocol:

- activity data at the more disaggregated level and the resulting implied emission factors (i.e., division of the reported emissions by the reported activity);
- other parameters (operational conditions such as climate or technical conditions, specific national characteristics) especially for the agriculture (e.g., typical animal mass, volatile solids daily excretion, etc.) and waste sectors (e.g., fraction of municipal solid waste disposed of at solid waste disposal sites, fraction of DCO in municipal solid waste, etc.).

Table 2.1 *Example of a CRF table: 2013 summary table 2 for the EU 15*

SUMMARY 2 SUMMARY REPORT FOR CO$_2$ EQUIVALENT EMISSIONS
(Sheet 1 of 1)

Inventory 2011
Submission 2013 v1.2
EUROPEAN UNION (15)

GREENHOUSE GAS SOURCE AND SINK CATEGORIES	CO$_2$ [1]	CH$_4$	N$_2$O	HFCs [2]	PFCs [2]	SF$_6$ [2]	Total
			CO$_2$ equivalent (Gg)				
Total (Net Emissions) [1]	2,823,473.21	289,255.56	263,657.09	70,745.43	3,460.73	6,072.75	3,456,664.76
1. Energy	2,831,237.46	39,095.39	27,395.68				2,897,728.53
A. Fuel Combustion (Sectoral Approach)	2,813,538.50	12,807.71	27,295.21				2,853,641.42
1. Energy Industries	1,030,350.25	2,901.20	7,875.15				1,041,126.60
2. Manufacturing Industries and Construction	469,545.81	1,500.58	5,498.51				476,544.90
3. Transport	787,083.80	1,110.66	7,539.75				795,734.22
4. Other Sectors	519,802.03	7,281.86	6,058.77				533,142.67
5. Other	6,756.60	13.41	323.02				7,093.04

Table 2.1 (*cont.*)

SUMMARY 2 SUMMARY REPORT FOR CO_2 EQUIVALENT EMISSIONS
(Sheet 1 of 1)

GREENHOUSE GAS SOURCE AND SINK CATEGORIES	CO_2 [1]	CH_4	N_2O	HFCs [2]	PFCs [2]	SF_6 [2]	Total
			CO_2 equivalent (Gg)				
B. Fugitive Emissions from Fuels	17,698.96	26,287.68		100.47			44,087.11
1. Solid Fuels	948.07	6,641.96		1.77			7,591.81
2. Oil and Natural Gas	16,750.89	19,645.71		98.70			36,495.30
2. Industrial Processes	163,455.50	638.53	8,861.13	70,745.43	3,460.73	6,072.75	253,234.07
A. Mineral Products	90,400.43	21.89	IE,NA,NE,NO				90,422.32
B. Chemical Industry	31,069.84	461.36	8,746.75	C,NA,NO	C,NA,NO	C,NA,NO	40,277.95
C. Metal Production	41,625.08	113.44	22.30	13.18	775.76	363.34	42,913.09

D. Other Production	21.08	6.26	80.68				108.02
E. Production of Halocarbons and SF$_6$				815.77	1,528.24	101.81	2,445.82
F. Consumption of Halocarbons and SF$_6$ [2]				69,747.25	1,156.73	5,607.60	76,511.58
G. Other	339.07	35.58	11.40	169.24	IE,NA,NO	IE,NA,NO	555.29
3. Solvent and Other Product Use	5,570.55		2,398.05				**7,968.59**
4. Agriculture		159,267.51	210,517.14				**369,784.65**
A. Enteric Fermentation		120,237.88					120,237.88
B. Manure Management		35,997.10	19,579.45				55,576.55
C. Rice Cultivation		2,536.56					2,536.56
D. Agricultural Soils[3]		9.23	190,823.88				190,833.11
E. Prescribed Burning of Savannas		NA,NO	NA,NO				NA,NO
F. Field Burning of Agricultural Residues		486.73	113.82				600.55
G. Other		NA,NO	NA,NO				NA,NO

Table 2.1 (*cont.*)

SUMMARY 2 SUMMARY REPORT FOR CO_2 EQUIVALENT EMISSIONS
(Sheet 1 of 1)

Inventory 2011
Submission 2013 v1.2
EUROPEAN UNION (15)

GREENHOUSE GAS SOURCE AND SINK CATEGORIES	CO_2 [1]	CH_4	N_2O	HFCs [2]	PFCs [2]	SF_6 [2]	Total
				CO_2 equivalent (Gg)			
5. Land Use, Land-Use Change and Forestry[1]	−179,342.15	2,095.40	3,254.29				−173,992.46
A. Forest Land	−271,251.49	790.36	359.01				−270,102.11
B. Cropland	72,201.61	141.49	2,664.38				75,007.49
C. Grassland	−9,648.87	276.97	116.81				−9,255.08
D. Wetlands	2,037.65	65.56	108.71				2,211.92
E. Settlements	34,533.42	63.58	5.23				34,602.24
F. Other Land	−3,804.26	1.43	0.15				−3,802.68
G. Other	−3,410.22	756.00	NA,NE,NO				−2,654.22
6. Waste	2,551.85	88,158.73	11,230.79				101,941.38
A. Solid Waste Disposal on Land	1.64	76,307.35	0.65				76,309.63

B. Waste-water Handling		10,767.41	10,047.68				20,815.09
C. Waste Incineration	2,532.00	77.27	167.22				2,776.49
D. Other	18.21	1,006.70	1,015.25				2,040.16
7. Other *(as specified in Summary 1.A)*	NA,NO	NA,NO	NA,NO	NA,NO	NA,NO	NA,NO	NA,NO
Memo Items: [4]							
International Bunkers	283,188.30	135.75	2,106.74				285,430.80
Aviation	129,114.80	25.41	1,154.85				130,295.07
Marine	154,073.50	110.34	951.89				155,135.73
Multilateral Operations	3.18	0.00	0.03				**3.21**
CO_2 **Emissions from Biomass**	366,078.37						366,078.37
Total CO_2 Equivalent Emissions without Land Use, Land-Use Change and Forestry							3,630,657.22
Total CO_2 Equivalent Emissions with Land Use, Land-Use Change and Forestry							3,456,664.76

Table 2.2 *Subcategories for combustion activities in the Energy sector*

GREENHOUSE GAS SOURCE AND SINK CATEGORIES
1. Energy
A. Fuel Combustion Activities (Sectoral Approach)
1. Energy Industries
    a. Public Electricity and Heat Production
    b. Petroleum Refining
    c. Manufacture of Solid Fuels and Other Energy Industries
2. Manufacturing Industries and Construction
    a. Iron and Steel
    b. Non-Ferrous Metals
    c. Chemicals
    d. Pulp, Paper and Print
    e. Food Processing, Beverages and Tobacco
    f. Other *(as specified in table 1.A(a) sheet 2)*
    Other non-specified
3. Transport
    a. Civil Aviation
    b. Road Transportation
    c. Railways
    d. Navigation
    e. Other Transportation *(as specified in table 1.A(a) sheet 3)*
    Other non-specified
4. Other Sectors
    a. Commercial/Institutional
    b. Residential
    c. Agriculture/Forestry/Fisheries
5. Other *(as specified in table 1.A(a) sheet 4)*
    a. Stationary
       Other non-specified
    b. Mobile
       Other non-specified

The requirements of common format and rules for the reporting respond to the need to facilitate the comparability of national inventories and their review (see Section 2.5) and contribute to the transparency of the national inventories.

Concerning the National Inventory Report, a common outline is provided in the UNFCCC guidelines (see Annex 1 of the reporting guidelines "FCCC/SBSTA/2006/9"). This outline fosters completeness, by reminding all Parties what is expected in the different chapters and their sections, and comparability, as all Parties using it then have the same elements in the same sections. A typical National Inventory Report thus consists of a report often exceeding several hundred pages, and is structured as follows:

- Chapter 1 introduces the inventory. It contains eight sections providing a description of the National Inventory System, the overview of methodologies and data sources, key category sources, QA/QC procedures, uncertainty and completeness evaluations, etc.
- Chapter 2 concerns emission trends. Its four sections explain GHG trends globally, per GHG gas, and per categories, for GHG and for indirect GHGs.
- Chapters 3–9 are the sectoral chapters for energy, industrial processes, solvent and other product use, agriculture, LULUCF, waste, and other. Different sections are expected to describe the related sources, their methodologies, source-specific information on uncertainties, QA/QC, recalculations and planned improvements.
- Chapter 10 details recalculations and improvements since the last submission, with sections for describing the reasons for recalculations, their implications on emission levels and trends, and the responses to the UNFCCC review process/improvement plan for the national inventory.
- Furthermore, eight annexes are defined for specific expected/extended issues (on key category assessments, complementary methodological issues, comparison between reference approach (global energy balance) and sectoral approach, assessment of completeness, uncertainty of the national inventory).

The six official UN languages can be used to write the National Inventory Report. Most of the inventory reports of Annex I Parties are in English, but for instance France, the Russian Federation and Spain use their mother tongue.

Annex I Parties have to submit their national GHG inventories by 15 April of the year N concerning the inventoried years 1990 up to the year N–2. This also applies to the EU as a whole. Accordingly, the EU sets the earlier deadline of 15 March for its Member States in order to have time to aggregate them and submit the EU inventory.

National variations

Generally the institutional arrangements for reporting issues are the same as arrangements for monitoring GHG emissions, i.e., the same agency which is in charge of calculating the estimates of GHG emissions is in charge of preparing the reporting documents (CRF Reporter submission and the National Inventory Report). In particular cases, the preparation of the National Inventory Report may be subcontracted to another body rather than the agency calculating the GHG emission estimates.

Even if the reporting of the GHG inventories is properly structured with common format (CRF reporting tool and well-structured NIR), inventories are not fully homogeneous. Differences between Parties may concern:

- **Completeness:** the reporting of the different Parties may be complete in varying degrees (some tables of the CRF or some sections of the NIR may be missing).
- **Level of detail/transparency:** within the CRF reporting tables, some background data may be missing. Within the national inventory report, more or less detail or explanations may be provided, especially concerning methodological descriptions for transparency purposes.
- **Comparability:** because of confidentiality issue or availability of only aggregated activity data, more or less notation key "IE" may be used (data Included Elsewhere). That represents possible non-homogeneous category allocations.

Different emission reporting requirements may be streamlined to reduce costs and increase consistency with other types of reporting such as those for EU ETS, E-PRTR (European Pollutant Release and Transfer Register – EU Regulation (EC) n° 166/2006), or national inventories of air pollutants (in the framework of the Gothenburg Protocol and the EU NEC Directive). Indeed much background information is (or should be) common to these different reporting requirements (background activity data, emission registry at plant level, etc.). The consistency between national GHG inventories and EU ETS reported emissions (see Chapter 5) is already more or less implemented by EU Member States. This consistency will become mandatory in 2015 under the "MMR" regulation[4] in order to assess the efficiency of the different policies in place to reach the EU self-assigned 2020 targets. It

---

[4] EU Regulation n° 525/2013 of 21 May 2013 also known as the "MMR Regulation," establishing a mechanism for monitoring and reporting greenhouse gas emissions and repealing Decision n° 280/2004/EC.

will enable low-cost reporting of non-EU ETS emissions by subtracting EU ETS emissions from the reported national inventory. This will allow the assessment of the non-EU ETS emissions reduction policies (see EU ESD – Effort Sharing Decision, on binding annual greenhouse gas emission targets for non-ETS sectors for the period 2013–2020).

In France for example, the Ministerial "SNIEPA" Order of 29 December 2006 was updated on 24 August 2011 to mandate the consistency of the national emission inventories with subnational inventories (see Chapter 3) and carbon/GHG balance at company or regional/local level. The French system was designed (drawing on the EU CORINAIR program implemented in the 1990s) to integrate the different EU and UN reporting requirements within a single National Inventory System (jointly managing GHG and air pollutants inventories) and by sharing the plant emission register information for the different national needs. A benchmark study on this issue of streamlining was performed in the EU comparing how the different Member States coordinate their different reporting requirements (see AEAT report ENV.C.1/SER/2007/0018, Jan. 2009).

2.5 Verification

As explained in Section 2.2, the stakes of verification for national GHG inventories are enhanced under the Kyoto Protocol, because of jurisdictional constraints and financial challenges. The three general compliance issues under Kyoto are: underestimations of GHG emissions for the Kyoto commitment period, non-transparent emission inventory and failure in the national system. In the event of an unsolved compliance problem, the Party may lose its eligibility to take part in the Kyoto flexibility mechanisms (especially emissions trading). For instance, six countries – Greece, Bulgaria, Croatia, Romania, Ukraine and Lithuania – have historically been suspended from flexibility mechanisms, most often due to a "failure in the national system." They have all managed to solve the issue within a few months and have therefore all been later reinstated.

But, before this last step of verification organized by the UNFCCC, other elements of verification are carried out at the national level.

Verification procedures at national level

At national level, verification procedures of the national GHG inventory involve quality assurance/quality control (QA/QC).

Timing, institutional organization

As recognized in the IPCC guidance, considering reasonable dedicated resources, it is not possible to check all aspects of inventory input data, parameters and calculations every year. Thus priorities should be focused annually on selected sets of data and processes relating to key category sources. Checks on all other source categories may be conducted through sampling and over a longer period of time than one year.

The inventory agency is responsible for coordinating the quality assurance/quality control (QA/QC) activities for the national inventory, especially following a quality plan.

The inventory agency should ensure that other organizations involved in the preparation of the inventory are following applicable QA/QC procedures.

QA/QC procedures, validation procedure and other possible verification

Under the UNFCCC and its Kyoto Protocol, no formal label of QA/QC is required for the procedures of the inventory agency, as long as the Party can prove that its QA/QC system is consistent with the IPCC Guidance on quality control and quality assurance. Nevertheless, the quality management system of some inventory agencies is certified under international standards such as ISO 9001.

Quality control (QC) refers to the different checks performed within the inventory agency as the inventory is being prepared:

- relevance of input data and assumptions (adequacy of activity data, emission factors and assumptions used to estimate GHG emissions);
- transcription errors of data and their reference (e.g., check of a sample of input data and its reference in inventory files versus the original data sources);
- correct calculations and units used (e.g., for a sample, comparison with an alternative equivalent calculation, or with a more aggregated equivalent calculation);
- data consistency (e.g., check of cross-sector consistency in the case of expected common used data across sectors; check of time series consistency of activity data, etc.);
- integrity of databases (check that expected database relationships and constraints are actually complied with, for instance in the case of automatic data import, etc.);
- reliable documentation (proper recording and archiving of procedures/files tracking how the inventory is made);

- justified recalculations (check the justification and relevance of recalculations);
- completeness checks (check that all emission sources are taken into account, and if not check the gap is documented and possibly managed in an improvement plan);
- comparisons with previous estimates (to identify possible unexpected changes due to the recalculations that need to be explained or corrected in case of mistakes);
- etc.

Quality assurance (QA) refers to the complementary review to QC driven at national level, which aims also at identifying areas of possible improvements. This review may be conducted as a whole or in parts. It is good practice that QA activities are carried out by reviewers that do not participate in the GHG inventory. These QA activities may be conducted through sectoral expert peer review focusing on the reliability of methodologies, or inventory audits focusing more on correct applications of specifications, guidelines, documented procedures, etc.

Based on the QA/QC activities carried out, the national authority, possibly with the support of an inventory monitoring group, ultimately validates the annual inventory prior to any communication on emissions results.

Other possible verification may be conducted at national level, especially the comparison of the national inventory with alternative estimates such as international projects or international datasets, emission estimates derived from inverse modeling, emissions factors of neighboring countries, etc.

Verification procedures at international level (UNFCCC)

The general and main objective of UNFCCC reviews is to assess the compliance of national GHG inventories with the IPCC guidelines/guidance and with the UNFCCC and Kyoto reporting requirements.

Institutional arrangements
UNFCCC reviews of national GHG inventories are coordinated by the UNFCCC Secretariat. Reviewers must obtain two accreditations: one from their country of origin, which sets its own criteria, and a second one from the UNFCCC which involves taking several exams in Bonn after several weeks of e-learning and one week of training in Bonn.

Reviewers from non-Annex I Parties receive financial support from the UNFCCC for their participation in the review process.

Timing and format of the UNFCCC review

After the April submissions of GHG inventories, the UNFCCC review process starts with the "initial check": the UNFCCC Secretariat checks that the submitted inventories are complete and correctly formatted. This stage I is scheduled to be finished (with a review report) seven weeks after the national submissions.

The UNFCCC Secretariat then moves on to "Synthesis and assessment." For this second review stage, emissions, activity data and implied emission factors are compiled and compared across Parties and over time, and "preliminary assessments" with potential problems are identified. A review report concludes this second stage ten weeks after the national inventory submissions.

The third and last review stage is the "individual review." It represents the most intensive review work and is performed by international expert review teams (ERT) who examine the data, methodologies and procedures of the different national GHG inventories (in the case of confidential data, a specific UNFCCC procedure is foreseen to manage the possible access by the ERT to the confidential data). Three formats of individual inventory review may be used.

- "Desk review": several national inventories are reviewed by experts from their own offices. This inexpensive kind of review had been abandoned for several years as it proved difficult to secure the time of unpaid reviewers when they are not gathered (see centralized and in-country reviews). The Secretariat however attempted to revive this format in 2013.
- "Centralized review": the expert review team meets for a week (generally in the UNFCCC Secretariat in Bonn) for the review of several national GHG inventories.
- "In-country review": the expert review team gathers in the reviewed country for one week. The review is hosted by the inventory agency of the reviewed country which allows for more direct interactions between reviewers and inventory compilers.

All Parties to the Kyoto Protocol undergo an in-country review prior to the determination of their Kyoto Assigned Amount, and then at least every five years. All questions and potential problems from the review process must be raised by 25 weeks after the national submissions.

English is the language used during the review for exchanges with the Parties and in the review reports.

The review report may contain two types of findings:

- recommendations for improvements, from non-mandatory "encouragements" to "strong recommendations," which have to be addressed in the following submissions (many recommendations cannot be addressed at once, especially as countries tend to receive them shortly before their next submission);
- "potential issues and questions," informally called a "Saturday Paper." In the event of potential underestimations, this paper lists the possible adjustments – i.e., emissions estimates which will be conservatively recalculated by the ERT if not addressed by the country in a resubmission. It may also list possible questions of implementation – i.e., possible failures of the national system.

The reviewed country must respond to the "Saturday Paper" within six weeks. Otherwise, the adjustments are applied and questions of implementations are forwarded to the Compliance Committee.

Role of Secretariat vs. ERT vs. Compliance Committee

The UNFCCC Secretariat coordinates the international reviews. It takes care of organizational matters, it ensures the geographical and expertise balance within review teams (e.g., choosing possible experts depending on their language background and the country to review) and it chooses the format of the individual reviews (centralized or in-country). It also provides the ERT with different tools to facilitate the reviews such as engines to search across Parties for emissions, activity data and implied emissions factors or to identify changes in completeness, that is subcategories that become or cease being reported.

The expert review team (ERT) is responsible for the technical findings resulting from the individual review activity. Expert review teams comprise lead reviewers, generalists and sectoral experts (for energy, industrial processes, agriculture, LULUCF and waste).

In case a Party does not agree with the issues of the individual review (e.g., an adjustment of its national GHG inventory or problem of compliance pointed out by the review process), the Party may also raise related questions to the Compliance Committee. The Compliance Committee will then examine the questions with the possible support of dedicated experts and the related documentation, before taking a decision.

2.6 MRV costs

Table 2.3 *MRV costs*

Monitoring	
Data collection by various national agencies	Several million euros per country per year, but in general for other primary objectives than monitoring emissions (e.g., policy design, economic intelligence, etc.)
Methodology design, update and implementation by the inventory agency	Included in reporting
Reporting	
Reporting by the inventory agency	€0.5–0.8 million per country per year
Support and coordination by the UNFCCC	Included in verification
Verification	
Support and coordination by the UNFCCC	€5.6 million per year overall, that is approximately €0.14 million per country per year
Funding of accredited reviewers from Annex 1 countries by their country of origin	€0.2–0.8 million per year overall, that is approximately €0.01 million per country per year
Response during and after the review by the inventory agency	20–30 man-days, included in reporting
Overall MRV costs	
Overall MRV cost per country per year	€0.8 [0.65–0.95] million
Overall MRV cost per tCO_2e[a]	€0.002/tCO_2e

[a] Based on the total 2011 emissions of Annex I countries including LULUCF: 17.87 Gt CO_2e. The €0.002/tCO_2e figure is likely an overestimate as the countries for which monitoring and reporting costs are available are large countries which tend to spend more than the average country on their GHG inventory.
Source: Authors (see explanations in the text below).

Monitoring costs: a difficult assessment

The cost of monitoring associated with national greenhouse gas inventories is impossible to assess in an objective manner. Indeed, most of the underlying data collection is not only, and often not primarily, carried out for monitoring greenhouse gas emissions. The energy sector is an obvious example: most countries collect data on energy sources and energy consumption because it is strategically important that the government and even the general public are regularly updated with reliable information on these topics. The US Energy Information Administration for example spent €22 million[5] on data collection in 2010 (Hogan et al., 2012). Similarly, the French National Forest Inventory received €12 million in 2012 to collect, analyze and publish forestry data in order to inform French forestry policy. And although this information underlies the forestry part of the national greenhouse gas inventory, it largely predates the GHG inventory which is not even explicitly listed in the law as one of the key purposes of the forest inventory.

Therefore, with minor exceptions including inventory improvements for which a dedicated funding can be identified, data collection for national GHG inventories can be considered to be almost free.

Then, the design, update and implementation of methodologies to convert this data into UNFCCC compliant emissions estimates generally incurs to the inventory agency. It is difficult to separate the cost of this step from the cost of reporting so these costs are included in reporting costs.

Reporting: €0.5–0.8 million per country per year

The cost of reporting is easier to estimate as it mainly falls on the Single National Entity (SNE) in charge of inventory coordination, also called the inventory agency. Hogan et al. (2012) provide estimates between €0.5 million – eight full-time equivalents – in Italy to €0.75 million in the US and €0.8 million in Germany although the latter figure includes third-party experts and research projects for GHG inventory preparation. This is corroborated by the number of people involved, although not full time, in France and

---

[5] All costs are converted into euros using the 2010 average exchange rate (e.g., €1 = US$1.3275).

Germany: 22 and 50 respectively. These figures are slightly under-estimated, as the inventory agency is not the only entity involved: it often relies on other entities for specific parts of the inventory, or at least interacts with them to obtain and understand the necessary data. Moreover, the UNFCCC itself incurs some reporting costs associated with the development and maintenance of reporting tools, and the aggregation and publication of national inventory data. Both sources of additional costs are nevertheless negligible compared with the costs borne by the inventory agency in most cases. The UNFCCC costs for reporting are however included in the estimate of verification costs.

For developing countries where labor costs are lower but where the necessary background information may not be as readily available, estimates are slightly different: Pacala et al. (2010) provides an expert judgment of €0.34 million for the data collection and training which is necessary for the first inventory, followed by €0.15 million per year annually to maintain capacity and updated data. These estimates are consistent with the €0.34 million grant provided by the Global Environment Facility for a National Communication under the UNFCCC.

Verification: €0.14 million per country per year

The costs of verification fall on several stakeholders: the UNFCCC – with the coordination of international reviews, the development and maintenance of review tools and services, and the training and accreditation of reviewers – bears the bulk of it. Taken together, the budget of the "Mitigation, Data and Analysis" department, the "supplementary activities" directly related to Annex I countries reporting and verification, the UNFCCC costs for national greenhouse gas inventories add up to €5.6 million annually for the biennium 2012–2013 (UNFCCC, 2012) i.e., €0.14 million per country per year.

Two other entities bear some verification costs: the inventory agency, which has to respond to questions during the review and potentially re-submit the inventory afterwards. This roughly amounts to 20–30 man-days per year. This time, as well as the resources put in by the inventory agency for internal verification (QA/QC), is already included in the reporting costs estimate. In addition, Annex II Parties (mostly OECD members) fund their accredited reviewers to conduct the reviews of other parties. Each reviewer takes about 15–25 days to review the sector for which he is accredited in 1–3 countries. This amounts to around 1,200 man-days per year,[6] that is €0.2–0.8 million depending on labor and travel costs. Reviewers from non-Annex I countries and Eastern Europe are already covered by the UNFCCC budget.

Table 2.4 summarizes the MRV costs of national GHG inventories for the different entities involved.

2.7 MRV ID table

Detailed definitions of the items of this table are provided in the appendix to Chapter 1.

Table 2.4 *MRV ID table*

Context	

Regulator	A. Official rules: UNFCCC and COP decisions (Conference of Parties)
	B. Advisory guidelines:
	- Up to 2012 (especially during 1st Kyoto commitment period 2008–2012):
	  • IPCC, Revised 1996 Guidelines for National GHG Inventories;
	  • IPCC Good Practice Guidance and Uncertainty Management in National Greenhouse Gas Inventories, 2000;
	  • IPCC Good Practice Guidance for LULUCF, 2003.
	- After 2012: IPCC 2006 Guidelines.

Type and level of incentive to comply	- Under the UNFCCC: "name and shame." A failure to comply results in a publicly available and derogatory review report. - Under the Kyoto Protocol: suspension from flexibility mechanisms (international emissions trading, clean development mechanism, joint implementation).

---

[6] 40 countries × 6 reviewers × 20 days per reviewer/2 countries per reviewer/2 (half of the reviewers are from non-Annex II and are therefore funded by the UNFCCC).

Table 2.4 (*cont.*)

Entities concerned	Type of entity, number of entities, related market value: 43 Annex 1 Parties. The value of AAU and ERU trading amounted to €1.1 billion in 2011 (Kossoy and Guigon, 2012) but will likely be close to zero in the coming years (Stephan et al., 2014).
Sectors concerned	All
Gases concerned	- 6 Direct GHGs: CO_2, CH_4, N_2O, HFC, PFC, SF_6. - 4 Indirect GHGs: NOx, CO, NMVOCs, SO_2. - Additional GHGs after 2012: NF_3 and other F gases.
Overall MRV costs	€0.65–0.95 million per country per year €0.002/tCO_2e
Monitoring	
Rules	Document references: - UNFCCC reporting Guidelines (FCCC/SBSTA/2006/9 18 August 2006); - Kyoto Protocol frame: "Kyoto Protocol Reference Manual on Accounting of Emissions and Assigned Amounts," UNFCCC Secretariat, February 2007; - Up to 2012 (especially during 1st Kyoto commitment period 2008–2012): IPCC Guidelines 1996, plus IPCC GPG 2000, plus IPCC GPG LULUCF 2003; - After 2012: IPCC 2006 Guidelines.
Other reference documents	- UNFCCC (e.g., art. 4.a), art. 7.d), etc.) - Kyoto Protocol (e.g., art. 3.1, 3.3 and 3.4 for LULUCF, 10.a), etc.) - COP decisions, e.g., Marrakesh agreements COP-7, 2001 for Kyoto rules and requirements).
Uncertainty requirements	No quantitative requirements.
Achieved uncertainty range	In level: - with LULUCF, 16% [2%–53%]; - without LULUCF, 9% [2%–25%]. In trend: - with LULUCF, 7% [2%–36%]; - without LULUCF, 4% [1%–19%]. See Section 3.4.1 for details.

Table 2.4 (*cont.*)

Cost range	Almost free, as long as one considers that the underlying data are produced essentially for other purposes (see Section 6.1).
Scope	A. Scope 1,2,3 (GHG Protocol): Scope 1 B. Territorial/jurisdictional C. NA.
Frequency	Unspecified, but reporting is annual
Source for activity data	- National energy statistics. - National general and specific sectoral statistics (industrial productions, transport statistics, agriculture statistics, national forest inventory, etc.). - National plant emission registry (when use of bottom-up approach, e.g., EU-ETS data). - Complementary information from sectoral federations. - Possible national specific inquiries. - etc.
Uncertainty range for activity data	On the basis of 35 Annex I reported information in submissions 2013, uncertainties on activity data can be summarized as follows: -> Uncertainty average for activity data (all sectors and all countries): 35%, standard deviation: ~90 points. Note: the given uncertainty average is an arithmetic average and not a weighted average taking into account the emission weights of the different sectors and/or countries. So it does not reflect the weights of possible important sectors with small uncertainties which may drive the uncertainties of total national inventories.
Sources for emission factors	- IPCC Guidelines: default EF (Tier 1); - IPCC Guidelines: equations of EF with national parameters (Tier 2); - other international literature/studies; - national literature/studies; - possible implied emission factors from plant emission registry (when available data and resources for bottom-up approaches); - sectoral emission model (international or national) (Tier 3); - EMEP/EEA Guidebook for indirect GHG (NOx, CO, NMVOC, SO_2).

Table 2.4 (*cont.*)

Uncertainty range for emission factors	On the basis of 35 Annex I reported information in submissions 2013, uncertainties on emission factors can be summarized as follows: -> Uncertainty average for emission factors (all sectors and all countries): 100%, standard deviation: ~200 points. Note: the given uncertainty average is an arithmetic average and not a weighted average taking into account the emission weights of the different sectors and/or countries. So it does not reflect the weights of possible important sectors with small uncertainties which may drive the uncertainties of total national inventories.
Direct measurement	Allowed but seldom used.
Incentives to reduce uncertainty	Small (see Section 2.3.3).
Is requirements stringency adapted to the amount of emissions at stake (materiality)?	Very little: the most important emissions sources (key categories) are prioritized in terms of inventory improvement.
Reporting	
Rules	Document references: - UNFCCC reporting Guidelines (FCCC/SBSTA/2006/9 18 August 2006); - Kyoto Protocol frame: "Kyoto Protocol Reference Manual on Accounting of Emissions and Assigned Amounts," UNFCCC Secretariat, February 2007.
Other reference documents	- UNFCCC - Kyoto Protocol - COP decisions, e.g., Marrakesh agreements COP-7, 2001 for Kyoto rules and requirements).
Format	- CRF format: Common Reporting Format for UNFCCC and Kyoto reporting of GHG emission inventories (FCCC/SBSTA/2006/9). - NIR: National Inventory Report with a defined structure format (FCCC/SBSTA/2006/9).

Table 2.4 (*cont.*)

Level of source disaggregation	- The level of source disaggregation for the reporting is defined by the CRF format. - The required level of source disaggregation for the emission estimation process is generally much more disaggregated and depends on the sector and the methodology implemented. It may depend on the structure of the activity statistics, its relevant split according to possible specific emission factors, the possible use of detailed models, etc.
Frequency	Annual
Timeline	- UNFCCC and Kyoto Protocol: emissions of year N–2 reported on 15 April N. - GHG national inventories for UE in case of UE Member States: emissions of year N–2 reported on 15 January and 15 March of year N (in advance to enable UE to report its GHG inventory to UNFCCC by 15 April year N as an Annex I Party).
Language	- National Inventory Report: any official UN language. - CRF emission inventory: English.
Is requirements stringency adapted to the amount of emissions at stake (materiality)?	No. In particular, all countries, no matter their size and amount of emissions need to report annually.
Cost range	€0.5m–€0.8m/country/year (see Section 6.2).
Verification	
Rules	Document references: - UNFCCC reporting Guidelines (FCCC/SBSTA/2006/9), especially point 17, 31, etc. - "Kyoto Protocol Reference Manual on Accounting of Emissions and Assigned Amounts," especially issues on QA/QC and verifications. - IPCC GPG 2000, especially QA/QC chapter, and annex on verifications.

Table 2.4 (*cont.*)

Other reference documents	Document references - Kyoto Protocol - COP decision
Format	Three reports: - Stage 1: Initial checks. - Stage 2: Synthesis & Analysis - Stage 3: Individual review
Frequency	Annual
Timeline	See Section 5.2.2
Language	English
Accredited entities for verification	Individual experts
Control of accredited entities	There is no procedure for maintaining accreditation once the UNFCCC exams have been passed.
Cost of accreditation	No financial cost, only the time resources for the training and the accreditation exam.
Support of accredited entities	Quite strong: the UNFCCC Secretariat conducts many initial checks and comparisons, coordinates the reviews, and provides many tools to navigate and extract specific information from the CRF tables.
Is requirements stringency adapted to the amount of emissions at stake (materiality)?	No. In particular, all countries, no matter their size and amount of emissions, are reviewed annually. There is no materiality threshold: any overestimate, no matter how small, can lead to an adjustment or a question of implementation during the review.
Cost range	€0.15 million per country per year (see Section 6.3).

2.8 What practitioners say about it

Three questions have been asked of stakeholders directly involved in MRV on national GHG inventories:

- Is there an incentive to improve accuracy/precision?
- What is the most important thing about MRV at national scale?
- What is the first thing you would change in the procedure?

Here is feedback from two experimented experts, one a national inventory compiler/manager and the other an accredited UNFCCC lead reviewer.

Feedback from Dr. Klaus Radunsky, Head of Unit Climate Change, UBA Austria – Point of view as a national inventory manager:

- Is there an incentive to improve accuracy/precision?
  - "When it comes to national GHG inventories the agreements on the so-called Kyoto Mechanisms (Emissions trading, CDM and JI) clearly have triggered significant improvement. E.g., the establishment of Good Practice Guidance, the introduction of the possibility of adjustments, the creation of eligibility criteria all where a driver to deliver better figures on time. Emission figures have become more complete, more transparent, more accurate, more consistent."
- What is the most important thing about MRV at national scale?
  - "A well working national system is key, that is supported by a QA/QC – including clear responsibilities and a management that recognizes the added value of robust GHG emission figures."
- What is the first thing you would change in the procedure?
  - "The current MRV framework under the Kyoto Protocol is fit for purpose. If something could be changed the change should be of those policy decisions that result in unnecessary burden for MRV. This burden is in particular high in the AFOLU sector. Another additional burden are regulations at the national and regional (EU) level that are not consistent with international regulations. More smart regional and national regulations would help to make the MRV framework easier to manage and more efficient. The last suggestion is to differentiate the review process depending on the significance of the GHG emissions – it is not good practice to use the same resources for countries that differ in national emissions by several orders of magnitude."

Feedback from Dr. Tinus Pulles, experienced Dutch environmental scientist and consultant, mainly active in the field of emissions of greenhouse gases and air pollutants and presently working part time at TNO – Point of view as an accredited UNFCCC lead reviewer:

- Is there an incentive to improve accuracy/precision?
  "I do not believe so. The uncertainties in any GHG inventory are in the order of magnitude of a few percent. The targets, as set in the Initial Reports to the Kyoto Protocol, are in almost all cases expressed in an accuracy that will never be reached by any inventory. Inventories are prepared to show compliance with the UNFCCC and KP targets. If a Party's distance to this target is larger than the uncertainty range of the full inventory, there is no problem. Accuracy seems to be important for emission trading, but this could most probably be best achieved by clear accounting rules, rather than by more precise or accurate inventories."
- What is the most important thing about MRV at national scale?
  "The understanding that this is a procedure, linked to deciding whether or not a target is being met. This is not a scientific activity but an accounting activity. The rules need to be very clear and unambiguous. Whether or not the inventory total is exactly representing the real world emissions (whatever that means!) is not very important."
- What is the first thing you would change in the procedure?
  "I would introduce the concept of 'insignificant source/sink.' This could probably be any source or sink whose estimated value is lower than the largest absolute uncertainty (in mass of CO_2 equivalents!) in the inventory. To be safe one could choose half or one fifth of this largest uncertainty. The scientific rationale for this would be that the probability that the estimate including this insignificant source or sink is statistically different from the one that does not include this category. The Expert Review Team would accept any tier 1 estimate for such a source without further investigation."

Acknowledgements

We are grateful to Jean-Pierre Fontelle (CITEPA, France) and Mark Tuddenham (CITEPA, France) for their useful comments on an early draft of this chapter. We also thank Dr. Klaus Radunsky (UBA, Austria) and Dr. Tinus Pulles (TNO, The Netherlands) for answering our "practitioners questions."

Bibliography

Dupont, M., Morel, R., Bellassen, V. and Deheza, M., 2013. International Climate Negotiations – COP 19: do not underestimate the MRV breakthrough (No. 33), Climate Brief. CDC Climat Research, Paris.

Hogan, P., Falconer, A., Micale, V., Vasa, A., Yu, Y. and Zhao, X., 2012. Tracking emissions and mitigation actions: current practice in China, Germany, Italy, and the United States (CPI Working Paper). Climate Policy Initiative, San Francisco.

Kossoy, A. and Guigon, P., 2012. *State and Trends of the Carbon Market 2012*. World Bank, Washington, DC.

Pacala, S., Breidenich, C., Brewer, P.G., Fung, I., Gunson, M.R., Heddle, G., Law, B., Marland, G., Paustian, K. and Prather, K., 2010. *Verifying Greenhouse Gas Emissions: Methods to Support International Climate Agreements Committee on Methods for Estimating Greenhouse Gas Emissions, National Research Council Report*. National Academy of Sciences, USA.

Stephan, N., Bellassen, V. and Alberola, E., 2014. Use of Kyoto credits by European industrial installations: from an efficient market to a burst bubble (No. 43), Climate Report. CDC Climat Research, Paris.

UNFCCC, 2012. *Programme Budget for the Biennium 2012–2013*. United Nations.

3 | *Variant 1: region/city geographical inventories*

IAN COCHRAN

3.1 Introduction

Greenhouse gas inventories and related measurement tools for quantifying emissions at the scale of a given territory or territory or administrative area can play an important role in local-scale climate action.[1] These tools can assist in a number of mandated and statutory strategic planning exercises, the development and provision of public services (transport, energy, waste) and provide a means for authorities to monitor changes in emission levels of all actors under their jurisdiction.

As of August 2013, no obligatory territorial-scale monitoring, reporting and verification of greenhouse gas emissions has been implemented at a subnational level. A number of different reasons may explain why no formal MRV of subnational territorial GHG emissions has been implemented with local governments instead implementing proactive, voluntary measures. First, local governments are not able to directly control the majority of the emissions under their jurisdiction, thus within the political economy of GHG management, subnational governments are unlikely to fully accept formal (and potentially binding) responsibility for actions beyond their direct control. Second, GHG inventories are increasingly being used as planning and management tools. However, to date the quantification of territorial emissions and their management at the subnational level remains disconnected from formalized measuring and reporting systems such as binding subnational GHG mitigation objectives,

---

[1] In France local governments are estimated to be directly responsible for 12 percent of national greenhouse gas emissions and are able to influence indirectly close to 50 percent of national emissions through policies such as regional development, transport, housing, etc.). Source: Centre de ressources pour les PCET de l'ADEME (www.pcet-ademe.fr/a-savoir/pourquoi-un-pcet).

national GHG inventories or the creation of monetized or fungible assets. As such, there is little incentive for actors to produce a full MRV given the limited added-value (access to finance, etc.) compared to potentially increased costs.

Nevertheless, over the last 15 years a wide variety of voluntary tools have been developed and implemented across the globe. While formalized MRV systems have not been put into place, different measuring and reporting frameworks and protocols have been developed with a number of efforts to foster harmonization across nations and continents. The different frameworks often are directly linked to national (Bilan Carbone® Territorial and PCIT in France), regional (Covenant of Mayors – see below) or "niche" markets dominated by different city-based networks (ICLEI, C-40).

Given current subnational and national territorial reporting systems, it is useful to explore what the state of practice is today to understand how future systems could potentially learn from each other. This section will present and analyze the dominant territorial GHG inventory methodologies and reporting frameworks currently in practice, focusing on how these tools respond principally to the operational needs of actors or city-based networks versus a formalized process requiring centralized reporting and verification. The issue of verification will not be addressed in detail in this chapter as little to no verification of territorial data has been identified to date.

3.2 Multiple methodologies and protocols based on actors' needs

The subnational quantification of greenhouse gas emissions plays a role in the voluntary, local-scale management of climate change by local public authorities. These tools allow local authorities to analyze the emissions of an entire geographical or administrative region over which they have direct and – depending on the jurisdictional or geographic perimeter – indirect influence. Different studies, indicators, inventories and other "tools" aid in a number of decision-making processes including:

- *Diagnostic and baseline* – profile of GHG emission sources within the area of study to identify principal sources and understand evolution over time without intervention;

- *Analysis of actions* – analysis of the direct and indirect impacts of emission–reduction policies, and when possible, linked to analyzing their cost efficiency in terms of cost per ton CO_2e. This may occur both ex ante and ex post;
- *Scenario analysis* – analysis and comparison of the mitigation (both direct and indirect) of potential policy "packages";
- *Tracking progress* – deployment of periodic or punctual indicators to track progress towards emission reduction goals.

Information tools are thus increasingly expected to perform a range of functions within the decision-making process (Cochran, 2010, 2012; OECD, 2010). Given the variety of functions that territorial emission inventories or tools are currently produced to perform, it is of little surprise that no single tool fulfills the multiple functions. A number of different methodologies have been developed to adapt the quantification exercise to specificities of the emissions and the sectors included, the measurement perimeter, data sources as well as time horizons and calculations methods. This may require the development of individual tools for each function.

As observed in France and many other European countries, territorial-scale greenhouse gas inventory tools appear to be most often part of territorial planning process – whether linked directly to the development of an over-arching "Climate Action Plan" – or linked to sectoral urban planning or transport planning. Territorial-scale GHG quantification is also relevant among a number of voluntary networks and programs – such as the *ICLEI- Local Governments for Sustainability*, the *Clinton Climate Change Initiative's C40 Cities Climate Leadership Group* of large urban areas, the European Union's *Covenant of Mayors* initiative or the increasing tendency for large urban governments to self-report their emissions through the CDP[2] cities reporting program.

Box 3.1 The Covenant of Mayors

Recognizing the importance of cities and local authorities in achieving its ambitious goal of reducing GHG emissions by

---

[2] Formerly Carbon Disclosure Project.

20 percent by 2020, the European Union launched the Covenant of Mayors initiative in January of 2008. A results-based voluntary process targeting cities and regions, signatories of the covenant formally commit to reduce the CO_2 emissions of their jurisdiction by at least 20 percent by 2020 (with a recommended baseline year of 1990).

The Covenant of Mayors requires that signatories develop a *Baseline Emission Inventory* and a *Sustainable Energy Action Plan* (SEAP) using the quantified GHG inventory and baseline as a point of departure. This inventory is a quantification of the amount of CO_2 emitted due to energy consumption and waste-related methane emissions in the territory of a Covenant signatory within a given period of time chosen by each signatory. It allows the identification of the principal sources of greenhouse gas emissions as well as reduction potential. The European Commission has developed recommended reporting guidelines for preparing the baseline emissions inventory. Nevertheless, local governments are not required to follow a strict set of methodological rules, but rather they should be in line with the principles outlined in the SEAP guidebook. Furthermore, two different approaches which can lead to substantially different results are accepted including a territorial or "IPCC approach" or a Life Cycle Assessment (LCA) approach which includes upstream emissions from energy produced and consumed within the territory. In terms of emissions reporting, the Covenant encourages an annual calculation and monitoring of emissions with a formal obligation to report emission levels every four years.

Both the commitment to join the Covenant and the produced action plan must be formal documents, officially approved by the respective City Council or decisional body in order to formalize and concretize the participation. While the European Commission and the Covenant do not provide grants for the development and implementation of the SEAPs, the European Investment Bank has created ELENA, a dedicated technical assistance facility to work with signatories in securing financing. It is the hope of the Covenant that raising the profile of local-level commitments and the development of concrete actions to reach emission reduction targets will assist local authorities in identifying and securing the necessary financing from both market and national-government sources.

Source: Covenant of Mayors (2014).

Territorial GHG emissions reporting remains principally a voluntary process or obligatory within the framework of a program that the local government has voluntarily opted into (see Box 3.1 concerning the Covenant of Mayors initiative in Europe). However, even when obligatory, this does not necessarily imply the use of a single, harmonized methodology, the systematic centralization of data through reporting mechanisms nor a formalized verification process.

A number of methodologies for quantification and reporting exist (Table 3.1). Different methodological approaches have been developed by the different networks, regional bodies or individual actors themselves. The variety of methodological approaches limits comparability of inventories from city to city or from city to national levels. Subnational governments are free in almost all cases to adapt methods to their individual needs, available data sources and other contextual factors. While this may render any effort to compare or aggregate subnational data difficult, it is important to remember that variations in approach result principally from the fact that local authorities produce these tools as a response to their own operational and communication-based needs and objectives.

The sections below will lay out a number of the most pertinent issues and challenges in the monitoring of GHG emissions at the subnational territorial scale. This discussion will draw on the comparison of three principal territorial methodologies in use today – the *Global Protocol for Community-Scale Greenhouse Gas Emissions;*[3] the *Bilan Carbone® Territorial*; and the *EC-Com methodology recommended by the Covenant of Mayors*. A comparison of these protocols is presented in Table 3.5 at the end of this chapter.

---

[3] Important steps have been taken towards harmonization with the development of the joint World Resources Institute/ICLEI/C40 Cities Climate Leadership Group quantification protocol supported by UNEP, UN Habitat and the World Bank. Currently being piloted in a number of large cities around the world, this protocol has become one of the references in terms of GHG quantification at the territorial scale.

Table 3.1 *Selected tools and methodological frameworks (those in bold are studied in detail below)*

Origin	Institutional body	Methodological frameworks
National/Regional	France: ADEME – ABC (since October 2011) (France)	**Bilan Carbone® Territorial**
	France: PCIT[a]	Methodological Guide for Territorial Atmospheric Emissions (*Guide méthodologique pour l'élaboration des inventaires territoriaux des émissions atmosphériques*)
	Denmark – Danish National Environmental Research Institute (NERI)	CO_2 Calculator
	Austria	The "CO_2 Grobbilanz" and the "EMSIG" tool
	UK/EU (through Metrex Network)	Greenhouse gas Regional Inventory Protocol (GRIP)
Membership-based Network	The Climate Registry[b]	Local Government Operations (LGO) Protocol[c]
	ICLEI	International Local Government GHG Emissions Analysis Protocol (IEAP)[d]
	Climate Alliance	ECORegion

Table 3.1 (*cont.*)

Origin	Institutional body	Methodological frameworks
Inter-governmental/ International Collaborations	World Resources Institute/ ICLEI/C40 supported by UNEP /UN Habitat/World Bank	**Global Protocol for Community-Scale Greenhouse Gas Emissions**
	EU Covenant of Mayors	**Covenant of Mayors Sustainable Energy Action Plan (SEAP) EC-Com**
	International Organisation for Standardisation (ISO)	Annex to Draft ISO 14069 for Community Emissions

[a] The *Pôle National de Coordination des Inventaires Territoriaux* in France has developed methodological guidelines for the preparation of an integrated assessment of atmospheric pollutants (including GHG emissions). In addition to responding to a number of other international, European and national reporting requirements, these guidelines are designed to be used by the 26 French Regions as part of their air, climate and energy plans to be updated every five years. However, there is to date no obligation to use these guidelines nor a formalized MRV of regional emissions.

[b] Note. The Climate Registry is a public-private partnership; some of its protocols have become institutionalized in US law and others, such as the Local Government Operations Protocol, have not.

[c] The Local Government Operations Protocol was developed through a partnership between the California Climate Action Registry (CCAR), the California Air Resources Board (CARB), ICLEI-US and The Climate Registry. It is based on the *Greenhouse Gas Protocol: A Corporate Accounting and Reporting Standard*, The Climate Registry's *General Reporting Protocol* and ICLEI's *International Emissions Analysis Protocol*.

[d] The methodology was promoted by ICLEI and served as the principal methodology promoted by the organization until the 2012 release of the *Global Protocol for Community-Scale Greenhouse Gas Emissions*.

Source: Based on Bader and Bleischwitz, 2009; Corfee-Morlot et al., 2009; Ibrahim et al., 2012.

3.3 Monitoring

At the territorial scale, choosing what to monitor can be a complex issue as it is closely linked by local authorities to both "normative questions" concerning responsibility for emissions and practical issues of who can directly influence levels. Clearly assigning responsibility for GHG emissions is key in resolving a number of methodological issues, such as double counting. However, it is rooted in a number of complex normative issues, as it requires a judgment as to whether "consumers" or "producers" are primarily responsible for the emissions stemming from the goods and services. While national inventories assign responsibility for emissions to the point of emission (inclusion of Scope 1), different territorial approaches account for emissions both within their territory as well as those linked to local activities – even if these emissions occur elsewhere (inclusion of Scopes 2 and 3). For example, is the energy utility producing electricity used within a given jurisdiction responsible for the resulting GHG emissions or are the local governments who can directly and indirectly influence energy consumption through regulations or other tools the responsible parties? The choice to use a direct emissions (Scopes 1 and 2 in most cases) versus a life-cycle approach (Scopes 1, 2, and 3) is rooted in different notions of who is responsible for the emissions. The quantification protocols for local-scale emissions often find a pragmatic "middle ground," taking into consideration the capacity of the actor producing the inventory to directly or indirectly mitigate emissions. Decisions establishing how responsibility for emissions is attributed, the emission scopes included and the sectors and gases included are often at the heart of the structure and base architecture.

While, as seen in Table 3.5, differences in monitoring greenhouse gas emissions exist between the protocols in use, a number of similarities can be established between approaches based along the lines of *whose* emissions are included, *what* sectors and sources are quantified and *how* this occurs in practice.

Whose emissions?

The perimeter of a territorial GHG inventory covers the emissions stemming from a range of actors across a given territory and can thus lead to a number of measurement challenges. These include not only local government operations, private companies and households, but equally "transit" emissions from individuals traversing the territory (airline, road, rail travel, etc.). In many instances, the definition of what emissions to include is influenced by the ability of the local authority to influence directly or indirectly – potentially extending beyond official competencies. It is important to note that while protocols may call for emissions to be included or excluded, in practice local governments often adjust methods to their needs and available data.

What sector?

All methodologies studied focus on the six greenhouse gases as defined by the Kyoto Protocol and typically address the five sectors laid out by IPCC guidelines: Energy (including Transportation); Industrial processes and product use; Agriculture, forestry and other land-use; Waste; and Other. The sectors included in an inventory will depend on the economic structure of the region in question. Inventories are likely to be dominated by IPCC energy subsectors, with the varying inclusion of the full range of sectors (industrial processes and land-use and land-use change and forestry (LULUCF)) when appropriate. Typically, territorial-scale methodologies focus on Scope 1 and Scope 2 emissions. Some approaches, such as the *Bilan Carbone® Territorial* as well as the more ambitious levels of reporting in the *Global Protocol for Community-Scale Greenhouse Gas Emissions*, place an emphasis on Scope 3 emissions. This approach borders on an urban metabolism/carbon footprint to understand the full range of direct, indirect and embodied emissions related to the social and economic activities in the territory – both upstream, at the point of consumption, and downstream.

How does this occur in practice?

Currently, compared to national emission inventories based solely on direct production and LULUCF (see Chapter 2), subnational territorial inventories require a combination of production- and consumption-based emissions attribution (Cochran, 2010; Corfee-Morlot et al., 2009; Ibrahim et al., 2012). As such, a range of data sources must be relied on. While the individual protocols provide recommendations on how to calculate greenhouse gas emissions and indicate what sectors are to be included, the choice is ultimately up to the local governments implementing the methodology. Similarly to what States do for national greenhouse gas inventories, local governments adapt the chosen protocol to the data sources available – often combining a mixture of direct emissions measurements ("tailpipe") if available from point sources as well as the emission-factor approach based on activity data. Further, local governments are equally able not to report emission levels for a given source or category if data are unavailable or deemed negligible. As it is likely that the aggregation of physical territorial data on energy use and other sectors may not correspond directly to the perimeter of a jurisdictional inventory, different methods of estimating emissions including modeling and economic input-output data will be used to fill gaps.

Monitoring uncertainty: making do with available data

Within current, voluntary territorial-emission quantification, uncertainty is a relatively loose concept with no established necessary levels of precision or in general calculation. Often, uncertainty is more connected with the level of precision necessary for a given use or decision-making process.

Data availability and the cost of collection create differences in the application of methodological approaches used by actors. Typically, as the number of covered emission sources, institutions and actors increases, so does the relative data requirements and, thus, in most cases, the cost of data collection and treatment. Moving from one inventory "perimeter" to another increases the number of emission sources involved, whether grouped into projects, entities or territories (Table 3.2). While bottom-up, detailed and verified physical data are preferable for calculations in terms of accuracy, these data concerning the different sources (fuel-specific consumption, passenger-km, etc.) are often not available and can rapidly increase costs as the number of sources increases. As such, it is often necessary to rely on a number of different solutions, including modeling and/or downscaling of top-down statistics.

Data sources and the means of calculating emissions can have a direct impact on the ability of inventories to respond to the needs of local authorities. In addition to measured physical activity data and statistical downscaling, actors may be obliged to rely on model outputs.

Table 3.2 *Principal data sources by inventory "level" categories**

Project	Entity	Territory
Physical Activity Data**	Physical Activity Data** Model Outputs***	Physical Activity Data** Model Outputs*** Down-scaling Statistical Data****

* While all methods of calculating activity data can be used at any level, this table attempts to indicate which are most common at each level.
** Physical data may include: electricity, fuel, energy consumption, passenger-km, production values, waste mass, cultivated area, size of herds, etc.
*** Model Outputs are the estimates of activity produced using modeling techniques calibrated to the territory. For example, transport/land-use models can be used to estimate passenger-km traveled at the level of the entire territory. It is important, however, to establish the margin of error introduced by modeling techniques.
**** The downscaling of statistical data (national or international) can be used to estimate the portion of activity for which the territory in question is responsible.

For example, the data used in the quantification of transport-related GHG emissions can have a double uncertainty, as they are calculated through modeling tools calibrated using data collected as much as a decade beforehand. While the use of statistical approaches is, in some cases, inevitable, the reliance on averages, whether national or regional, may not capture the specificities of a given territory. Thus, emission reductions stemming from policies fostering, for example, the composition of the vehicle park across the entire territory or certain behavioral changes may not be captured by GHG inventories. While often necessary, these approaches to estimating emissions can introduce additional uncertainty into the final results as the margin of error increases.

The same holds true for the uncertainty of the emission factors used to quantify emissions. The uncertainty of the result is dependent on the calibration of the emission factor used. The most accurate quantification may require that context-specific or *Tier 3* emission factors[4] be developed for activities – taking into consideration the

---

[4] Tier 3 factors will need to be calculated principally for those emission factors representing aggregate characteristics of the entity in question. This corresponds principally to electricity (when it varies from national/regional averages) and the local vehicle fleet (given high levels of non-fossil technology, hybrid, biofuels, etc., penetration).

specific context and technologies used in a given place. However, in many instances, context-specific emission factors are not available or cannot be calculated (due to a lack of funds or data). As such, actors must decide among a number of nationally established emission factors (provided nationally, for example in France by the ADEME in their *Base Carbone®* or the CITEPA in the OMINEA guide) or international emission factors (developed by the International Panel on Climate Change). Emission factors are important to ensure accuracy, as the greenhouse gas intensity of activities may vary widely over time and across locations as well as be directly modified by policies.[5]

This lack of data, whether stemming from availability or the cost of production, can influence the uncertainty of the resulting quantified information. In many instances, actors will establish their specific quantification approach based on what data are available –particularly when the information tool must be developed within a relatively short period of time.

Monitoring costs

To date, no comprehensive data are available concerning the cost of subnational territorial greenhouse gas quantification. While a number of anecdotal examples can be identified, the cost can vary greatly depending on the level of detail and precision required by the local authority conducting the inventory; the amount and quality of the data available ex ante; the size of the territory; and the ability to conduct the quantification exercise internally or employ a consultant to do so.

The Association Bilan Carbone has recently collected survey data from users of the Bilan Carbone which gives a general idea of the costs involved when a local government contracts with an external consultant. Their survey indicates that the use of the Bilan Carbone® Territorial tool requires approximately 15 full-time days for an urban area with 1–50,000 residents and approximately 26 days for an urban area greater than 50,000 residents. Their estimates indicate that the

---

[5] For example, due to policies focusing on the deployment of renewable energy sources, the carbon intensity of the local energy mix may vary from national and international averages.

average consultant rate is between €600 and €800 per day. Thus, the use of the Bilan Carbone Territoire® tool averages between €10,500 and €18,200. Typically, this covers only Scope 1 and Scope 2 emissions with further Scope 3 analysis requiring additional time and resources (ABC, 2013). If produced internally, it is equally important to factor in the one-time training cost of €1,750 for the Bilan Carbone Territoire® tool and an annual operating license of between €350 and €700. Assuming that internal staff takes as much time as a consultant to compile the inventory,[6] the internal use of the Bilan Carbone Territoire® tool averages between €8,000 and €12,400. In addition, having internal expertise on this tool and its local implementation is likely to generate informal and long-term benefits to the local authority.

Estimations calculated using these average costs are used to assess the per CO_2e costs for five local authorities in France, assuming a yearly update of the inventory (Table 3.3). Removing "Chamonix-Mont-Blanc" which is a clear outlier due to its small size, these costs are estimated to 0.003 [0.001–0.007] €/tCO_2e. Costs appear to mainly be driven by city size since the inventory costs are largely fixed costs. When applied to administrative regions rather than cities, these costs would therefore likely be much lower.

While the Covenant of Mayors has estimated and centralized data on the total cost of the implementation of the SEAP plans,[7] no information is currently available in terms of the cost of measuring and tracking greenhouse gas emissions.

A number of means of reducing these costs may be available such as the combining of resources to produce regional-scale inventories with resolution at the city or other administrative perimeter scale. For example, in France, the Air Quality organizations (AASQA) carry out regional inventories with a city-level resolution. This allows cities to have an inventory at a lower cost, given that the majority of the development and calculations being centralized.

---

[6] The first inventory may be produced faster by an experienced consultant, but subsequent inventories could be produced more efficiently by internal staff who will likely be better acquainted with local data, especially when the inventory is updated after the first year.

[7] See *The Covenant of Mayors in Figures – 5 Years Assessment* (www.eumayors .eu/IMG/pdf/com_in_figures_jrc.pdf).

Table 3.3 *Cost of subnational GHG inventories*

Local authority name	Population	Method used	Total GHG emissions (tCO2e/yr)	Estimated average cost of inventory (€/yr)	Average cost of inventory (€/tCO₂e)
Dunkerque Grand Littoral	197,858	Méthode globale (Scope 1, Scope 2, Scope 3) type Bilan Carbone®	21,000,000	18,200	0.001
Lille Metropole	1,154,861	Méthode globale (Scope 1, Scope 2, Scope 3) type Bilan Carbone®	10,000,000	18,200	0.002
Marseille Provence Métropole	1,140,000	Méthode globale (Scope 1, Scope 2, Scope 3) type Bilan Carbone®	9,000,000	18,200	0.002
Grand Chalon	106,224	Méthode globale (Scope 1, Scope 2, Scope 3) type Bilan Carbone®	2,615,000	18,201	0.007
Communauté de communes de la Vallée de Chamonix-Mont-Blanc	13,468	Méthode globale (Scope 1, Scope 2, Scope 3) type Bilan Carbone®	12,500	10,500	0.84

Source: Author based on ABC (2013), Communauté de Communes Vallée de Chamonix (2011), Communauté urbaine de Dunkerque (2009), Grand Chalon (2013), Lille Metropole (2014) and Marseille Provence Metropole (2014).

3.4 Reporting

Given the current use of subnational territorial greenhouse gas inventories as typically tools serving the management needs of local authorities, few obligatory reporting standards currently exist. While a number of protocols provide suggested reporting formats, to date, only the EU Covenant of Mayors has set formal requirements for signatory local authorities to report. In general, both suggested and formal reporting formats focus more on what data and information to include (activity data, emission factors, breakdown between territorial and operational emissions) than on a harmonized format.

Nevertheless, the issue of how to aggregate and organize emission data has been addressed by local authorities and the developers of different methodologies. Reporting typically occurs along two lines. First, emission data are aggregated by scope. Second, emission data are aggregated along sectoral lines with emphasis paid to the identification of categories that correspond to the operational divisions of local governments rather than a less-relevant purely sector-based framework. Further, all of the protocols studied call for an inclusion in final reports of the emission factors used, and if possible, the base activity data used for calculation.

Reporting procedure

The basis for many territorial-scale reporting is the UNFCCC Common Reporting Framework (see Chapter 2). This framework provides guidance for reporting "complete, consistent and transparent" national greenhouse gas inventories, regardless of the method used to produce the data (IPCC, 2006). The guidelines and reporting framework establish and resolve what is included, and what must not be included, in order to produce comparable information across applications by different countries. In addition to defining what gases should be included and how different anthropogenic emissions sources should be treated, the Common Reporting Framework presents a method of aggregating and reporting GHG estimates into five categories: Energy (including Transportation); Industrial processes and product use; Agriculture, forestry and other land-use; Waste; and Other. Each category is then disaggregated into a number of subcategories corresponding to specific sources, classified by type of activity.

In general, reporting frameworks have adopted many of the basic elements of the IPCC-devised UNFCCC Common Reporting Framework. Nevertheless, different levels of aggregating and disaggregating data can influence the usefulness and policy-relevance of the produced data for local authorities. As such, it is important to stress that inventories are typically produced for *internal* purposes rather than *external* reporting where strict homogeneity is necessary to assure coherence.

Inventories conducted for *internal* uses, whether planning measures or tracking ex post, adapt approaches to the aggregation and categorization of sectors that respond to specific policy sectors and actions to facilitate the tracking of progress, including: buildings; lighting and traffic signals; water delivery facilities; etc. This type of categorization presents inventory results in a form more conducive to adjusting locally-controlled policies. As a result, they may not precisely follow IPCC-established sectors as they are less useful for local-level use and action. Nevertheless, the association of these categories with the larger IPCC system should be indicated. An important issue is level of disaggregation of emissions. It is important that these categories be contextualized for local actors, corresponding to their operational activities and division (Table 3.4).

While currently rare, homogeneity and comparability would be central to required external use reporting frameworks. *The Global Protocol for Community-Scale Greenhouse Gas Emissions* has attempted to bridge the need for a reporting format that corresponds to local needs, but nevertheless ties into national reporting formats. As such, this protocol suggests that for each emission source, the corresponding IPCC classification number is also provided – but also goes beyond IPCC reporting requirements to include Scope 2 and 3 emissions. This enables local authorities to have a more active collaboration with their national governments in the preparation of national GHG inventories that are submitted to the UNFCCC.

Verification

Internal verification procedures may be recommended by different methodologies and put into place ad hoc by local governments. However little to no required formal verification of subnational territorial greenhouse gas inventories currently occurs involving external third-party entities.

Table 3.4 *Example of disaggregated emissions sectors for local governance and decision-making*

IPCC macro sector	IPCC detailed category	Theoretical local reporting framework (disaggregated by fuel or energy source, including Scope 1 and 2 emissions)
Energy	Commercial/ Institutional	Buildings and facilities: - Municipal buildings, equipment/facilities - Municipal public lighting - Tertiary (non-municipal) buildings, equipment/ facilities - Industries (excluding industries involved in the EU Emission trading scheme – ETS)
	Residential	- Residential buildings - Social housing
	Public electricity and heat production	Local electricity production: - Wind power - Hydroelectric power - Photovoltaic - Combined heat and power - Other
		Local heat/cold production: - Combined heat and power - District heating plants - Other
	Other – stationary	- Water/sewer (energy only)
	Road transportation (disaggregated per fuel type)	- Municipal fleet - Public transport - Private commercial transport - Private vehicle use
	Fugitive emissions	Other

Table 3.4 (*cont.*)

IPCC macro sector	IPCC detailed category	Theoretical local reporting framework (disaggregated by fuel or energy source, including Scope 1 and 2 emissions)
Industrial Processes and Product Use		Other
Agriculture, Forestry and Other Land Uses		- Parks and land under municipal management - Agricultural and forestry land in jurisdiction - Land-use change in jurisdiction
Waste		- Waste (non-energy emissions)

Source: Author based on EC (2010), GHG Protocol (2013), ICLEI (2009) and IPCC (2006).

3.5 Conclusions: local needs currently prevail over harmonization

To date, there may be few immediate incentives for subnational actors to develop and adopt a harmonized protocol, particularly if the existing range of tools fit their current local needs and uses. While in recent years broad efforts at the international level have pushed for harmonization in practice, a number of obstacles to harmonization also exist at the local level. First, local authorities may oppose the deployment of an obligatory standard because it could be perceived as a means for the central government to exercise more control over their operations. In particular, local authorities may perceive a harmonized methodological framework as only being of use to national authorities to collect data, rather than as a tool for local-level action. With the increasing recognition of the immensity of the task for some national governments to meet increasingly ambitious climate goals, local authorities may fear that a harmonized inventory system is a step towards the imposition by national governments of binding local emission reduction targets. If these targets came without the provision of additional resources, local governments would potentially be constrained in decisions about how to use already "thin" local finances across a growing number of policy objectives.

Second, local authorities may also be uncomfortable with the notion of comparisons or standardized performance assessment across regions. They fear that such data could result in negative comparisons between themselves and other areas, given that the potential for emissions reduction and emission intensities can vary significantly depending on the context. For example, it would be inappropriate to compare aggregated emissions from an urban region with energy-intensive, heavy industry to another urban region with an economy based largely in the service sector. On the other hand, one could argue that the same issue exists for comparison between countries and did not prevent the emergence of comparable and verified national greenhouse gas inventories. Furthermore, as financing mechanisms such as CDM or NAMAs may require territorial inventories (at least sectorally), such as the REDD system and the World Bank's initiative on citywide CDM methodologies, movement towards harmonization may occur through a "carrot"-based approach.[8]

Finally, a number of local governments have already actively deployed methodologies and quantification tools for their own use and these may be embedded in their efforts to manage emissions. The prospect of shifting to a different methodology or using a different tool may be expensive and disruptive, particularly when no technical or financial resources are provided to aid in the transition.

These barriers present a relatively complex challenge to harmonization. To date most local-level action on GHG mitigation has remained voluntary and, thus, a top-down mandating of a single accepted methodology, in most cases, may be unfeasible. Harmonization efforts acceptable to all actors should be flexible enough to be adaptable to produce numbers useful to both local and national mitigation efforts.

---

[8] While formal MRV systems have not been deployed, there is nevertheless ongoing reflection as to how a system could function such as the BASEMIS-MRV project in France. This joint project between the Nantes-Saint Nazaire Metropolitan Area, the Lyon Urban Community and the Strasbourg Urban Community aims to produce a methodology that responds to multiple reporting requirements to which the cities are subjected as well as serving as a basis for potential MRV needs (performance-based payments, etc.).

Table 3.5 *MRV ID table*

Context	Global Protocol for Community-Scale Greenhouse Gas Emissions (GPC)[a]	Bilan Carbone® Territorial[b]	EC-Com[c]
Regulator	Created by: C40 Cities, ICLEI Support: World Resource Institute, UNEP, UN-HABITAT	Created by: Agence de l'Environnement et de la Maîtrise de l'Energie (ADEME) Transferred to the: Association Bilan Carbone (ABC) in October 2011	European Commission Covenant of Mayors
Type and level of incentive to comply	- Reputation within network - Voluntary tool/engagement	- Voluntary tool - Highly recommended by the ADEME in the construction of a PCET (Plan Climat Energie Territoire)	- Reputation - Binding engagement after voluntary commitment
Entities concerned	- Subnational governments, principally urban - Local authorities[d]	- The "territory" module that evaluates emissions from all activities taking place on the territory of the community (version 7 update in April 2013). It is designed to apply to any local authority administering French territory (municipalities, region, etc.) And more generally to any entity organized around a territory with unambiguous boundaries (Country, NRP, etc).	- Subnational governments

Table 3.5 (*cont.*)

Context	Global Protocol for Community-Scale Greenhouse Gas Emissions (GPC)[a]	Bilan Carbone® Territorial[b]	EC-Com[c]
Sectors concerned	Dependent on level of detail selected (three options): - GPC 2012 BASIC: Energy production and use, transport, waste, industrial processes - GPC 2012 BASIC+: BASIC as well as agriculture, forestry and land-use - GPC 2012 EXPANDED: trans-boundary emissions from the exchange/use/consumption of goods and services (Scopes 1, 2 & 3)	- Structured in a significantly different manner from the other protocols, encompasses upstream and embodied emissions, and as such produces a larger value for GHG emissions. - All sectors. A specific tool – ClimAgri – was developed by the ADEME and has been available since 2011.	Energy consumption: - Municipal buildings, equipment/facilities; - Residential buildings; - Tertiary buildings, equipment/facilities; - Public lighting; - Industry not involved in EU ETS; - Transport (aviation and fluvial transport excluded); - Non-energy emissions from wastewater and solid waste treatment.
Gases concerned	CO_2, CH_4, N_2O, HFCs, PFCs and SF_6 in metric tons and in tons of CO_2 equivalent should be reported.	- CO_2, CH_4, N_2O, HFCs, PFCs and SF_6, converted in tons of CO_2 equivalent. - All the other GHGs are considered such as: Montreal Protocol gases (CFC), stratospheric water vapor (produced by planes), etc.	- Required: CO_2, CH_4 and N_2O if sources are addressed in the Sustainable Energy Action Plan

				Monitoring	
Overall MRV costs	No data available			€8,000–20,000 per Bilan Carbone Territorial 0.003 [0.001–0.007] €/tCO$_2$e (assuming a yearly update of the inventory)	No data available
Rules	GPC 2012 BASIC	GPC 2012 BASIC+: guidance for accounting and reporting of agriculture, forestry and land use in urban spaces, as well as appropriate accounting and allocation of GHG emissions due to inter-city and international transport.	GPC 2012 EXPANDED includes all Scope 3 categories based on full consumption-based and production-based accounting.	Bilan Carbone® "Territoire" Version 7: A methodology guide associated with tools for the operational assessment of the GHG emissions associated with a territory (Scope 1, 2 & 3), and the definition of a reduction action plan.	How to Develop a Sustainable Energy Action Plan (SEAP) – Guidebook – EU Covenant of Mayors www.eumayors.eu/IMG/pdf/seap_guidelines_en-2.pdf

Table 3.5 (*cont.*)

Context	Global Protocol for Community-Scale Greenhouse Gas Emissions (GPC)[a]	Bilan Carbone® Territorial[b]	EC-Com[c]
Other reference documents	Based on: - *ICLEI: International Local Government GHG Emissions Analysis Protocol* - *UNEP/WB/UN-HABITAT: International Standard for Determining Greenhouse Gas Emissions for Cities;*[2] - *WRI/WBCSD: GHG Protocol Standards;*[3] - *Covenant of Mayors: Baseline Emissions Inventory/ Monitoring Emissions Inventory methodology;*[4] - *ICLEI USA: Local Government Operations Protocol5.*	Based on and compatible with ISO 14064 standard, - GHG Protocol Initiative - Directive "permit" No 2003/87/ EC concerning the exchange of CO_2 quota system. - Internationally recognized and integrated into existing systems standards (e.g., ISO 14000) and future (e.g., ISO 14069).	Not stated
Uncertainty requirements	No specific requirement, however: "The calculation of GHG emissions should not systematically overstate or understate actual GHG emissions. Accuracy should be sufficient to give decision makers and the public reasonable assurance of the integrity of the reported information. Local authorities should reduce uncertainties in the quantification process to the extent that it is possible and practical." (GHG Protocol, 2013)	No specific requirement, however: "The Bilan Carbone ® is a tool for decision support and thus satisfies a system based on the order of magnitude reasoning." The Bilan Carbone® helps the user to evaluate the uncertainty associated with the calculation (based on the combination between the uncertainty on the emissions factors and the activity data used, and in line with the IPCC guidelines.	No specific requirement
Achieved uncertainty range	Not formally assessed	Not formally assessed	Not formally assessed

Cost range					
Scope	**GPC 2012 BASIC:**	**GPC 2012 BASIC+:**	**GPC 2012 EXPANDED:**		
A	Covers all *Scope 1* and *Scope 2* emissions of stationary units, mobile units, wastes, and Industrial Processes and Product Use (IPPU), as well as *Scope 3* emissions of waste sector.	Covers GPC 2012 BASIC as well as agriculture, forestry and land use (AFOLU) and *Scope 3* emissions for mobile units.	Covers the entirety of *Scopes 1, 2,* and 3 emissions including trans-boundary emissions due to the exchange/use/consumption of goods and services.	While the Bilan Carbone® Methodologies do not use the Scope terminology, it nevertheless covers Scopes 1–3 depending on user: A global method based on lifecycle analysis (LCA), it allows to quantify the anthropogenic emissions of greenhouse gases that are generated: – directly by the activities and services specific to the entity (producer approach: transport, use of buildings, energy, waste, etc.) – indirectly, "incorporated" in the products or services required for the activity of the entity and that are issued outside of the entity (consumer approach: consumer goods and materials, capital equipment, etc.).	Scope 1. Direct emissions due to fuel combustion in the territory in the buildings, equipment/facilities and transportation sectors. Scope 2. (Indirect) emissions related to production of electricity, heat, or cold that are consumed in the territory. Scope 3 (User Dependent). Other direct emissions that occur in the territory, depending on the choice of sectors. Option to include lifecycle as an alternative to a standard inventory (IPCC fuel combustion emission factors) through the use of lifecycle-derived emission factors.
B	Territorial	Territorial	Territorial	Territorial	Territorial

Table 3.5 (*cont.*)

Context	Global Protocol for Community-Scale Greenhouse Gas Emissions (GPC)a			Bilan Carbone® Territorialb	EC-Comc
C	Not Applicable			Not Applicable	Not Applicable
Frequency	Annual monitoring encouraged	Not Applicable	Not Applicable	Annual monitoring encouraged	Annual monitoring encouraged First inventory (so-called Baseline Emission Inventory) must be conducted within one year after signature of the Covenant as part of the Sustainable Energy Action Plan.
Source for activity data	Not specified			Encourages the use of Physical Activity Data. If PAD are not available, then encourages the use of Model Outputs. If MO not available, encourages the use of Downscaling Statistical Data	Encourages activity data specific to the study municipality and discourages estimates based on national averages
Uncertainty range for activity data	Not specified, but the quality of data is to be self-evaluated according to: High (H): localized emission factors and detailed activity data; Medium (M): national emission factors or generic activity data; Low (L): international/national emission factors and generic activity data.			Not specified, but the quality of data is to be self-evaluated in % of uncertainty following the IPCC guidelines	Not specified

Source for emission factors	See above	- *Base Carbone* ® – emission factors calculated by the ADEME for France - IPCC international estimates	Not specified. Allows use of IPCC default emission factors (IPCC Tier 1 & IPCC Tier 2) or the use of LCA internationally standardized ISO 14040 series
Uncertainty range for emission factors	See above	Assessed in % of uncertainty	Not specified
Direct measurement	Preferred when possible, but not required	Preferred when possible, but not required	Preferred when possible, but not required
Incentives to reduce uncertainty	None	None	None
Is requirements stringency adapted to the amount of emissions at stake (materiality)?	No	No	No
Reporting			
Rules	GPC 2012 Accounting and Reporting Framework	Common reporting format provided by Bilan Carbone® Territoire	European Commission Covenant of Mayors

Table 3.5 (*cont.*)

Context	Global Protocol for Community-Scale Greenhouse Gas Emissions (GPC)[a]	Bilan Carbone® Territorial[b]	EC-Com[c]
Other reference documents			
Format	Suggested format: - For each source, the corresponding IPCC classification number in the national greenhouse gas inventory is also provided (e.g., 1.A.3.b Road transportation). This enables local authorities to have a more active collaboration with their national governments in the preparation of national GHG inventories that are submitted to UNFCCC. - Report source or sector-specific quantification methods used. Suggested information to include: **Emissions by Sources:** Total GHG emissions (in tCO_2e). For sources included in GPC 2012 BASIC; if quantification is not possible, Notation Keys should be used. The total number of occurrences of each Notation Key and relevant GPC reference number should be indicated. If GPC 2012 BASIC+ or EXPANDED is chosen, sources that are included should be clearly indicated. **Emissions by Scopes:** Indicate the scope of each emission source, and separate total emissions by *Scope 1*, *Scope 2* and *Scope 3*. It is noted that in reporting by "scopes," complete Scope 1 emissions must be reported including emissions from Energy Generation (GPC I.3.1). **Gases:** Data for CO_2, CH_4, N_2O, HFCs, PFCs and SF_6 in metric tons and in tons of CO_2 equivalent should be reported.	The Association Bilan Carbone issued a reporting template (www.associationbilancarbone.fr/private/325/field-fichier/trame_de_rapport_type_bilan_carboner_-_fevrier_2013.pdf). The key points to report are: -**Context and objectives:** Description of the study area; Motivations, expectations and objectives; Scope, phasing and schedule. -**Methodology and vocabulary:** Reminder of the Bilan Carbone® methodology and accounting principles (GES, GWP, emission factors, etc.). -**Presentation of territory's GES emissions:** Dashboard by categories, subcategories or SCOPE, ratios; qualitative commentaries for each category. -**Carbon vulnerability assessment:** Assessment of additional costs related to the increase in oil prices or a tax on the GES emissions.	Reporting template provided. Local authorities must also provide: - inventory year; - number of inhabitants in the inventory year; - choice of emission factor approach (standard IPCC or LCA); - emission reporting unit (CO_2 or CO_2-equivalent); final energy consumption and emissions by each sector addressed and by energy carrier; - emission factors used; - identification of local electricity generation plants; - identification of local heat/cold plants; Local authorities are also encouraged to provide: - information on data collection methods;

-Data quality:
- *High (H):* localized emission factors and detailed activity data;
- *Medium (M):* national emission factors or generic activity data;
- *Low (L):* international/national emission factors and generic activity data.
- **Year:** Year of inventory or emission data
-**Quantification:** Report source or sector-specific quantification methods used

-Reduction actions plan:
Presentation of the reductions objectives and plan.
The Bilan Carbone ® summary sheet: global emissions calculated in carbon equivalent (equ.C) and CO_2 equivalent (equ.CO_2) results for each position for which emissions data input are required.

- assumptions made;
- references used;
- information on any changes related to approach/ methodology/data sources, etc. since the previous inventory;
- eventual comments that would help to understand and interpret the inventory. For example, it may be useful to provide exploitations on which factors have influenced CO_2 emissions since last inventories, such as
- economic conditions or demographic factors;
- names and contact information of people who provided information for the inventory.

Table 3.5 (*cont.*)

Context	Global Protocol for Community-Scale Greenhouse Gas Emissions (GPC)[a]	Bilan Carbone® Territorial[b]	EC-Com[c]
Level of source disaggregation	User-dependent: - At least six main categories close to those of national greenhouse gas inventories: Stationary units, Mobile units (in the *IPCC Guidelines* these two categories are grouped under 'energy'), Waste, IPPU (industrial process and product use), AFOLU (agriculture, forestry, and land use), and Other indirect emissions. These emission sources are further categorized by scopes (see *Section 3 Boundary Setting*) to distinguish direct and indirect impacts. Indicate the scope of each emission source, and separate total emissions by *Scope 1, Scope 2 and Scope 3*. - Regardless of whether local authorities choose to report BASIC, BASIC+ or EXPANDED, the GHG data are aggregated and reported by *Scope 1, Scope 2 and Scope 3* separately.	- Results are presented by sectors including: Energy production, Industrial processes, Tertiary emissions, Residential, Agriculture and fisheries, Freight transport, Passenger transport, Construction of buildings and infrastructure, Waste and end of life materials, Creation of future waste and Food-related emissions. - The Bilan Carbone ® method does not directly use the Scopes terminology to disaggregate emissions totals.	- Total territorial emissions disaggregated by sector of activity and by energy carrier (the level of disaggregation is user-dependent). - Separate reporting of emissions associated with municipal operations (also known as corporate emissions).
Frequency	Not specified	Not specified	Every four years
Timeline	Not specified	Not specified	Not specified
Language	English	French and English	The reporting template is completed in English, while the Sustainable Energy Action Plan document can be in other languages.

Is requirements stringency adapted to the amount of emissions at stake (materiality)?:	No	No	No	No
Cost range	No average data available	No average data available	No average data available	No average data available
Verification	No required verification process	No required verification process	No required verification process	SEAPs are analyzed by the EU Joint Research Center based on data coherence and consistency checks, however there is no required verification process.

[a] Information from GHG Protocol (2013).

[b] Information comes from: Bader and Bleischwitz (2009); Bilan Carbone® Territoire 6; DRIEA- IDF (2013); Ibrahim et al. (2012).

[c] Baseline emissions inventory guidelines developed with the European Commission's Covenant of Mayors (EC-CoM), Part II in How to Develop a Sustainable Energy Action Plan (European Commission, 2010), referred to hereon as "EC-CoM" (information drawn from: Ibrahim et al., 2012).

[d] Local authority, as defined by ISO/TR-14069, is a public body recognized as such by legislation or by the directives of a higher level of government to set general policies, plans or requirements. GPC can also be useful for subnational entities such as towns, districts, counties, prefectures, provinces and states pursuant to appropriate modifications.

Source: Author based on European Commission (2010), GHG Protocol (2013) and ICLEI (2009).

Bibliography

ABC, 2013. *Synthèse Enquête Flash 2013*. Association Bilan Carbone. www.associationbilancarbone.fr/sites/default/files/enquete-flash-2013-bc-2012.pdf. Accessed May 19, 2014.

Bader, N. and Bleischwitz, R., 2009. *Study Report: Comparative Analysis of Local GHG Inventory Tools*. Produced for the College of Europe and Institut Veolia Environnement.

Cochran, I., 2010. A use-based analysis of local-scale GHG inventories (No. 2010–7), Working Paper. CDC Climate Research, Paris.

2012. Towards a hierarchy of GHG information tools: implications for harmonization, production and appropriation, in I. Cochran, *The Local-Level Management of Climate Change: The Case of Urban Passenger Transportation in France*. Doctoral Thesis: Université Paris-Dauphine, Paris. www.cdcclimat.com/spip.php?action=telecharger&arg=1734. Accessed May 19, 2014.

Communauté de Communes Vallée de Chamonix, 2011. *Plan Climat Energie Territorial – Présentation du diagnostic énergie/climat du territoire*. www.cc-valleedechamonixmontblanc.fr/documents/communaute/grands_programmes/pdf/reunion_publique_29_03_2011.pdf. Accessed May 19, 2014.

Communauté urbaine de Dunkerque, 2009. *Stratégie climat de la Communauté urbaine de Dunkerque*. www.communaute-urbaine-dunkerque.fr/fileadmin/user_upload/pdf/Institution/Plan-climat/Strategie_PCT.pdf. Accessed May 19, 2014.

Corfee-Morlot, J., Kamal-Chaoui, L., Donovan, M.G., Cochran, I., Robert, A. and Teasdale, P.J., 2009. Cities, climate change and multilevel governance (No. 14), OECD Environmental Working Papers. OECD publishing, Paris.

Covenant of Mayors, 2014. *Covenant of Mayors – Committed to local sustainable energy*. www.eumayors.eu/index_en.html. Accessed May 19, 2014.

DRIEAL-IDF, 2013. Étude comparative des outils carbone territoriaux dans les démarches de développement local et d'aménagement. Direction Régionale & Interdépartementale de l'Equipement et de l'Aménagement d'Ile-de-France. www.driea.ile-de-france.developpement-durable.gouv.fr. Accessed May 19, 2014.

European Commission, 2010. *How to Develop a Sustainable Energy Action Plan*. Publications Office of the European Union, Luxembourg.

GHG Protocol, 2013. *The Global Protocol for Community-Scale Greenhouse Gas Emissions*. www.ghgprotocol.org/city-accounting. Accessed May 19, 2014.

Grand Chalon, 2013. *Plan Climat Energie Territorial du Grand Chalon.* www.legrandchalon.fr/fileadmin/user_upload/mediatheque/ Ressources/Livret_blanc.pdf. Accessed May 19, 2014.

Ibrahim, N., Sugar, L., Hoornweg, D. and Kennedy, C., 2012. Greenhouse gas emissions from cities: comparison of international inventory frameworks. *Local Environment: The International Journal of Justice and Sustainability* 1: 1–19.

ICLEI, 2009. *International Local Government GHG Emissions Analysis Protocol.* Release version 1.0. www.iclei.org/index.php?id=8154. Accessed August 2009.

IPCC, 2006. *IPCC Guidelines for National Greenhouse Gas Inventories. Revised 1996 IPCC Guidelines for National Greenhouse Gas Inventories*; 1997, in H.S. Eggleston, L. Buendia, K. Miwa, T. Ngara and K. Tanabe, eds. Prepared by the National Greenhouse Gas Inventories Programme. IGES, Japan.

Lille Metropole, 2014. *Le Bilan Carbone.* www.communaute-urbaine-dunkerque.fr/fileadmin/user_upload/pdf/Institution/Plan-climat/ Strategie_PCT.pdf. Accessed May 19, 2014.

Marseille Provence Metropole, 2014. *Bilan carbone du territoire.* www .planclimat-mpm.fr/evaluer/bilan-carbone/bilan-carbone-du-territoire. Accessed May 19, 2014.

OECD, 2010. *Cities and Climate Change.* Organisation for Economic Co-operation and Development, Paris.

4 | Variant 2: sectoral MRV at the jurisdictional level – forestry (REDD+) in the VCS and the UNFCCC

MARIANA DEHEZA AND
VALENTIN BELLASSEN

4.1 Context

Ever since avoided deforestation came back on the agenda of international climate negotiations in Montreal in 2005, there has been a forefeeling that only a large-scale approach, national or jurisdictional, would eventually be acceptable. This was confirmed by the 16th Conference of the Parties in 2010 (Decision 1/CP.16), and this is the approach that the World Bank has been pursuing with its Forest Carbon Partnership Facility (FCPF). Accordingly, the Verified Carbon Standard (VCS) – the leading standard for REDD+ (Reduction of Emissions from Deforestation and Degradation of Forests and the role of conservation, sustainable management and enhancement of forest carbon stocks) projects in 2012 – has been trying to upscale its project-scale approach over the last couple of years. This resulted in the Jurisdictional and Nested REDD+ (JNR) Framework which undertook public consultation in 2012 and was officially released in 2013.

The Verified Carbon Standard (VCS) is one of the most widely used standards in the voluntary market, with 55 percent of transacted credits (56 MtCO$_2$e) according to Peters-Stanley et al. (2013). So far, however, all these credits have been coming from individual projects, including those that allow for the REDD+. As of October 1st, 2013, the JNR was still too recent and the first programs and credits to pass it had still to materialize. Yet, eight pilot programs (at the national and regional level) using these requirements were being developed. Five of these pilot programs[1] are funded by a US$1.4 million grant from the

---

[1] These pilot programs are expected to be implemented at a national level in Costa Rica and at a subnational level in the States of Acre (Brazil), San Martín and Madre de Dios (Peru) and Mai Ndombe Province (the Democratic Republic of the Congo).

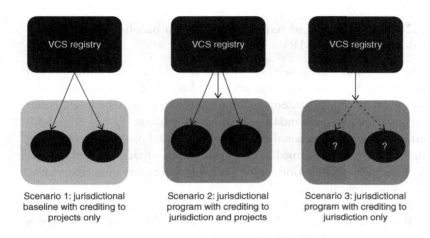

Scenario 1: jurisdictional baseline with crediting to projects only

Scenario 2: jurisdictional program with crediting to jurisdiction and projects

Scenario 3: jurisdictional program with crediting to jurisdiction only

Note: Only one jurisdictional level is shown, yet multiple levels may exist and receive VCUs simultaneously

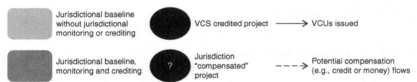

Figure 4.1 VCS JNR simplified crediting scenarios
Source: VCS (2013a).

Norwegian International Climate and Forest Initiative (NICFI) given to the VCS over a three-year period (2013–2015) to develop and pilot integrated JNR accounting and verification frameworks.

As such, it was at that time the most operational MRV framework for jurisdictional REDD+, and to our knowledge, the most advanced sectoral MRV framework. This is why it has been chosen as a "variant" from national greenhouse gas inventories for MRV at territorial scale in this chapter. It remains to be seen whether the VCS JNR keeps its headway or is overtaken by the World Bank's FCPF or, more likely, by the UNFCCC thanks to the breakthrough decisions of the 19th Conference of the Parties in Warsaw (Dupont et al., 2013). No matter the outcome, the future leading standard for jurisdictional REDD+ MRV will likely retain some, if not most, of the VCS JNR requirements.

4.2 Variable scope of requirements: from baseline only to full jurisdictional MRV

The JNR requirements released by the Verified Carbon Standard (VCS) are applicable at the national and/or subnational level and may also include nested projects. Subnational jurisdictions may be based either on administrative boundaries or other boundaries (e.g., eco-region) established by the national government. "Nested projects" refer to initiatives that are developed at the project scale – that is possibly a finer scale than the jurisdiction – but that could ultimately integrate a jurisdictional program.

Different crediting scenarios could be envisioned (Deheza and Bellassen, 2012) but the VCS decided to simplify three eligible cases where its requirements are applicable (Figure 4.1).

Scenario 2 and scenario 3 are fully jurisdictional as credit flows are expected at the jurisdictional level. As such, they require a full MRV procedure across the entire jurisdiction (i.e., across all included carbon pools, activities and areas).

4.3 Monitoring requirements

Activity-based vs. land-based accounting

The monitoring requirements first and foremost depend on the crediting scenario (see Section 4.2). If scenario 1 is applied, monitoring will apply to specific activities – e.g., reforestation, small-scale mosaic deforestation, large-scale commercial deforestation, and it may be restricted to specific locations within the jurisdiction. The JNR refers to this option as *activity-based accounting*. *Land-based accounting*, which corresponds to a full jurisdictional MRV procedure, including all forestry activities across the whole jurisdiction, must be used if scenario 2 or 3 are applied (Table 4.1).

Differentiation of sources of emissions/sequestration

A REDD+ jurisdictional baseline and program may be broken down into any of the broad activities[2] depicted in Table 4.2. For the purposes

[2] The VCS defines these categories based on UNFCCC decisions.

Table 4.1 *Monitoring requirements and accounting approaches*

	Applicable crediting scenarios	Monitoring requirements
Land-based accounting	Scenario 2, Scenario 3	Historical GHG emissions shall be calculated from changes in carbon stocks. Such a historical level shall form the basis of the baseline projection. This applies to jurisdictions where no baseline (or reference level) has been established by the UNFCCC for crediting purposes. Changes within and between all land-use categories shall be regularly monitored, using methods to ensure the consistent treatment of land areas over time. Land-based accounting may use sample plots, remote sensing techniques, modeling approaches, or some combination of these to produce an estimate of emissions and removals for the entire geographic area over the specified time period.
Activity-based accounting	Scenario 1	A historical level of GHG emissions across the historical reference period shall be calculated for each selected activity. Such historical level shall form the basis of the baseline projection. Historical rates for gross deforestation shall be determined using remote sensing imagery, except for large-scale commercial deforestation which must be separated out when exceeding 10% of total deforestation.[a] Historical rates for all other activities may optionally use remote sensing imagery. Examples of other data sources that may be used include surveys, relevant statistics and inventories.

[a] This is mandatory for scenario 1 and recommended as best practice for scenario 2. The rationale behind this requirement is that commercial deforestation may bias spatial baselines and project accounting for all other types of deforestation, mainly because commercial deforestation is less dependent on location than other deforestation activities, making it hard to estimate accurately when a project area will be deforested for commercial purposes.

of jurisdictional and nested REDD+, these categories are defined in terms of the UNFCCC REDD+ activities as depicted in the first column of Table 4.2.

These reporting categories of activities are not rigidly imposed; jurisdictional proponents can choose which broad activities set out in Table 4.2 will be accounted for within their jurisdictional REDD+ program, except for deforestation which must be accounted for regardless of which other activities are included. Proponents must separately monitor each broad activity. In the case where deforestation is included but degradation is not, accounting for eventual leakage from deforestation to degradation is mandatory. This breakout requirement also exists in UNFCCC requirements, with the exception of leakage from deforestation to degradation. UNFCCC requirements however require "completeness," that is the monitoring of all activities.

As stated for reforestation and improved forest management, carbon sequestration/emissions in REDD+ activities can occur in seven compartments or carbon pools, although not all seven necessarily need to be monitored:

- **Above-ground woody biomass:** including stems, branches and the foliage of trees as well as non-woody vegetation and shrubs.
- **Above-ground non-woody biomass.**
- **Below-ground biomass:** including living roots.
- **Deadwood:** including non-living biomass such as standing or lying on the ground stumps or buried dead roots.
- **Litter:** non-living biomass with a diameter less than a certain threshold defined in the methodologies. It also includes decomposing lying deadwood.
- **Soil organic carbon:** including all soil components derived from plants and animals and peats.
- **Harvested wood products.**

Under the UNFCCC, the first two categories cannot be reported separately (IPCC, 2006).

The JNR requires project developers to be conservative when choosing the pools and sources that will be accounted for, in the sense that all the pools that could decrease in the future compared to the jurisdictional baseline need to be included in the accounting as well as those that are deemed above *de minimis*. There is no specific definition of what can be considered a *de minimis* source except that in the overall

Table 4.2 *Activities to be accounted for by jurisdictional REDD+ programs*

UNFCCC REDD+ activities/Broad VCS jurisdictional and nested REDD+ activities	Broad VCS project activities	Specific VCS project activities	Major activities
RED (Reducing Emissions from Deforestation)	REDD (Reduced Emissions from Deforestation and Degradation)	APD (avoided planned deforestation)	Reducing deforestation (conversion of forest to non-forest).
		APD + RWE (avoided planned deforestation plus wetland restoration)	
		APD + CIW (avoided planned deforestation and wetland conservation)	
		AUD (avoided unplanned deforestation)	
		AUD + RWE (avoided unplanned deforestation plus wetland restoration)	
		AUD + CIW (avoided unplanned deforestation and wetland conservation)	
REDD (Reducing Emissions from Degradation)		AUDD (avoided unplanned degradation)	Reducing emissions from forests remaining forests.
		AUDD + RWE (avoided unplanned degradation plus wetland restoration)	
		AUDD + CIW (avoided unplanned degradation and wetland conservation)	

Table 4.2 (*cont.*)

UNFCCC REDD+ activities/Broad VCS jurisdictional and nested REDD+ activities	Broad VCS project activities	Specific VCS project activities	Major activities
	IFM (Improved Forest Management)	RIL (reduced impact logging)	Increasing removals from forests remaining forests / increasing conversion to forests.
		LtPF (logged to protected forest)	
		ERA (extended rotation age)	
		IFM + RWE (improved forest management plus wetland restoration)	
		IFM + CIW (improved forest management and wetland conservation)	
REDD+ (Sustainable management of forests and enhancement of forest carbon stocks)		LtHP (low productive to high-productive forest)	
	ARR (Afforestation, Reforestation and Revegetation)	ARR (afforestation, reforestation and revegetation)	
		ARR + RWE (afforestation, reforestation and revegetation plus wetland restoration)	

Source: VCS (2013a).

excluded sources shall not collectively represent more than 10 percent of total emissions.

Depending on the size of the jurisdiction, the VCS also requires the calculation of emissions or removals not only within the jurisdictional boundary, but also the calculation of emissions indirectly affected by the jurisdictional program, most commonly referred to as "leakage." If the jurisdiction is national then there is no need to account for leakage. However, subnational jurisdictions do need to account for emissions that may occur inside the same country but outside the jurisdiction. Activity-shifting, market and ecological leakage are three types of leakage considered.[3] Leakage emissions may be determined either directly from monitoring, or indirectly when leakage is difficult to monitor directly but where scientific knowledge or research provides credible estimates of likely impacts. The *JNR Leakage Tool* provides guidance on how to perform these calculations and jurisdictional proponents can also justify the use of their own methods.

Criteria for the jurisdictional baseline

A jurisdictional baseline needs to be developed in any of the crediting scenarios. It is fixed for a period of 5–10 years after which it must be updated and re-validated by an auditor.

A jurisdictional baseline may be divided into any of the following broad activities:[4]

- reduced emissions from deforestation (including most REDD activities, set out in VCS document AFOLU Requirements);
- reduced emissions from degradation (which may include some REDD and most IFM activities set out in VCS document AFOLU Requirements);

---

[3] Market leakage occurs when projects significantly reduce the production of a commodity resulting in a shift of production elsewhere to make up for the lost supply. Activity-shifting leakage occurs when the actual agent of deforestation displaces its deforestation or degradation activities outside the project boundary. Finally, ecological leakage occurs in wetland restoration and conservation projects where a project activity causes changes in GHG emissions or fluxes of GHG emissions from ecosystems that are hydrologically connected to the project area.

[4] The VCS defines these categories based on the UNFCCC REDD+ activities defined in Decision 1/CP.16.

- carbon stock enhancement (e.g, ARR, assisted natural regeneration and IFM Low-productive to High-productive Forest set out in VCS document AFOLU Requirements).

The selected activities will also be accounted for within the jurisdictional REDD+ program. In order to develop the baseline the jurisdictional proponent must develop at least two fixed alternative baseline scenarios: historical annual average emissions or removals over an 8–12 year period and a historical trend of emissions or removals based on changes over at least 10 years. Both of these scenarios must end within 2 years of the start of the current jurisdictional baseline period.

In order to ensure that baseline emissions are not overestimated due to exceptional events that are unlikely to reoccur in the next ten years, some instances of forest loss in the historical reference period should be excluded: areas impacted by significant geological and weather-related natural disturbances[5] and large infrastructure projects.[6]

Other alternative baseline scenarios may include modeled adjustments reflecting national or subnational circumstances which may include the determination of deforestation projections based on changes in potential deforestation drivers (e.g., GDP, road infrastructure, population growth, agricultural commodity prices, etc.) or committed national (and subnational) policies and development plans. The justification of performing such adjustments is required and should demonstrate that there is greater certainty in projecting the chosen independent variable rather than performing a direct projection of deforestation.

In some cases where a jurisdictional baseline exists but does not cover some of the selected activities, a project baseline covering these activities needs to be developed. In those cases the geographic areas of both areas should not overlap. Out of these baselines, the jurisdiction must determine the most plausible one and justify its selection. A no-objection letter from the jurisdictional authority is required if

---

[5] Referring to areas larger than 1,000 hectares of forest loss due to volcanos, landslides, hurricanes, and other events that have a return interval greater than ten years.

[6] Large infrastructure projects are those that imply the loss of more than 1,000 hectares of forests. These projects may include the flooding from a new dam or the footprint of a new mine. Roads are not considered as large infrastructure projects. More generally, this exclusion is accepted for infrastructure projects that are not part of a pattern that will likely be replicated in the future.

the program proponent is not itself an entity with legislated control or authority over the jurisdiction. In all cases, a stakeholder consultation must be conducted.

Monitoring requirements at jurisdictional scale

The activities and carbon pools that need to be monitored are the same ones that were selected in the jurisdictional baseline. Monitoring needs to be conducted at least every five years at the jurisdictional level. By default, the entire forest area of the jurisdiction needs to be monitored. Exceptionally, two types of forest areas may be excluded:

- if they are not impacted by the program (e.g., remote forests that will likely not be touched by deforestation);
- areas excluded from the baseline due to significant natural disturbances or large-scale infrastructure projects should also not be accounted for.

Specific monitoring requirements are set for some activity data such as land-use changes and for some emission factors such as the carbon stocks of major carbon pools (Table 4.3).

At project scale

Nested projects on their side need to follow the monitoring requirements of the VCS at the project level that are set by each methodology. For example, methodology VM007 allows an uncertainty of ±10 percent at estimation of land-use and land-cover change for REDD projects through the use of remote sensing data. Methodology VM015 includes requirements regarding accuracy of each class or category when using Land-Use and Land-Cover Map and Land-Use and Land-Cover Change Map. They should be 80 percent accurate.

The incorporation of lower-level monitoring results – project level – results into higher level – jurisdictional level – results is considered best practice under some conditions:

- Lower-level monitoring results from activities such as deforestation or afforestation can be used directly as part of high-level monitoring as long as this incorporation does not impact the estimates for other activities or other areas at the higher monitoring level. This would

Table 4.3 VCS JNR monitoring requirements for activity data and emission factors

Monitoring element	Method/approach to be used
Activity data: land-use changes	Spatially explicit land conversion information, following IPCC Approach 3 (IPCC, 2006). This can be achieved by stratifying the jurisdiction into more homogeneous strata such as municipalities and repeated sampling consistent with the stratification. Alternatively, remote sensing and/or cadastral information can be used to provide wall-to-wall land-use change maps.
	A minimum 75 percent accuracy is required for land-use classification.
	Proxies can be used instead of such direct measurements. In that case, the program proponent shall demonstrate transparently:
	• their correlation with actual land-use change;
	• that they represent an equivalent or better method than direct measurement of land-use change.
	The "equivalent or better" requirement must take into account reliability, consistency or practicality. As the use of a proxy is certainly more practical than performing an actual measurement the stringency of this requirement is dissolved.

Activity data: degradation and enhancements in forest carbon stocks (including afforestation, reforestation, improved forest management, and revegetation)	*Direct methods* such as remote sensing or forest inventory or *indirect methods* such as survey data or statistical data on timber harvesting. Community-based monitoring methods are encouraged where appropriate and results of such monitoring shall be subject to the same accuracy assessment and uncertainty deductions as all methods (see Chapter 5).
Emission factors	IPCC Tier 2 – that is country-specific default values, or Tier 3 – that is country-specific methods, usually peer-reviewed modeling, shall be used. IPCC Tier 1 (IPCC default values) may be used for carbon pools representing less than 15 percent of total carbon stocks. Jurisdictions shall document the precision level for each emission factor. Emission factors used in monitoring shall be consistent with those used to set the baseline.

Table 4.4 *Deduction factor for uncertain estimates*

Estimated uncertainty range at 95% confidence level for total emission reductions	Deduction factor
±15% to ±30%	0.943
±30% to ±50%	0.893
±50% to ±100%	0.836
> ±100%	to be addressed in the methodology

Source: 32nd meeting Report – CDM Methodology Panel.

be the case for example if deforestation in area B – where there is no lower-level project – was monitored as total deforestation minus deforestation within project area A.

- For other activities such as reductions in degradation, the monitoring of lower and higher levels may impact one another. Total GHG emission reductions and removals from the lower level (within the same boundary, i.e., scope and carbon pools) shall be deducted from the higher level's total emissions reductions and removals to prevent any double counting.

Uncertainty requirements depend on the accounting approach at the jurisdictional level

Similarly to the VCS requirements for projects, the JNR mandates an uncertainty assessment at jurisdictional level. The assumptions, parameters and procedures that have significant uncertainty need to be presented and the approaches for reducing uncertainty should be described. In terms of uncertainty requirements:

- the accuracy of forest versus non-forest classification shall be at least 75 percent;
- where *land-based accounting* is applied, the 95 percent confidence interval of historical emissions shall be calculated. If it exceeds 50 percent of the estimated value, a deduction factor is applied to the amount of carbon credits issued. The deduction factor to be applied should be based on the recommendations of the 32nd meeting of the CDM Methodology Panel (Table 4.4);

- where *activity-based accounting* is elected, the uncertainty of emissions and removal factors shall meet the requirements of the latest version of the VCS Standard (Version 3.4 in October 2013). These requirements indicate that if the 95 percent confidence interval is within the allowed 30 percent, no deduction is required. Otherwise, a deduction is applied to the amount of carbon credits issued following the rationale described in Box 4.1.

Box 4.1 Uncertainty deduction

Where activity-based accounting is elected, the GHG emission and removal factors shall have a precision that meets the requirements set out in the VCS Standard.

For example, in Province A significant deforestation pressure exists in a given stratum. Field monitoring is conducted to develop an emission factor for activity–based accounting. The carbon stock is equivalent to 550 tCO_2e/ha, post deforestation land use is pasture with no remnant trees and clearance does not involve biomass burning.

High measurement effort is applied and the 95 percent confidence interval is equal to 20 percent of the mean (110 tCO_2e/ha), which is within the allowable 30 percent (as set out for activity-based accounting in the VCS Standard) and so no deductions are required.

Alternatively, a lower measurement effort could be applied and the resulting uncertainty is reflected in a 95 percent confidence interval equal to 50 percent of the mean (275 tCO_2e/ha). Given the allowable uncertainty of 30 percent of the mean (165 tCO_2e/ha), an appropriate (i.e., conservative) uncertainty deduction could be based on the half width of the confidence interval: (275 − 165)/2 = 55. This would give an emission factor in the baseline case of 550 − 55 = 495 tCO_2e/ha, and in the monitored case 550 + 55 = 605 tCO_2e/ha.

Source: VCS JNR Requirements.

4.4 Reporting

In order to apply for the issuance of credits, the project/program developer needs to prepare a monitoring report according to the VCS Standard or the VCS JNR Monitoring Report Template. The monitoring report must include the following details on the data and parameters monitored in order to calculate baseline and project emissions and removals, as well as leakage:

- recording frequency;
- original sources for data and measurement procedures, including all the data collected in the field using permanent sample plots.

Information on how social and environmental safeguards have been addressed is also required as well as information on the implementation of internal allocation or benefit sharing mechanisms which are needed for the implementation of crediting scenarios 2 and 3. Concerning reporting frequency, the jurisdictional proponent must submit a monitoring report for verification at least every five years. In the case where nested projects and jurisdictions are included, they can monitor and report at different intervals but need to synchronize their reporting with the higher-level jurisdiction at least every five years.

In crediting scenarios 2 and 3, the project developer also needs to prepare a non-permanence risk report applying the *JNR Non-Permanence Risk Tool*. This tool provides guidance on how to document and substantiate the risk analysis that will ultimately be performed by the auditor in order to determine the "risk rating" and therefore the number of credits to be withheld in the buffer account.

4.5 Verification

The verification procedure of JNR programs is described in the *Jurisdictional and Nested REDD+ (JNR) Validation and Verification Process*. Compared to the verification of individual projects, other stakeholders than the auditor are involved. The validation and verification of REDD+ JNR programs undergo public stakeholder consultations for a period of 60 days prior to the release of the verification report by the auditor. In the case where the jurisdictional baseline is renewed, the review of a JNR expert panel (see below) may also be required.

At the end of the public stakeholder consultation period, the jurisdictional proponent must either update its documentation, taking account of these comments, or demonstrate the insignificance or irrelevance of the comments. The auditor and the JNR expert panel must verify that comments have been accordingly addressed.

The auditor – Validation and Verification Body (VVB) in the VCS jargon – must have been accredited by the VCS before contracting its services with the jurisdictional proponent. The VCS does not have an accreditation procedure of its own, however: it automatically grants accreditation to entities accredited either for the Clean Development Mechanism of the UNFCCC or under ISO 14065, scope VCS.

Where a review by the JNR expert panel is required, the auditor addresses a draft verification report to the JNR expert review panel. The JNR review panel evaluates the scientific rigor and appropriateness of underlying data and assumptions used by the jurisdictional proponent in its monitoring report and in the development of the baseline. This panel should consist of three JNR experts (one local and two international). A list of potential local experts must be provided by the jurisdictional proponent. The VCA Association eventually reviews this list and selects the local expert together with a couple of international JNR experts that are recruited through continuous calls for experts set up by the VCS.

As well as in VCS projects, the auditor is also in charge of determining a risk rating for the jurisdiction following the *JNR Non-Permanence Risk Tool* across five broad categories: political and governance risk; program design and strategy risk; carbon rights and use of carbon revenues; funding risk; and natural risk. As jurisdiction may propose the implementation of risk mitigation strategies, the auditor is also responsible for assessing their credibility and robustness. In general the auditor has to perform a survey among relevant agents and in some cases general indicators may be used to estimate risks. For instance, for the determination of the political risk factor where the tool allows for the calculation of an overall governance score based on the latest available data of the World Bank Institute's

Worldwide Governance Indicators (WGI) and the World Bank's All Indicators for One Country tables.

4.6 Comparison between VCS and UNFCCC requirements for REDD+

The 19th COP which took place in Warsaw in November 2013 provided an operational MRV framework for REDD+ under the UNFCCC. Applicants to performance based funding coming from the Green Climate Fund must comply with this framework. In addition, public funding agencies, which are currently the main source of funding for REDD+ activities, are also likely to require compliance with this framework in the near future. After all, the framework has been negotiated and accepted by their own government under the UNFCCC. Such a "UNFCCC" label for REDD+ is therefore a serious competitor to the VCS JNR.

Decision 14/CP.19 sets the MRV requirements for REDD+ under the UNFCCC. In terms of monitoring, it requires developing countries to use:

- the latest IPCC guidance;
- and, "as appropriate," a combination of remote sensing and ground-based forest carbon inventory approaches.[7]

Reporting is due every other year, as part of the larger "biennial update reports" which cover all sectors but without many specific requirements. No common reporting format is established, contrary to what is in place for national greenhouse gas inventories of Annex 1 countries, but a series of elements must be included: the activities included; the territorial forest area covered; the period over which emissions have been assessed; the description of the national forest monitoring system; and "necessary information that allows for the reconstruction of the results."

Verification is conducted by two LULUCF experts accredited by the UNFCCC and follows the same criteria as the review of national greenhouse gas inventories, that is mostly consistent with IPCC guidance (see Chapter 2).

Although these UNFCCC requirements are too recent to have been implemented, Table 4.5 highlights the main differences between them and the VCS JNR.

---

[7] These are "requests" from decision 4/CP.15. Decision 14/CP.19 simply requires that MRV "be consistent" with decision 4/CP.15.

Table 4.5 *Comparison between VCS JNR and UNFCCC requirements for MRVing REDD+*

VCS JNR	UNFCCC
Monitoring	
Approach 3 (spatially explicit information) only for activity data on land-use changes.	Approach 1 and 2 can also be used (net changes or gross changes in land-use areas at the national level).
Proxies can be used for activity data on land-use changes if they are "equivalent or better" in terms of reliability, consistency or practicality.	When proxies are used, the correlation must be statistically significant and established based on country-specific data.
	Unless "inappropriate," countries must use a combination of remote sensing and ground-based forest carbon inventory approaches.
Deforestation must be monitored, other activities are optional.	All activities should be covered.
De minimis sources need not be monitored (up to an aggregated total of 10 percent). Activities or pools for which emissions will not increase over time need not be monitored.	No materiality threshold. Only activities and pools for which IPCC (2006) proposes a methodology must be monitored.
Forest areas not impacted by the program or excluded from the baseline (significant natural disturbance, large-scale infrastructure) need not be monitored (see Chapter 4).	Unmanaged forests be monitored, except when they are subject to deforestation.
Default emission factors (IPCC Tier 1) can only be used for pools representing less than 15 percent of total carbon stocks.	Key categories (see Chapter 1.1) must use country-specific emission factors (IPCC Tier 2 or 3).

Table 4.5 (*cont.*)

VCS JNR	UNFCCC
Minimum accuracy of 75 percent for forest vs. non-forest classification.	No quantitative requirement.
Deduction factor applied to carbon credits when total uncertainty is higher than 50 percent on the baseline (see Chapter 6). Where activity-based accounting is elected, uncertainty of emissions and removal factors should be within an allowed 30 percent at a 95 percent confidence level.	No quantitative requirement.

Reporting	
Large-scale commercial deforestation must be separated out when exceeding 10 percent of total deforestation.	
Separation between above-ground woody and non-woody biomass.	

Verification	
Conducted by an accredited auditing company, together with a JNR expert panel composed of one local expert and two international experts from the VCS roster of experts.	Conducted by review team composed at least of two UNFCCC accredited LULUCF experts, one from a developed country and one from a developing country.
At least every five years.	Every two years.

4.7 MRV costs

Monitoring costs

Given the young age of these requirements no programs have been registered so far at the jurisdictional level. We therefore refer to three studies that present data on per hectare monitoring costs in order to estimate per tonne monitoring costs at the project level and at the country level and use them to estimate monitoring costs (Table 4.6). The estimates correspond to large-scale projects with sizes over 100,000 hectares comparable with eventual programs at jurisdictional scale. Country-level cost estimates were calculated based on simulations performed by Plugge et al. (2013) in order to show the effect of the inclusion of uncertainties and monitoring costs in REDD estimates. These authors refer to FAO's Global Forest Resources Assessment to select five countries which show small to large forest areas and various deforestation rates. In the estimation of the monitoring cost per country which could mostly consist of the interpretation of remote sensing data supported by ground-based measurements a variable and a fixed component were included. The variable component corresponds to a perhectare assessment cost of €0.01 that Plugge et al. (2013) set as the one corresponding to an uncertainty level of 10 percent. The fixed component was set to US$100,000 (€78,300)[8] and includes inter alia the costs for remote sensing imagery.

As the "project level" costs are based on existing projects – whereas "country level" costs are only ex-ante estimates – and as these projects are large enough to be representatives of jurisdictions, they are retained for the MRV ID table.

The country estimates presented in Table 4.6 slightly differ from those of Hardcastle and Baird (2008) quoted by UNFCCC (2009). The Hardcastle and Baird (2008) estimates are higher for Colombia, Indonesia and Ghana, and lower for Cameroon than those of Plugge et al. (2013). The application of the country costs of Hardcastle and Baird (2008) to the estimated yearly emission reductions lead us to per tonne monitoring costs ranging between 0.001 and 0.023 €/tCO$_2$

---

[8] All costs are converted to euros where necessary, using either the 2013 annual average exchange rate of 0.783 US$/€ or the 2010 annual average exchange rate of 0.785 US$/€, depending on the relevant study year.

Table 4.6 *Literature review on monitoring costs for REDD+*

	Project/country name	Size (ha)	Yearly emission reductions (tCO$_2$e)	€/ha/yr	€ (project or country/ yr)	€/tCO$_2$/yr
Rendon Thompson et al. (2013)	Tambopata National Reserve and Bahuaja Sonene National Park	548,489	403,293	0.12	64,420	0.16
	Sustainable Forest Management in Forestry Concessions	98,932	847,382	0.27	27,112	0.03
Project level	Noel Kempff	642,184	114,901	0.07	45,254	0.39
	Juma	329,483	379,272	0.09	30,958	0.08
Pearson et al. (2013)	REDD project South East Asia	300,000	600,000	N/A	131,880	0.22
Average Monitoring cost at the project level					60,000	0.18

Plugge et al. (2013)	Ghana (DR: −23.36%)	4,940,000	32,633,920	0.01	117,279	0.004
	Cameroon (DR: −11.05%)	19,916,000	109,232,933	0.01	234,841	0.002
Country level	Indonesia (DR: −5.27%)	94,432,000	251,531,830	0.01	819,791	0.003
	Colombia (DR: −1.67%)	60,499,000	41,669,283	0.01	553,417	0.013
	Suriname (DR: −0.12%)	14,758,000	1,392,600	0.01	194,350	0.140

Average monitoring cost at the country level | | | | | | 0.032

Figures were converted into euros when necessary based on the annual average exchange rate of the original figure if provided, and of the corresponding study year otherwise. DR refers to ten-year deforestation rates reported for each country in the FAO's FRA report (2010) which authors used to determine yearly emission reductions by halting deforestation.

Source: Authors.

(average: 0.01 €/tCO$_2$). The REDD project estimates presented in Table 4.6 are consistent with Böttcher et al. (2009) who present a survey of monitoring costs using different MRV technologies.

These comparisons increase our confidence in the presented cost ranges. As we observe in the results the average value at a country level is six times lower. This can be explained by the economies of scale that can be achieved by monitoring very large surfaces but also regarding the monitoring techniques that are applied. At the project level they concern mostly ground measurements combined with some interpretation of remote sensing imagery, while country-level estimates concern mostly remote sensing supported by ground-based measurements. On the other hand, the costs reported at the project level correspond to ex-post case studies and as such are far more reliable.

Overall MRV costs

In order to perform the calculations of the range of overall per tonne MRV costs that appear in the MRV ID table, we add to the costs of monitoring, the following costs of reporting and verification and apply them to our example projects (see Chapter 11 and Chapter 13):

- €10,000–15,000 for preparation of monitoring reports (Beaurain and Schmidt-Traub, 2010).
- The absolute cost of periodic verification is estimated at €20,000–50,000 per verification (Chenost and Gardette, 2010). These costs are higher than the one estimated at €5,000–15,000 per verification (Guigon et al., 2009; Krey, 2005; Michaelowa and Stronzik, 2002; UNEP, 2007). We however consider costs presented by Chenost and Gardette (2010) more pertinent given the complexity and large scale of jurisdictional REDD projects. Note that under the UNFCCC framework where verification is conducted by UNFCCC accredited reviewers, verification costs will likely be cheaper and be borne by the UNFCCC rather than the REDD+ jurisdiction.
- Issuance fees of €0.08 per tCO$_2$e, thus ranging from €10,000 to €70,000 per project for the project sizes were considered here.

4.8 Conclusion

The VCS JNR framework has largely derived its procedures and requirements from what has been developed by the standard at the project level. The main difference is that this framework accepts different crediting scenarios that determine the scope and perimeter of monitoring as well as the scope of the baseline. Depending on the chosen crediting option, the monitored perimeter varies: jurisdiction for both baseline and actual emissions for options 2 and 3, and project/activity for actual emissions for option 1. Monitoring requirements also vary accordingly, with more stringent requirements when emissions are monitored at project/activity level.

Given that jurisdictional programs will likely have a higher reach than individual REDD projects, additional requirements have been set for verification, mostly in the cases where a jurisdictional baseline needs to be validated or updated. In these cases a JNR expert review panel is included in addition to the work of the auditor.

The MRV requirements for REDD+ in the UNFCCC context are more challenging to analyze as they have just been agreed in December 2013 in Warsaw. They are however very similar to the MRV requirements applying to the forestry part of national greenhouse gas inventories for Annex 1 countries. They are somewhat less demanding than the VCS JNR requirements: in particular, quantitative requirements are set for land classification accuracy and total emissions uncertainty in the baseline and a separation is required for large-scale commercial deforestation. The equations used are however likely to be roughly similar as both refer to IPCC good practice guidance (IPCC, 2006) on this point.

4.9 MRV ID table

Detailed definitions of the items of this table are provided in the appendix to Chapter 1.

Table 4.7 *MRV ID table*

	VCS JNR requirements
Regulator	- The VCS program is managed by the VCS Association (VCSA), an independent organization. VCSA is responsible for the management, the review and establishes the rules and requirements that operationalize the VCS to enable the validation of GHG projects and the verification of GHG emission reductions and removals. The VCSA is also responsible for the methodology approval process. - VCS JNR requirements were developed by the VCS Jurisdictional and Nested REDD+ Initiative (JNRI), overseen by an advisory committee and technical expert groups. This committee included representatives from national and subnational governments, leading experts in REDD+ and representatives from NGOs and the private sector.
Type and level of incentive to comply	**For project proponents:** - Positive incentives ("carrots"): issuance of VCS credits to projects and jurisdictions depending on the crediting scenario (timeliness and quantity). - Negative incentives ("sticks"): credit discounting due to high monitoring uncertainty.
Entities concerned	*Project/program proponents:* - Due to the recent publication of these requirements, no JNR programs have been registered as of September 2013. However, eight pilot programs are currently under development.
Sectors concerned	REDD+ - Reduced emissions from deforestation; - Reduced emissions from degradation (including REDD and most IFM activities); - Carbon stock enhancement (e.g., reforestation, assisted natural regeneration and IFM Low-productive to High-productive Forest).

	Monitoring
Gases concerned	All Kyoto Protocol gases (CO_2, CH_4, N_2O, HFC-23, PFC, SF_6, plus NF_3 as of 2013)
Overall MRV costs	145,000 [85,000–250,000] €/jurisdiction/year 0.4 [0.15–0.9] €/tCO_2 (see section h.2)
Rules	*JNR Requirements, v3.1* *VCS Program Guide, v3.4* *VCS Standard, v3.3* JNR Non-Permanence Risk Tool, v3.0 AFOLU Requirements, v3.3 JNR Leakage Tool
Other reference documents	- IPCC Fourth Assessment Report: Climate Change 2007 (2007) for global warming potentials of GHGs - *IPCC Guidelines for National Greenhouse Gas Inventories* (2006) - Good Practice Guidance for Land Use, Land-Use Change and Forestry (2003) for statistical approaches used in monitoring - All REDD and IFM VCS Methodologies - Peer-reviewed literature - National forestry inventories and statistics - GOFC-GOLD Sourcebook
Uncertainty requirements	Historical emissions from changes in carbon stocks must be calculated with a 95 percent confidence interval lower than 50 percent of the estimated value to avoid a deduction in the amount of carbon credits issued.

Table 4.7 (*cont.*)

Achieved uncertainty range	No jurisdictional programs registered so far. At project level, three REDD projects registered by the VCS have reached uncertainty levels ranging between less than 15% and 18% at a 95% confidence level.
Cost range	0.18 [0.08–0.39] €/tCO$_2$e/yr 60,000 [25,000–130,000] €/jurisdiction/yr (see section h.1)
Scope	Scope 1 Territorial/jurisdictional
Frequency	At least every five years.
Source for activity data	Field measurements (such as DBH, height, number of trees, etc.), remote sensing, surveys and statistics.
Uncertainty range for activity data	The accuracy of forest versus non-forest classification shall be at least 75 percent.
Source for emission factors	IPCC Guidelines on National GHG Inventories, peer-reviewed literature, measurements, surveys, etc.
Uncertainty for emission factors	IPCC default values may be used for carbon pools representing less than 15 percent of total carbon stocks. Where activity-based accounting is elected, uncertainty of emissions and removal factors should be within an allowed 30 percent at a 95% confidence level.

Direct measurement	Direct measurement can be used and may include for example: - areas of strata; - tree dimensions (forest inventory plots); - remote sensing.
Incentive to reduce uncertainty	Avoid an eventual uncertainty deduction of credits if the required precision level is not reached. See Box 4.1. for an example of a deduction.
Is requirements stringency adapted to the amount of emissions at stake (materiality)?	Yes, to some extent. Carbon pools which can be demonstrated not to be a source of emissions need not be monitored if no credits are claimed for the corresponding sink. Emission sources can be considered *de minimis*, and therefore neither accounted nor monitored, up to a cumulated 10% of the net project reductions.

Reporting

Rules	*VCS Program Guide, v3.4* *VCS Standard, v3.3* AFOLU Requirements, *v3.3* *JNR Requirements, v3.1* JNR Monitoring Report, *v3.2*
Other reference documents	
Format	Following the format of JNR Monitoring Report template

Table 4.7 (*cont.*)

Level of source disaggregation	Disaggregation down to single carbon pools, activity and strata (e.g., above-ground biomass from reforestation in a given municipality).
Frequency	At least every five years
Timeline	No available data
Language	English
Is demand stringency adapted to the amount of emissions at stake (materiality)?	See "Monitoring." In addition, there is no mandatory reporting frequency beyond the five-year minimum which allows smaller jurisdictions to report less often than larger ones.
Cost range	€10–15,000 for preparation of monitoring reports; see Chapter 3.1 (Beaurain and Schmidt-Traub, 2010). 0.04 [0.01–0.1] €/tCO$_2$e/yr
VCS	
Rules	*VCS Program Guide, v3.4* *VCS Standard, v3.3* AFOLU Requirements, v3.3 Verification Report, v3.2 JNR Validation and Verification Process, v3.0 JNR Non-Permanence Risk Tool, v3.0

Other reference documents	World Bank Institute's Worldwide Governance Indicators (WGI) World Bank's All Indicators for One Country
Format	Following the format of the JNR *Verification Report* (upcoming).
Frequency	Verification takes places at every reporting event, that is, after the publication of the monitoring report.
Timeline	No available data. The 60-day consultation period as well as eventual review time of the peer review panel needs to be added.
Language	English
Accredited entities for verification	Named validation and verification bodies (VVB): 22 entities accredited by the VCS. Certain entities have reached ISO validation, mostly smaller structures. All CDM entities credited for the AFOLU sector are accepted by the standard.

For some programs a peer review panel may be constituted and must be composed of one local expert chosen by the VCSA from a list proposed by the jurisdictional proponent and two international experts that have been selected by the VCSA through an approval and selection process. |
| Control of accredited entities | Accredited V/VBs shall undergo surveillance during the first and second years after the year of their initial accreditation or reaccreditation. ANSI may decide to conduct surveillance visits out of sequence and without prior notice or with short notice if a complaint is received regarding the performance of the V/VB. |

Table 4.7 (*cont.*)

Cost of accreditation	Temporary accreditation: non-refundable fee of €6,500 for seven sectoral scopes, plus €1,000 for each additional sectoral scope thereafter. VVBs pay an annual fee to maintain accreditation depending on their gross annual revenues (€1,175 if they are below €294,000, 0.4% of their revenue if revenues are above €294,000 and below €10.8 million and €43,175 for revenues above €10.8 million). Assessment and surveillance fees are €980 per day per assessor plus travel expenses.
Support of accredited entities	None
Is requirements stringency adapted to the amount of emissions at stake (materiality)?	The VCS incorporates the definition given by ISO, whereby there is a materiality threshold established that allows verification to focus on reaching a reasonable level of assurance of the accuracy of their validation with respect to material errors, omissions and misrepresentations. The threshold for materiality with respect to the aggregate of errors, omissions and misrepresentations relative to the total reported GHG emission reductions and/or removals shall be 5% for projects and 1% for large projects. Where: - Projects: Less than or equal to 300,000 tonnes of CO_2e per year. - Large projects: Greater than 300,000 tonnes of CO_2e per year.
Cost range	Difficult to estimate as no program has been certified so far at the jurisdictional level; €78,300 for a REDD project in Southeast Asia according to Pearson et al. (2013). For MRV overall calculations, we refer to Chenost and Gardette (2010) who estimate the absolute cost of periodic verification at €20,000–50,000 per verification (0.12 [0.04–0.33] €/tCO_2e/yr). Issuance fees for the VCS of 0.08 €/VCU are added.

Bibliography

Beaurain, F. and Schmidt-Traub, G., 2010. *Developing CDM Programmes of Activities: A Guidebook*. South Pole Carbon Asset Management Ltd, Zurich.

Böttcher, H., Eisbrenner, K., Fritz, S., Kindermann, G., Kraxner, F., McCallum, I. and Obersteiner, M., 2009. An assessment of monitoring requirements and costs of Reduced Emissions from Deforestation and Degradation. *Carbon Balance and Management* 4(1): 7.

Chenost, C. and Gardette, Y.M., 2010. *Bringing Forest Carbon Projects to the Market*. UNEP, Paris.

Deheza, M. and Bellassen, V., 2012. Delivering REDD+ incentives to local stakeholders: lessons from forest carbon frameworks in developed countries (No. 35), Climate Report. CDC Climat Research, Paris.

Dupont, M., Morel, R., Bellassen, V. and Deheza, M., 2013. International Climate Negotiations – COP 19: do not underestimate the MRV breakthrough (No. 33), Climate Brief. CDC Climat Research, Paris.

Guigon, P., Bellassen, V. and Ambrosi, P., 2009. Voluntary carbon markets: what the standards say... Working Paper, Mission Climat. Caisse des Depots.

IPCC, 2006. *2006 IPCC Guidelines for National Greenhouse Gas Inventories*. IGES, Hayama, Japan.

Krey, M., 2005. Transaction costs of unilateral CDM projects in India – results from an empirical survey. *Energy Policy* 33(18): 2385–2397.

Michaelowa, A. and Stronzik, M., 2002. Transaction costs of the Kyoto mechanisms. HWWA Discussion Paper, No. 175.

Pearson, T., Brown, S., Sohngen, B., Henman, J. and Ohrel, S., 2013. Transaction costs for carbon sequestration projects in the tropical forest sector. *Mitigation and Adaptation Strategies for Global Change* (May): 1–14.

Peters-Stanley, M., Gonzales, G. and Yin, D., 2013. *Covering New Ground: State of the Forest Carbon Markets 2013*. Forest Trends' Ecosystem Marketplace, Washington, DC.

Plugge, D., Baldauf, T. and Köhl, M., 2013. The global climate mitigation strategy REDD: monitoring costs and uncertainties jeopardize economic benefits. *Climatic Change* 119(2): 247–259.

Rendon Thompson, O., Paavola, J., Healey, J., Jones, J., Baker, T. and Torres, J., 2013. Reducing Emissions from Deforestation and forest Degradation (REDD+): transaction costs of six Peruvian projects, ecosystem services, governance and stakeholder participation. *Ecology & Society* 18(1).

UNEP, 2007. *Guidebook to Financing CDM Projects*. United Nations Environment Programme.

UNFCCC, 2009. Cost of implementing methodologies and monitoring systems relating to estimates of emissions from deforestation and forest degradation, the assessment of carbon stocks and greenhouse gas emissions from changes in forest cover, and the enhancement of forest carbon stocks. Technical paper.

VCS, 2013a. JNR Requirements v3.1.

2013b. JNR Validation and Verification Process, v3.0.

2013c. The JNR Registration and Issuance Process, v3.0.

2013d. Non-Permanence Risk Tool, v3.0.

PART II

MRV of industrial sites and entities

5 | Trendsetter for companies and industrial sites: the EU Emissions Trading Scheme

GUILLAUME JACQUIER AND
VALENTIN BELLASSEN

5.1 Context

Lineage and birth of the EU ETS

Almost like a living organism, the European Union Emissions Trading Scheme (EU ETS) is one of the final lines of an elaborate and complex process. This process began years ago with the formal acknowledgment at international level "that change in the Earth's climate and its adverse effects are a common concern of humankind" (United Nations, 1992) and the recognition "that human activities have been substantially increasing the atmospheric concentrations of greenhouse gases, that these increases enhance the natural greenhouse effect, and that this will result on average in an additional warming of the Earth's surface and atmosphere and may adversely affect natural ecosystems and humankind" (United Nations, 1992). This recognition led to setting a goal, namely the "stabilization of greenhouse gas concentrations in the atmosphere at a level that would prevent dangerous anthropogenic interference with the climate system" (United Nations, 1992).

From this awareness and with this general objective in mind, a first operational step was taken with the highly publicized Kyoto Protocol (United Nations, 1997) which sets quantified emission reduction targets for each developed country. In order to fulfill these commitments while taking into account the technical, political and economic constraints, several tools were created including MRV procedures, flexibility mechanisms and a compliance committee.

The role of the MRV procedures is to ensure that the developed Parties to the UNFCCC monitor and submit their annual emissions in a way which assures comparability and consistency with the rules of the Protocol (see Chapter 2 on national GHG inventories under the UNFCCC). The market-based mechanisms intend to provide

139

Parties with the possibility to abate emissions where it is cheapest. The compliance committee ultimately judges whether Parties complied with the rules and mechanisms. In particular, it solves disputes between Parties, or between a Party and an expert review team (see Chapter 2 on national GHG inventories under the UNFCCC).

The three market-based mechanisms included in the Kyoto Protocol are:

- **Joint Implementation** (JI), defined in article 6, which allows a country with an emissions reduction commitment under the Kyoto Protocol (Annex B Party) to earn carbon credits from financing a project which reduces emissions in another Annex B Party;
- **the Clean Development Mechanism** (CDM), defined in article 12, which allows an Annex B Party to earn carbon credits from financing a project which reduces emissions in a developing country (see Chapter 11 on the CDM);
- **International Emissions Trading** (IET), defined in article 17, which allows Annex B Parties to trade among themselves the allowances which materialize their emissions reductions commitments.

This latter mechanism facilitates the emergence of emissions trading schemes at regional or international level. This was the path chosen by the European Union in 2003 with the establishment of a "scheme for greenhouse gas emission allowance trading ... in order to promote reductions of greenhouse gas emissions in a cost-effective and economically efficient manner" (European Commission, 2003).

The ETS Directive is the key legislative act of the EU ETS. Amended several times, thus reflecting the evolution of the system, the Directive was modified for the first time in 2004 before the scheme even started to operate. The main purpose of this first amendment, the so-called "Linking Directive" (European Commission, 2004b), was to authorize installations to surrender carbon credits – generated by CDM or JI projects – instead of emission allowances – distributed by the European Commission – for compliance purposes. This directive connects JI and the CDM to the EU ETS, thus reinforcing the relationship between the EU ETS and the Kyoto Protocol. Other amendments were gradually adopted during the different phases of the EU ETS and are presented in the relevant sections.

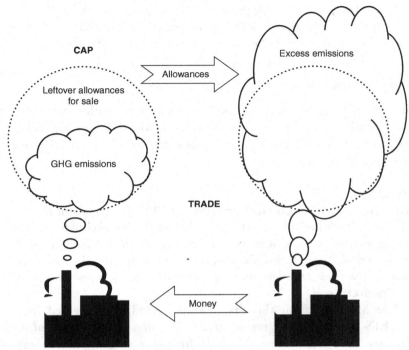

Figure 5.1 The cap-and-trade principle

The cap-and-trade principle

The EU ETS operates on the cap-and-trade principle. A cap is set on the maximum amount of greenhouse gases that can be emitted by all installations covered by the regulation. Allowances for each ton of CO_2 equivalent within the cap are then allocated for free to covered installations or auctioned off. These allowances (or EUA, standing for EU Allowances) can then be traded between relevant stakeholders, in practice covered businesses and financial institutions, which allows a price to emerge. Each year, installations must surrender a number of allowances equivalent to their verified emissions. An installation which has emitted less than the number of its allowances can keep the spare allowances for later or sell them. Conversely, an installation which has problems keeping its emissions in line with its allowances can either invest to reduce its emissions, or buy additional allowances to cover its need, or both (Figure 5.1).

Beyond the cap-and-trade principle, which remains unchanged at the core of the scheme, the EU ETS has undergone several changes during its development, as it has become more mature and comprehensive.

Development and evolution

Started on January 1st, 2005, the EU ETS operates within periods of time called "phases." To provide installations with a reasonable visibility, most rules are fixed within each phase, and only allowed to change from one phase to another.

Phase I

The first trading period ran from 2005 to 2007. It was meant to be a "learning by doing" phase, which would enable all stakeholders to get acquainted with the system before entering the first Kyoto commitment period. Though this phase is therefore often described as a test phase, it was nevertheless fully operational and the money involved was perfectly real.

The MRV rules for this first trading period, implemented from the ETS Directive, were set out in the Decision 2004/156/EC of 29 January 2004 establishing guidelines for the monitoring and reporting of greenhouse gas emissions (European Commission, 2004a). Concerning verification, each Member State was in charge of ensuring that reports submitted by operators were verified in accordance with the criteria set out in Annex V of the ETS Directive.

More than 10,000 installations, from energy and manufacturing industry sectors, representing about 40 percent of EU greenhouse gases emissions, were part of this first trading period. The cap, i.e., the total quantity of allowances to be issued, was determined by each country in its National Allocation Plan (NAP), which defined how many EUA were to be allocated in total and to each EU ETS installation on their territory. The European Commission then considered whether the NAPs met the criteria set out in Annex III of the original text of the Directive, the first of them to be in line with the country Kyoto target. If needed, the NAPs were modified by the Member States until they were approved by the Commission.

Considering it was a "trial phase," the caps were not intended to be stringent, and the overall amount was set at what the European Commission deemed to be the 2004 level of emissions. By the end of the first MRV cycle, that is in April 2006, when 2005 verified emissions data were published by the Commission, it became obvious that the 2004 level had been overestimated, mainly due to the lack of precise verified emissions for installations before the EU ETS was launched.

The remaining allowances could not be used in phase II, so the price of EUA dropped close to zero at the end of 2007. At the end, the first phase of operation of the EU ETS provided a mixed picture. Due to this over-allocation, the scheme largely failed to put a meaningful price on greenhouse gases emissions over the last year. However, the main purpose of this phase was not yet to achieve important reductions in greenhouse gases emissions, but to implement and test the EU ETS, in order to prepare for the first commitment period of the Kyoto Protocol. From this point of view, phase I was a success. Apart from allowing all stakeholders to become acquainted with the system's operation, it has yielded reliable verified emissions as a solid basis for the next phase, as well as lessons to be learned to avoid the pitfalls seen above.

Phase II

The second phase, from January 1, 2008 to December 31, 2012, coincided with the first commitment period under the Kyoto Protocol. This phase saw a sectoral enlargement of the scope, with the inclusion of aviation in the second amendment to the ETS Directive, the so-called "Aviation Directive" (European Commission, 2008b) "to include aviation activities in the scheme for greenhouse gas emission allowance trading within the Community" from 2012 onwards. MRV rules for aviation are quite different from those concerning stationary installation sectors and will not be described in this chapter.

Drawing lessons from the test phase, the MRV rules of Decision 2004/156/EC were replaced by a new text, Decision 2007/589/EC of 18 July 2007, for "it was apparent that the guidelines laid down in that Decision [2004/156/EC] required several changes in order to render them more clear and cost-efficient" (European Commission, 2007). The main changes to the MRV rules for this second trading period were:

- better adjustment of the appropriate balance between cost-effectiveness and accuracy, introducing exemptions and simplifications to facilitate the application of the guidelines for plants using pure biomass fuels and small emitters (installations with average verified reported emissions of less than 25,000 tons of fossil CO_2 per year, that is 75 percent of covered installation during phase II) as well as setting new requirements more in line with technical constraints;

• greater harmonization based on international guidance developed by the Intergovernmental Panel on Climate Change (IPCC), the International Organisation for Standardisation (ISO), the Greenhouse Gas Protocol Initiative of the World Business Council on Sustainable Development (WBCSD) and the World Resources Institute (WRI);

• the introduction of a fall-back approach with maximum uncertainty thresholds in order to provide an alternative route for the monitoring of emissions from very specific or complex installations;

• an expansion and update of the list of reference emission factors.

The cap was also significantly lowered, to ensure that phase II would result in real emission reductions and that the countries would meet their Kyoto targets. However, it was still determined via the national allocation plans, as it was for the first trading period. Three more countries participated in phase II of the EU ETS: Norway, Iceland and Liechtenstein. For all countries which had been involved in the first phase, the average annual amount of allowances for the second phase was about 3 percent lower than the average annual verified emissions during the first phase.

Unfortunately, despite this willingness to set a limit unequivocally inducing the facilities to reduce their emissions, history would repeat itself, and the system would face serious criticism of its credibility and effectiveness at the end of phase II in the same way it had at the end of phase I, but for different reasons. In phase I over-allocation was mainly the consequence of lacking reliable emissions data to establish a baseline beforehand, and the fact that it was a "test" phase. The significant amount of allowances in excess at the end of phase II resulted from a combination of economic crisis and the expansion of renewable energy driven by the "renewable energy" directive. Because of this unexpected situation, average annual verified emissions during the years 2009–2012 were 10 percent lower than 2008 verified emissions, and the price of allowances gradually fell from an average 18 €/tCO_2e in 2008 to 7.4 €/tCO_2e in 2012. Unlike the previous phase, allowances from phase II could be carried over to phase III. As a result, the dramatic emissions reductions partly obtained from the economic crisis still weigh on the supply/demand imbalance of emissions allowances in 2013. Whether this imbalance reveals the adequacy or the inadequacy of the scheme is a matter of interpretation, but the amount of criticism certainly harms the credibility of the EU ETS.

The end of phase II was marked by many uncertainties about the future of the EU ETS, with outstanding queries such as the management of phase II allowances in excess, the inclusion of international flights due to many objections from outside the EU, and more widely the overall effectiveness of this instrument considering the technical and economical constraints on operators.

Phase III

The third phase of the EU ETS began on January 1st, 2013, and will last until December 31st, 2020. The key rules for this third phase were passed in 2009 in a third amendment to the ETS Directive, the so-called "Revised ETS Directive" (European Commission, 2009).

Although the issues raised at the end of phase II have not yet been solved, many deep changes occurred in this phase, in accordance with the path set in 2009 by the Revised ETS Directive.

First, the cap is no longer determined at the national level through the NAPs, but is globally set at EU level, and it gradually decreases from year to year. This gives coherence and meaning to the EU cap, which is no longer simply a sum of national caps but an actual clearly defined goal. The cap for 2013 for stationary sectors was set in Decision 2010/634/EU to 2,039,152,882 EUAs, and will decrease by 1.74 percent per year. This limit includes all allowances, those auctioned and those issued free of charge.

Second, auctioning of allowances is now the rule, free allocation being the exception. Nevertheless, all sectors but energy are covered by the exception and receive a variable amount of free allowances, depending on whether the cost of carbon significantly threatens the international competitiveness of the sector.

Third, the scope had been considerably extended, both in industrial sectors covered by the EU ETS and in the greenhouse gases taken into account. Although Annex II of the ETS Directive refers to the "basket" of the six greenhouse gases of the Kyoto Protocol (CO_2, CH_4, N_2O, HFC, PFC and SF_6), the EU ETS had focused for the first two trading periods on CO_2 alone, for the sake of simplicity and because it is the most important anthropogenic GHG. The most notable extensions are N_2O emissions from fertilizer manufacturing and CO_2 emissions from other metals than steel (see below, Section 5.2).

In terms of geographical scope, it is also worth noting that Croatia joined the EU ETS for this phase, bringing the number of countries participating in the scheme to 31.

These changes in the structure of the system, and the experience gained during the second trading period, necessitated a new rewriting of MRV rules for the third period. Thus the Decision 2007/589/EC was repealed, and replaced by two Regulations:

- Regulation 601/2012 (European Commission, 2012b) on the monitoring and reporting of greenhouse gas emissions (noted below, MRR, for Monitoring and Reporting Regulation);
- Regulation 600/2012 (European Commission, 2012c) on the verification of greenhouse gas emission reports and tonne-kilometre reports and the accreditation of verifiers (noted below, VR, for Verification Regulation).

The main principles which these two regulations emphasize for the third trading period are:

- Harmonization at all levels, in order to avoid different applications of MRV rules between Member States. Thus, the two texts insist among other things on a definition of biomass consistent with the Directive 2009/28/EC, a more transparent and consistent manner of determining unreasonable costs, a better balance between measurement-based methodology and calculation-based methodology, a more consistent estimation of missing data, harmonized rules to determine whether a verifier is competent, independent and impartial, and harmonized requirements for the verification reports and the performance of the verification activities.
- Reinforcement of the central role of the monitoring plan, setting out detailed, complete and transparent documentation concerning the monitoring methodology, as well as a strengthening of the improvement principle, requiring operators to regularly review their monitoring methodology for improvement and to consider recommendations made by verifiers.
- Flexibility provided to allow a combination of measurement methodologies, standard calculation methodology and mass balance within the same installation.
- Simplification with regard to the uncertainty assessment requirement, where measuring instruments are used under type-conform

conditions, and in particular where measuring instruments are under national legal metrological control, and also with respect to installations with low emissions to avoid a disproportionate monitoring effort.

The rest of the chapter focuses on MRV in the EU ETS. The detailed MRV rules are described, with a dedicated section on M, R and V, and analyzed against the two key trade-offs of *cost vs. uncertainty* and *information relevance vs. comparability* identified in the introduction to this book.

5.2 Monitoring

Scope: what does the EU ETS encompass?

The EU ETS covers entities with significant emissions, clearly identified, and which can be effectively supervised by the administration. Phases I and II focused on only 11 industrial activities, nonetheless representing 40 percent of EU GHG emissions.[1] Phase III has more than doubled the number of industrial sectors involved from 11 to 28, not to mention the inclusion of aviation since 2012 (Table 5.1). In absolute quantities though, the amount of emissions covered has only slightly increased, reaching around 45 percent of EU GHG emissions.

The basic entity on which the ETS focuses is the installation, as defined in article 3(e) of the ETS Directive:

Installation means a stationary technical unit where one or more activities listed in Annex I are carried out and any other directly associated activities which have a technical connection with the activities carried out on that site and which could have an effect on emissions and pollution.

Beyond this definition, most of the time, a site actually consists of only one ETS installation which includes several technical units. However, in some cases (for the most complex sites), the site may be split into several ETS installations. In practice the limits of an ETS installation

---

[1] EU-27 total GHG anthropogenic emissions, excluding LULUCF (Land Use, Land Use Change, and Forestry). Note that this included not only industrial emissions but also those from transportation, waste management, agriculture, and other non-industrial sectors.

Table 5.1 *Activities covered by the EU ETS (summary of Annex I of the Directive)*

Activities	Threshold (total rated thermal input of combustion units or production capacity)	Activities	Threshold (total rated thermal input of combustion units or production capacity)
Combustion	20 MW	*Drying or calcination of gypsum*	20 MW
Refining of mineral oil	–	Production of pulp	–
Production of coke	–	Production of paper or cardboard	20 t/day
Metal ore roasting or sintering	–	*Production of carbon black*	20 MW
Production of pig iron or steel	2.5 t/h	*Production of nitric acid*	–
Production or processing of ferrous metals	20 MW	*Production of adipic acid*	
Production of primary aluminum	–	*Production of glyoxal and glyoxylic add*	
Production of secondary aluminum	20 MW	*Production of ammonia*	–
Production or processing of non-ferrous metals	20 MW	*Production of bulk organic chemicals by cracking, reforming, partial or full oxidation*	100 t/day
Production of cement clinker	500 t/day (rotary kilns) or 50 t/ day (other furnaces)	*Production of hydrogen (H_2) and synthesis gas by reforming or partial oxidation*	25 t/day

Table 5.1 (*cont.*)

Activities	Threshold (total rated thermal input of combustion units or production capacity)	Activities	Threshold (total rated thermal input of combustion units or production capacity)
Production of lime or calcination of dolomite or magnesite	50 t/day	*Production of soda ash (Na_2CO_3) and sodium bicarbonate ($NaHCO_3$)*	–
Manufacture of glass	20 t/day	*Capture of greenhouse gases for the purpose of transport and geological storage*	–
Manufacture of ceramic products by firing	75 t/day	*Transport of greenhouse gases by pipelines for geological storage*	
Manufacture of mineral wool insulation material	20 t/day	*Geological storage of greenhouse gases*	–

Note: Activities in italic are newly included sectors for the third trading period.

are usually those defined in the GHG emissions permit and the interpretation may vary between Member States.

It is acknowledged that the approach to setting the installation boundaries laid down in GHG emissions permits differ between Member States. ... In some Member States, industrial sites (e.g., in the chemical industry) receive one overarching GHG emissions permit for the total site and are thus regarded as a single installation, whereas in other Member States, the same site could receive separate GHG emissions permits and thus be seen as more than a single installation.

(European Commission, 2010)

In any case, when determining the coverage of the EU ETS, the activities and thresholds listed above are the only relevant criteria.

The threshold of 20 MW is appreciated by adding the rated thermal inputs of all combustion units within the installation, excluding units under 3 MW and units using exclusively biomass. However, if the threshold is reached after performing this calculation, it is then necessary to note that the units excluded from the calculation are NOT excluded from the scope of the scheme and must be taken into account in the MRV process.

For all these activities, the CO_2 must obviously be monitored. However, the third trading period also introduced other greenhouse gas emissions to take into account for specific activities. Thus, in the case of primary aluminum production, PFC emissions resulting from anode effects must also be monitored, as well as N_2O emissions from adipic acid, caprolactam, glyoxal and glyoxylic acid production.

When the threshold of any activity listed above is found to be exceeded in an installation, monitoring and reporting shall be complete and cover all process and combustion emissions from all emission sources and source streams belonging to all activities listed (article 5 of the MRR). The emissions considered are Scope 1 site-level emissions, that is to say directly emitted to the atmosphere by the units of the installation. The "indirect" emissions, such as those associated with the production of electricity consumed, for instance, are not part of the scope of the ETS.

Exclusions to the scheme are installations or parts of installations used for research, development and testing of new products and processes, and installations exclusively using biomass (clause 1 of Annex I to the ETS Directive). Moreover units for the incineration of hazardous or municipal waste are also excluded (clause 6 and definition of the combustion activity in Annex I to the ETS Directive).

Monitoring methodology: choose your path

In order to effectively monitor the greenhouse gases, and according to the MRR, several approaches are open to the operator. The monitoring of emissions can thus be carried out either by calculation from activity data (consumption of fuels and materials), or by measuring with equipment for continuous measurement of gaseous effluents, or by a "fall-back methodology" with maximum uncertainty thresholds

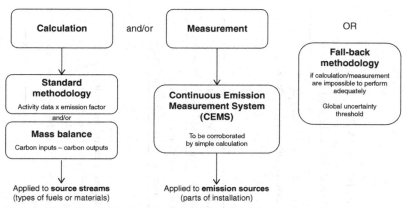

Figure 5.2 Authorized monitoring methodologies

if the requirements induced by the previous approaches are impossible to satisfy (Figure 5.2).

The calculation-based approach is itself composed of two possible methodologies: the standard methodology set out in article 24 of the MRR, and the mass balance methodology set out in article 25 of the MRR.

Thanks to the flexibility provided by the MRR for the third trading period, a combination of calculation-based approach and measurement-based approach within the same installation is also allowed provided that neither double counting nor data gaps in the emissions occur.

Activity-specific monitoring methodologies, however, are often imposed. It is the case for instance for the determination of N_2O emissions from nitric acid production where continuous measurement must be used.

Table 5.2 indicates which type of methodology must be used for the different ETS activities (detailed specific monitoring rules are in Annex IV of the MRR).

The standard methodology is based on the quantities of fuels or materials used to determine CO_2 emissions (N_2O emissions are usually determined by measurement and for PFC specific calculations are made). This methodology is usable for combustion as well as process emissions.

$$E_{CO2_{combustion}} = AD(TJ : amount\,combusted * NCV) * EF\left(t_{CO_2} / TJ\right) * OF$$

Equation 5.1

Table 5.2 *Methodologies to be used for the different ETS activities (summary of Annex IV of the MRR)*

Activities	Methodology to be used	Activities	Methodology to be used
Combustion processes	measurement-based methodology or standard methodology (unless the fuels are included in a mass balance)	*Drying or calcination of gypsum*	standard methodology or measurement-based methodology
Refining of mineral oil	all	Production of pulp	standard methodology or measurement-based methodology
Production of coke	all	Production of paper or cardboard	standard methodology or measurement-based methodology
Metal ore roasting or sintering	all	*Production of carbon black*	all
Production of pig iron or steel	all	*Production of nitric acid*	CO_2 by standard methodology or measurement-based methodology; N_2O concentration by continuous emissions measurement and flow measurement by mass balance

Activity	Methodology
Production or processing of ferrous metals	measurement-based methodology or, either mass balance, where carbon from fuels or input materials remains in the products or other outputs, or standard methodology otherwise
Production of adipic acid	CO_2 by standard methodology or measurement-based methodology; N_2O by measurement-based methodology for abated emissions and mass balance for temporary occurrences of unabated emissions
Production of primary aluminum	process CO_2 by mass balance or measurement-based methodology; no restriction for combustion CO_2; PFC by specific calculation
Production of glyoxal and glyoxylic acid	CO_2 by standard methodology or measurement-based methodology; N_2O by measurement-based methodology for abated emissions and mass balance for temporary occurrences of unabated emissions
Production of secondary aluminum	standard methodology or measurement-based methodology
Production of ammonia	standard methodology or measurement-based methodology
Production or processing of non-ferrous metals	measurement-based methodology or, either mass balance, where carbon from fuels or input materials remains in the products or other outputs, or standard methodology otherwise
Production of bulk organic chemicals by cracking, reforming, partial or full oxidation	measurement-based methodology or standard methodology where the fuels used do not take part in or stem from chemical reactions; otherwise no restriction

Table 5.2 (*cont.*)

Activities	Methodology to be used	Activities	Methodology to be used
Production of cement clinker	standard methodology or measurement-based methodology	*Production of hydrogen (H₂) and synthesis gas by reforming or partial oxidation*	measurement-based methodology or **standard methodology** for emissions from combustion and from fuels used as process inputs; measurement-based methodology or mass balance for emissions from the production of synthesis gas
Production of lime or calcination of dolomite or magnesite	standard methodology or measurement-based methodology	*Production of soda ash (Na₂CO₃) and sodium bicarbonate (NaHCO₃)*	measurement-based methodology or mass balance for process emissions; no restriction for combustion
Manufacture of glass	standard methodology or measurement-based methodology	*Capture of greenhouse gases for the purpose of transport and geological storage*	measurement-based methodology
Manufacture of ceramic products by firing	standard methodology or measurement-based methodology	*Transport of greenhouse gases by pipelines for geological storage*	measurement-based methodology
Manufacture of mineral wool insulation material	standard methodology or measurement-based methodology	*Geological storage of greenhouse gases*	measurement-based methodology

$$E_{CO_{2process}} = AD\left(t \, or \, Nm^3\right) * EF\left(t_{CO_2}/t \, or \, t_{CO_2}/Nm^3\right) * CF$$

Equation 5.2

Where:

AD is activity data, expressed as terajoules (TJ) for combustion, related to amount of fuel combusted, in tonnes (t) or normal cubic metres (Nm^3) times the net calorific value (NCV); for process emissions the activity data can be either an input material (e.g., limestone or soda ash), or the resulting output of the process (e.g., the cement clinker or burnt lime). The MRR refers consequently to Method A (input based) or Method B (output based) (Annex II, section 4 of the MRR). Both methods are considered equivalent, the operator can therefore choose the one that best suits the installation and its constraints;

EF is emission factor, expressed as tonnes CO_2 per terajoule (t CO_2/TJ);

OF is oxidation factor, dimensionless, used to take into account the unburned carbon not released to the atmosphere during combustion;

CF is conversion factor, dimensionless, following the same logic as the oxidation factor, used to take into account the entering carbon not released to the atmosphere during process due to incomplete chemical reactions.

The mass balance is another calculation-based approach, used when the standard methodology is not applicable because of significant amounts of carbon ending up in the products, and the difficulty of linking final emissions to individual inputs. Therefore in such cases (for instance integrated steel plant or chemical industry), an oxidation or a conversion factor is not enough to account for the amount of carbon not released to the atmosphere. The mass balance is described by the following equation:

$$E_{CO_2} = 3.664 * \left(\sum_{inputs} AD * CC - \sum_{outputs} AD * CC \right)$$

Equation 5.3

Where:

AD is the activity data, related to the amount of material (input or
    output);
CC is the carbon content of said material;
3.664 is the factor for converting the molar mass of carbon to CO_2.

The measurement-based approach remains the most direct way to get
greenhouse gas emissions. This approach is mandatory in some cases
(N_2O emissions and quantifying CO_2 transferred with the purpose
of long-term geological storage), and allowed otherwise. However,
if such an approach is chosen for all or part of emission sources, the
MRR requires that the operator corroborate these emissions by calculating the annual emissions of each considered greenhouse gas for
the same emission sources and source streams (but without applying
any of the uncertainty requirements of calculation-based approach)
(article 46 of the MRR). The measurement-based approach is currently used by a very few installations. It is not further detailed in
this chapter, but Chapter 10 explores the issue of direct measurement
in the EU ETS.

These methodologies are to be applied to basic items of the installation
resulting in emissions from different types of fuels or materials in the case
of calculation-based approach or from different locations in the case of
measurement-based approach. These items are defined in the MRR as
source stream and emission source (article 3 of the MRR).

A source stream is "a specific fuel type, raw material or product giving rise to emissions of relevant greenhouse gases at one or more emission sources as a result of its consumption or production." Considering
source streams is relevant for calculation-based approaches because
each type of input or output will have its specific calculation factors
(EF or CC), regardless of the number of emission sources where it
is used.

An emission source is "a separately identifiable part of an installation
or a process within an installation, from which relevant greenhouse
gases are emitted or, for aviation activities, an individual aircraft."
Considering emission sources is relevant for the measurement-based
approach because they define the measurement point where the instruments of a continuous measurement system are installed.

Dual classification: categorization of installations and source streams

In order to adapt the system requirements to the scale of emissions from different installations, the EU ETS defines three categories of installations (article 19 of the MRR).

- **Category A:** average annual emissions $\leq$ 50,000 t CO_2e
- **Category B:** 50,000 t CO_2e < average annual emissions $\leq$ 500,000 t CO_2e
- **Category C:** average annual emissions > 500,000 t CO_2e

The average annual emissions are *verified* emissions in the previous trading period 2008–2012, excluding biomass (as biomass is considered to have an emission factor equal to zero in the context of the ETS), but before subtraction of transferred CO_2.

It may occur that, in some cases, verified emissions reports are not available (e.g., facilities entering for the first time in the EU ETS as a result of the extension of the scope) or not relevant (e.g., facilities that changed their installations or their mode of operation). The operator shall therefore use a conservative estimate of annual average emissions, i.e., a conservative set of assumptions to avoid underestimation of annual emissions.

Category A installations are far more numerous than categories B or C installations, as shown in Figure 5.3 as an example for 2012. However, they are responsible for a small proportion of overall emissions: 4 percent for 2012, while category C installations account for 85 percent (Figure 5.3).

Moreover, even within a given installation, the requirements for the monitoring of emissions are also proportionate to the individual impact of the different source streams on the total emissions. Thus the operator has to classify all source streams for which a calculation-based approach is used according to article 19 of the MRR, into major, minor and *de minimis* source streams (Figure 5.4).

This dual classification allows determining the minimum requirements for tiers, i.e., "a set requirement used for determining activity data, calculation factors, annual emission and annual average hourly emission, as well as for payload" (article 3 of the MRR).

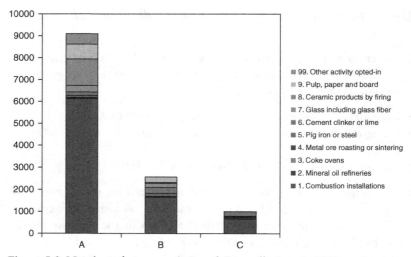

Figure 5.3 Number of category A, B and C installations in 2012
(all countries)
Source: Author based on European Environment Agency (EEA) data viewer (2012).

Determining parameters

The tier system

According to the dual classification described above, the operator must determine the activity data and the various calculation factors in accordance with requirements (tiers) more or less restrictive depending on his installation category and the categorization of his source streams.

The tiers are rated from 1 to a maximum of 4, 1 being the least accurate. Tiers of the same number (e.g., tier 2a and 2b) are considered equivalent. Figure 5.5 gives for instance the different possible tiers for combustion emissions in a calculation-based approach.

Which tier is to be applied depends on installation category (A, B or C) and categorization of the source stream considered (*de minimis*, minor or major), as illustrated by Table 5.3 and Table 5.4.

Uncertainties and allowed references

The numbers associated with tiers therefore characterize the expected exactness on the determination of the parameter considered, and result in different requirements to be met.

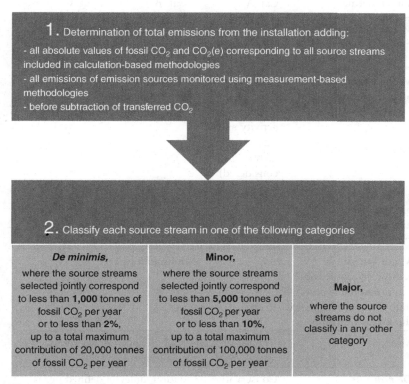

Figure 5.4 Classification of source streams

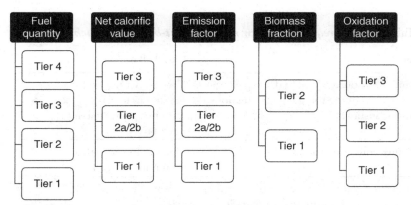

Figure 5.5 Tier system for calculation-based approaches (combustion emissions)

Table 5.3 *Tier requirements for calculation-based approach*

Source stream	Cat. A	Cat. B	Cat. C
Major commercial standard fuel	Minimum tier 2 for activity data, net calorific value and emission factor, and tier 1 for oxidation factor		
Major not falling in other categories	Minimum tier 1 or tier 2 (depends on activity and calculation factor considered)	Highest (from 1 to 4 depending on activity and calculation factor considered)	
Major but technically not feasible or unreasonable costs	Minimum tier 1	Up to two tiers lower with a minimum of tier 1	One tier lower with a minimum of tier 1
Major but still technically not feasible or unreasonable costs; improvement plan (max. three-year transition)	Minimum tier 1		
Minor	Highest tier technically feasible and without unreasonable costs (minimum tier 1)		
De minimis	Conservative estimation, unless a defined tier is achievable without additional effort		

Table 5.4 *Tier requirements for measurement-based approach*

Source	Cat. A, B and C
Emission source > 5,000 tCO_2e per year or > 10% of the total annual emissions of the installation	Highest (CO_2: tier 4, i.e., maximum uncertainty 2.5%; N_2O tier 3, i.e., maximum uncertainty 5%)
Other emission sources	One tier lower with a minimum of tier 1
Technically not feasible or unreasonable costs, and application of a calculation methodology technically not feasible or incurs unreasonable costs	Minimum tier 1

For **activity data,** tier levels are directly related to an **uncertainty threshold,** i.e., the maximum uncertainty allowed for the determination of the quantity of fuel or material over a reporting period. For instance definitions of tiers for activity data of major source streams for combustion of fuels are given below.

This uncertainty must be assessed by the operator and submitted to the competent authority together with the monitoring plan.

The assessment shall comprise the specified uncertainty of the applied measuring instruments, uncertainty associated with the calibration, and any additional uncertainty connected to how the measuring instruments are used in practice. Uncertainty related to stock changes shall be included in the uncertainty assessment where the storage facilities are capable of containing at least 5% of the annual used quantity of the fuel or material considered.

(Article 28 of the MRR)

For **calculation factors,** tier levels define what principle can be used to determine them. There are basically two possibilities:

- use of **default values;** or
- **measurement (typically by laboratory analyses).**

The use of default values corresponds to tiers 1 or 2. The MRR lists the allowed values in its article 31 (Table 5.6).

Laboratory analyses correspond to tier 3, which is the highest for calculation factors. In this case the laboratory used to carry out analyses must be accredited in accordance with EN ISO/IEC 17025 (or meets requirements equivalent to EN ISO/IEC 17025 if access to an accredited laboratory is technically not feasible or would incur unreasonable costs). There is no uncertainty requirement on analyses themselves, but the operator must respect minimum frequencies given in Annex VII of the MRR depending on fuel or material used (Table 5.7).

Moreover, the operator must also write a sampling plan and get it approved by the competent authority (article 33 of the MRR).

Technical feasibility and unreasonable costs

Although the requirements described above are progressive and in theory adapted to the magnitude of emissions of the installation and its different source streams, it may happen that they still cannot be met. In accordance with the increasing harmonization effort in the

Table 5.5 Tiers for activity data of major source streams for combustion of fuels

Installation category	A		B		C	
Type of source streams	Tier	max. uncertainty	Tier	max. uncertainty	Tier	max. uncertainty
Commercial standard fuels	2	± 5.0%	2	± 5.0%	2	± 5.0%
Other gaseous and liquid fuels	2	± 5.0%	4	± 1.5%	4	± 1.5%
Solid fuels	1	± 7.5%	4	± 1.5%	4	± 1.5%
Flaring	1	± 17.5%	3	± 7.5%	3	± 7.5%
Scrubbing: carbonate (Method A)	1	± 7.5%	1	± 7.5%	1	± 7.5%
Scrubbing: gypsum (Method B)	1	± 7.5%	1	± 7.5%	1	± 7.5%

Table 5.6 *Values allowed for calculation factors according to required tiers*

Tier	Values allowed
1	• standard factors and stoichiometric factors listed in Annex VI; • values specified and guaranteed by the supplier of a material where the operator can demonstrate to the satisfaction of the competent authority that the carbon content exhibits a 95% confidence interval of not more than 1%; • values based on analyses carried out in the past, where the operator can demonstrate to the satisfaction of the competent authority that those values are representative for future batches of the same material;
2	• standard factors used by the Member State for its national inventory submission to the Secretariat of the United Nations Framework Convention on Climate Change; • literature values agreed with the competent authority, including standard factors published by the competent authority.

development of the EU ETS, the MRR clarifies the cases of possible derogation. An operator may derogate from a specific requirement (such as the required tier level) only when it is technically not feasible or induces unreasonable costs.

"Technical inability" to fulfill a specific requirement must be justified by the operator to the competent authority. As for the criterion of excessive cost, being for its part more easily quantifiable, it responds to a precise definition, still for the sake of consistency. "The competent authority shall consider costs unreasonable where the cost estimation exceeds the benefit" (article 18 of the MRR). Figure 5.6 illustrates the principle of unreasonable costs with numerical examples.

Operator's instruments vs. supplier's instruments
The operator remains the main actor to perform the monitoring of his emissions. However, the MRR, in order to maintain an acceptable cost-effectiveness ratio, does accept the use of instruments which are under the control of fuel or material suppliers.

Table 5.7 *Minimum frequency of analyses*

Fuel/material	Minimum frequency of analyses
Natural gas	At least weekly
Process gas (refinery mixed gas, coke oven gas, blast-furnace gas and convertor gas)	At least daily – using appropriate procedures at different parts of the day
Fuel oil	Every 20,000 tonnes and at least six times a year
Coal, coking coal, petroleum coke	Every 20,000 tonnes and at least six times a year
Solid waste (pure fossil or mixed biomass fossil)	Every 5,000 tonnes and at least four times a year
Liquid waste	Every 10,000 tonnes and at least four times a year
Carbonate minerals (including limestone and dolomite)	Every 50,000 tonnes and at least four times a year
Clays and shales	Amounts of material corresponding to 50,000 tonnes of CO_2 and at least four times a year
Other input and output streams in the mass balance (not applicable for fuels or reducing agents)	Every 20,000 tonnes and at least once every month
Other materials	Depending on the type of material and the variation, amounts of material corresponding to 50,000 tonnes of CO_2 and at least four times a year

This could be the case not only for activity data (fuel or material consumption) but also for other calculation factors for which analyses carried out by suppliers can be used.

If the operator uses supplier's instruments, he has to provide evidence to the competent authority that the supplier's instruments allow compliance with at least the same tier compared to the use of instruments within his own control. Moreover, supplier's instruments must give more reliable results and be less prone to control risks than the methodology based on his own instruments.

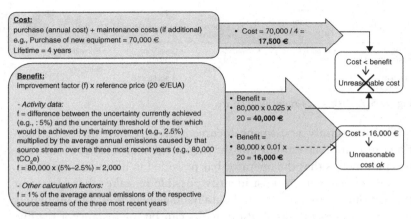

Figure 5.6 Illustration of the principle of unreasonable costs

If this is the case, the operator may rely either upon amounts from invoices, or direct readings from the measurement systems, if it is possible.

The monitoring plan

Based on the monitoring rules outlined above, and on the methodological choices made, the operator writes all the elements necessary to understand the monitoring of his emissions in a monitoring plan. This key document is the reference that will be used by all stakeholders to understand and follow the monitoring of the installation's emissions. The operator writes, implements and updates the monitoring plan in accordance with the requirements defined in the MRR; the competent authority must approve the document and any changes; and the verifier refers to it to assess its proper implementation.

The mandatory content of the monitoring plan is given in Annex I of the MRR and is divided into two main parts: general information about the installation, and detailed description of the monitoring methods applied, including data used, uncertainties achieved, calculation formulae, tiers applied, etc.

Moreover, the monitoring plan is backed by several supporting documents. These are an uncertainty assessment, a risk assessment and various procedures.

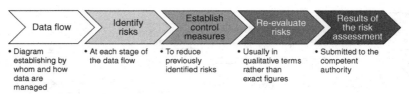

Figure 5.7 Risk assessment procedure

The uncertainty assessment document must contain all the calculations and rationale establishing the numerical uncertainties of the various parameters that the operator has provided in his monitoring plan.

The risk assessment must identify possible mistakes that can occur throughout the monitoring and data management flow and ultimately induce errors in the declaration. Risks can be for instance a reading error on a meter, the loss of recording documents, copy and paste errors, etc. Once the risks are identified, the operator also assesses what measures could be set to reduce those risks, such as control check by another person, electronic transmission, back-up files, etc. These measures are implemented and the reduced risks are then re-evaluated.

Procedures describe in detail the various steps performed by the operator in every practical aspect related to the monitoring of emissions. As these elements could change frequently without being crucial to the monitoring methodology, procedures are briefly described in the monitoring plan but are not considered part of it. Of course, they must be available to the competent authority or the verifier upon request.

The monitoring plan, backed by these supporting documents, is therefore supposed to be a solid basis describing the monitoring choices and operation, and as such not prone to frequent modifications. Theoretically, the monitoring plan could in fact remain unchanged during an entire ETS phase.

However, this is not the case in practice. It is common that modifications occur in a facility, and the monitoring plan must reflect at all times the current status of the installation. Any change in data sources, fuels or materials used, source stream or installation classification, or monitoring management, for instance, will demand that the operator review his monitoring plan accordingly. Some of these changes are considered "significant" by the MRR and must be notified as soon as possible to the competent authority; others are judged "non-significant" and the operator has until the end of the current year to declare them.

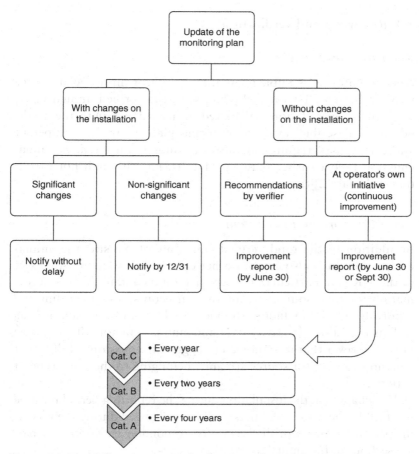

Figure 5.8 The different scenarios leading to update of the monitoring plan

Moreover, even if there are no changes in the installation, the monitoring plan will nevertheless have to be updated in certain circumstances (see Figure 5.8). One of them is the case of recommendations issued by the verifier, which must be taken into account by the operator (article 9 of the MRR). The other case is the requirement that the operator regularly check whether the monitoring methodology can be improved (article 14(1) and article 69(1)-(3) of the MRR), thus introducing the continuous improvement principle in the monitoring process.

5.3 Reporting and verification

Reporting deadlines

Once monitoring is implemented, the operator must declare every year by March 31st the following year, the verified annual emissions of his installation, calculated in accordance with the methodologies described in the monitoring plan. However, competent authorities may require operators to submit the verified annual emission report earlier than by March 31st, although not earlier than February 28th.

Reporting format and content

In addition to the total verified emissions of the site, the annual declaration must also contain other elements as stated in Annex X of the MRR. In particular, the report should contain detailed information for each source stream and emission source regarding the reporting period, including the methodology and tiers applied, as well as the value of activity data and emission factors. It should be noted however that it is allowed to aggregate emissions of different emission sources (or source streams) belonging to the same type of activity.

Also changes in the installation during the reporting period must be notified. In the case where tiers used have changed during the reporting period, the operator shall report corresponding emissions as separate sections of the annual declaration.

In line with the objectives of harmonization and to assure effective integration of these elements required in the annual emissions reports, the European Commission has provided an electronic template for the reporting. However, Member States may require their operators to use specific file formats such as internet-based forms, as long as the required information is included. Several Member States have made this choice such as France with the web-based GEREP[2] system or the UK with the ETSWAP[3] system.

---

[2] Gestion Électronique du Registre des Émissions Polluantes (electronic management of pollutant emissions register).
[3] Emissions Trading Scheme Workflow Automation Project.

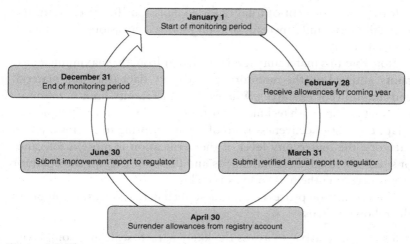

Figure 5.9 The compliance cycle

Verification: who and how?

Before the March 31st deadline, the operator must have had his emissions report verified. The verifier must be independent and have a sufficient knowledge of the Directive, regulations, and other relevant legislation and guidelines, as well as experience of data and information auditing, and of the sector-specific technical monitoring aspects. An accreditation system is in place in each Member State to ensure that verifiers possess these competences.

The goal of verification is to assess if:

- the operator's report is complete and meets the requirements of the MRR;
- the operator has acted in compliance with his monitoring plan;
- the data are free from material misstatements.

A material misstatement is a "misstatement that, in the opinion of the verifier, individually or when aggregated with other misstatements, exceeds the materiality level or could affect the treatment of the operator's or aircraft operator's report by the competent authority" (MRR, article 3(5)). The materiality level is different depending on the category of the installation.

It is set to 5 percent of total reported emissions for category A and B installations, and 2 percent of total reported emissions for category C installations.

Note that this materiality level is different from the maximum uncertainty allowed on the monitoring of activity data (fuel and material consumption for example). Whereas the uncertainty limit in monitoring is set to cope with technical constraints, and with the willingness to adapt the cost-effectiveness ratio of the monitoring to the installation category, the materiality level of the verification is more a tolerance of small unintended misstatements and does not exempt the operator from correcting them as soon as possible.

The verification process itself is described in the AVR, and comprises the following steps:

- a strategic analysis to assess the likely nature, scale and complexity of the verification tasks;
- a risk analysis to identify and analyze the relevant inherent risks and control risks;
- a verification plan commensurate with the information obtained and the risks identified during the strategic analysis and the risk analysis, and including a verification program, a test plan and a data sampling plan.

During this process, the verifier also has to conduct a site visit, in order to assess the operation of measuring devices and monitoring systems, the boundaries of the installation, as well as the completeness of source streams and emission sources.

The site visit can be waived under certain conditions, if all relevant data can be remotely accessed by the verifier, and if the conditions established by the Commission for not carrying out site visits are met. These conditions are quite restrictive as they apply only to category A or category B installations having one single source stream, or to an unmanned site with telemetered data, or to remote or inaccessible locations with a high level of data centralization.

A site visit is nonetheless mandatory at least every three years, or if the verifier has changed since the previous verification, or if changes on the installation have occurred.

At the end of the verification, the verifier issues a verification report containing one of the following conclusions:

- the report is verified as satisfactory;
- the report contains material misstatements that were not corrected before issuing the verification report;
- the scope of verification is too limited (due to missing data or insufficient information) and the verifier could not obtain sufficient evidence to issue a verification opinion with reasonable assurance that the report is free from material misstatements;
- non-conformities, individually or combined with other non-conformities, provide insufficient clarity and prevent the verifier from stating with reasonable assurance that the report is free from material misstatements.

In the case of a non-satisfactory verification report (i.e., one of the last three conclusions), the competent authority eventually estimates the emissions.

Determination of emissions by the competent authority

The competent authority shall make a conservative estimate of the emissions of an installation in any of the following situations:

- no verified annual emissions report has been submitted by the operator by the deadline;
- the verified annual emissions report is not in compliance with the MRR;
- the emission report of the operator has not been verified in accordance with the AVR.

This calculation made by the competent authority is usually very disadvantageous for the operator and this situation remains quite rare.

Accreditation of verifiers

Verifiers are accredited by the national accreditation bodies of countries (such as UKAS[4], COFRAC[5], etc.) according to the standards described in the AVR and in Regulation 765/2008/EC (setting out the

---

[4] United Kingdom Accreditation Service.
[5] Comité français d'accréditation.

requirements for accreditation and market surveillance relating to the marketing of products).

It is worth noting that accreditation can be requested by either a legal person or a legal entity, which can lead to different administrative structures. Although most of the accreditations are organizational based (i.e., delivered to verification bodies), individual accreditation does exist (in Germany for instance).

However, considering the wide variety of activities targeted by the EU ETS, accreditation of verifiers is divided into sectoral scopes, corresponding to activities referred to in Annex I of the ETS Directive. As a result, a verifier shall only issue a verification report to an operator whose installation activity matches its accreditation scope.

In addition to delivering accreditation, national accreditation bodies also carry out an annual surveillance of each verifier. This surveillance consists of a visit to the premises of the verifier – to review a representative sample of the internal verification documentation and to assess the implementation of the verifier's quality management system – and witnessing the performance and competence of a representative number of the verifier's staff.

Improvement reports

In addition to the emissions report, the operator has other reporting obligations in order to fully be in line with the MRR. The third period of the EU ETS places special emphasis on continuous improvement and the operator must regularly submit an improvement report to the competent authority as mentioned in Section 5.2.

The improvements proposed could either come from the verifier's recommendations (see Figure 5.10) or from the operator himself. In the case of improvements responding to the verifier's recommendations, an improvement report has to be submitted to the competent authority by June 30th of the same year. In the case of improvements at the operator's own initiative, the deadline is June 30th as well (though it may be extended to September 30th by the competent authority), but the mandatory periodicity of the report depends on the installation category (from every year to every four years, see Figure 5.8).

These two improvement reports may be merged if both are relevant for a given year.

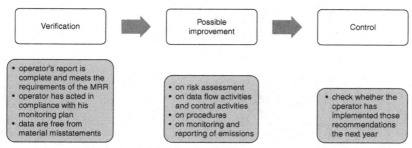

Figure 5.10 Improvement based on verifier's recommendations

5.4 MRV costs

Each year, MRV costs an average €22,000 per installation and €0.07/tCO₂e

Average MRV costs per installation are €15,000–32,000 per year, and average MRV costs per emitted ton of CO_2e are in the order of €0.04–0.08 per tCO_2e (Table 5.8). These figures are however somewhat uncertain and very variable between installations.

Most studies attempting to quantify the costs of MRV in the EU ETS rely on industry surveys. The resulting estimates are therefore subject to at least three large sources of uncertainty: biased sample – large companies, or companies most impacted by MRV costs may be more inclined to fill in the survey; approximate answers – most companies do not keep a precise record of internal costs; and conversion of time spent into monetary costs – the applicable labor cost is difficult to determine.

Four robust qualitative conclusions on MRV costs in the EU ETS

Four qualitative conclusions nevertheless prove to be robust across existing studies:

- MRV costs constitute the bulk – between 65 percent and 95 percent depending on the studies – of the overall transaction costs for participating in the EU ETS (Heindl, 2012; Jaraité et al., 2010; King et al., 2010). The other transaction costs include administrative fees, access to information and trading costs. It was already the case for the UK ETS (Jaraité et al., 2010).

Table 5.8 *Literature review on MRV costs in the EU ETS*

	Years considered	MRV cost per installation (€/yr)			MRV cost per emitted ton (€/tCO$_2$e/yr)			Cost per installation (€/yr)		
		Average	Min	Max	Average	Min	Max	Monitoring	Reporting	Verification
Best estimate based on literature review		22,148	9,378	75,365	0.07	0.03	1.20	26%	34%	40%
King et al. (2010)	2009	19,109	6,991	94,731	0.082	0.047	1.282	3,249	5,351	5,160
AEA (2006)	na	7,963	5,851	10,074	0.006					
ETG (2008)	2005–2007	9,316			0.014					
European Commission (2008a)	na	8,500	2,000	15,000						
Graus & Voogt (2007)	2005–2006	11,725	1,570	21,880						
Jaraité et al. (2010)	2005–2007	31,913	13,493	100,106	0.044	0.023	1.561	8,936	9,255	13,722

Heindl (2012)	2010–2011	15,423	7,648	31,259	0.082	0.031	0.765		
European Commission (2012a)	na								900
For US GHG Reporting rule:									
US EPA (2009)		11,448	3,952	64,767	0.020	0.001	0.137	7,890	275	3,984

Figures in bold come from the most reliable studies, i.e., those with most methodological information. Averages in italic are approximations based on minimum and maximum values. The information for the US GHG Reporting rule, at the bottom, does not apply to the EU ETS and is only provided as a basis for comparison. Figures were converted into euros when necessary based on the annual average exchange rate of the original figure if provided, and of the corresponding study year otherwise. One-off costs incurred for setting up the MRV system are spread over ten years (only 10 percent of these costs are added to the annual figure provided in the table).[6]

Source: Authors.

[6] One-off costs are generally lower than recurring costs, and in the very worst case equal to three times the recurring costs. Therefore, even if these costs are only spread over five years, the annual estimate does not significantly change.

- Large economies of scale exist for MRV: the cost per emitted ton of CO_2 decreases exponentially with the amount of verified emissions (Heindl, 2012; Jaraité et al., 2010; King et al., 2010). For smaller firms, verification constitutes the bulk of incompressible MRV costs (Jaraité et al., 2010; King et al., 2010): the tier approach is therefore more efficient at reducing costs for small installations than the provisions on verification.
- MRV, and in particular monitoring, is much more costly in some specific sectors such as refining and cement production, due to the complexity of the processes involved (King et al., 2010; US EPA, 2009). King et al. (2010) also identify high monitoring costs for power plants but this is likely due to an outlier which invested heavily in fuel sampling.
- On average, MRV costs are almost evenly distributed between monitoring, reporting and verification, although verification tends to be a little more expensive than the first two. Installation size strongly influences this distribution, as verification can represent as much as two-thirds of MRV costs for installations below 25,000 tCO_2e/yr and as little as one-fourth for installations above 500,000 tCO_2e/yr (Jaraité et al., 2010; King et al., 2010).

While the phase II changes likely largely decreased monitoring and reporting costs for small installations (see Section 5.1), they probably did little to decrease verification costs as all installations are still verified every year, although small ones may waive the site visit two years out of three in most cases (see Section 5.3).

Direct measurement, inclusion threshold and cost vs. uncertainty trade-off

The use of direct measurement could strongly influence the *cost vs. uncertainty* trade-off: in the American context of the US GHG Reporting rule, the US EPA (2009) assesses that the systematic use of direct measurement could reduce uncertainty by up to 65 percent, but would multiply costs by a factor of 10. A hybrid approach, mandating direct measurement only for emitters – generally larger ones – who already practice it to comply with an existing regulation, reduces uncertainty by 50 percent while doubling the costs.

The US EPA (2009) also assessed the effectiveness of a minimum threshold for inclusion in the perimeter of the regulation. Compared to the 25,000 tCO_2e/yr threshold retained in the US, a 10,000 tCO_2e/yr threshold increases costs by 35% and covers only 1% more emissions. To the contrary, decreasing the inclusion threshold to 100,000 tCO_2e/yr saves 23% of the costs and covers 2.5% fewer emissions. This is difficult to compare with the EU ETS where the inclusion threshold depends on rated thermal input, in MW, rather than estimated emissions, in tCO_2e/yr. Interestingly, however, one can note that during phase II, 64% of installations had average emissions below 25,000 tCO_2e/yr.[7]

Costs of MRV for other entities than the covered installations

Assessments of MRV costs for other entities than the reporting installation are much rarer. The European Commission assesses the public costs – for the Commission and the Member States – of the legislative process and its subsequent implementation between €3,000 and €10,000 per installation and per year (European Commission, 2008a) and the cost of accreditation – for auditors – around €10,000 per year and per verifier (European Commission, 2012a). Ultimately, these costs are borne by installations through "subsistence fees" such as those associated with the issuance of permits for emitting GHGs, or through verification costs for annual audits. Subsistence fees and verification costs are consistent with the estimates provided by the European Commission (2010).

5.5 MRV ID table

Table 5.9 *MRV ID table*

Context	
Regulator	Official rules and Advisory guidelines: European Commission Member State administration on some country-specific points

---

[7] Only years with active participation, that is verified emissions higher than zero, are taken into account.

Table 5.9 (*cont.*)

Type and level of incentive to comply	Default emissions calculated by the competent authority in case of non-satisfactory reporting, and a penalty of 100€/ton of CO_2e emitted for which the operator has not surrendered allowances. This penalty does not release the operator from the obligation to surrender an amount of allowances equal to those excess emissions.
Entities concerned	Stationary technical units where activities listed in Directive 2003/87/EC are carried out: 11,500 installations. Auditors: 200 active entities across the countries involved.
Sectors concerned	Combustion; refining; metal ore sintering; production of coke, pig iron, steel, ferrous or non-ferrous metals, aluminum, cement clinker, lime, pulp, paper, carbon black, nitric acid, adipic acid, glyoxal, glyoxylic acid, ammonia, bulk organic chemicals, hydrogen, soda ash, sodium bicarbonate, plaster boards, gypsum products; manufacture of glass, ceramic products, mineral wool; drying of gypsum; capture, transport and geological storage of GHG.
Gases concerned	CO_2 (always), N_2O (specific cases), PFC (specific cases)
Overall MRV costs	22,000 €/installation per year on average; 0.07 €/tCO_2e on average
Monitoring	
Rules	Commission Regulation n° 601/2012
Other reference documents	Guidances provided by the Commission services
Uncertainty requirements	No overarching requirement, with the exception of fall-back methodology (see Section 2.2)
Achieved uncertainty range	No estimation available

Table 5.9 (*cont.*)

Cost range	3,000–9,000 €/installation per year
	0.02 €/tCO$_2$e on average
Scope	Direct emissions of stationary technical units (Scope 1/operational/site)
Frequency	From continuously to yearly (depends on installation and source streams categories)
Source for activity data	Operator's instruments, supplier's instruments, invoices
Uncertainty range for activity data	1.5%–15% (depends on installation and source streams categories).
Source for emission factors	Standard factors from regulation or used by the Member State for its national inventory submission, literature values, values specified and guaranteed by the suppliers, values based on analyses (depends on installation and source streams categories).
Uncertainty range for emission factors	No overall quantitative requirement. However, there are qualitative or quantitative requirements for the various components of emission factors, which depend on the type of installation (e.g., 1% at 95% confidence interval for the carbon content of a fuel if the installation chooses to use a default factor).
Direct measurement	Mandatory for all emissions of N$_2$O and for quantifying CO$_2$ transferred; otherwise allowed if overall uncertainty lower than calculation-based methodology but not frequently used.
Incentives to reduce uncertainty	Almost none in practice. In principle, however, operators are supposed to aim for the highest achievable accuracy/precision, unless this is technically not feasible or incurs unreasonable costs following the principle of "continuous improvement" in monitoring and reporting which is introduced in article 9 of the Directive 2003/87/EC.

Table 5.9 (*cont.*)

Is requirements stringency adapted to the amount of emissions at stake (materiality)?	Yes: threshold for inclusion and then more stringent requirements for larger installations and source streams. In addition, "unreasonable costs" authorizing a coarser monitoring are easier to demonstrate for smaller installations.

Reporting	
Rules	Commission Regulation n° 601/2012
Other reference documents	Guidances provided by the Commission services
Format	standardised electronic reporting language based on XML
Level of source disaggregation	11,500 installations. Annual emission reports of installations must contain information for all emissions sources and source streams
Frequency	Yearly
Timeline	Year Y − 1 emissions reported at year Y
Language	Member State language
Is requirements stringency adapted to the amount of emissions at stake (materiality)?	Partly: although basic requirements – monitoring report – are the same for all installations, the frequency of the reporting on the improvements of the monitoring plan is more frequently required for larger installations.
Cost range	5,000–9,000 €/installation per year 0.02 €/tCO$_2$e on average

Verification	
Rules	Commission Regulation n° 600/2012
Other reference documents	Guidances provided by the Commission services
Format	Verification report
Frequency	Yearly
Timeline	Year Y − 1 emissions verified at year Y

Table 5.9 (*cont.*)

Language	Member State language
Accredited entities for verification	Verifier shall be independent of the operator, and have sufficient knowledge of the Directive and regulations, of the requirements relevant to the activities being verified, and of the generation of all information related to each source of emissions in the installation. The tasks related to accreditation are carried out by the national accreditation bodies.
Control of accredited entities	The national accreditation body carries out an annual surveillance of each verifier to which it has issued an accreditation certificate, witnessing the performance and competence of a representative number of the verifier's staff. The national accreditation body may conduct an extraordinary assessment of the verifier at any time to ensure that the verifier meets the requirements of the regulation.
	Examples of reason for suspension: the verifier has committed a serious breach of the requirements of the Regulation or has persistently and repeatedly failed to meet the requirements of the Regulation
Cost of accreditation	€10,000 per accredited entity per year
Support of accredited entities	None
Is requirements stringency adapted to the amount of emissions at stake (materiality)?	A materiality level of 5% of the total reported emissions is set for categories A and B installations, and a materiality level of 2% of the total reported emissions is set for category C installations. In some cases, small installations can also waive the site visit two years out of three (see Section 5.3).
Cost range	€5,000–14,000/installation per year; €0.03/ tCO_2e on average

Box 5.1 MRV for free allocation[8]

From the third period of the EU ETS, allocations of free allow-ances have no longer been based on historical emissions from installations (except in special cases), but on the product of a benchmark (product-based benchmark, heat-based benchmark or fuel-based benchmark) and of data of historical activity (European Commission, 2011).

Operators must submit an application for allocation, which must be verified as satisfactory by a verifier before being trans-mitted to the competent authority, and then to the European Commission.

To that end, sites have to be split into subinstallations, each sub-installation corresponding to a specific allocation regime to which a benchmark is associated:

- product benchmark (if relevant): value set as the average of the 10 percent most greenhouse gas efficient installations, in terms of CO_2 emitted per ton of product produced at European level in the years 2007–2008;
- heat benchmark (if relevant and if no adequate product bench-mark exists): value set as 62.3 tCO_2/TJ of heat;
- fuel benchmark (if relevant and if no adequate product bench-mark exists): value set as 56.1 tCO_2/TJ of fuel;
- process emissions approach (for some specific cases): value set as 97 percent of historical emissions (tCO_2).

Activity data needed for the calculation of free allocation (tonnes of product produced, fuel or heat consumption, etc.) are based on previously verified historical data if they are available and relevant. If not (basically because the site is a new entrant), then activity data for free allocation are based on new activity data which must also be verified (Table 5.10).

---

[8] National Implementation Measures. To allocate free allowances to installations, all Member States have carried out a preliminary calculation based on application forms submitted by operators and have notified these so-called national implementation measures (NIMs) to the Commission.

Table 5.10 *Relevant period of time taken into account for activity data for the calculation of free allocation for 2013–2020*

Status of the installation	Relevant period for activity data
incumbent installation (i.e., start of operation before June 30, 2011)	2005–2008 or 2009–2010 (operator's choice)
new entrant (i.e., start of operation after June 30, 2011)	90 days following the start of normal operation

The verification process and the requirements upon the verifier are similar to those for the annual report, although the two verifications (the one concerning the free allocation application and the one for the annual emissions report) are separate. In the case of new entrants, it should be noted that the allocation request and its verification can only take place after the start of normal operation and the subsequent 90 days period to determine the relevant activity level. The operator will then receive his free allocations the following year, covering both the current and the previous year.

The amount of free allowances for the installation is the sum of all subinstallations free allowances. This amount may be adjusted during the period in case of significant changes in the installation or cessation of operations. Moreover, in line with the objectives set in the ETS Directive, free allowances decrease each year by equal amounts with a view to reaching no free allocation in 2027.

5.6 What practitioners say about it

Different practitioners involved in the EU ETS were asked three questions. Their responses, which are not always consistent with one another, enlighten the issues discussed in this chapter in a concrete and operational way, and situate the rules outlined above in the European industrial reality.

According to you, is there a significant incentive to improve accuracy/precision?

Rémi Bussac, Environment, Health and Consumers, EDF – European Affairs
"Yes. The entry into force of the ETS and the implementation of the MRV guidelines back in 2005 have significantly changed the way operators of large combustion plants monitor CO_2 emission.

The costs associated with CO_2 emission (and the penalties foreseen by EU regulations in case of unverified emissions) are obviously strong incentives for operators to improve the accuracy and precision of their GHG emissions reporting.

The MRV, originally designed for GHG only, opened the path for better emissions determination at installation level (for instance for SO_2, NOx and dust, that are also commonly subject to taxes or market-based instruments or annual mass emission limits in the frame of the European industrial emission regulation – NERP, TNP, …)."

Eric Dugelay, Partner, Global Sustainability Services Co-Leader, Deloitte
"Today's pricing of a ton of CO_2eq being what it is (low), there is not much of an incentive to increase the accuracy of the measurement and valuation of the GHG emissions. In fact the levels of precision, as they are today, are perceived as sufficient by the industrial sites Deloitte visits to conduct its detailed verification work in the context of the EU ETS. And from an audit profession standpoint, the tolerances proposed by the ETS are very comparable to the ones in place in the context of the audit of financial information. So, our views converge with those of our clients: there is not a significant incentive to improve accuracy/precision."

Yann Martinet, Agro Industry & Environment Project Manager, COOP de France Déshydratation
"Rather than *encouraging* industry to improve accuracy in terms of monitoring GHG emissions, the EU ETS *requires* it to do so. The many different regulations controlling air emissions require industry to monitor several dozens of substances and it would not be possible to apply these demanding requirements covering GHGs to each of these substances as it is so extensive. This may seem paradoxical as quantifying carbon is easy within the frame of a heat benchmark, such as the one applying to fodder drying sites – new entrants in the ETS

third trading period – compared with substances much more difficult to address, such as NOx, NMVOCs, TSP and persistent organic pollutants affecting human health."

Anonymous operator, UK
"There is always a significant incentive to improve accuracy owing to the financial implications over-reporting entails for installations which emit significant amounts of CO_2. However, any improvement in accuracy should not add any extra complication – currently, the EU-ETS process is excessively onerous considering any benefits seen by operators and requires substantial work to demonstrate compliance with uncertainty allowances as it is and we would rather see this process simplified than made more challenging."

Based on your experience, what is the most important thing about MRV at the industrial plant scale?

Rémi Bussac, Environment, Health and Consumers, EDF – European Affairs
"All the basic principles settled by the MRV are important: Completeness, Consistency, Transparency, Trueness, Cost effectiveness, Faithfulness and Improvement of performance in monitoring and reporting emissions.

The full integration of MRV within the Environment Management System at the installation level (ISO 14001…) is definitely helpful.

It is important to try keeping the MRV approach as simple and straightforward as possible at the installation level (for instance by assessing the emissions only at the site level, and not at the unit level, if it is not required by your local regulation).

When calculating the CO_2 emission based on the fuel consumption, an important part of the MRV is probably the fuel management system of the plant, which will handle the supply, the stocks, the consumption and the fuel analysis."

Eric Dugelay, Partner, Global Sustainability Services Co-Leader, Deloitte
"Based on our experience at the industrial plant level, the quality of the monitoring plan is probably the most obvious objective since ultimately the reporting of the emissions is to be accurate. The control of this key framework by the national and regional environmental

authorities is expected to provide areas of continuous improvement that are expected by the industrialists."

Yann Martinet, Agro Industry & Environment Project Manager, COOP de France Déshydratation
"For the fodder drying sector that *COOP de France Déshydratation* represents, monitoring GHG emissions involves sound fuel sampling and careful monitoring of the associated tests. The procedures put in place by the competent authorities to establish monitoring plans and online emissions reporting meet the first two requirements (monitoring and reporting). The verification requirement weighs the heaviest in this triple approach, particularly at national level. It is vital that, beyond the controls carried out by local authorities, an overall vision be applied at Member State level regarding key parameters of the reporting conducted (e.g., NCV of the fuel, emissions factors, etc.), and more widely, that this be linked up with sectoral energy balances and even national emissions inventories."

Anonymous operator, UK
"The most important thing about the MRV process at an industrial plant scale would probably be the ongoing maintenance of monitoring equipment. It is important to ensure that EU-ETS critical equipment is calibrated and functioning correctly – it requires stringent quality control checks to identify any problems in activity or quality data, and this becomes a big issue if errors aren't picked up until the verification process. Thus, having the resource available to check the data regularly is vital."

What is the first thing you would change in the procedure?

Rémi Bussac, Environment, Health and Consumers, EDF – European Affairs
"In EU, the MRV guidelines have been significantly improved from the phase I (2005–2008) to the phase III (2013–2020). Simplified requirements have for instance been introduced for smaller installations.

However, proving that the maximum level of uncertainty is not exceeded is still very heavy for operators, as well as time consuming, and often fragile from a scientific point of view.

We think that commercial transactions should be considered by default as complying with uncertainty requirements for GHG determination."

Eric Dugelay, Partner, Global Sustainability Services Co-Leader, Deloitte
"We would positively perceive a reinforcement of the dialogue between the national and regional environmental authorities on one hand, the accreditation bodies on the other hand, and finally the accredited verifiers such as Deloitte. In that respect, the dialogue that is in place in the United Kingdom should probably inspire our practices in some other countries."

Yann Martinet, Agro Industry & Environment Project Manager, COOP de France Déshydratation
"The development of national applications for reporting emissions, their updating after each amendment in the regulations in force and the resulting extensive data processing before they are made available to the national expertise centres could be centralized at EU level. This would present the triple advantage of harmonizing reporting procedures between Member States, rationalizing reporting costs and speeding up the lengthy procedure, even though the reporting timeframe in place is extremely tight. Moreover, companies located in several Member States would meet these requirements more effectively. The system of remote reporting established in France since the start of the first trading period in 2005 seems to constitute a sound base for further work."

Anonymous operator, UK
"In terms of changing the procedure, having been participating in EU ETS for a number of years, we have honed our processes to align with the MRV requirements. Currently, one of the biggest challenges is demonstrating the uncertainty of third party meters subject to NLMC. It would improve the process if suppliers were legally obliged to provide information relating to their supply meters. Guidance which has been provided by the EA has not addressed this issue."

Bibliography

AEA, 2006. "Costs of Compliance with the EU Emissions Trading Scheme." AEAT/ENV/R/2192. UK Environment Agency.
European Environment Agency (EEA). "EU Emissions Trading System (ETS) data viewer", 2012. www.eea.europa.eu/data-and-maps/data/data-viewers/emissions-trading-viewer. Accessed March 2013.

ETG, 2008. "Administrative Cost of the Emissions Trading Scheme to Participants." Emissions Trading Group.

European Commission, 2003. "Directive 2003/87/EC of the European Parliament and of the Council of 13 October 2003 Establishing a Scheme for Greenhouse Gas Emission Allowance Trading within the Community and Amending Council Directive 96/61/EC."

2004a. "Decision 2004/156/EC of 29 January 2004 Establishing Guidelines for the Monitoring and Reporting of Greenhouse Gas Emissions."

2004b. "Directive 2004/101/EC of the European Parliament and of the Council of 27 October 2004 Amending Directive 2003/87/EC Establishing a Scheme for Greenhouse Gas Emission Allowance Trading within the Community, in Respect of the Kyoto Protocol's Project Mechanisms."

2007. "Decision 2007/589/EC Establishing Guidelines for the Monitoring and Reporting of Greenhouse Gas Emissions pursuant to Directive 2003/87/EC of the European Parliament and of the Council."

2008a. "Impact Assessment – Accompanying Document to the Proposal for a Directive of the European Parliament and of the Council Amending Directive 2003/87/EC so as to Improve and Extend the EU Greenhouse Gas Emission Allowance Trading System." SEC(2008) 52. Commission Staff Working Document. Brussels.

2008b. "Directive 2008/101/EC of the European Parliament and of the Council of 19 November 2008 Amending Directive 2003/87/EC so as to Include Aviation Activities in the Scheme for Greenhouse Gas Emission Allowance Trading within the Community."

2009. "Directive 2009/29/EC of the European Parliament and of the Council of 23 April 2009 Amending Directive 2003/87/EC so as to Improve and Extend the Greenhouse Gas Emission Allowance Trading Scheme of the Community."

2010. "Guidance on Interpretation of Annex I of the EU ETS Directive (excl. Aviation Activities)."

2011. "Decision 2011/278/EU – Determining Transitional Union-Wide Rules for Harmonised Free Allocation of Emission Allowances pursuant to Article 10a of Directive 2003/87/EC."

2012a. "Impact Assessment – Accompanying the Document COMMISSION REGULATION (EU) No .../.. of XXX on the Monitoring and Reporting of Greenhouse Gas Emissions pursuant to Directive 2003/87/EC of the European Parliament and of the Council and COMMISSION REGULATION (EU) No .../.. of XXX on the Verification of Greenhouse Gas Emission Reports and Tonne-Kilometre Reports and the Accreditation of Verifiers pursuant to Directive 2003/87/

EC of the European Parliament and of the Council." SWD(2012) 177 final. Commission Staff Working Document. Brussels.

2012b. "Commission Regulation (EU) 601/2012 of 21 June 2012 on the Monitoring and Reporting of Greenhouse Gas Emissions pursuant to Directive 2003/87/EC of the European Parliament and of the Council."

2012c. "Commission Regulation 600/2012 on the Verification of Greenhouse Gas Emission Reports and Tonne-Kilometre Reports and the Accreditation of Verifiers pursuant to Directive 2003/87/EC of the European Parliament and of the Council."

Graus, W. and Voogt, M., 2007. "Small Installations within the EU Emissions Trading Scheme." ECS04079. European Commission & Ecofys.

Heindl, P., 2012. "Transaction Costs and Tradable Permits: Empirical Evidence from the EU Emissions Trading Scheme." Discussion Paper 12–021. ZEW (Center for European Economic Research).

Jaraité, J., Convery, F. and Di Maria, C., 2010. Transaction costs for firms in the EU ETS: lessons from Ireland. *Climate Policy* 10(2): 190–215.

King, K., Pye, S. and Davison, S., 2010. *Assessing the Cost to UK Operators of Compliance with the EU Emissions Trading System*. Aether, Abingdon, UK.

United Nations, 1992. "United Nations Framework Convention on Climate Change."

1997. "Kyoto Protocol to the United Nations Framework Convention on Climate Change."

US EPA, 2009. *Regulatory Impact Analysis for the Mandatory Reporting of Greenhouse Gas Emissions Final Rule (GHG Reporting)*. United States Environmental Protection Agency, Washington, DC.

6 | Variant 1: the waste sector in Australia's Carbon Pricing Mechanism, another ETS at site level

MARION AFRIAT AND EMILIE ALBEROLA

Acknowledgements: We are grateful to Mark Hunstone (National Inventory Systems and International Reporting Branch) for his answers to our questions and his review of the NGER Measurement Determination elements.

6.1 Context

In 2010, the waste sector in Australia reported emissions of around 15 Mt CO_2e – mainly in the form of methane and nitrous oxide – and was responsible for 3 percent of Australia's greenhouse gas (GHG) emissions.[1] Although this may appear as a negligible part of national emissions, Australia chose to include this sector in its Carbon Pricing Mechanism (CPM) as an incentive to promote recycling, alternative waste treatment, composting and capturing methane for destruction or use in electricity generation. In addition, the waste sector presents a number of opportunities for cost-effective abatement according to Australia's plan for a Clean Energy Future (Ministry of Finance, 2011). For example, methane capture is a common practice in the solid waste and wastewater sectors in order to generate renewable energy. More explicitly, the scheme covers carbon dioxide, methane and nitrous oxide emissions from solid waste (accounting for 80 percent of the waste emissions[2]), wastewater treatment (most of the remainder) and incineration (0.2 percent of the waste emissions[3]).

---

[1] Climate change and the resource recovery and waste sector, Department of the Environment, Water, Heritage and the Arts, MMA, April 2010.
[2] Waste emissions projections, Department of Climate Change and Energy Efficiency (2012).
[3] Ibid.

The CPM is directly inspired by the Carbon Pollution Reduction Scheme bill (CPRS) which failed to gain adequate support in either the Australian Parliament or the Senate (2008–2010). The CPRS was supposed to be an emissions trading scheme covering 80 percent of GHG emissions (767 facilities).

Australia's Carbon Pricing Mechanism was launched on July 1st, 2012 and was terminated by the new government on July 17th, 2014. It consists of a carbon tax over the first three years and was initially intended to be recast as a cap-and-trade mechanism from July 1st, 2015. As of September 2013, Australia's CPM was the only Carbon Pricing Mechanism worldwide to directly cover the whole waste sector. However, in 2015, the new South Korean Emission Trading Scheme (ETS) will also cover the waste sector but, as of February 1st, 2014, we are not aware of further details on the associated MRV procedures. Since 2013, New Zealand's ETS has also covered a part of the waste sector, namely methane emissions from solid waste disposal.

The waste sector differs from sectors more commonly covered by carbon pricing mechanisms in several ways:

- most of its emissions are non-CO_2 gases;
- its emissions are laden with higher uncertainty than the energy sector, although this uncertainty is comparable to some industrial sectors;
- a large share of its emissions are "legacy emissions," that is emissions due to past activities: while other sectors emit in proportion to their present level of activity, the waste sector largely emits in proportion to the amount of waste deposited in landfills over the previous years.

To facilitate the reading, even though the CPM was repealed in July 2014, the entire chapter is written in the present tense. Indeed the National Greenhouse and Energy Reporting System (House of Representatives, 2007) is still in place and will continue to require covered waste sector entities to have measurement and reporting procedures after July 2014. Moreover, the Australian decision to include the waste sector is an interesting counter-example to the European decision not to include it in its ETS, especially as the EU's decision was motivated by the large monitoring uncertainty of the waste sector (European Commission, 2006).

6.2 The waste sector covered by the Carbon Pricing Mechanism

Scope and general MRV requirements

The waste sector covered by the Carbon Pricing Mechanism (CPM) includes emissions from landfills, wastewater treatment, waste incineration and the biological treatment of solid waste. All waste facilities with direct emissions of at least 25,000 tonnes of CO_2e a year are liable under the CPM.[4] This inclusion threshold is the same for all the sectors covered by the CPM. Most of the emissions released from the waste sector are methane (CH_4) emissions. CO_2 emissions generated from waste management or produced from the flaring of methane are considered to be from biomass sources and do not need to be estimated. For example, landfill gas comprises both methane and carbon dioxide but only the methane component should be reported. The only CO_2 emissions to be reported in the waste sector are those from waste incineration as they may be from fossil sources (e.g., plastics). Nitrous oxide (N_2O) must also be reported by wastewater treatment plants. Indeed, the treatment of human waste in municipal wastewater facilities generates N_2O whereas organic waste decomposition in landfills generates negligible amounts of this gas (IPCC, 2006).

In terms of monitoring, reporting and verification, the waste sector included in the CPM has to meet the requirements set by the 2007 National Greenhouse and Energy Reporting Act (NGER) and the 2008 National Greenhouse and Energy Reporting Measurement Act (Measurement Determination). Carbon price liability is established by the 2011 Clean Energy Act (CEA). The Carbon Pricing Mechanism (CPM) and the National Greenhouse and Energy Reporting scheme

---

[4] Avoiding displacement of waste from covered to non-covered facilities, the "prescribe distance rule" applies. Indeed, all facilities emitting more than 10 kt CO_2e/year are also covered by the CPM if they are located in the vicinity of a covered facility (emitting more than 25 kt CO_2e/year or more). The aim is to ensure that there is no diversion of waste from large landfills to smaller landfills in order to avoid the cost impact of the carbon price. The Department of Climate Change publishes a list of designated larger landfills through regulations, and smaller landfills which accept the same type of waste as the covered larger landfill and are within a certain distance from the larger one.

(NGER) are administered and regulated by the Clean Energy Regulator. The Climate Change Department oversees the NGER and the CPM legislations and may propose revisions. Information collected through the NGER scheme helps in assessing which waste facilities are liable for the Carbon Pricing Mechanism.

There are some common requirements for the three subsectors (landfills, wastewater and waste incineration). The minimum information required to determine GHG emissions from waste facilities is the amount of waste or wastewater that the facility has handled (in tons), the amount of methane flared, captured and transferred (for landfills and wastewater handling), the financial year when the facility commenced operation and the State or Territory where the facility is located.

The distinction between legacy and non-legacy waste

With the implementation of the Clean Energy Act, on July 1st, 2012, landfill operators need to distinguish between legacy waste and non-legacy waste. This distinction determines whether the emissions are:

- covered by the Clean Energy Act – non-legacy emissions;
- or, for abated legacy emissions, eligible for carbon credits under the Carbon Farming Initiative (CFI), a domestic offset scheme rewarding emissions reductions which occur outside of the CPM regulated perimeter.

CPM liability only applies to emissions from waste deposited after July 1st, 2012 which is called "non-legacy waste emissions." Emissions from waste deposited before July 1st, 2012 are defined as "legacy waste emissions." Hence, landfill operators are not liable for emissions generated from historic waste streams (legacy waste). However, legacy waste emissions do count for the purpose of determining whether a landfill facility exceeds the 25,000 tonnes per year threshold.

6.3 Monitoring the waste sector's GHG emissions

IPCC guidelines propose methods, criteria and emissions factors to estimate emissions from waste (IPCC, 2006). The methane emission estimation methods from landfills are estimated principally using data on the receipt of solid waste materials at the landfill and the First Order Decay Model provided in these guidelines, except in certain circumstances. Emission factors more specific than the IPCC defaults are provided. The Measurement Determination is also updated annually to reflect improvements in estimation methods and respond to industry feedback as required.

Choice of the monitoring methodology: default factor or not?

As of February 2014, the Measurement Determination does not allow the direct measurement of emissions with one exception: CO_2 emissions from waste incineration. However, the extension of direct measurement is being considered: there is a commitment in the technical guidelines[5] to work towards the inclusion of a method framework for the direct measurement of emissions from solid waste disposal on land. In addition, in the NGER Measurement Determination review response paper (May 2011), the Climate Change Department was advised that some wastewater treatment plants have the capacity to monitor and report nitrous oxide emissions based on continuous direct measurement. The Climate Change Department intended to continue the ongoing dialogue with the Water Service Association of Australia (WSAA) in the development of a framework for direct measurements.

The methods and criteria for calculating direct (Scope 1) GHG emissions from solid waste disposal on land are included in chapter 5 of the Measurement Determination as amended to July 1st, 2012. Methane in landfill gas captured for consumption onsite, transferred offsite or flared is deducted for calculation of total emissions of methane released by the landfill during the year. As specified by Conolly (2013), composting activities at a landfill are covered only if they form part of a liable landfill facility. A waste to energy facility that burns green waste is also not covered by the CPM as biomass is deemed renewable.

---

[5] www.environment.gov.au/climate-change/greenhouse-gas-measurement/ publications/nger-technical-guidelines-2013. To work towards the inclusion of a method 4 framework for solid waste disposal on land.

Common elements to all methods for monitoring GHG emissions from landfill

First of all, a distinction must be made between waste received at landfill and waste disposed of in landfill: only the amount of waste disposed of in a landfill has to be reported, even if both have to be monitored. Waste disposed of in landfill is the waste received at the landfill minus waste diverted from disposal, that is the material which is composted, recycled or used onsite. In 2008–2009 54 percent of the waste generated in Australia was recovered.[6]

Second, the operators need to estimate the tonnage of solid waste. This estimate is usually based on calibrated measuring equipment, respecting at least the state or territory legislation applying to the landfill. Invoices, when they exist, are considered to be sufficient evidence.

Third, the operators need to estimate the opening stock of Degradable Organic Carbon (DOC) following Equation 6.1. The DOC of material is defined as the fraction of that material made up of organic carbon that can degrade biologically to form organic compounds including methane. Therefore, estimating the opening stock of degradable organic carbon is the cornerstone of the estimate of emissions from a landfill.

Equation 6.1 – The monitoring equation for emissions from landfill

CH_4 gas generation released from landfill = (Decomposable DOC from newly deposited waste + Decomposable DOC from waste left) × Emission Factor × conversion factor from Carbon to a mass of CH_4.

Where decomposable DOC is given in tons of carbon; Emission Factor (EF) is the proportion of decomposable DOC that turns into methane annually, set at 0.5; and the conversion factor (CF) is 1.3336×21 tCH$_4$ tC^{-1}.

Source: NGER (Measurement) Determination, 2008.

---

[6] Recovery rate is the addition of the amount of recycling and energy recovery divided by the waste generation. Waste and recycling in Australia 2011, National report, Department of Sustainability, Environment, Water, Population and Communities, p. 41.

There is an alternative method to estimate methane generated from a landfill. It applies to facilities that capture methane generated by the landfill and where the estimates of the quantity of methane captured for combustion (either at the landfill or elsewhere) and for flaring exceed 75 percent of the estimated emissions generated by the landfill according to the application of the Tier 2 of the 2006 IPCC Guidelines (First Order Decay Model).[7] Then, amount of methane generated by the landfill is estimated as [1/0.75] multiplied by the quantity of methane captured. This alternative approach aims at replacing the First Order Decay Model where a more accurate estimate of emissions generated by the landfill – i.e., based on the quantity of emissions captured – is available. It is also an incentive for these landfills to upgrade to less uncertain emission factors: when using method 2, facilities which have higher methane collection rates than 75 percent – the quantity of methane captured, transferred offsite or flared exceeds 75 percent of the estimated methane generated at the landfill – may replace 0.75 with the actual collection rate. This reduces the estimated amount of methane generated, and thus the facility's liability under the CPM.

Finally, the last common element of the three methods option is the classification of the composition of solid waste received at a landfill. Solid waste is made up of both waste stream and waste mix types. Section 5.10 of the Measurement Determination describes the three waste streams by which the composition of solid waste must be classified, namely:

• Municipal Solid Waste (MSW);
• Commercial and Industrial Waste (C&I); and
• Construction and Demolition Waste (C&D).

Section 5.11 of the 2008 Measurement Determination details nine different waste mix types: food, paper and paper board, garden and park, wood and wood waste, textiles, sludge, nappies, rubber and leather,

---

[7] The Revised 1996 IPCC Guidelines for National Greenhouse Gas Inventories (1996 Guidelines, IPCC, 1997) and the Good Practice Guidance and Uncertainty Management in National Greenhouse Gas Inventories (GPG2000, IPCC, 2000) describes two methods for estimating CH_4 emissions from solid waste disposal sites: the Mass Balance Method (Tier 1) and the First Order Decay (FOD) Method (Tier 2). The use of the Mass Balance Method is strongly discouraged as it produces results that are not comparable with, and less accurate than, the FOD method.

inert waste including concrete, metal, plastic and glass. Emissions generated at the landfill will vary according to tonnage of each waste mix type deposited in the landfill: waste mix types release more or less methane, more or less quickly.

These variations are governed by the following two parameters:

- Degradable Organic Carbon content (DOC): the fraction of DOC describes the amount of organic carbon contained within a material that will readily decay and transform to either methane or carbon dioxide.
- The methane generation constant (k) determines the rate at which the breakdown of DOC occurs. k varies with both waste type and climatic conditions to reflect that organic decay is principally a biogenic process affected by ambient moisture and temperature conditions.

Default values are provided in Table 6.2 and Table 6.3 for the waste streams and waste mix types and for the default value of k, see Section 5.14 of the Measurement Determination.

Calculating GHG emissions from waste deposited on a landfill: three method options

Beyond these common requirements, facility operators can choose between three methods for monitoring landfill emissions (Table 6.1).

Method 1 provides the option for default waste composition data (waste streams and waste mix types) and k values (methane generation constants) specific to Australia. The minimum data required for Method 1 are location by State/Territory, annual waste accepted in tons, and annual amount of methane gas flared or otherwise captured in standard cubic meters.

Methods 2 and 3 are similar to Method 1 except that they require the measurement of a facility-specific methane generation constant (k). The facility-specific value of k changes the profile of methane emissions over time but does not change the total amount of emissions from a site. To calculate k, the operator needs to select and sample a representative zone. The difference between Methods 2 and 3 is that Method 3 uses the more stringent sampling requirements of the US Environmental Protection Agency instead of those from the IPCC 2000 Good Practice Guidance and Uncertainty Management in National Greenhouse Gas Inventories. The use of facility-specific waste composition data is an option available under all methods.

Table 6.1 *Summary of methods for monitoring GHG emissions of waste sector in Australia*

Methods of monitoring/ Type of waste	Method 1	Method 2	Method 3
Landfill (CH_4)	Default values for both waste composition and decomposition rate	Facility-specific estimates for decomposition rate k, allowing the division of the sampled zone into gas flow rate categories	Facility-specific estimates for decomposition rate k, applying US EPA or equivalent standards for the direct measurement of gas flow rate
Waste water (CH_4, N_2O)	Calculation based on the amount of wastewater treated and default values for COD and other parameters	Site-specific COD and organic nitrogen content from industry practices	Site-specific COD and organic nitrogen content from Australian or equivalent standards
Waste incineration (CO_2)	Calculation based on the amount of waste incinerated and default values		

Source: Authors from NGER (Measurement) Determination, 2008.

Table 6.2 *Default values of composition of solid waste* (%)

Waste stream	New South Wales	Victoria	Queensland	Western Australia	South Australia	Tasmania	Australian Capital Territory	Northern Territory
Municipal solid waste	31	36	43	26	36	57	43	43
Commercial and industrial	42	24	14	17	19	33	42	14
Construction and demolition	27	40	43	57	45	10	15	43

Source: Authors from NGER (Measurement) Determination, 2008.

Table 6.3 *Default values of waste mix type of each waste stream (%)*

Waste mix type/ waste stream	Municipal solid waste default	Commercial and industrial waste default	Construction and demolition waste default
Food	35.0	21.5	0.0
Paper and paper board	13.0	15.5	3.0
Garden and park	16.5	4.0	2.0
Wood and wood waste	1.0	12.5	6.0
Textiles	1.5	4.0	0.0
Sludge	0.0	1.5	0.0
Nappies	4.0	0.0	0.0
Rubber and leather	1.0	3.5	0.0
Inert waste	28.0	37.5	89.0

Source: NGER (Measurement) Determination, 2008.

As noted by Conolly (2013), there is a time lag between waste deposition in a landfill and the moment when methane from that waste starts being formed and emitted. In the CPM, this lag is assumed to be six months: no emissions are calculated for waste deposited in landfill during the reporting year. This means that during the first year of operation, a liable landfill facility will have a Provisional Emissions Number (PEN = covered emissions from a facility) of zero (no liability), unless it hosts composting activities or other covered emissions, in which case the PEN will be greater than zero to cover these emissions. This has implications for reporting and future liability where operational control changes halfway through a reporting year.

Wastewater handling: a different emission calculation between domestic/commercial wastewater and industry wastewater

The Measurement Determination applies to GHG emissions released from the decomposition of organic material, nitrification and denitrification processes or flaring of sludge biogas occurring in wastewater collection and treatment systems, or from discharge into surface waters. It covers the methane (CH_4) emissions from sludge and the nitrous oxide (N_2O) from treated human sewage and proposes different methodologies to calculate these two types of emissions.

Calculations strongly rely on the Chemical Oxygen Demand (COD) of the sludge wastewater entering the plant. The COD is the total material available for chemical oxidation (both biodegradable and non-biodegradable) measured in tons. It is commonly used to indirectly measure the amount of organic compounds in water.

There are two distinctions between wastewater plants dealing with domestic and commercial wastewater[8] and wastewater plants coping with industrial wastewater[9] (restricted to industries identified in the Australian-New Zealand Standard industrial classification – ANZIC[10]). First, industrial plants are allowed to deduct the COD leaving the treatment site as effluent. They are therefore only liable for site-level emissions, whereas domestic wastewater plants are liable for both on-site and downstream emissions. Second, for industrial wastewater treatment plants, the regulation has not determined N_2O calculation methods.

The methodology used for both domestic/commercial wastewater and industrial wastewater is similar to the methodology applied to landfills: in method 1, the calculation of emissions is based on default emission factors while in methods 2 and 3, operators have to calculate these emission factors through sampling and analysis.

Method 1 is based on the National Greenhouse Accounts Methods.[11] This is the default method option where COD values, methane emission factors, nitrous oxide factors and correction factors are given. The method takes into account GHG emissions released from wastewater treatment plant and methane emissions released from flaring.

- **Calculating CH_4 emissions released from wastewater handling:** the methodology provides a method for estimating emissions in the absence of data on Chemical Oxygen Demand (COD) for on-site wastewater and sludge. Emissions are calculated as the difference between the estimated amount of methane generated at the wastewater treatment plant – based on the amount of

---

[8] Domestic or commercial wastewater means liquid wastes and sludge from housing or commercial premises.

[9] Industrial wastewater means liquid wastes or sludge resulting from the production of a commodity, by an industry.

[10] The industries identified in the ANZIC are dairy products, pulp-paper-and-paperboard, meat and poultry, organic chemicals, raw sugar, beer, wine and other alcoholic beverages, fruit and vegetables.

[11] Australian national greenhouse accounts, National Greenhouse accounts factors, July 2013, www.climatechange.gov.au/ sites/climatechange/files/documents/07_2013/national-greenhouse-accounts-factors-july-2013.pdf.

treated wastewater and default emission factors – and the actual amount of methane measured in the captured sludge biogas.

- **Calculating N_2O emissions released from wastewater handling (only for domestic or commercial plant):** N_2O emissions are calculated following Equation 6.2.

Equation 6.2 – The monitoring equation for nitrous oxide emissions from wastewater treatment

N_2O emissions from human sewage treated by the plant = (quantity of N entering the plant – quantity of N transferred out of the plant – quantity of N leaving the plant) x EF_{secij} + quantity of N leaving the plant differentiated by discharge environment x EF_{disij}

Where Nitrogen (N) is given in tonnes; EF_{secij} is the emission factor of N treated by the plant set at 4.9 tCO_2e of N_2O per tonne of N; Emission Factor (EF_{disij}) is the proportion N differentiated by discharge environment that turns into nitrous oxide annually, set at 4.9 (for enclosed waters), 1.2 (for estuarine waters) and 0 (for open coastal waters).

Source: NGER (Measurement) Determination, 2008.

- **Calculating GHG emissions from flaring sludge biogas:** 70 percent of sludge biogas is assumed to be methane which is then flared.

Equation 6.3 – The monitoring equation for methane emissions from flaring sludge biogas

$$GHG\ emissions\ from\ flaring = \sum_j 0.7 \times EC \times EF_j$$

Where Energy content factor of sludge biogas is given in gigajoules per cubic meter of flared methane (EC);[12] Emission Factor (EF_j) for GHG type (j) is given in tCO_2e per gigajoule.[13] As biogas is considered renewable, $EFCO_2$ is set to zero.

Source: NGER (Measurement) Determination, 2008.

---

[12] For the Energy content factor, see Schedule 1 of the 2008 NGER (Measurement) Determination, pp. 212–218.
[13] Ibid.

Methods 2 and 3 are similar to Method 1 except that they require the calculation of Chemical Oxygen Demand concentrations in wastewater (for methane emissions) and the calculation of nitrogen quantity in the wastewater and sludge through sampling and analysis, conducted in accordance with listed Australian or international standards or an equivalent standard (e.g., ISO 6060:1989, APHA (1995)... see 2008 NGER Section 5.28 for detailed list).

Waste incineration: only one method to calculate GHG emissions based on default factors

The 2008 Measurement Determination currently only provides two methods for waste incineration.

Method 1 is the default method option and uses IPCC default values for proportion of carbon per waste type and oxidation factor.[14] The quantity of each waste type incinerated by the plant during the year measured in tonnes of wet weight value is the only variable to be monitored.

Method 4 is based on direct measurement (for details, see part 1.3.3 of the 2008 NGER Determination Act).

Monitoring accuracy and uncertainty

Section 1.13 of the Measurement Determination sets a general principle on accuracy and uncertainty: "Having regard to the availability of reasonable resources by a registered corporation and the requirements of this Determination, uncertainties in emission estimates must be minimized and any estimates must neither be over nor under estimates of the true values."

Therefore, no quantitative threshold is required for uncertainty. The only obligation is to estimate and report uncertainty defined as the "95 percent confidence level or interval."

Section 8.10 of the Measurement Determination allows for two ways of estimating uncertainty. For facilities using method 1, default aggregated uncertainty levels are provided (Table 6.4). But facilities may also perform their own calculations, and those using method 2, 3 and 4 are even obliged to do so. In that case, waste operators are required to estimate the overall uncertainty of their emissions

---

[14] Department of Industry, Innovation, Climate Change, Science, Research and Tertiary Education (2013b: 565).

Table 6.4 *Aggregated uncertainty level by waste activities (%)*

Waste activity	Aggregated uncertainty level (%)
Solid waste disposal on land	35
Wastewater handling (industrial)	65
Wastewater handling (domestic or commercial)	40
Waste incineration	40

Source: NGER (Measurement) Determination, 2008.

calculating according to the GHG Protocol guidance on uncertainty.[15] This protocol uses the First Order Error Propagation Method and requires waste operators to:

- first, assess uncertainty at a source level by aggregating the uncertainty of the emission factor, the energy content factor and the activity data for the source;
- second, assess uncertainty at a facility level by aggregating the total uncertainty of each source associated with the facility;
- finally, assess uncertainty at the corporation level (the waste operator) by aggregating the total uncertainty for each facility under the operational control of the operator.

As of February 1st, 2014, no waste reporters have used higher-order methods to estimate their emissions under the NGER.

As detailed by Sinclair Knight Merz (2012), the management of waste in Australia is primarily the responsibility of the states, territories and local governments, which regulate and manage waste according to their respective legislation, policies, plans and programs. The Australian Commonwealth government has responsibility for national legislation such as the NGER Act and the 2011 Clean Energy Act (Carbon Pricing Mechanism), strategies and policy frameworks for waste. Therefore, variations in the way waste is classified and defined between jurisdictions can present difficulties for reporting at the national level on waste activities.

---

[15] GHG Protocol team, GHG Protocol guidance on uncertainty assessment in GHG inventories and calculating statistical parameter uncertainty, www.ghgprotocol.org/files/ghgp/tools/ghg-uncertainty.pdf

The National Waste Policy has identified this issue as a key challenge. Indeed, strategy 4 and strategy 16 of this policy support the introduction of a national definition and classification system for waste that aligns with definitions in international conventions (strategy 4 of the National Waste Policy), and the development of a national waste data system and publication of a three-yearly current and future trends waste and resource recovery report – the National Waste Report (Sinclair Knight Merz, 2012). Some improvements have been made but the specificity of Australian waste management still raises issues of comparability and completeness due to this mass of reporting obligations.

6.4 Reporting

EERS: *an online reporting mechanism*

Reports are due by October 31st following the reporting period (financial year) for which a corporation is reporting. To submit reports, NGER reporters must use an online system, the Emissions and Energy Reporting System (EERS), which replaced OSCAR (Online System for Comprehensive Activity Reporting) in April 2013.[16] For landfills and wastewater treatments plants, a separate Microsoft Excel-based Calculator must be filled in and returned to the regulator.

General principles for reporters under the NGER Act

All reporters must prepare their estimates of emissions in accordance with the principles in the *2008 Measurement Determination*, Section 1.13:

- **Transparency:** emission estimates must be documented and verifiable.
- **Comparability:** emission estimates using a particular method and produced by a registered corporation in an industry sector must be comparable with emission estimates produced by similar

---

[16] https://sts.cleanenergyregulator.gov.au/adfs/ls/?wa=wsignin1.0&wtrealm
=urn%3acer%3aportal%3aprod&wctx=http%3a%2f%2fportal
.cleanenergyregulator.gov.au%2f_layouts%2fAuthenticate.aspx%3fSour
ce%3d%252fPages%252fHome.aspx

corporations in that industry sector using the same method and consistent with the emission estimates published by the Department in the National Greenhouse Accounts.

- **Accuracy:** reporters must minimize the uncertainty (see Section 6.3).
- **Completeness:** all identifiable emission sources (landfills, wastewater handling and incineration) must be reported.

General requirements for reporting

The report must include general information about the facility: facility name, address, the State or the Territory in which the facility is located, the industry sector to which the activities constituting the facility are attributable and facility identification number (if it has been issued by the Clean Energy Regulator).

The report must also include detailed information on emissions estimates: type of source, criteria used to estimate the amount of waste disposed for the source, the method used to estimate emissions from the source, the amount of each greenhouse gas emitted in CO_2e and the total amount of greenhouse gas emitted from the source, in CO_2e.

Finally, the report must include the uncertainty associated with the estimate for the total amount of Scope 1 emissions (the aggregated uncertainty level).

Monitoring and reporting costs

The House of Representatives, "National Greenhouse and Energy Reporting Bill 2007 – Explanatory Memorandum" is an ex-ante regulation impact statement for the whole scheme. According to this explanatory memorandum, the monitoring and reporting cost per facility per year depends on the amount emitted by the facility. All the waste facilities covered by the CPM emit more than 25,000 CO_2e per year. Thus, the covered waste facilities are included in two categories:

- Emitting more than 25,000 CO_2e per year and less than 50,000 CO_2e per year. The annual reporting cost is estimated at AUS\$4,500 (€2,664).[17]

---

[17] All annual reporting costs are in Australian dollars or euro of the year 2007 due to the fact that the NGER Bill 2007 – Explanatory memorandum was released in 2007. The exchange rate was AUS\$1 = €0.592.

- Emitting more than 50,000 CO_2e per year. The annual reporting cost is estimated at AUS$10,000 (€5,920).

Given the proportion of larger and smaller landfills, the average monitoring and reporting cost is estimated at €4,862 per landfill per year. A survey conducted in 2011 found that this figure was likely underestimated, but was not able to provide an alternative one (Australian National Audit Office, 2011).

The average monitoring and reporting cost per tCO_2e is estimated at €0.08. This estimate is based on solid waste disposal only, a category representing 9,997 million tonnes of CO_2e which is 78 percent of the total waste emissions in 2011 (Department of Industry, Innovation, Climate Change, Science, Research and Tertiary Education, 2013b). Since 20 percent of landfills emit 80 percent of the emissions (Australia's plan for Clean Energy Future),[18] the cost per tCO_2e was assumed to be dominated by landfills with more than 50,000 tCO_2e per year (133 out of the 197 landfills emitting more than 10,000 tCO_2e per year, with an average 60,132 tCO_2e emitted per year).

6.5 Verification

As with most existing carbon pricing mechanisms, Australia's CPM provides for the verification' part an independent, third-party verifier which has been accredited. As opposed to the EU ETS or the Californian ETS, however, verification is not systematic: only a subsample of liable entities with aggregated emissions above 125,000 tonnes per year are actually verified in any given year.

Sampling-based verification

The Clean Energy Regulator (CER) can initiate greenhouse and energy audits for two reasons:

a. **Suspected breach of the legislation**: if the CER suspects non-compliance with the NGER legislation, it can compel a corporation to be audited. In this case, after receiving a written notice from the CER, the corporation shall appoint a greenhouse and

---

[18] Ministry of Finance (2011), "Australia's plan for clean energy future," regulation impact statement.

energy auditor of its own choice (unless specified otherwise in the CER note). The corporation pays for these audits. As these audits occur in cases where the CER suspects non-compliance, an audit may be undertaken as a precursor to the application of enforcement measures, including investigations by authorized officers, civil penalties and criminal proceedings.

b. **General compliance strategy**: even if there is no suspicion of non-compliance, the CER may still organize an audit as part of the broader compliance strategy. In this case, the CER sends written notice advising that the CER will appoint a greenhouse and energy auditor to audit a corporation's compliance. The CER pays for these audits.

There is only one situation when the greenhouse and energy audit is mandatory. It is for liable entities with an emissions number exceeding 125,000 tonnes of CO_2e a year. Contrary to the EU ETS, the threshold is defined at the company level. Entities are required to submit a reasonable assurance audit (a type of greenhouse and energy audit) with their liable entity report. Finally, another situation when a GHG and energy audit occurs is when the liable entity does one voluntarily.

Requirements for auditing service

The 2009 National Greenhouse and Energy Reporting Audit Determination provides for two types of greenhouse and energy audits:

a. **An assurance engagement**: its purpose is to provide an independent conclusion (called an assurance conclusion) on whether the audited body has complied, in all material respects, with specified requirements of the legislation.

b. **A verification engagement**: it is an independent assessment of specific areas of compliance, presented in the form of factual findings. Indeed, the audit team performs a predetermined set of procedures agreed between the audit team leader and the CER or the audited body, before the engagement starts. Thus, the audit team provides a report of factual findings based on the specific procedures requested. No assurance conclusion is expressed. Instead the users of the report draw their own conclusions.

Assurance engagement process

The assurance process is divided into four key phases: preparing, planning, performing and reporting.

a. **Preparing the assurance engagement**

The auditor team leader must decide whether the team is able to accept the client and engagement by assessing the inherent risks and the auditor's independence from the client.

b. **Planning the assurance engagement**

The auditor assesses whether the assurance engagement is possible by evaluating what will be audited (the subject matter) and what it will be audited against (the criteria). Then, the auditor develops audit procedures for the performing phase to appropriately address the assurance risks. This is the assurance engagement plan (nature, timing and extent of evidence). Then, the auditor discusses information gaps and risks with the CER or engaging body. If there is no gap, the auditor is unable to undertake an audit, and, consequently, to form a conclusion. The assurance engagement process stops here.

c. **Performing the assurance engagement**

During this stage, the auditor attempts to obtain evidence which will reduce the assurance risk to an acceptable level. The auditor aims to assess whether the evidence shows that the audited body has complied with all the relevant NGER legislation in all material aspects. The objective is to provide the audit team leader with sufficient evidence to enable them to issue the conclusion.

d. **Final step – reporting**

The auditor obtains management's sign-off on the completeness and accuracy of the reported greenhouse and energy information and the representations made by management to the auditor. Then, by using the evidence gained during the audit, the auditor evaluates the final reported greenhouse and energy information against the legislation and methodology.

An audit report must include three elements: a cover sheet, an audit opinion (Part A, which is the conclusion) and detailed findings (Part B).

The audit team leader can give different conclusions:

• **A reasonable assurance conclusion:** the audited body has respected all the requirements of the NGER legislation (positive form).

- **A qualified reasonable assurance conclusion:** when misstatements are present or there is a lack of evidence but it is not pervasive enough to affect the matter being audited as a whole.
- **A limited assurance conclusion:** there is no misstatement in the matter being audited that is material or pervasive enough to affect the matter being audited as a whole (negative form is used).
- **An adverse conclusion:** there are misstatements that are material and pervasive enough to affect the matter being audited as a whole.
- **A conclusion that unable to form an opinion about matter being audited:** the effect of a limitation on scope or significant circumstance is so material and pervasive that the auditor has not been able to obtain sufficient appropriate assurance evidence.

Verification engagement process
The purpose of a verification engagement is to conduct agreed-upon procedures and report factual findings arising from those procedures. Indeed, the audit team performs a predetermined set of procedures agreed between the audit team leader and the CER or the audited body, before the engagement starts.

There are the same four steps in the verification engagement process. The main difference is that in the reporting steps, the auditor provides a document with factual findings and there is no conclusion. Instead the users of the report draw their own conclusions.

Accreditation procedure

Under the legislation, only the audit team leader must be registered as a greenhouse and energy auditor of category 2 or 3 (see below). Other members of the audit team do not need to be registered. However, the NGER Regulations do contain requirements for other members of an audit team. There are three types of accredited auditors but regular auditors can also be in the audit team:

- **Category 1: NGER technical auditor or non-technical auditor.** A technical auditor must have obtained at least 150 hours technical training and have participated for 700 hours of audits in the five years immediately preceding the day of his application. For a non-technical auditor application, the auditor must have obtained at least 350 individual hours of experience in auditing and preparing audit reports.

- **Category 2 and 3: Audit team leader.** He or she is responsible for ensuring the requirements of legislations and standards are satisfied. The audit team leader should be personally involved in the assurance or verification engagement so that they are part of the process as a whole. An audit team leader must have obtained at least 700 individual hours' experience as an audit team leader or a professional member of an audit team in auditing and preparing audit reports. They also must have obtained at least 490 individual hours' experience as an audit team leader of an audit team that has three or more other members. A category 3 auditor must have been registered as a category 2 before applying.

Verification costs

Australia's plan for a Clean Energy Future is an ex-ante regulation impact statement for the whole scheme. For the covered entities (all sectors), total verification costs were estimated to be around 32 million dollars per year. For the government, the total costs related to verification were estimated at around 5–9 million dollars per year. The administrative costs represent the costs to the government of undertaking audits for a selection of emissions reports submitted by liable entities in order to double-check the reports of large emitters and to ensure the accuracy of reports by small liable entities.

For the liable entities required to obtain third party audits – i.e., those operating facilities which emit more than 125,000 CO_2e emissions per year, the verification cost is estimated to be US$161,500 (€95,608) which includes the audit cost and the cost associated with liaising with the auditors. Australia's plan for a Clean Energy Future estimated that the CPM covered around 500 liable entities. Around 300 liable entities do not have the obligation to organize an audit every year. The cost of verification for these entities – which is actually paid by the regulator – is not provided. It is necessarily lower than the total administration costs[19] divided by this number of facilities: 23,333 dollars per year (€17,368).

It is difficult to assess how many waste entities lie above the 125,000 tCO_2e threshold: in the published reports for 2012–2013, we managed to identify only five entities for which waste management is a major

---

[19] This includes all aspects of NGER administration, not only verification.

activity. Three of them were above the threshold. The cost of verification per ton of CO_2e is therefore estimated at €120–208 per year, assuming that half of the waste emissions covered by the scheme come from companies with cumulated emissions above 125,000 tCO_2e per year, with an average 335,515 tCO_2e per year per company based on the three companies identified in the 2012–2013 report.

6.6 Uncertainty related to waste emissions: is it an issue? Should it be reduced?

Three large sources of uncertainty: classification, emission factors and decay rate

Compared with energy and most industrial sectors, the direct and indirect emissions of the waste sector are laden with large uncertainties. In Chapter 8 of the Measurement Determination, for the industrial process sources, the lower uncertainty levels are for soda ash use (5% of emission factor uncertainty level and 1.5% of activity data uncertainty) and the highest uncertainty level is for nitric acid production (40% emission factor uncertainty level and 1.5% of activity data uncertainty). In comparison, the Measurement Determination quotes an aggregated uncertainty level of 35% for solid waste disposal on land, of 65% for the industry wastewater handling, of 40% for the domestic or commercial wastewater handling and of 40% for the waste incineration when using the default calculation emissions method. Uncertainty comes from two main sources: the differences in waste definitions and waste classifications and the timing of GHG emissions.

The first source of uncertainty is the difference in waste definitions and classifications in the Australian state jurisdictions. For instance, South Australia uses the same waste streams as the NGER Act, namely municipal solid waste, commercial and industrial waste and construction and demolition waste (see Section 6.4). However, Tasmania sets more detailed waste streams: municipal waste, inert waste, construction and demolition waste, commercial and industrial waste, and controlled waste. Unless clear guidance is provided on which waste stream should inert waste and controlled waste be included, Tasmanian landfills may generate artificial differences among themselves as they reclassify these waste streams in order to comply with the NGER Act.

The second source of uncertainty is related to the timing of the release of the carbon quantities into the atmosphere (k) and concerned only landfill (see Section 6.3).

The Australian legislation allows for, but does not incite, uncertainty reduction

The Australian legislation provides some guidance to reduce uncertainty in the waste sector. To reduce the uncertainty stemming from default parameters, the NGER Act always provides the opportunity to use site-specific values, with the exception of waste incineration emissions (Section 6.3).

Where higher-order methods are used to estimate emissions and calculate the associated uncertainty, the data used to generate the assessment of uncertainty will more accurately reflect the actual range than when using Method 1.

Beyond obvious incentives for landfills which would by chance obtain a lower amount of emissions when using higher-order methods, the Australian CPM provides only one incentive for lower uncertainty, namely the case of landfills capturing or flaring more than 75 percent of their gas (see Section 6.3).

Australia and the European Union: diverging views on the importance of uncertainty

The waste sector is not included in the EU ETS. In this regard, the Australian CPM is an interesting counter-example. Indeed, the main explanation provided by the European Commission to keep the waste sector outside the EU ETS is the high uncertainty of its emission factors and the lack of detailed activity data (European Commission, 2006).[20]

The only waste subsector considered for inclusion in the European Commission report assessment is waste incineration. In the waste incineration options assessment, the European Commission made a distinction between incineration of hazardous waste and municipal solid waste. The inclusion of the municipal solid waste in the EU ETS could accelerate the retrofitting or renewal of outdated municipal

---

[20] European Commission, Directorate General for Environment, Inclusion of additional activities and gases into the EU-emissions trading scheme, report under the project "Review of the EU emissions trading scheme," October 2006.

incinerators to enhance the level of energy recovery. Nevertheless, in the report, the Commission evaluates that waste incineration is well covered by a large number of environmental schemes at the national and EU level. As of February 1st, 2014 no legislative action has been undertaken however to include the waste incineration (municipal waste) in the EU ETS.

By covering the waste sector, Australia seems to deem that the level of uncertainty is not a key argument when considering whether to cover the waste sector in a carbon pricing mechanism. Based on economics theory, this stance is perfectly understandable, unless asymmetrical information between agents and the regulator make it likely that reported figures are biased (Shishlov and Bellassen, 2014).

6.7 Conclusion

As confirmed by Conolly (2013), the major challenges with monitoring, reporting and verifying waste sector emissions within the Australian CPM are:

- Waste is categorized as legacy and non-legacy waste. There is no way of accurately back-casting waste data from the present to when the landfill opened where there are no records although defaults can be used.
- Default k decomposition rates do not necessarily accommodate states with a vast difference in landscapes, topographies and weather conditions.
- Composting activities at a landfill are covered if they form part of a liable landfill facility. A stand-alone composting facility that does not form part of a liable landfill facility is not covered under the Clean Energy Act and therefore does not report emissions.

Compared with energy and industrial sectors, the waste sector has two main original features. First, the bulk of its emissions are "legacy emissions" from waste deposited in previous years contrary to most other sectors where emissions occur only when the facility produces an output. A practical consequence of this feature is that some landfills may enter the CPM several years after operations started, when their legacy waste emissions are large enough to push the facility above the 25,000 tCO_2e threshold. Then, emissions from the waste sector are laden with much larger uncertainties than other sectors. The 2008 Measurement

Determination offers several guidelines and options to reduce uncertainty but stops short of offering incentives to do so. More generally, the Australian legislator did not see the large uncertainty of this sector as a reason to keep it out of the CPM, whereas European legislators did keep it out of their EU ETS. A rational explanation for these diverging views remains to be found.

6.8 MRV ID table

Table 6.5 *MRV ID table – waste sector in the Australian Carbon Pricing Mechanism*

Context	
Regulator	Clean Energy Regulator
Type and level of incentive to comply	Penalties for not complying with the MRV requirements: NGER Act 2007, Part 5 - Civil penalties for non-compliance: up to 2000 penalty units – AUS\$230,000 (€173,599)[a] - Include cumulative civil penalties (per day of non-compliance: up to 100 penalty units per day – AUS\$12,000 (€9,057)[b]
Entities concerned	Facilities which emit at least 25,000 t CO_2e per year. Exception: *"prescribed distance rule"* = the threshold lowers to 10,000 t CO_2e per year and covers smaller landfills which are within a certain distance of a larger landfill (emitting over 25,000). This is to avoid waste being diverted from the liable landfill to a small nearby landfill. In 2010, there were 459 landfills. 197 emitted more than 10,000 tonnes per year. In 2011, the waste sector emitted around 11,7 Mt CO_2e and was responsible for 3% of Australia's greenhouse gas emissions.
Sectors concerned	Energy sector, industrial sectors, mining activities, transport (voluntary inclusion started in 2013) but this chapter focuses on the waste sector

Table 6.5 (*cont.*)

Gases concerned	CO_2e, CH_4, N_2O
Total MRV costs	€4,862 [2,664–5,920] per landfill per year, without verification (only applicable for landfills owned by large companies, see Section 6.5). 0.22 [0.08–0.37] €/tCO_2e depending on whether verification is mandatory.
Monitoring	
Rules	Clean Energy Regulation Act 2011 (Part 3. Division 2. Subdivision B) National Greenhouse and Energy Reporting Act 2007 National Greenhouse and Energy Reporting Regulations 2008 (Chapter 5 Waste) National Greenhouse and Energy Reporting (Measurement) Determination 2008
Other reference documents	NGER System measurement technical guidelines July 2013 CER, Supplementary guideline – Estimating an emissions profile at a landfill CER, Solid waste disposal land, User Guide V2.2
Uncertainty requirements	None beyond estimating uncertainty. Uncertainty must be reported as the 95% confidence level.
Achieved uncertainty range	Not available
Cost range	Included in reporting
Scope	A. Scope 1 (direct emission) B. Operational emissions C. Entity ("facility/unit")
Frequency	Yearly
Source for activity data	Amount of waste deposited, in tonnes, per waste stream: - Municipal solid waste - Commercial and industrial waste - Construction and demolition waste
Uncertainty range for activity data	Not available

Table 6.5 (*cont.*)

Source for emission factors	- National Greenhouse and Energy Reporting (Measurement) Determination 2008 - NGER System measurement technical guidelines July 2013 - Clean Energy Regulation Act 2011 (Part 2. Division 2. Subdivision F)
Uncertainty range for emission factors	If using Method 1: the Measurement Determination gives default aggregate uncertainty levels for the source: - 35% for solid waste; - 65% for wastewater handling (industrial); - 40% for wastewater handling (domestic or commercial) and for waste incineration. If using Method 2, 3 or 4, the Measurement Determination referred to the Uncertainty Protocol. As of February 1st, 2014, no waste reporters have used higher-order methods to estimate their emissions. Therefore, there is not currently information on the uncertainty associated with the use of these methods.
Direct measurement	Only allowed for waste incineration as of February 1st, 2013, but extension to landfills and wastewater is being considered.
Incentives to reduce uncertainty	Almost none, except for landfills with methane capture and flaring systems which may gain from upgrading to method 2 or 3 (see Section III.A.1).
Is requirements stringency adapted to the amount of emissions at stake (materiality)?	No, except for the lower threshold of 25,000 tCO_2e/yr under which facilities are not covered by the CPM.
Reporting	
Rules	National Greenhouse and Energy Reporting Regulations 2008 (Chapter 5 Waste) National Greenhouse and Energy Reporting Act 2007
Other reference documents	

Table 6.5 (*cont.*)

Format	A National Greenhouse and Energy Report registered in the Emissions and Energy Reporting System (EERS). EERS is a web-based data collection tool.
Level of source disaggregation	→ Solid waste disposal on land/wastewater handling/ waste incineration - Facility: Municipal/Commercial & industry/ Construction & demolition → From facility → From flaring
Frequency	Yearly
Timeline	**July 1st:** start of the reporting year. **August 31st:** Nominate operational control if required. **October 31st:** report on forecast emissions for current reporting year and actual emissions for previous reporting years. **February 1st:** surrender units to cover reported emissions from previous reporting year. **June 30th:** end of the reporting year.
Language	English
Is requirements stringency adapted to the amount of emissions at stake (materiality)?	No: yearly reporting required in a common format, no matter the size of the landfill.
Cost range	For landfills: 5,020 € [2,750–6,110] per entity per year and 0.08 €/tCO_2e on average
Verification	
Rules	NGER 2008 Division 6.3 to 6.6 NGER (Audit) Determination 2009 NGER (Auditor Registration) Instrument 2012
Other reference documents	Greenhouse and energy auditor registration guidelines November 2012

Table 6.5 (*cont.*)

Format	The greenhouse and energy audit is an **assurance engagement**: (NGER Audit determination 2009 Part 3, NGER 2008 Division 6.04A-3) providing the audit team leader's independent opinion on the matter being audited. The format is an assurance conclusion.
Frequency	Yearly for businesses which emit more than 125,000 tonnes CO_2e per year. Random otherwise.
Timeline	Same as reporting (October 31st).
Language	English
Accredited entities for verification	Three types of auditors: - Category 1: NGER technical auditor or non-technical auditor - Category 2 and 3: Audit team leader → All applicants must take training courses (verification and assurance engagements), have participated for a number of hours in at least five audits (350 hours for category 1,700 hours for category 2 and 3). For category 2 and 3, applicants must successfully complete training courses (team leadership, assurance engagement, verification engagement). List of accredited auditors: www.cleanenergyregulator.gov.au/National-Greenhouse-and-Energy-Reporting/Auditors/register-of-greenhouse-and-energy-auditors/Pages/default.aspx
Control of accredited entities	Inspections of auditors during or after the completion of a greenhouse and energy audit. The inspection may be conducted up to five years after the completion of the audit.
Cost of accreditation	Not available
Support and control of accredited entities	-**Before being accredited**: must follow training courses (verification, assurance engagement, compliance engagement, greenhouse and energy audit). -**After being accredited**: must complete at least 15 days of continuing professional development every three years and attend regular trainings relevant to continuing professional development.

Table 6.5 (*cont.*)

Is requirements stringency adapted to the amount of emissions at stake (materiality)?	Verification is not systematic, except for sites with emissions higher than 125,000 tonnes of CO_2e a year. Smaller sites do not pay for verification, unless they are suspected of breaching the law.
Cost range	0.14 [0–0.29] €/tCO_2e Small, and borne by the regulator for companies below the 125,000 tCO_2e threshold for annual verification (see Section 6.5). For companies above the 125,000 tCO_2e threshold, verification costs are estimated to be around €95,608.

[a] The conversion rate in July 2011 was AUS$1 = €0.75478.
[b] Ibid.

Bibliography

Australian National Audit Office, 2011. "Administration of the National Greenhouse and Energy Reporting Scheme," Audit Report No. 23 2011–2012, 124pp.

Clean Energy Regulator, 2012a. "Estimating an emissions profile at a landfill," Supplementary guideline, 11pp.

2012b. "National greenhouse and energy reporting (auditor registration) instrument," 20pp.

2013. "Audit determination handbook," 180pp.

Conolly, F., 2013. Greenhouse Gas Emission Inventory (2009), Clean Energy Regulator interviewed by M. Afriat, August 24, 2013.

Department of Climate Change and Energy Efficiency, 2012a. Exposure draft regulations – Clean energy amendment regulation 2012 and National Greenhouse and Energy Reporting Amendment Regulation 2012, Explanatory note, p. 155.

2012b. "National greenhouse and energy reporting system measurement," technical guidelines for the estimation of greenhouse gas emissions by facilities in Australia, 488pp.

Department of Industry, Innovation, Climate Change, Science, Research and Tertiary Education, 2013a. "Australian national greenhouse accounts," National Inventory Report 2011, Volume 3, 227pp.

2013b. "National greenhouse and energy reporting system measurement," technical guidelines for the estimation of greenhouse gas emissions by facilities in Australia, 665pp.

Encycle consulting, 2013. "A study into commercial and industrial waste and recycling in Australia." 158pp.

European Commission, Directorate General for Environment, Ecofys, 2006. "Inclusion of additional activities and gases into the EU-emissions trading scheme," report under the project review of the EU ETS.

Federal Register of Legislative Instruments, 2010, National Greenhouse and Energy Reporting (Auditor) Determination 2009, F2010L00053, 29pp.

2012, National Greenhouse and Energy Reporting (Auditor Registration) Instrument, F2012L02295, 20pp.

2013a, Clean Energy Regulations 2011, F2013C00315, 312pp.

2013b, National Greenhouse and Energy Reporting Act 2007, F2013C00521, 139pp.

2013c, National Greenhouse and Energy Reporting (Measurement) Determination 2008, F2013C00661, 390pp.

GHG Protocol team, GHG Protocol guidance on uncertainty assessment in GHG inventories and calculating statistical parameter uncertainty, www.ghgprotocol.org/files/ghgp/tools/ghg-uncertainty.pdf. Accessed April 11, 2013.

House of Representatives, 2007. National Greenhouse and Energy Reporting Bill, Explanatory Memorandum.

Hyder, 2009. "Australian landfill capacities into the future," Final report.

2011. "Waste and recycling in Australia," Final report.

IPCC, 2006. 2006 IPCC Guidelines for National Greenhouse Gas Inventories. IGES, Hayama, Japan.

Ministry of Finance, 2011. "Australia's plan for clean energy future," regulation impact statement.

Shishlov, I. and Bellassen, V., 2014. "Review of monitoring uncertainty requirements in the CDM." Working Paper No. 16. CDC Climat, Paris, 33pp.

Sinclair Knight Merz, 2012. "Review of Australia's international waste-related reporting obligations," Final report, 148pp.

Waste Contractors and Recyclers Association of NSW, 2012. Carbon pricing and the waste industry, position letter, 4pp.

7 | Variant 2: non-site level emissions in an ETS – the case of electricity importers in the California cap-and-trade

MARION AFRIAT AND EMILIE ALBEROLA

Acknowledgements: We are grateful to Wade McCartney (California Air Resource Board) and David Edwards (California Air Resource Board) for their answers to our questions.

7.1 Context

Electricity in carbon pricing mechanisms

Most cap-and-trade schemes developed or in development in the world at least regulate CO_2 emissions from the electricity sector. Several specifications may facilitate the inclusion of this power sector under this kind of regulation:

- the electricity sector is usually responsible for a large share of CO_2 energy emissions – 12 billion tons or 40 percent CO_2 energy emissions globally;
- some low-cost CO_2 emission reductions opportunities exist within the sector such as fuel-switching (Ellerman et al., 2010; IEA, 2012);
- the electricity sector is usually not at risk of carbon leakage, as international electricity trades are greatly limited by grid connections, and operators can therefore pass on the costs of carbon allowances to consumers in the price of electricity.

In terms of monitoring, reporting and verification of its CO_2 emissions, the power sector offers some inherent advantages: large point sources, relatively few flows to monitor, fuel inputs traded and therefore measured, some data and reporting structures available from pre-existing regulation and a limited number of companies involved.

In most developed or developing cap-and-trade schemes, the electricity sector is covered at the production level – electricity producers rather than consumers are capped – and the regulation only applies to power plants located within the regulator's jurisdiction. However, the cap-and-trade scheme in California presents a specificity for the power sector: the regulation also covers the electricity imported from neighboring States. Another example of covering Greenhouse Gas (GHG) emissions from electricity consuming emissions and entities located outside the regulator's jurisdiction is the Shenzhen Emission Trading Scheme (ETS) pilot[1], see Chapter 8. From this angle, the Californian law is – to our knowledge – the first instance of a border carbon adjustment and, as such, a very interesting testing ground. In February 2014, the California Air Resources Board (ARB) will discuss the potential inclusion of cement importers in the California market. This new proposal confirms the stake of carbon border adjustment for California.

The Californian ETS

Genesis and design
In 2006, California approved the Global Warming Solution Act (AB 32) which aims at reducing GHG emissions to 1990 levels by 2020 and assigns the responsibility to ARB for developing a strategy and implementing the necessary measures to meet the 2020 target. One of these measures was a cap-and-trade program.

In 2007, ARB developed and adopted the Mandatory Reporting of Greenhouse Gas Emissions Regulation (ARB MRR, 2007) pursuant to the AB 32 Act (2006). 2008 was the first year of the implementation of the MRR. The 2008–2010 first reporting years helped to improve California's GHG emission inventory and provided an emission trends tracking mechanism which supports emission reduction strategies. In December 2010, the ARB Board adopted amendments to the MRR in order to harmonize with the GHG reporting requirements of the US EPA (40 CFR part 98) to support California's cap-and-trade system, and to ensure consistency with the Western Climate Initiative reporting structure.

---

[1] The Shenzhen ETS pilot covers emissions from Scope 1 and Scope 2 (indirect emissions from electricity consumption). Covered entities can be liable for their emissions occurring outside the physical boundaries of Shenzhen municipality. For example, the Shenzhen ETS pilot covers a Chinese utility company named SEC which operates in and out of Shenzhen. Thus, covered emitters purchasing electricity from SEC will have to surrender allowances for their indirect emissions (from electricity consumption).

The final rules of the cap-and-trade program were finalized by ARB in October 2011 and approved by the California Office of Administrative Law (OAL) in December 2011. The cap-and-trade program establishes an aggregate cap covering 85 percent of the state's GHG emissions. The program is divided into three compliance periods. During the first phase, 2013–2014, it covers emissions from industrial facilities and main electricity suppliers to the Californian grid (which emit 25,000 metric tons or more of carbon dioxide equivalent [CO_2e] annually). Over the second compliance period, 2015–2017, emissions associated with fossil transportation fuels and retail sales of natural gas will be included. During the third phase, 2018–2020, some possible voluntary inclusions could be added.

ARB must take into account existing and proposed international, federal and state GHG emission reporting programs. By this mission, ARB reviewed the MRR regulation in August 2012 to ensure consistency with the cap-and-trade-program regulation and with the updates of the US EPA rules. The latest review of MRR rules appeared in November 2013 and was implemented in January 2014.

In 2011, power generation in California represented approximately 20% of the total GHG emissions.[2] However, in the same year, the imported electricity from Arizona, Nevada, Utah, Oregon and Washington made up 30% of the Californian electricity supply.[3] For a comparison, the imported electricity in the European Union (27) was 0.05% of the electricity consumption in 2007.[4] In addition, in 2011, the GHG emissions from imported electricity amounted to 54.1% of the Californian electricity emissions and 10.45% of the Californian total GHG emissions.[5] Such a large share of emissions could not be

---

[2] www.arb.ca.gov/cc/inventory/data/tables/ghg_inventory_scopingplan_00-12_2014-03-24.pdf
[3] www.energyalmanac.ca.gov/overview/energy_sources.html
[4] Electricity imports and ETS, business case studies, HEC students.
[5] The Californian GHG inventory data includes estimates for carbon dioxide (CO_2), methane (CH_4), nitrous oxide (N_2O), sulfur hexafluoride (SF_6), nitrogen trifluoride (NF_3), hydrofluorocarbons (HFCs) and perfluorocarbons (PFCs). Data sources include California and federal agencies, international organizations and industry associations. The calculation methodologies are consistent with the 2006 IPCC guidelines. The current inventory uses global warming potential (GWP) values from the IPCC Second Assessment Report, consistent with USEPA's national inventory. www.arb.ca.gov/cc/inventory/doc/methods_00-09/ghg_inventory_00-09_technical_support_document.pdf and www.arb.ca.gov/cc/inventory/data/tables/ghg_inventory_scopingplan_00-11_2013-08-01.pdf

ignored by the Californian cap-and-trade program. In particular, this specificity of the Californian electricity market does not protect it from carbon leakage, contrary to the general case of electricity production described above. Recognizing that an accurate accounting of California's GHG regulation would need to include emissions from imported electricity, the California Legislature wrote a provision into AB 32 directing ARB to account for all emissions from out-of-state electricity delivered to and consumed in California. Covering imported electricity was particularly important given the Californian air pollution context. Due to a high air pollution in California (seven out of ten most polluted cities in the United States by ozone are located in California[6]), ARB passed strict air pollution regulations regarding power plants. Yet, due to softer legislations outside California, some new power plants were located close to the Californian border, constituting an air pollutant leakage. By covering electricity importers, ARB tries not to repeat for GHGs the pollution leakage which took place for air pollutants. This inclusion is a significant difference from the "trendsetter," that is the European Union Emission Trading System (EU ETS, see Chapter 5).

AB 32 requires the adoption of a regulation for the mandatory reporting of GHG emissions. This regulation was approved by the California OAL in December 2008 and contains a specific methodology for electricity importers. This chapter focuses on the general rules for monitoring, reporting and verification (MRV) of emissions from electricity importers in California, and how these differ from the EU ETS. The key challenge is that although electricity importers operate in California, the emissions to be monitored are occurring outside the Californian jurisdiction.

Challenges from setting MRV requirements in the Californian ETS
In California's cap-and-trade, setting MRV requirements for an electricity importer raises three challenges.

First, completeness of reporting between power entities, by enforcing the mandatory reporting of emissions for importers that are responsible for the emissions associated with the power plants located outside of California. For example, out-of-state entities could simply

---

[6] State of the Air 2013, the American Lung Association, www.stateoftheair.org/2013/city-rankings/most-polluted-cities.html

choose not to report emissions associated with sales into the California Independent Systems Operator ("CAISO") territory at out-of-state entities, under the pretext that ARB does not have jurisdiction over these sales (and correspondingly, the emissions associated with these sales).[7] Thus, in the event ARB cannot determine whether there are missing emissions from its reports, or if ARB is unable to fully assert its jurisdiction over such sellers, there would likely be damaging effects on the GHG and electricity markets.

Second, consistency with established policies and requirements from the regulations of other States. These regulations being already implemented and clearly understood by power entities, consistency helps reduce monitoring costs for the regulated entities.

Finally, coordination with three separate but interrelated regulations:[8] the Mandatory Reporting of Greenhouse Gas Regulation (article 95111 is dedicated to power entities' MRV obligations including electricity importers), the California Cap on Greenhouse Gas Emissions and Market-based Compliance Mechanisms Regulation (article 95852 (b) details the first deliverers of electricity's obligations covered by the Californian cap-and-trade program including electricity importers) and the AB 32 Cost of Implementation Fee Regulation (article 95201(a)(4)(A).

7.2 Monitoring electricity importers under the GHG Inventory Program

Recognizing that an accurate accounting of California's GHG emissions would need to include emissions from imported electricity, and

---

[7] This example was quoted by Southern California Edison (SCE) in its comments on "ensuring completeness of reporting from power entities" in the Final statement of reasons for rulemaking including a summary of comments and ARB responses, November 2012, www.arb.ca.gov/regact/2012/ghg2012/ghg2012finalfsor.pdf

[8] The three regulations were originally developed pursuant to the California Global Warming Solutions Act of 2006 (the Act): Mandatory Reporting of Greenhouse Gas Emissions (title 17, California Code of Regulations, section 95100 et seq.) (reporting regulation or MRR), as well as conforming amendments to the definition sections of the AB 32 Cost of Implementation Fee Regulation (title 17, California Code of Regulations, section 95200 et seq.) (fee regulation) and the California Cap on Greenhouse Gas Emissions and Market-Based Compliance Mechanisms (title 17, California Code of Regulations, section 95800 et seq.) (cap-and-trade regulation).

wary of emissions leakage, the California Legislature wrote a provision into AB 32 directing ARB to account for all emissions from out-of-state electricity delivered to and consumed in California.

However, California's limited jurisdiction does not allow for the direct regulation of out-of-state generation facilities. In order to meet the aforementioned statutory obligation of AB 32 on imported electricity, ARB developed a hybrid approach to regulating the electric sector (Bushnell et al., 2013). Under this hybrid approach, the regulated entity is the "first deliverer" of electricity into the California grid, instead of the power plant in the EU ETS. For in-state generation the facility operators are considered as the first deliverers: operators of in-state facilities report facility emissions and net generation directly to ARB. Therefore, the source and its associated emissions, of the electricity is known. For out-of-state generation, first deliverers of imported electricity are the retail providers and power marketers who import energy into the California grid. The retail providers are entities that provide electricity to end users in California such as investor-owned utilities, publicly owned utilities, multi-juridictional utilities, electric service providers, Community Choice Aggregators and the Western Area Power Administration. The power marketers are purchasing/selling entities that do not provide power to end users but are listed as the purchasing/selling entity at the "first Point of Receipt" for power imported into California.

One significant limitation of this approach is the uncertainty associated with which emissions factor to attribute to imported power. For instance, due to the nature of interconnection in California, electricity imports do not, in general, travel directly from generation facility to the California grid. According to Bushnell et al. (2013), it is generally not possible to identify the source of imported electricity with sufficient granularity to assign a specific emissions obligation. Although the identification of sources based on the North American Electric Reliability Corporation (NERC) E-tagging system "has its limitations, through continued use and with constructive regulatory requirements, it will continue to improve" according to W. McCartney.[9] California regulators address this uncertainty of the emissions factor by providing first deliverers the option of

[9] Following an email exchange with W. McCartney, ARB, Climate change program data section.

reporting either a default emission factor – unspecified source – or a facility-specific emissions factor – specified source – associated with the energy they are importing.

Scope: *imported electricity from specified and unspecified sources*

Tracking electricity transactions to identify importers

The mandatory reporting of GHG emissions regulation (MRR) applies to all power entities – also called electricity deliverers, including electricity importers and exporters. Whereas electricity exporters generate electricity inside the State of California and deliver it to a load located outside the State, electricity importers deliver imported electricity from neighboring States. Electricity importers are identified through the e-tags regulated by the NERC. E-tags were initially introduced in 1997 in response to the need to track the increasingly complicated energy transactions which were produced as a result of the beginning of electric deregulation in North America. They allow the monitoring of electricity imports: indeed, when electricity is delivered across balancing authority areas, NERC e-tags are created to request, to approve and to document the interchange transaction from source (generation) to sink (load), designating the market path and physical path from first Point of Receipt (POR) to final Point of Delivery (POD). Therefore, electricity importers are identified on the NERC e-tag as the Purchasing Selling Entity (PSE) on the last segment of the tag's physical path with the point of receipt located outside the State of California and the point of delivery located inside the State of California (see Figure 7.1).

In the MRR Regulation, ARB considers that the existing NERC e-tag system provides a consistent and reliable source of data on electricity trades and independent documentation of electricity delivered across balancing authority areas (electricity importations, exportations and wheels). Based on this reliable information on the tracking of electricity transactions, ARB identified 64 electricity importers[10] covered by the cap-and-trade program in 2011.

---

[10] www.arb.ca.gov/cc/reporting/ghg-rep/reported_data/ghg-reports.htm

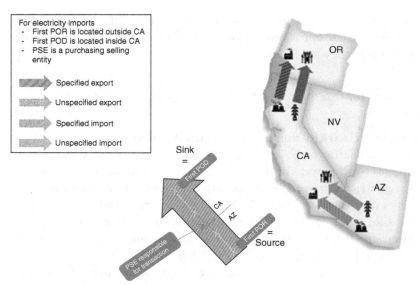

Figure 7.1 Electricity imports and exports from specified and unspecified sources among the e-tag market path.
Source: Final Statement of Reasons for Rulemaking (2013), ARB.

A *different treatment for specified and unspecified sources of electricity*

There is no emissions threshold associated with the requirements of the MRR regulation regarding an electricity importer.[11] Even if an entity imports 1 MWh, the associated emissions must be reported and verified. Nevertheless, under the Cap-and-Trade Regulation, the inclusion threshold for an electricity importer is based on the annual direct emissions from each of the electricity importer's sources of electricity: as long as one of the sources exceeds 25,000 tCO$_2$e per year, the importer is covered by the regulation.

There is a distinction between imported electricity from specified sources of electricity, which are covered if facilities emit 25,000 metric tons or more of CO$_2$e per year, and unspecified sources from which all direct emissions are considered as covered. Emissions from specified sources are all emissions from imports that can be traced back to

---

[11] Initial Statement of Reasons for Rulemaking (2010), ARB.

a specific generating facility. Emissions from unspecified sources are imported electricity's emissions from a source that cannot be identified at the time the electricity enters into the Californian grid.

Electricity importers who want to be treated as a specified source must meet the following criteria:[12]

1. The electricity importer must be the facility operator or have right of ownership or a written power contract for electricity generated by the facility or unit. Indeed, a power contract is used for the purpose of documenting specified sources of imported electricity versus unspecified sources.

2. The imported electricity must be "directly delivered"[13] to the California grid. Electricity must be delivered across a Californian balancing authority.[14] For example, electricity is directly delivered when the facility which imports the electricity has a first point of interconnection with a Californian balancing authority (itself or a distribution facility inside this balancing authority).

3. If Renewable Energy Certificates (RECs) were created for the electricity generated and reported pursuant to MRR regulation, then the RECs must be verified and retired pursuant to MRR regulation.

Since the implementation of the 2013 legislation review in January 2014, the electricity importer, claiming that its power imports come from a specified source, has to comply with a new "seller warranty" requirement. Indeed, there must be a verification that each sale in the market path or chain was made pursuant to a specified source contract (see Figure 7.2).

Nevertheless the seller warrant term is not a required contract term. The original seller does not need to provide an additional separate

[12] CRR, Title 17, Chap. 1 ARB, Subchapter 10 Climate Change, Article 5. Cap-and-Trade Regulation, Section 95852(b)(3) and CCR, Title 17, Chap.1 ARB, Subchapter 10 Climate Change, Article 2. Mandatory Greenhouse Gas Emissions Reporting (MRR), section 95111(g).

[13] Definition in Section 95102(b)(125).

[14] A Balancing authority is the responsible entity that integrates resource plans ahead of time, maintains load-interchange generation balance and supports interconnection frequency in real time. In California, there are eight balancing authorities: Balancing authority of northern California (BANC), California independent system operator (CAISO), Imperial irrigation district (IID), Los Angeles department of water and power (LADWP), Pacific Corp-Waste, Sierra pacific power (SPP), Turlock irrigation district (TID) and Western area lower Colorado (WALC). See definition Section 95102(a)(25) of the MRR.

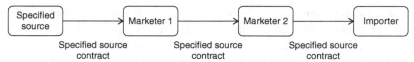

Figure 7.2 Direct delivered, specified, unspecified, imported and exported electricity under California's cap-and-trade program
Source: California Environmental Protection Agency, Air Resources Board.

warrant. The specified source transaction itself will effectively provide the warranty as the electricity was procured from the generation source by the buyer pursuant to ARB requirements as long as the sale contract clearly identifies the designated source and the contract is contingent upon delivery from that source.[15] However, for resale transactions, resellers are obligated to warrant that the power transaction is specified by offering some documentary proof of contract for verification purposes. Absent such warranties, the import will have to be designated as "unspecified," with the consequence that the importer would have to report the potentially higher "default" emissions factor (see Section 7.4). The implementation of a seller warrant is necessary to ensure that specified power claims are supported by contract documentation.

Determining which electricity imported transactions are specified or unspecified relies on written power contracts, supporting records, settlement data and invoices.[16] Thus, due to the high level of documentation required, in many cases electricity importers will likely not be able to provide these documents (Bushnell et al., 2013). Most electricity importers will have an incentive not to "specify" if the value of the default emission factor is generous and to claim as a specified source if the default emission factor is conservative. Hence, the value of the default emission factor should be central to an accurate accounting of emissions from importers (see Section 7.4).

The reporting entities claiming specified sources have to respect the registration calendar to provide all data to ARB for the calculation of their associated emission factors.

---

[15] Final Statement of Reasons for Rulemaking (2013), ARB.
[16] MRR, Section 95105(d)(6) and Final Statement of Reasons for Rulemaking (2012), ARB.

Table 7.1 *Registration calendar for power entities for 2014*

Date	Activity
February 1	Power entities must register specified facilities outside California. Then they obtain associated emission factors calculated by ARB.
April 10	Reporting deadline for submitting emissions data report for electricity generation facilities producing over 25,000 metric tons of CO_2e from combustion sources, suppliers and others.
June 2	Reporting deadline for submitting emissions data report for electricity importers.
July 15	Deadline for corrections to RPS adjustment data required for power entity data reports.
September 2	Final verification statements due for all reports, including emissions, supplier data, and product data.

Source: California Environmental Protection Agency, Air Resources Board.

Two possible adjustments for renewables sources and sources imported and exported in the same hour

The Californian Renewable Portofolio Standard (RPS) requirement predates the Californian ETS, mandating that each power entity sources a fixed share of its electricity from renewable energies. The objective is to increase the amount of electricity generated from eligible renewable energy resources by 30 percent of the total retail sales of electricity in California per year by 2020. To certify that one megawatt hour of electricity was generated and delivered by an eligible renewable energy resource, the California Energy Commission established Renewable Energy Certificates (REC).

Hence, among specified sources of electricity, electricity procured by an electricity importer from renewables sources is included in the calculation of the Renewable Portfolio Standard adjustment (RPS adjustment) and therefore excluded from the calculation of imported electricity emissions under the MRR.

This deduction is called "RPS adjustment." The RPS adjustment applies to electricity that is not directly delivered to California,[17] and

---

[17] If directly delivered, the electricity source can be specified and therefore be attributed an emission factor of zero if it is indeed renewable.

therefore is not included in statewide GHG emissions accounting. The aim of this adjustment is to reduce the cost of the RPS compliance that would be borne directly or indirectly by entities that must comply both with AB 32 and with California's RPS program.

Imported electricity from an eligible renewable energy resource must meet the following conditions to be included in the calculation of the RPS adjustment.[18] The importer has either (1) ownership or contract rights to procure the electricity generated from the eligible renewable energy source or (2) a contract to import this electricity on behalf of a Californian entity that has the ownership or contract rights to the electricity generated from the eligible renewable energy source. RECs associated with the RPS adjustment must be retired during the same year in which the adjustment is claimed. This requirement aims to avoid double-counting in the event a tradable REC (alone) is sold. It ensures that the entity does not claim an RPS adjustment tied to a specific REC, then sells the tradable REC to a buyer who could also claim it for the RPS adjustment. In the event of a linking of California's cap-and-trade program with other GHG emissions trading systems approved by the Board, such as the Quebec cap-and-trade program, no RPS adjustment can be claimed for an eligible renewable energy resource when its electricity is directly delivered or is generated in this linked jurisdiction.

For any entity claiming an RPS adjustment, registration information and the amount of electricity claimed in the RPS adjustment must be fully reconciled and corrections must be certified by ARB, along with the rest of the annual report (see Section 7.2). The registration[19] requires the importer's general information about the renewable facility or unit, such as its nature, its ARB identification number, its status (new specified source, continuing specified source or no longer a specified source), the primary technology or fuel type use,[20] the number of

---

[18] CRR, Title 17, Chap.1 ARB, Subchapter 10 Climate Change, Article 5. Cap-and-Trade Regulation, Section 95852(b)(4).

[19] CCR, Title 17, Chap. 1 ARB, Subchapter 10 Climate Change, Article 2. Mandatory Greenhouse Gas Emissions Reporting (MRR), section 95111(g)(1).

[20] Variable renewable resources by type, defined for purposes of this chapter as pure solar, pure wind and run-of-river hydroelectricity; hybrid facilities such as solar thermal; hydroelectric facilities ≤ 30 MW, not run-of-river; hydroelectric facilities > 30 MW; geothermal binary cycle plant or closed loop system; geothermal steam plant or open loop system; units combusting biomass-derived fuel, by primary fuel type; nuclear facilities; cogeneration by

RECs, their vintage date and their serial number and to retain meter generation data for verification purposes.

Similarly, a Qualified Export adjustment[21] to the compliance obligation allows the exclusion of the imported electricity and the exported electricity[22] during the same hour by the same purchasing-selling entity from the accounted amount. Only qualified exports, a subset of exports limited to simultaneous imports, are included in the calculation of covered emissions and reduce the compliance obligation of the electricity importer pursuant to the cap-and-trade regulation. The aim of the Qualified Export adjustment is to address leakage from in-state generation under limited conditions[23] CO_2 emissions and MWhs included in the Qualified Export adjustment must nevertheless be reported and verified pursuant to MRR regulation, and must be documented by hourly import and export data.

A specified monitoring documentation for power entities

Instead of filling in a GHG Monitoring Plan for industrial facilities, all power entities which import or export electricity must prepare a GHG Inventory Program Documentation.[24] This documentation must be completed, maintained and made available for verifiers and ARB auditors pursuant to the recordkeeping requirements. The main specificity of the GHG Inventory Program Documentation compared to the GHG Monitoring Plan is the inclusion of electricity imports. Monitoring the out-of-state electricity generation delivered and consumed in California indeed requires the following specific information:

---

primary fuel type; fossil sources by primary fuel type; co-fired fuels; municipal solid waste combustion.

[21] The definition of the Qualified Export can be found in article 95802(a)(225) of the California Cap-and-Trade Regulation and its obligations in article 95852(b)(5) of the California Cap-and-Trade Regulation.

[22] Exported electricity must be reported separately from unspecified sources and each specified source according to the MRR Regulation. However, in the cap-and-trade regulation, exported electricity is only mentioned to explain qualified export. Exported electricity is not included in the California cap-and-trade program.

[23] Final Statement of Reasons for Rulemaking (2011), ARB, 107pp.

[24] The obligations under the GHG Inventory Program for electricity importers are found in article 95105(d) of the MRR Regulation.

- **General information on the power entity:** information on entity location, operations and electricity transactions.[25]
- **Calculation of imported electricity:** a query of NERC e-tag source data to determine the quantity of electricity (MWh) imported, exported and wheeled[26] for transactions (query description, access to the raw e-tag data for review and a tabulated summary), a description of steps taken and calculations made to aggregate data into reporting categories (unspecified electricity delivery, specified electricity delivery, specified asset-controlling supplier and multi-juridictional retail provider).
- **Management:** management policies or practices applicable to reporting and to other independent or internal data management systems and records, a list of key employees involved in data compilation and in the preparation of the emission data report as well as training sessions for these employees.
- **Control:** records of preventive and corrective actions, identify modifications made in the emissions data report after initial certification, and write a description of an internal audit program (including data report review and documents ongoing efforts to improve GHG Inventory Program).

The calculation of covered emissions for electricity importers

The treatment of six emissions sources

Calculating the imported electricity is based on the distinction of electricity sources (specified or unspecified source). Regarding the uncertainty associated with which emission factor to attribute to imported power, California's regulator provides to first deliverers the possibility of reporting a facility-specific emission factor associated with the energy they are importing.

The power entity must calculate and report covered emissions pursuant to the following equation:

---

[25] Electricity transactions as defined in article 95102(a)(141) of the MRR Regulation It means the purchase, sale, import, export or exchange of power.
[26] Wheeled electricity is the electricity generated outside California which is delivered into and passed through California but the final point of delivery is situated outside California. according to article 95102(a)(142) of the MRR regulation.

$$CO_2e_{covered} = CO_2e_{unspe} + (CO_2e_{spe} - CO_2e_{specified\ not\ covered})$$
$$- CO_2e_{RPS\ adjs} - CO_2e_{QE\ adjust} - CO_2e_{linked}$$

Each component of this equation is calculated using the following equation:

$$CO_2e = MWh \times TL \times EF$$

Specified and unspecified sources' emission factors: the main source of uncertainty

The amount of unspecified power sources and the value of the default emission factor are the main sources of uncertainty in the overall accounting of emissions from imported power. All deliveries of electricity not meeting the requirements for specified sources pursuant to MRV must indeed use the default emission factor for unspecified electricity. The default emission factor provided by ARB for unspecified electricity importers is 0.428 MtCO$_2$e/MWh. The default emission factor is based on the method adopted by the Western Climate Initiative (WCI)[27] and corresponds to the emission factor of a relatively efficient natural gas combined cycle power plant (see Section 7.4). For a comparison, the default emission factor for a coal plant is 0.87 MtCO$_2$e/MWh and for a natural gas plant, the default factor is 0.36 MtCO$_2$e/MWh.[28] Table 7.2 provides a summary of the emission factors used for the different sources in order to calculate the emissions covered by the California cap-and-trade program.

Historically unspecified power made up a substantial share of imports. In the 2008 GHG Emissions Inventory, of the total GHG

[27] Default emission factor calculator (2010), WCI. The default emission factor is calculated as the average emission factor for power plants outside of California located in the Western Electricity Coordinating Council (WECC) that are available on the margin, i.e., they are not dedicated to serving baseload. Baseload plants are considered to have a capacity factor greater than 60 percent. The factor is lower than some high-emitting sources available in the western region bulk power market. Absent other measures, there could, in some cases, be an incentive to dispatch higher-emitting resources. However, this incentive is mitigated by the higher costs of operating higher-emitting less efficient plants relative to lower-emitting efficient plants. Final Statement of Reasons of Rulemaking (2011), ARB.

[28] Highlights, Key figures on climate, France and worldwide, 2014 Edition. Service de l'observation et des statistiques, Ministère de l'Ecologie, du Développement durable et de l'Energie.

Table 7.2 *The emission factors used for the different imported electricity sources*

TYPES OF SOURCES

Emissions from unspecified sources

Definition	A source of electricity that is not a specified source at the time of entry into the transaction to procure the electricity.
EF	Default emission factor for unspecified electricity imports = 0.428 MtCO$_2$e/MWh
TL	= 1.02 to account for transmission losses between the power plant and measurement at the first point of delivery in California

Emissions from specified sources

Definition	A facility which is permitted to be claimed as the source of electricity delivered: the reporting entity must have either full or partial ownership in the facility/unit or a written power contract as defined in MRR section 95102(a) to procure electricity generated by that facility/unit. Specified facilities/units include cogeneration systems.
Emission factor (EF)	The EF for specified sources above the GHG emissions compliance threshold is calculated by the Executive Officer (ARB) and published on ARB's Mandatory Reporting website using the following equation: $EF_{sp} = E_{sp}/EG$ Where: E_{sp} = CO$_2$e emissions for a specified facility or unit for the report year (MtCO$_2$e). EG = Net generation from a specified facility or unit for the report year reported to ARB under this section (MWh). EF = 0 MtCO$_2$e for specified sources below the GHG emissions compliance threshold.
Transmission loss correction factor (TL)	= 1.0 when deliveries are reported as measured at the specified power plant. = 1.02 when deliveries are not reported as measured at the power plant to account for transmission losses between the power plant and measurement at first point of receipt in California.

Emissions from imported electricity supplied by Asset-Controlling Suppliers (ACS)

Definition "Asset Controlling Supplier" is a subcategory of specified source. An ACS is an entity that owns, operates or exclusively markets resources that are interconnected. The output of these resources could then be mixed and directly delivered to California on a single tag. ACS must be identified on the physical path of NERC e-tags as the purchasing-selling entity at the first point of receipt. ACSs are assigned a supplier-specific identification number and system emission factor by ARB for the wholesale electricity procured from its system and imported into California. Electricity imported from ACSs must be monitored and reported separately from the other specified sources covered by the cap-and-trade. Indeed, the CO_2e emissions from electricity imported from ACSs do not need to be matched with allowances under the cap-and-trade program.

EF Based on annual reports submitted to ARB, the ARB regulator calculates and publishes on the ARB Mandatory Reporting website the annual emission factor for *all* asset-controlling suppliers recognized by ARB (Section 95852.2 and 95111 b (3)).[a]

TL = 1.02 when deliveries are not reported as measured at a first point of receipt located within the balancing authority area of the ACS.

TL = 1.0 when deliveries are reported as measured at a first point of receipt located within the balancing authority area of the ACS.

Emissions from Renewables Portfolio Standard (RPS adjustment)

Definition The annual metric tons of CO_2e from imported electricity are calculated for electricity generated by each eligible renewable energy resource located outside the state of California and registered with ARB by the reporting entity pursuant to section 95111(g)(1) (see requirements for claims for eligible renewable energy resources in the Renewable Portfolio Standard (RPS) adjustment).

EF EF_{unsp} = Default emission factor for unspecified electricity imports = 0.428 MT of CO_2e/MWh.

Table 7.2 (*cont.*)

TYPES OF SOURCES

Emissions from Qualified Export adjustment

Definition   During any hour in which an electricity importer claims qualified exports and corresponding imports, the maximum amount of QE adjustment for the hour shall not exceed the product of:

[Lower quantity of imports or export (MWh) for the relevant hours] × [lowest EF of any portion of the QE or corresponding imports for the hour]

Emissions from linked market

Definition   Annual metric tons of CO_2e from electricity with a first point of receipt located in a jurisdiction where a GHG emissions trading system has been approved for linkage by the Board pursuant to subarticle 12 of the C&T regulation.

Note: This table does not take into account the retail provider subcategory "multijurisdictional retail provider."

[a] For data year 2012, ARB has recognized only one asset-controlling supplier: Bonneville Power Administration (BPA) which is a federal agency responsible for marketing electricity power from all of the federal-owned hydroelectric projects in the Pacific Northwest. While the BPA service territory does extend into California, it only does it at the distribution level and power is only provided at the level at one entity, Surprise Valley Electric (an electric cooperative). The MRR specifies that the asset-controlling suppliers system emission factor assigned to BPA is 20 percent of the default emission factor for unspecified sources.

For data year 2013, ARB has recognized and approved two asset-controlling suppliers Bonneville Power Administration and Powerex. Powerex is the wholly-owned electricity marketing subsidiary of BC – Canada's third largest electricity utility – responsible for marketing BC Hydro's surplus electricity in the western United States.

Emission factor for BPA for data year 2012 = 0.0856 $MtCO_2e$/MWh.
Emission factor for BPA for data year 2013 = 0.0249 $MtCO_2e$/MWh.
Emission factor for Powerex for data year 2013 = 0.0293 $MtCO_2e$/MWh.

Source: Authors from MRR regulation.

emissions associated with imported electricity, 43 percent was attributed to facilities outside California that are under contract or ownership obligation to serve California customers (specified sources). The remaining 57 percent was attributed to unspecified sources that contribute to the Western Region power pool. Unspecified power emissions is about 6 percent of Californian GHG emissions. Given the large uncertainty associated with the default factor, unspecified power is a likely large contributor to the overall uncertainty of emissions accounting under the Californian ETS.

Specified facilities and relevant regulation

In the case of specified sources, the considered level of CO_2e emissions is different according to the relevant mandatory reporting regulation: the mandatory reporting of GHG emissions in California (MRR Regulation), the US EPA GHG Reporting Rule or none. The relevant regulation obviously depends on the location of the specified facility (California, other State, foreign country). Table 7.3 summarizes the calculation of the emission factor.

7.3 Reporting: a separate report for imported electricity according to sources

Web-based reporting

Reporting entities shall submit emissions data reports through the California Air Resources Board's Greenhouse Gas Reporting Tool (e-GGRT) approved by the Executive Officer. This e-GGRT is a web-based system developed to support reporting under the article 40 Part 98 of the US Code of Federal Regulation (CFR) related to Mandatory Reporting of Greenhouse Gases. Electricity importers must use e-GGRT to register facilities or suppliers and submit both the certificate of representation and the annual GHG emission data report.

General requirements for reporting

Each year, reporting entities must develop, certify and submit to the Air Resources Board GHG data reports in compliance with the following requirements.

Table 7.3 *The calculation of the emission factor for specified facilities depending on their mandatory reporting regulation*

	Mandatory reporting of GHG emissions (MRR) (California)	US EPA GHG Reporting Rule (other US, facilities with more than 25,000 tCO₂e/yr)	No mandatory reporting regulation (other, fuel consumption report available)	When a US EPA GHG Report or EIA fuel consumption report is not available (other)
For specified facilities or units whose operators are subject to …				
Considered CO$_2$e emissions (Esp) for the calculation of the emission factor	Esp = CO$_2$e emissions reported (pursuant to section 95112	Esp = GHG emissions reported to US EPA (pursuant to 40 Code of Deferral Regulation CFR Part 98). Emissions from combustion of biomass-derived fuels will be based on EIA data, when not reported to US EPA	Esp is calculated using heat of combustion data reported to the Energy Information Administration (EIA)	The assignment of an emission factor by the Executive Officer based on the type of fuel combusted or the technology.

Source: Authors from MRR regulation.

- **General information of the electricity entity:** ARB identification number, country, geographic location and indicate whether the reporting entity qualifies for small business status (California Government Code 11342.610), Energy Information Administration and California Energy Commission identification numbers.
- **Designated a representative person for the reporting process named a "data reporter."**
- **Corporate Parent and North American Industry Classification System (NAICS) Codes:** report the NAICS code that most accurately describes the facility or supplier's primary product/activity/service.
- **Facility Level Energy Input and Output:** the operator must include in the emissions data report information about the facility's energy acquisitions and energy provided or sold as detailed in section III.C.

GHG emissions data reports for electricity importers

In the GHG emissions data report, the power entity must report GHG emissions and delivered electricity (imported, exported and wheeled) in MWh.

- **Reporting categories:** power entities must report imported, exported and wheeled electricity in MWh **disaggregated by first Point of Receipt (POR) or final Point of Delivery (POD)**, as applicable, and must also separately report imported and exported electricity from unspecified sources and from each specified source. Substitute electricity[29] must be separately reported for each specified source, as applicable. First Points of Receipt and final Points of Delivery must be reported using the standardized code used in NERC e-tags, as well as the full name of the POR/POD.
- **GHG emissions:** the power entity must report GHG emissions separately for each category of delivered electricity required, in metric tons of CO_2 equivalent (Mt of CO_2e).

---

[29] MRR Section 95102(a)(442): substitute electricity means electricity that is provided to meet the terms of a power purchase contract with a specified facility or unit when that facility or unit is not generating electricity.

For imported electricity, the power entity must separately report as follows:

- **Imported electricity from unspecified sources:** the power entity must report for each first Point of Receipt the following information: location of the first POR in or out of a linked jurisdiction published on ARB's website, amount of electricity measured at the first POD in California and GHG emissions including those associated with transmission losses.
- **Imported electricity from specified facilities or units:** the power entity must report electricity deliveries from a specified source and associated GHG emissions by facility or unit and by first POR, as applicable. The specified facility or unit must also report substitute electricity received from specified or unspecified sources and if any of the following conditions apply for electricity deliveries:
  - deliveries previously reported as consumed in California;
  - deliveries from existing federally owned hydroelectricity facility by exclusive marketers or allocated by contract;
  - deliveries from new facilities;
  - deliveries from existing facilities with additional capacity.
- **Imported electricity supplied by asset-controlling suppliers:** the power entity must separately report imported electricity supplied by ACS recognized by ARB. The reporting entity must report delivered electricity from ACS as measured at the first point of delivery in the State of California.
- **Imported electricity through exchange agreements**[30]: power entities must report delivered electricity under power exchange agreements consistent with imported and exported electricity reporting requirements. Electricity delivered into the State of California under exchange agreements must be reported as imported electricity and electricity delivered out of California under exchange agreements must be reported as exported electricity.

---

[30] MRR, Section 102(a)(160): commitment between electricity market participants to swap energy for energy. Exchange transactions do not involve transfers of payment or receipts of money for the full market value of the energy being exchanged, but may include payment for net differences due to market price differences between the two parts of the transaction or to settle minor imbalances.

Confidentiality, when requested, must be demonstrated by reporters

California recognizes GHG emissions as publicly available information: all the emissions data submitted to ARB under the reporting process is public information and shall not be designated as confidential (MRR, section 95106). However, any entity submitting information to the Executive Officer may claim such information as "confidential" by clearly identifying such information as "confidential." Any claim of confidentiality by an entity submitting information must be based on the entity's belief that the information marked as confidential is either trade secret or otherwise exempt from public disclosure under the California Public Records Act (Government Code section 6250 et seq.). The responsibility to defend confidentiality is on the facility, and not on the program administrator (Bode, 2012). Power entities do not differ from other entities covered by the MRR in this respect.

Verification

Programs underpinning trading schemes tend to favor third-party verification owing to their need for confidence in the robustness and completeness of data from each reporter (Singh and Mahapatra, 2013). California's MRV regulation, similarly to the EU ETS, requires verification from an independent, third-party verifier who has been accredited by a designated body.

Annual verification: from a full to a less intensive verification

All power entities that import power into California are annually verified, no matter their size (MRR, sections 95130 and 95131). In order to limit the verification costs for power entities, two types of verification services are indicated in the regulation:

- **A full verification** is required in the first year of each compliance period. The key element of a full verification is that the verification team must undertake a site visit of the headquarters or other location of central data management (for retail provider or marketer). During this visit, the verifiers must check and review all emission sources, product data and facility operations used to write the GHG

Inventory Program Documentation. The verifiers must also evaluate the data management system of the reporting entity.

- However, beyond the first year of each compliance period, a full verification is required when there is a change in the verification body, a change of ownership of the reporting entity, an adverse or a qualified positive verification statement and when there are changes in sources or emissions. In this last case, the verification team is not obliged to conduct a full verification. Yet, if it chooses a less intensive one, the verification body must provide information on the causes of the emission changes if the total reported GHG emissions differ by more than 25 percent from the preceding year's emissions data report.

- **A less intensive verification:** the reporting entity may choose a less intensive verification for the remaining years of the compliance period. This type of verification only requires data checks and document reviews of the entity's GHG inventory program documentation. This assessment is based on the most current sampling plan's analysis and risk assessment which comes from a full verification. In a less intensive verification there is no site visit required.

The key steps of a verification procedure

Whatever the type of annual verification chosen by the reporting entity, the verification process includes some key steps that must be undertaken by the verification team.

1. Verifiers must develop **a verification plan** which summarizes information from the reporting entity such as the timing of verification services, documentation of planned activities and document reviews. The verification plan must be submitted to ARB with a notice of verification services. The objective of the notice is to allow ARB staff to plan in advance for any additional oversight of the verification, with particular dates of verification activities proposed in advance.

2. Verifiers must check and review all emission sources, product data and facility operations. Thus, the verification team must develop a sampling plan based on a strategic analysis developed from document reviews and interviews to assess the likely nature, scale and complexity of the verification services for the reporting entity. The

sampling plan is a very important document for the verification process. It includes all the assessments of the development of the GHG inventory program documentation, the rigor and appropriateness of data management systems, and the coordination within the reporting entity's organization to manage the operation and maintenance of equipment and systems. The sampling plan also includes a qualitative narrative of uncertainty risk assessment on the reliability and accuracy of the data (equipment, frequency, sampling, calculation, reporting, etc.) and describes potential issues emerging with material misstatement or nonconformance. The sampling plan must be retained by the verification body and be available to ARB upon request.

3. The reporting entity must make any possible improvements or corrections to the submitted emissions data report as a result of data checks by verifiers. Then, the reporting entity must submit a revised emissions data report to ARB.

4. Verifiers must complete two verification statements (one for emissions data and one for product data) and provide them to the reporting entity and ARB by September of the year (see Table 7.4). There are two types of statements:

   • a qualified positive verification statement which indicates that the verification team has found no material misstatement in the emissions data report and that the report meets the requirements of the regulation;
   • an adverse verification statement which explains all nonconformances and material misstatements.

   In case of failing to receive a verification statement by the applicable deadline or in case of receiving an adverse emissions data verification statement, the ARB officer will make a final decision before October 10th of the year. To make this decision, the ARB officer develops an assigned emissions level for the data year for the reporting entity. The ARB officer will consider at a minimum:

   • the reporting entity operations characteristics for the data year (operation duration and schedule) and the potential maximum fuel used during operating hours;
   • any previous emissions data reports and verification statement;
   • wholesale and retail transactions that would affect an assigned emissions level;

Table 7.4 *Key dates for verification*

Date	Activity
March	Contract with verification body (and schedule site visit if applicable)
July	Suggestion made by ARB: the reporting entity should get answers to all questions from ARB and from verifier request on final issues
September	Final verification statements on emissions data and product data

Source: California Environmental Protection Agency, Air Resources Board.

- emissions, electricity transactions, fuel use or product output information reported to ARB or other State, federal or local agencies.

Reporting entities must not use the same verification body or verifier(s) for a period of more than six consecutive years. The reporting entities can start re-using the same verification body or verifier(s) after at least a period of three years.

Accreditation procedure

ARB issues accreditation to three types of verifiers (MRR, section 951132):

- **Verification body:** a firm accredited by ARB that is able to render a verification statement and provide verification services for reporting entities subject to reporting under this article. A verification body must be composed of at least five staff members, including two lead verifiers, and carry liability insurance.
- **Lead verifier:** a person who may act as the lead verifier of a verification team providing verification services or as a lead verifier providing an independent review of verification services rendered. He must have been an ARB accredited verifier for two continuous years and have worked as a verifier in at least three completed verifications under the supervision of an ARB accredited lead verifier.

Table 7.5 *The impact of meter monitoring error in the verification procedure*

Meter monitoring			
Source's emissions (errors)	Total facility's emissions (errors)	Using missing data	Verification decision
Whatever the % of the source's emissions	< 5%	Can be used	No adverse verification statement
Whatever the % of the source's emissions	> 5%	Cannot be used	Adverse verification statement

Source: California Environmental Protection Agency, Air Resources Board.

- **Verifier:** the applicant must take an ARB approved general verification training and receive a passing score of greater than an unweighted 70 percent on an exit examination. ARB order for accreditation is valid for a period of three years, whereupon the applicant may re-apply for accreditation and re-pass ARB verification training and examination to have the accreditation renewed by ARB. During all the accreditation period of three years, lead verifiers and verifiers must demonstrate proficiency during ARB annual audits and must attend regular training webinars.

Uncertainty requirement – avoiding a material misstatement: 5 percent for electricity importers and electricity producers

Power entities have an incentive to avoid Material Misstatement, as defined in section 95102(a)(277) of the MRR Regulation: for any error or combination of errors on total reported covered emissions or product data with an impact higher than 5 percent, power entities receive an adverse verification statement.[31] In addition, there is a

---

[31] For more information, see Section 95103(k) on Measurement Accuracy Requirement.

specific requirement for the measurement of the metering accuracy[32] in the case of a meter failing calibration. Three situations are described depending on the meter calibration scope (see Table 7.5).

MRV costs €73,000 per facility and €0.14/tCO$_2$e to electricity deliverers

The calculation of the global cost of the MRR is estimated from successive Initial Statements of Reasons for Rulemaking (ISRR) issued by ARB for each amendment in 2007, 2010, 2012 and 2013. The cost estimation is an ex-ante assessment. The annual average cost per facility and per tonne of CO$_2$e is obtained by adding up the incremental costs of each amendment to the initial – and by far largest – cost estimated in the 2007 IRR. One-off costs are spread over ten years without applying a discount rate to be consistent with the other estimates provided in this book.

Electricity importers, included in "electricity deliverers" (Table 7.6), incur a larger MRV cost than the average reporting entity. Likely due to the need to keep track of numerous transactions and to associate a relevant emission factor to each of these, electricity deliverers are indeed considered to be among the most complex facilities by ARB, together with petroleum refineries.

The average costs per tCO$_2$e were for the average reporting entity divided by three after the inclusion of fuel and gas suppliers in 2011. Indeed, fuel and gas suppliers report huge amounts of emissions per facility – on average 25–40 million tCO$_2$e per facility – which allows them to benefit from large economies of scale.

7.4 Uncertainty in the Californian cap-and-trade program: the carbon leakage issue

Based on a hybrid approach to regulate out-of-state facilities, the inclusion of the imported electricity, under the Global Warming Solution Act (AB 32) of California, raises two issues: the uncertainty of emission factors for emissions from out-of-state generation facilities and resources shuffling. Both issues are related to carbon leakage.

---

[32] MRR Section 95131(b)(13).

Table 7.6 *MRV costs of the MRR*

	State-wide cost (€/yr)	Cost per facility ((€/yr)			Cost per tCO_2e (€/yr)		
		Average	Min	Max	Average	Min	Max
Electricity deliverers	6,386,306	72,572	25,594	111,549	0.14	0.05	0.24
Average reporting entity	24,796,676	34,778	10,893	58,663	0.06	0.02	0.10
Administration	789,493	1,120			0.002		

Note: Costs were converted from dollars to euros using the 2010 annual average exchange rate of €1 = US$1.3275. As the costs have not significantly altered since the initial MRR of 2006, especially for electricity deliverers, the minimum and maximum costs are based on the range provided in the initial ISRR. To obtain the per facility and per tCO_2e costs, state-wide costs are divided by the number of facilities and the total amount of emissions in 2012, except for electricity deliverers for which the relevant ISRR uses an assumed 88 facilities (against 103 in 2012).

Source: Authors from the ARB ISRRs.

The uncertainty of electricity importers' emission factors

For out-of-state facilities, the first deliverers of imported electricity which face the compliance obligation for emissions are the marketers and retail providers who import energy into the California grid. One significant limitation of this approach is the uncertainty associated with the emission factors attributed to imported power. Due to the nature of the Western Interconnection, electricity imports do not, in general, travel directly from a generation facility to the California grid (Bushnell et al., 2013). According to them, it is generally not possible to identify the source of imported electricity with sufficient granularity to assign a specific emissions obligation. As seen in Section 7.2, this is likely a major source of uncertainty in the total emissions covered by the Californian ETS.

First deliverers with contract for clean energy (lower emission factors) will wish to specify their actual emissions factor in order to minimize the carbon costs. If the emission factor is set too low firms will have an incentive to "launder" their higher emitting resources through the market to attain the lower, unspecified, emission factor (Bushnell et al., 2013). Indeed, if the first deliverer cannot identify the source of the imported electricity, a default emission factor is set at 0.428 $MtCO_2e/MWh$, which is representative of a fairly clean natural gas plant according to the WCI group (Bushnell et al., 2013). Hence, first delivers who received electricity from dirty sources will have an incentive to choose to not identify these dirty sources and be assigned the default emission factor than a higher one. This biased behavior of deliverers will likely result in an overall underestimation of emissions from imported electricity. It could also lead to carbon leakage, if Californian coal power plants relocate in neighboring states to benefit from the default emission factor.

Whether this is a failing of ARB to comply with the Assembly Bill 32 – which requires the California Air Resources Board to minimize leakage to the extent feasible and in furtherance of achieving the state-wide GHG emissions limit – remains to be seen. Indeed, using a generous default factor for out-of-jurisdiction emissions is a key recommendation of Cosbey et al. (2012) to avoid WTO challenges in the case of international carbon border adjustment. Similarly, it may have been employed by ARB to avoid a constitutional challenge under the inter-State commerce article of the US constitution. In addition, ARB plans to reevaluate the default emission factor prior to each compliance period based on updated data reported to the Energy Information Administration.[33]

The confusing concept of resource shuffling

Resource shuffling is another mechanism which can undermine the effectiveness of reducing leakage and a fair calculation of electricity importers' emissions. Resource shuffling is a form of carbon leakage which is specific to the electricity sector. The idea is that out-of-state producers may reconfigure their transmission by substituting imports from a low-emitting source for imports from a high-emitting source to the California grid while re-directing the higher emitting power to other States without carbon limits. The Californian Cap-and-Trade Regulation[34] requires first deliverer emitters to vow by a written attestation, under penalties, that they are not simply funneling more of their clean electricity into the California grid.

In August 2012, ARB suspended for 18 months[35] the enforcement of the resource shuffling prohibition provision that requires importers of electricity to annually attest that they have not engaged in resource shuffling during the previous year of a compliance period. In October 2012, ARB staff, in consultation with the California Energy Commission, the California Public Utilities Commission, the California Independent System Operator and stakeholders, refined the definition of resource shuffling by identifying situations which are not considered as resource shuffling activities, named "Safe Harbor activities."[36] A safe harbor activity is a scenario involving substitutions of low-emitting imports that ARB will not consider as resource shuffling. According to ARB

---

[33] Final Statement of Reasons for Rulemaking (2011), ARB.
[34] California cap-and-trade regulation, Section 95852(b)(2).
[35] 01.01.2013 to 06.30.2014.
[36] California cap-and-trade regulation instructional guidance, Appendix A: what is resource shuffling, ARB November 2012, www.arb.ca.gov/cc/capandtrade/guidance/appendix_a.pdf

staff, there are 13 situations which are identified as a safe harbor activity such as RPS compliance, termination of contracts for
"other reasons than resource shuffling," expiration of contract, or
electricity deliveries due to operational emergencies or distribution
constraints. Nevertheless, it seems difficult to distinguish between
transactions motivated by resource shuffling or by other reasons. In
July 2013, ARB staff released draft proposed amendments on the
resource shuffling and the safe harbor activities concepts. Due to
the controversial attestation provision, ARB is considering removing it. However, this proposal does not remove the ambiguity of the
resource shuffling concept.

The amount of resource shuffling could have a large impact on the
CO_2 price and on the amount of carbon leakage. Caron et al. (2012)
estimated that the allowance price would skyrocket to US\$65/
tCO_2 and the leakage to electricity exporters would be −35 percent if resource shuffling is banned and if the ban can be enforced
(scenario C). Indeed, due to the Renewable Portfolio Standard, the
Californian electricity production is on average less CO_2-intensive
than imported electricity. So, the implementation of a cap-and-trade
program and a rule which forbids resource shuffling led to the
increase of electricity production in California at the expense of
electricity imports. The leakage in this first situation is lower than
the leakage in the situation where California does not have some
electricity tariffs (scenario A) or where California does have electricity tariffs but no legislation to prevent resource shuffling (scenario
B); see Table 7.7.

Resource shuffling and the opportunistic choice of electricity
importers to specify their sources are two interrelated issues: if the
resource shuffling ban is ineffective, importers will easily find renewable sources of electricity, and will therefore have a strong incentive
to specify their sources. Hence, carbon leakage will be high, but
the underestimate from "opportunistically unspecified" sources will
be low. To the reverse, if the resource shuffling ban is effective, it
will reinforce the incentive for importers to "launder" their imports
by claiming the default rate of unspecified sources for their dirtier
imports.

Table 7.7 *The leakage according to the implementation or not of an electricity tariff and a ban on resource shuffling*

	Electricity tariff	Legislation to forbid resource shuffling	Economic effects	Leakage
Scenario A	No	No	The Californian electricity production decreased and is replaced by the increase of electricity importations	The aggregate leakage to electricity exporters is 46%
Scenario B	Yes	No	All renewable and nuclear powers from out-of-state producers are exported into the California grid. The Californian electricity production decreased and is replaced by the increase of electricity importations	The aggregate leakage to electricity exporters is 48%
Scenario C	Yes	Yes	The Californian power production is on average less carbon-intensive than out-of-state power production. The Californian production increased and the electricity imports decreased	The aggregate leakage to electricity exporters is −35% but is partially offset by positive leakage (29%) to other US regions due to changes in both trade and fossil fuel prices

Sources: Caron et al. (2012).

However, as the regional scope of the program grows, concerns about leakage and contract shuffling will decline. Indeed, the expansion of the cap-and-trade program will increase the percentage of electricity purchases which are located within the ETS or a linked ETS. Thus, resource shuffling will become more difficult. One of California's upcoming challenges will be the ability of its ETS to integrate with broader regional initiatives.

7.5 Conclusion

The Californian cap-and-trade program offers an interesting case by covering electricity importers. Due to the specific feature of Californian power generation (30 percent of the electricity supply came from imported electricity in 2011), the inclusion of electricity was needed. Thus, the California MRV legislation is adjusted to take into account this special feature and try to frame rules which embrace the full scope of border carbon adjustment. On the monitoring side, the first step is to identify the imported electricity though the NERC e-tag system or through a power contract. The second step is to determine if the imported electricity comes from a specified or an unspecified source. This distinction is essential in the calculation of covered emissions and is embodied by the emission factor used in this calculation (specified emission factor or default emission factor). On the reporting side, the power entities must prepare a GHG Inventory Program Documentation instead of a GHG Monitoring Plan which is the common document expected from entities covered by the cap-and-trade program. Finally, the verification process is identical to that for entities from other sectors.

At this stage, the California Air Resource Board is still working on its regulation in order to reduce the uncertainty associated with the inclusion of energy importers. Indeed, the challenge is becoming even more important with the inclusion of transportation fuels and natural gas suppliers during the second compliance period started in 2015.

7.6 MRV ID table

Table 7.8 MRV ID table

	Context
Regulator	A. California Air Resources Board (Executive officer) Title 17, CRR, sections 95100–95158 B. Advisory guidelines: Chapter 3 – What does my company need to do to comply with the cap-and-trade regulation?: 3.8 Additional requirements of Electric Distribution Utilities
Type and level of incentive to comply	Penalties (Title 17, CCR, 95107): if deadline is missed or there is a shortfall, four allowances must be provided for every ton of emissions that was not covered in time.
Entities concerned	Electricity importers: 2013: 279 electricity power entities[a] 2013: 102 electricity importers and 60 covered electricity importers[b] In 2011, 29.7% of the Californian electricity was imported electricity (89,686 Gigawatts-hours[c]) In 2011, Electricity Generation (Import) was 10.45% of the total GHG emissions[d]
Sectors concerned	Electricity
Gases concerned	CO_2e, CH_4, N_2O
Overall MRV costs	**Ex-ante cost assessment:**[e] Average cost per electricity deliverer: €73,000 per year Average cost per t CO_2e: €0.14

Table 7.8 (*cont.*)

	Monitoring
Rules	California Global Warming Solutions Act (AB 32, 2006).
	CRR, Title 17, Chap.1 ARB, Subchapter 10 Climate Change, Article 5. Cap-and-Trade Regulation, **section**
	95812(c)(2)(B) and 95852(b).
	CCR, Title 17, Chap.1 ARB, Subchapter 10 Climate Change, Article 2. Mandatory Greenhouse Gas
	Emissions Reporting (MRR), section 95111(b)(5).
Other reference documents	Senate Bill 1368 Emission performance standards 2006
	Original equipment manufacturers (OEM) documentation.
Uncertainty requirements	No overall uncertainty requirement
Achieved uncertainty range	Not available (2012 was the first year of operation, monitoring reports were to be submitted in June 2013).
Cost range	Not available: the system is too recent, no study covered this part.
Scope	A. Scope 2 (direct emissions and emissions related to electricity consumption)
	B. Operational emissions
	C. Entity ("facility/unit")
Frequency	Yearly
Source for activity data	Electricity transactions as monitored by e-tags (MWh) from unspecified sources and specified sources
Uncertainty range for activity data	None, except when meters are used. In that case, measurement uncertainty must be lower than 5%.

Source for emission factors	- ARB website: www.arb.ca.gov/cc/reporting/ghg-rep-power/ghg-rep-power.htm - MRR, **Section 95111(b)(1),(2),(5).** - C&T Regulation, **Section 95852(b)(1)(B).**
Uncertainty range for emission factors	No uncertainty requirement for emission factors.
Direct measurement	Possible, conditions: **MRR, Section 95103(k)(1)_(11)**
Incentives to reduce uncertainty	There is an incentive for electricity importers to claim a specified source if its emission factor is lower than the default value (see Section 7.2). This incentive may increase precision but decrease accuracy as it is biased: importers from a "high carbon" source have an incentive to remain "unspecified" and apply the default emission factor.
Is requirements stringency adapted to the amount of emissions at stake (materiality)?	No. All importers face the same monitoring requirements, no matter their size. However, facilities with emissions lower than 25,000 tCO_2e/yr are not covered by the carbon pricing regulation (AB 32).

Reporting	
Rules	CCR, Title 17, Chap.1 ARB, Subchapter 10 Climate Change, Article 2. Mandatory Greenhouse Gas Emissions Reporting (MRR), section 95103(h), section 95104, section 95105. CRR, Title 17, Chap.1 ARB, Subchapter 10 Climate Change, Article 5. Cap-and-Trade Regulation, section 95852(b).
Other reference documents	EPA 40 CFR §98.3 and §98.4

Table 7.8 (*cont.*)

Format	**GHG Emission data report registered in the Cal e-GGRT (California Electronic Electronic Greenhouse Gas Reporting Tool)** Electric power must report GHG emissions separately for each category of delivered electricity required: - Imported electricity from unspecified sources - Imported electricity from specified facilities or units - Substitute electricity

Level of source disaggregation	**Section 95111(a)(3) and (4)**
	→Direct delivery electricity:
	  →Facility or unit:
	  - Unspecified source
	  - Specified source
	  →POR
	Quantitative explanation (number of sites, productions units, spatial resolution/aggregation)
	→If difference between required reporting level of disaggregation and the published level of aggregation

Frequency	Yearly
Timeline	**By February 1, of each year**: power entities must register their anticipated specified facilities and units outside California. Deadline to submit GHG reports to ARB: **June 1 of each year**. Reports Year n−1 emissions (June 3 for 2013). All revisions should be made well before **August 15 of each year.**
Language	English
Is requirements stringency adapted to the amount of emissions at stake (materiality)?	No. All the power entities are required to report. Zero emissions must be reported until cessation requirements are met.
Cost range	Not available: the system is too recent, no study covered this part.

Verification

Rules	CCR, Title 17, Chap.1 ARB, Subchapter 10 Climate Change, Article 2. Mandatory Greenhouse Gas Emissions Reporting (MRR), section 95130 to 95133
Other reference documents	GHG Inventory program, section 95105(d)
Format	Verification of Emissions data report
Frequency	Yearly But two types of verification: **Section 95130(a)(1)** - Full verification (2013, 2015): first year of each compliance period. - Less intensive verification (2014, 2016, 2017): for the remaining years of the compliance period.
Timeline	**July 15 of each year:** Deadline for corrections to RPS Adjustment data required for power entity data reports. **August 15 of each year:** Verification body start their review **September 1 of each year:** Deadline for submitting verification (September 3 for 2013)
Language	English
Accredited entities for verification	**Section 95132.(b)(1)** Three types of accreditation applications: - *The Verification Body (VB).* - *The lead verifier (LV).* - *The verifier:* → All applicants must take an ARB approved general verification training and receive a passing score of greater than an unweighted 70% on an exit examination. There are some additional requirements for offset verifier. Accreditation valid for a period of three years. List of Accredited VB: www.arb.ca.gov/cc/reporting/ghg-ver/arb_vb.htm

Table 7.8 (*cont.*)

Control of accredited entities	After the end of the three years accreditation, the applicant (VB, LV or Verifier) may re-apply for accreditation and re-pass ARB verification training and examination to have the accreditation renewed by ARB. During all the accreditation period of three years, lead verifiers and verifiers must demonstrate proficiency during ARB annual audits.
Cost of accreditation	Not available: the system is too recent, no study covered this part.
Support and control of accredited entities	-**Before being accredited**: must fellow a general verification training. -**After being accredited**: must demonstrate proficiency during ARB annual audits and attend regular training webinars.
Is requirements stringency adapted to the amount of emissions at stake (materiality)?	Essentially no: all importers are verified. However, a materiality threshold is set at 5% of facility-level emissions: errors with an impact below this threshold do not lead to a negative verification statement (see Section 7.3).
Cost range	Not available: the system is too recent, no study covered this part.

a www.arb.ca.gov/cc/reporting/ghg-rep/reported-data/ghg-reports.htm

b Ibid.

c www.energyalmanac.ca.gov/electricity/electricity_generation.html

d www.arb.ca.gov/cc/inventory/doc/methods_00–09/ghg_inventory_00–09_technical_support_document.pdf and www.arb.ca.gov/cc/inventory/data/tables/ghg_inventory_scopingplan_00–11_2013-08-01.pdf

e ARB, Initial Statement of Reasons for Rulemaking (2012), Initial Statement of Reasons for Rulemaking (2010), Initial Statement of Reasons for Rulemaking (2007).

Bibliography

ARB, 2013. California cap on greenhouse gas emissions and market-based compliance mechanisms regulation, www.arb.ca.gov/cc/capandtrade/c-t-reg-reader-2013.pdf, p. 396. Accessed March 28, 2013.

[2007]2013. Mandatory Reporting of Greenhouse Gas Emissions Regulation (Mandatory reporting regulation or MRR). The MRR was originally approved in 2007 and revised in 2010, 2012 and 2013. The current regulation became effective on January 1, 2014. www.arb.ca.gov/cc/reporting/ghg-rep/regulation/mrr-2013-clean.pdf. Accessed March 28, 2013.

2011. Staff report, Final Statement of Reasons for Rulemaking, amendments to the regulation for the mandatory reporting of greenhouse gas emissions, No. 10-11-12, p. 436.

2013. Staff report, Final Statement of Reasons for Rulemaking, amendments to the regulation for the mandatory reporting of greenhouse gas emissions, No. 13-9-8, p. 261.

2012. Staff report, Final Statement of Reasons for Rulemaking, amendments to the regulation for the mandatory reporting of greenhouse gas emissions and conforming amendments to the definition sections of the AB 32 cost of implementation fee regulation and the cap-and-trade regulation, No. 12-6-2, p. 99.

2013. Staff report, Initial Statement of Reasons for Rulemaking, amendments to the regulation for the mandatory reporting of greenhouse gas emissions, p. 113.

2012. Staff report, Initial Statement of Reasons for Rulemaking, amendments to the regulation for the mandatory reporting of greenhouse gas emissions and conforming amendments to the definition sections of the AB 32 cost of implementation fee regulation and the cap-and-trade regulation, p. 97.

2007. Staff report, Initial Statement of Reasons for Rulemaking, a proposed regulation for mandatory reporting of greenhouse gas emissions pursuant to the Global Warming Solutions Act of 2006, p. 232.

2010. Staff report, Initial Statement of Reasons for Rulemaking, revisions to the regulation for mandatory reporting of greenhouse gas emissions pursuant to the Global Warming Solutions Act of 2006, p. 292.

Verification of GHG Emissions Data Reports, ARB website, www.arb.ca.gov/cc/reporting/ghg-ver/ghg-ver.htm. Accessed December 2013.

Bode, R., 2012. Chief, Greenhouse Gas Emission Inventory Branch. Interviewed by A. Mahapatra, July 26, 2012.

Bushnell, J., 2008. The design of California's cap-and-trade and its impact on electricity markets, *Climate Policy* 8(3): 17.

Bushnell, J., Chen, Y. and Zaragoza-Watkins, M., 2013. Emissions in California's Electricity Sector, University of California Energy Institute at Haas, working paper series, E3 WP-049, p. 31.

Caron, J., Rausch, S. and Winchester, N., 2012. Leakage from subnational climate initiatives: the case of California. MIT Global Change Unit report No. 220, p. 37. http://globalchange.mit.edu/files/document/MITJPSPGC_Rpt220.pdf. Accessed April 18, 2013.

Cosbey, A., Droege, S., Fischer, C., Reinaud, J., Stephenson, J., Weischer, L. and Wooders, P., 2012. A Guide for the Concerned: Guidance on the elaboration and implementation of border carbon adjustment, Entwined Policy Report No. 03, Stockholm, Sweden, p. 22.

Edwards, D., 2013. Greenhouse Gas Emission Inventory Branch. Interviewed by M. Afriat, June 24, 2013.

Ellerman, A.D., Convery, F.J. and De Perthuis, C., 2010. *Pricing Carbon: the European Union Emissions Trading Scheme*, Cambridge University Press, p. 368.

IEA, 2012. 2012 Annual report, www.iea.org/publications/freepublications/publication/IEA_Annual_Report_publicversion.pdf, p. 21. Accessed April 29, 2013.

MEDDE, Highlights, Key figures on climate, France and worldwide, 2014 Edition. Service de l'observation et des statistiques.

Singh, N. and Mahapatra, A., 2013. Designing Greenhouse Gas Reporting Systems: Learning From Existing Programs. Working Paper. World Resources Institute, Washington, DC, p. 24.

US EPA, 2009. Regulatory Impact Analysis for the Mandatory Reporting of Greenhouse Gas Emissions Final Rule (GHG Reporting), Final report, p. 219.

    2010. Mandatory Greenhouse Gas Reporting Rule, presentation at EPRI CEM User Group Meeting, Cleveland, Ohio, p. 28.

    2011. Greenhouse Gas Reporting Rule, training presentation, p. 75. www.epa.gov/ghgreporting/documents/pdf/2010/Part-98-Training-Complete.pdf. Accessed April 25, 2013.

    2011. Why Are Both Downstream and Upstream Reporting Required?, FAQ, US EPA website, www.ccdsupport.com/confluence/pages/viewpage.action?pageId=91553964. Accessed April 25, 2013.

WECC, 2011. Ten Year Regional Transmission Plan, Executive summary, p. 20.

8 | Variant 3: emissions of a company/ institution rather than a site: the case of the Shenzhen ETS

CASPAR CHIQUET

8.1 China's domestic emissions reduction policy

China's unparalleled economic growth has brought with it a massive increase in fossil fuel consumption: China uses almost as much coal as the rest of the world put together.[1] Unsurprisingly, its annual greenhouse gas emissions surpassed those of the US in 2006 (WRI, CAIT 2.0, 2014).[2] Still, China's negotiators insist on the principle of "common but differentiated responsibility," stating that industrialized nations have been polluting the atmosphere for the last 150 years and China and other developing countries should therefore have a lesser burden when it comes to reducing consumption of fossil fuels. The failure to include the world's largest emitters – China and the US amount to at least 42 percent of global emissions[3] – into a binding agreement remains one of the major roadblocks of international climate change negotiations.

Interestingly, China's domestic policy is more ambitious than one would assume from its stance on the international stage. While its Copenhagen pledge to reduce its carbon intensity by 40–45 percent compared to 2005 by 2020 was a promising step in the right direction, it was merely a restatement of previously approved domestic policy. China's policy roadmap has included energy intensity targets for already more than a decade, with detailed breakdowns for different sectors and industries. These intensity targets allow continued economic growth, while addressing energy consumption and emissions. Consequently, China has so far not been willing to commit itself to an absolute cap (even assuming a rising trajectory) internationally, although domestically absolute caps on energy consumption or certain fuels are under discussion.[4]

---

[1] 2013 US EIA data.
[2] Washington, DC: World Resources Institute. Available at: http://cait2.wri.org.
[3] 2008 US EPA data.
[4] See for example State Council 2013-2: www.gov.cn/zwgk/2013-01/23/content_2318554.htm.

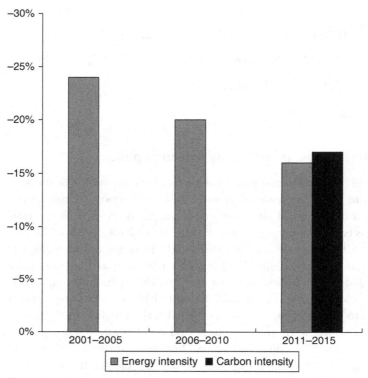

Figure 8.1 Energy intensity targets in recent 5-Year Plans. Base years are 2000, 2005 and 2010 respectively
Source: Author. Based on data from National Bureau of Statistics of the People's Republic of China.

The 10th 5-Year Plan (2001–2005) for example contained an overall energy intensity reduction target of 24 percent against the baseline year 2000. The target under the 11th 5-Year Plan (2006–2010) was a 20 percent reduction against 2005 levels, a target China barely managed to achieve, having to resort to drastic measures in the last year, such as cutting off electricity supply for factories which had used up their quota (see Box 8.1 "Forced shutdowns under the 11th 5-Year Plan"). The current 12th 5-Year Plan (2011–2015) sets slightly less ambitious goals than the previous ones, but for the first time explicitly introduces a separate carbon intensity target[5] (Figure 8.1).

---

[5] The small difference between energy intensity and carbon intensity is attributable to the energy mix, which is over time slowly shifting to a less emission-intensive configuration.

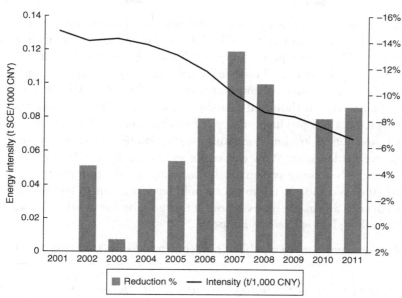

Figure 8.2 Energy intensity 2001–2011 in tons Standard Coal Equivalent (SCE)

Source: Author. Based on data from National Bureau of Statistics of the People's Republic of China.

Overall, the energy intensity of China's economy has actually halved over 2001–2011 according to top-down statistics from the Chinese Bureau of Statistics (Figure 8.2).[6]

Box 8.1 Forced shutdowns under the 11th 5-Year Plan

Testimony by a plant operator in Changxing, Huzhou, Zhejiang province:

Because energy saving and emission reduction measures have so far not been systematically implemented, targets set by superior ministries have not been met. Now the workgroup came [for an

---

[6] A controversy persists around the discrepancy between top-down and bottom-up accounting of Chinese GDP and energy consumption data. Researchers have estimated the resulting error in China's carbon inventory to be as high as 1.4 gigatonnes (Guan et al., 2012).

inspection], the leaders panicked and now the ordinary people and enterprises have to pay the bill. Nobody would have thought that they decided to cut power supply 24h a day for 50 days in a row! This has been enforced now for a week already. Because the textile industry is the most important industry branch in Changxing, there are several thousand factories located here. All these factories facing a full production stop led to chaos in the domestic market and lots of trading companies with pending orders are facing numerous lawsuits. Who will cover such huge losses? If one had from the beginning systematically restricted production for only 5 to 10 days a month, the impact would have been much less severe than such a brusque intervention. If this goes on for another week, something bad is likely to happen.

Source: www.tianya.cn/publicforum/content/develop/1/470284.shtml

Cap-and-trade as the policy instrument of choice

In addition to specifying a carbon intensity reduction target for the first time, the 12th 5-Year Plan also calls for the implementation of market-based instruments and emission trading as a means to achieve the energy- and carbon-intensity goals, and together with a 2011 regulation from the National Development and Reform Commission,[7] sets the stage for seven regional ETS pilots in China (Map 8.1).

The seven pilot cap-and-trade schemes are located in five cities (Beijing, Shanghai, Tianjin, Shenzhen, Chongqing) and two provinces (Guangdong, one of the manufacturing hubs of China, and Hubei, one of the hubs for the car industry in China). The cap-and-trade pilots are still in their early stages, with most of the legislation still taking shape. The tentative roadmap is to process pilot transactions as early as 2013, and transition towards a national cap-and-trade by 2015, although government officials have already admitted that this timeline may be too ambitious.

On a national level, Beijing has issued a few important guidelines regulating emission exchanges, verifiers and offset projects. The ETS pilots mostly mirror these rules at the local level. Furthermore,

[7] NDRC Climate Change 2011–2601: www.ndrc.gov.cn/zcfb/zcfbtz/2011tz/ t20120113_456506.htm.

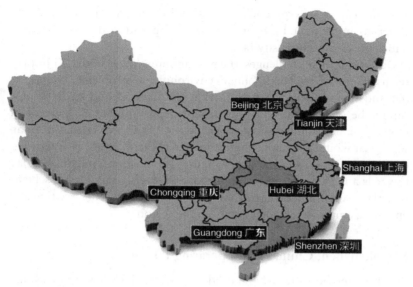

Map 8.1 The seven Chinese emissions trading pilot schemes
Source: IETA (2013).

starting with the 12th 5-Year Plan, Beijing has improved the method-ology according to which the national target is distributed and passed down to provinces and municipalities.[8] But provincial governments are now struggling to align their intensity-based relative targets under the 5-Year Plan with the requirements of a cap-and-trade system. Additionally, in an economy that is still heavily regulated, there is a lot of friction to be expected, as costs cannot be passed on easily and mar-ket distortions are abundant. The electricity price for example is set by the Chinese state, and forces (state-owned) utilities to operate at a loss if coal prices rise above a certain threshold. It is therefore possible that Beijing will hold back on the implementation of a nation-wide ETS until certain market reforms have been realized, such as a liberaliza-tion of the power sector, which would make carbon pricing in general easier, as costs could be imposed on generation and then passed down. An alternative would be to turn the current intensity targets into an

[8] LBNL & ERI 2011: http://china.lbl.gov/publications/
target-allocation-methodology-china%E2%80%99s.

absolute cap on energy consumption. With such a cap,[9] it would be easier to implement local and national cap-and-trade systems than under the current intensity target.

Despite all these challenges, the new administration under Xi Jinping seems determined to tackle China's environmental problems. The potential and importance of a nation-wide Chinese cap-and-trade scheme cannot be overstated. Not only would it put another 23 percent of global emissions under a cap, dwarfing the EU ETS or the Californian scheme, it would also unlock international climate change negotiations, denying the United States further excuses for inaction. And on the road towards a truly global price for carbon, China's cap-and-trade scheme will play a very important role in its interaction with other existing and emerging emission trading systems in the region.

8.2 Shenzhen, China's first operating ETS pilot

As of November 1st, 2013, only the Shenzhen ETS has already commenced operations, and is therefore an ideal example to examine the characteristics of a Chinese MRV system and its administrative infrastructure.

Shenzhen is a large municipality with a population of 10 million, located adjacent to Hong Kong in Guangdong province, South China. Shenzhen has the status of a "Special Economic Zone" with considerably more legislative autonomy than other municipalities in China. It gained this status in 1979 as part of China's ambitious reform program after the Cultural Revolution and was designed to experiment with free markets and a less regulated economy. This special status greatly benefitted Shenzhen's economic development, and it is now one of China's most developed regions, with annual emissions in the range of 80 million tonnes of CO_2, a per capita GDP of US\$20,000 and per capita emissions of 8 tonnes. This compares with 450 million tonnes of CO_2, US\$45,000 and 12 tonnes respectively for California.

The special status of Shenzhen makes it predestined to run one of the Chinese ETS pilots. However, Shenzhen was initially not listed among the original six ETS pilots, when NDRC was to announce the plan to run the trials in 2011. It took considerable effort from

---

[9] An absolute cap on energy consumption and emissions would likely keep rising for the next few years, with peak emissions projected for the time frame around 2025 (ERI, e.g., Jiang Kejun in an interview with Xinhua: http://news .xinhuanet.com/energy/2013-08/12/c_125151095.htm).

Figure 8.3 Organizational setup of the Shenzhen ETS
Source: Author.

Shenzhen to finally make it on that list, and the fact that Shenzhen is now the first and only scheme already in operation shows the ambition of Shenzhen's administration. The institution in charge of running the ETS is Shenzhen's Development and Reform Commission (DRC), with strong support from the city government and vice-mayor Tang Jie's office (Figure 8.3). Partially thanks to Shenzhen's relative autonomy, the People's Congress of Shenzhen (the legislative body) promulgated the "Provisions on Carbon Emission Management for the Special Economic Zone Shenzhen" as early as October 2012, marking the first and, as of November 1st, 2013, still the only legal framework for running an ETS in China.[10] All other pilots will have to operate based on administrative decrees,[11] limiting their ability to oversee and enforce compliance. As in most of the other Chinese ETS pilots, an Emission Trading Exchange[12] is in charge of administrating all technical aspects of the scheme (including operating the registry, technical aspects of MRV, etc.).

The scheme was launched on June 18, 2013 with a first batch of allowance allocation, and opening of the trading platform for allowances. Guangdong province, to which Shenzhen belongs, has its own ETS pilot. The anomaly of an ETS operating within the administrative and geographical boundaries of another ETS creates a lot of questions, especially in the context of MRV at the company level, some of which will be examined in more detail below.

[10] Several other pilots are currently trying to pass similar laws through legislation.
[11] Administrative decrees are issued by the administration directly, without going through a legislative process. They grant the government the authority to enforce previous legislation by defining procedures without the need for additional legislation. The trade-off is a set of limits, including upper bounds on fines that can be imposed based on administrative decrees.
[12] www.cerx.cn/en/

The Shenzhen ETS covers 635 companies in 26 sectors; about 38 percent of Shenzhen's overall Scope 1 and 2 emissions are under the cap. Further, 197 large public buildings will also be part of the trial ETS, but account for only 1–2 percent of total emissions.

In the first few months following the launch, allowance trading has involved small volumes and has been mostly driven by private speculators who can also register on the exchange. Prices went as high as CNY 130 (€15.50) per permit,[13] prompting concerns from emitters who have mostly held back from trading so far, waiting for more clarity regarding allocation rules and better visibility on compliance obligations.

8.3 Capping direct and indirect emissions

Like the other Chinese ETS pilots, Shenzhen imposes a cap on both Scope 1 (direct emissions) and Scope 2 emissions (indirect emissions from electricity consumption). On the reporting side, this is familiar territory for companies under the cap: for energy intensity reporting under current and previous 5-Year Plans, they had to report both electricity and fuel consumption for several years and these monitoring procedures are well established. Given the heavily regulated nature of the Chinese power sector, it is virtually impossible for electricity producers to pass down costs to consumers without major pricing reforms, which are politically unviable at the moment. Hence the pragmatic solution was to simply include Scope 2 and cap the demand side instead of the supply side.

The anomaly however is the inclusion of power plants into the cap. One can only assume that the Shenzhen government has the long-term ambition to move the cap directly to emission sources (as is the case in other major ETS systems), and that the involved utilities are not too concerned about the short-term costs arising from the inability to pass on costs, and the capacity buildup for a future national ETS is the main motivation for them to participate in the ETS.[14] Among others, the scheme also covers a large utility, SEC, with an installed capacity of 4.6 GW in and around Shenzhen. SEC has also considerable previous

---

[13] CERX: www.szets.com/Portal/home.seam?cid=316722 on October 17, 2013.
[14] Chinese utilities are state-owned and therefore have considerable influence on policy design.

experience with emission trading thanks to its participation in several CDM projects.

The implication of including SEC under the cap is that emitters purchasing electricity from SEC will have to surrender allowances for their Scope 2 emissions, and SEC itself has to surrender allowances again for its Scope 1 emissions resulting from the production of that sold electricity. Moreover, when SEC sells electricity to Guangdong enterprises falling outside of the municipality's jurisdiction, the corresponding Scope 2 emissions will be accounted for within the provincial ETS of Guangdong province according to the draft Guangdong ETS legislation.

This kind of double counting does not harm the effectiveness of the tool in reducing emissions, as long as it is accounted for in the cap setting: the overall cap should indeed consider more than the total emissions covered as some are counted twice. How this is taken into account for the cap setting exactly is an open question and unfortunately not documented publicly, but it can be assumed that provinces and municipalities have procedures for dealing with such double counting issues, since the same questions arise for the energy intensity reporting and accounting under the 5-Year Plans.

For the Guangdong ETS, sources with the Guangdong DRC stated that they are considering modifying their reporting rules for utilities to account only for emissions from self-use. This would avoid the double counting, but, since self-use emissions are extremely minor, questions the inclusion of utilities in the first place. There are no such plans publicly under discussion for Shenzhen.

8.4 MRV and compliance at company level

Prevalent reporting practice under existing regulation prompted Shenzhen policymakers to make the legal person the compliance unit, and not the installation. Again, this design decision is shared by all Chinese ETS pilots. The advantages of this approach are the many synergies with existing reporting infrastructure, previous experience with energy consumption and energy intensity reporting, and the possibility for compliance enforcement based on crosschecks with similar reporting.

The main implication for emitters under the cap is that they can be liable for their emissions occurring outside the physical boundaries of Shenzhen municipality, depending on the ownership structure of assets. Partial ownership and holding structures are not taken into account, and there are many theoretical possibilities for "emission footprint minimization" through the use of project companies, indirect ownership and other legal structures. Contrary to what would happen in a western economy, this possibility of carbon leakage will likely remain theoretical in Shenzhen:

- For one, it is commonly mandatory in China to form a project company for industrial assets, which makes the company-based accounting very similar to the EU ETS installation-based accounting, provided consolidation on group/holding level is not required. The latter point is not yet clear from the published rules.
- Furthermore, the heavily regulated market environment likely creates enough indirect barriers to prevent such behavior.

In some cases, it can also complicate things for the cap setters: there is at least one instance where a company headquartered in Shenzhen has been put under a cap in both the Shenzhen ETS and the Guangdong ETS, although it is operating out of Shenzhen with factories beyond the municipality's borders.

The second implication for MRV in particular is that it provides an additional incentive for emitters to report fuel consumption paired with default emission factors. While the MRV regulations allow for a whole range of different monitoring approaches, including mass balance, modeling or even direct measurements,[15] the "default emission factors" approach is probably the cheapest *per se*. But company-level reporting will reinforce this feature as this approach is likely to fit in best with existing reporting structures for energy consumption and thus further minimize reporting costs for participating emitters.

8.5 Intensity-based cap and allowances

National policy dictates the relative intensity targets in relation to GDP output. These targets are then broken down to provincial targets, and again, at the provincial level, handed down to the municipalities. Shenzhen has accordingly been allocated a target of 21 percent

---

[15] See SZDB/Z 69, 8.1.

reduction in CO_2 emissions per unit of GDP by 2015 compared to 2010 levels. This reduction trajectory is then translated into an absolute number of allowances, which are allocated in advance for the trial phase 2013–2015.

The Shenzhen government will have to intervene in the market to fine-tune the number of allocated allowances in relation to actual GDP output. The "Interim Administrative Measures for Carbon Emission Allowance Trading" specify that up to 10 percent of annual allocations can be bought back by the government, and there is a special fund for such interventions. Likewise, up to 10 percent of the preliminary allocation can be added for an emitter under the cap, if it fulfills its carbon intensity target, but needs additional allowances due to higher than estimated economic output.[16] What would happen if interventions beyond 10 percent of initial allocation were required is not specified in the draft "Interim Measures."

The 2010 emissions of the 635 companies under the cap amount to 31.73 million tons. Allocations in the first phase, which started in mid-2013 and will last into 2015, total around 100 million tons (Figure 8.4).

The result is a 9.6 percent *increase* in total emissions as compared to 2010, which is the baseline year for the 12th 5-Year Plan, but a *decrease* of 23.7 percent in carbon intensity, in line with the reduction targets for Shenzhen municipality.

According to the Shenzhen DRC, allocations will happen in one batch for the entire first pilot phase 2013–2015. Since there is no public registry and no visibility on allocation methodologies, it is impossible to determine exactly how many allowances have been allocated to date. This lack of transparency is a recurring characteristic of all Chinese ETS pilots, and will very likely have major implications on trading activity and behavior of ETS participants.

Intensity-based allowances

The intensity-based cap has implications for the compliance cycle. Emitters under the cap have received or will receive a certain number of allowances either based on their historical emissions, or reported

---

[16] Interim Measures, para 17–20. http://fzj.sz.gov.cn:8080/cms/templates/fzb/ fzbDetails.action?siteName=fzb&pageId=4442

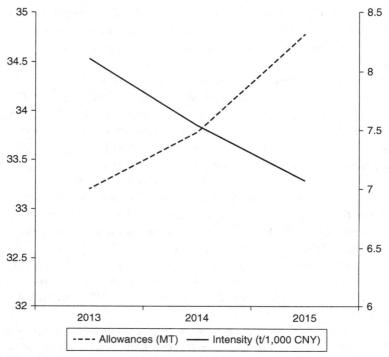

Figure 8.4 Allowance allocation versus carbon intensity
Source: Author. Based on data from National Bureau of Statistics of the People's Republic of China.

expected economic output[17] and carbon intensity of their production (the exact allocation method depends on the sector, but methodologies have not been made public). At the end of the compliance year, however, actual output (profit) and actual carbon intensity of production need to be reported, and the Shenzhen authorities will then adjust the amount of allocated allowances based on actual carbon intensity of a given year. Shenzhen DRC has stated that it will coordinate with utilities and other departments (bureaux of statistics, energy, tax) to crosscheck reported information from enterprises. How exactly that process works has not been disclosed so far. In particular, the process for removing excess allowances will prove crucial for an effective cap.

---

[17] The exact methodology is not published, but likely does not take into account wages and other contributions to the economy.

Box 8.2 Intensity-based allowances for a laptop manufacturer

Company A produces laptops, which it sells for a profit of CNY 500 per unit. Assuming the carbon footprint (production) of one laptop is 100 kg, then the carbon intensity of one laptop is 0.2 kg/CNY or 5,000 CNY/t. Company A expects to produce and sell 100,000 laptops, thus its expected carbon footprint is 10,000 tons and its expected added value (profit) is CNY 50 million. Based on that projection, the allowance allocation system will distribute for free a preliminary allocation of 10,000 allowances to Company A based on its expected production, but locks in the calculated carbon intensity, presumably to a lower value than 0.2 kg/CNY in order to be in line with the overall carbon intensity target.

Now, if Company A produces and sells only 50,000 laptops throughout the year at the same margin, resulting in a profit of CNY 25 million, the amount of allowances will be adjusted based on the locked-in intensity of 5,000 CNY/t, and Company A will only have 5,000 allowances available for compliance at the end of the year. Let's assume the footprint of producing one laptop increases to 200 kg, then the company will actually have to buy 5,000 allowances at the end of the compliance cycle to compensate for the doubled carbon intensity of its products.

This contrasts with the free allowance allocation methods previously used in the EU ETS, where Company A would still have 5,000 excess allowances left if production fell to 50,000 units and emission levels stayed the same.

Consequently, the system works the other way around: if Company A manages to produce and sell more units while maintaining the same carbon intensity, or if it even achieves a lower carbon intensity of its output, it will receive additional allowances from the government which it can use to cover its emissions or sell to other emitters.

Source: Stutz (2010).

8.6 Reporting, confidentiality and disclosure

Observers from Europe frequently identify a lack of transparency as one of the most pressing problems of the emerging Chinese ETS. Indeed, compared to the EU ETS, the amount of publicly available information and interaction of policymakers with stakeholders and participating emitters is relatively low. Also, important information is not made publicly available, such as allocation rules, accreditation criteria for verifiers and details on compliance procedures and surrendering of allowances. The reason for this lack of transparency is often very simple: things are just not ready yet. Being a trial, during the current phase of the Shenzhen ETS, regulation is often created on the spot as a problem occurs, and documented in internal memos for the regulator's eyes only.

A second reason is the fact that emitters are very sensitive about sharing data related to their production, fearing the disclosure of valuable information to their competitors much more than the inconvenience of having no visibility on participating emitters and the overall compliance rate during the compliance cycle. Since the Shenzhen ETS features a carbon-intensity cap, carbon intensity data from the same industry with a comparable product lineup will hint at profit margins. Therefore, there are currently no plans whatsoever to make emission data of individual companies publicly available. The Shenzhen DRC is contemplating whether or not to disclose emission data for the 26 different sectoral scopes throughout the year. But it is possible that, in the end, only aggregated information on compliance levels will be made public, with the result that it will be impossible to directly determine at a given moment during the compliance cycle whether the allowance market is short or long. The allowance price on CERX should nevertheless provide a proxy for the demand/supply equilibrium for allowances.

Taken together with the absence of future contracts (Shenzhen, as well as the other ETS pilots, allows only spot trading in the first phase), a forward price signal, which could influence investment decisions, will hardly establish itself under such circumstances.

8.7 Enforcement of compliance

Shenzhen is the first trial ETS to have a firm legal basis for enforcing compliance with the "Provisions on Carbon Emission Management for the Special Economic Zone Shenzhen,"[18] which went through the municipal legislative body in October 2012. The most important enabling function of this piece of legislation is giving Shenzhen DRC the authority to enforce compliance, and to fine non-complying emitters at three times the market price.[19] Without this additional piece of legislation, the DRC would have been limited to administrative fines, which are capped at CNY 30,000 (€3,500). Compared to the compliance cost, that level of administrative fines is clearly too low. Other ETS pilots lacking such legislation are currently struggling to find ways to allow their local DRC to fine non-complying emitters at a higher rate.

Another way to enforce compliance is to embed it into other administrative procedures where the DRC has more leverage. A good example is the neighboring ETS in Guangdong province, where the DRC makes ETS compliance a prerequisite for approval of any kind of new project for a company. This elevates ETS compliance to the same status as compliance with environmental impact assessment (EIA) regulations and/or final construction acceptance procedures, which are – at least in South China – usually well enforced. Whether Shenzhen plans to adopt similar measures is currently not known.

Apart from these "sticks," there are also "carrots." The Shenzhen Provisions are not very specific in that regard, but they provide a basis for setting incentives for complying companies.[20] Such incentives will likely include preferential access to bank loans (again, following Guangdong's example). The concept of "green credit" is already well established in China, where banks issue loans at preferential interest rates to companies meeting certain "green" criteria. It is likely that continued ETS compliance will also guarantee access to such loans. The Guangdong draft regulations also mention other financial incentives, such as preferential access to provincial-level subsidies and grants.[21]

8.8 MRV ID table

[18] www.sz.gov.cn/zfgb/2013/gb817/201301/t20130110_2099860.htm
[19] The concept of market price has not been defined in exact terms in the Shenzhen Provisions; however, in the draft regulations for Guangdong province, it is defined as the average market price for the compliance year. Shenzhen is likely to adopt that definition as well.
[20] Provisions para 8.
[21] "Guangdong Province Carbon Emission Allowance Management and Trading Regulations," para 21. Currently undergoing stakeholder consultation and not yet published.

Table 8.1 *MRV ID table*

	Context
Regulator	Shenzhen DRC, appointed by People's Congress of Shenzhen (legislative body) as implementing agency.
Type and level of incentive to comply	Preferred access to loans, funding initiatives, etc. Penalty of three times the market price for each metric ton in case of non-compliance.
Entities concerned	635 companies, representing about 38% of Shenzhen's total emissions (Scope 1 and 2); 197 large public buildings, representing about 1–2% of Shenzhen's total emissions.
Sectors concerned	26 sectors in total; most important sectors are power, water & gas (utilities) and manufacturing.
Gases concerned	CO_2 only
Overall MRV costs	Low – during the pilot phase, MRV will be heavily subsidized with resources from DRC, and verification costs only partially to be covered by emitters.

	Monitoring
Rules	SZDB/Z 69[a]
Other reference documents	ISO 14064
Uncertainty requirements	Not yet specified, SZDB/Z 69 para 9.2.2 states no specific requirements beyond the reporting of uncertainty. Uncertainty calculation follows ISO and IPCC guidelines and is only used to improve future reporting quality.

Achieved uncertainty range	Not yet specified, SZDB/Z 69 para 9.2.2 states no specific requirements
Cost range	Negligible – most emitters will likely use fuel consumption and default emission factors, leveraging existing monitoring and reporting infrastructure
Scope	A. Scope 1, 2 B. Operational C. Company-level emissions
Frequency	Annually
Source for activity data	Company monitoring data, documents, purchase contracts, receipts, etc.
Uncertainty range for activity data	N/A
Source for emission factors	SZDB/Z 69 annex F (different sources); Chinese National EFs IPCC values Equipment Manufacturer EFs Direct measurements
Uncertainty range for emission factors	6 Categories from international default EFs (lowest) to measured (highest); however no specific requirements
Direct measurement	Can be used, but no direct incentive to do so (apart from potentially lower EFs)
Incentives to reduce uncertainty	Currently none, SZDB/Z 69 para 9.2.2
Is requirements stringency adapted to the amount of emissions at stake (materiality)?	Not specifically

Table 8.1 (*cont.*)

	Reporting
Rules	SZDB/Z 69 and SZDB/Z 70
Other reference documents	ISO 14064
Format	Electronic and paper (both mandatory); no XETL or data transmission standard, non machine-readable data entry form from regulator
Level of source disaggregation	Company level
Frequency	Annually
Timeline	Annual reporting in Q1
Language	Chinese
Is requirements stringency adapted to the amount of emissions at stake (materiality)?	No
	Verification
Cost range	Minimal – reporting via electronic interface on registry and standard templates on paper
Rules	SZDB/Z 70
Other reference documents	ISO 14064

Format	Electronic and paper (both mandatory); no XETL or data transmission standard, non machine-readable data entry form from regulator
Frequency	Annually
Timeline	Annual verification in Q2
Language	Chinese
Accredited entities for verification	Locally accredited verifiers. No public accreditation standard or procedure
Control of accredited entities	DRC
Cost of accreditation	Accreditation process not public, opaque appointment directly by DRC
Support of accredited entities	DRC
Is requirements stringency adapted to the amount of emissions at stake (materiality)?	No
Cost range	~10,000 CNY (€1,100) per company per year[b]

[a] "Specification with guidance for quantification and reporting of the organization's greenhouse gas emissions," SZDB/Z 69 –2012.
[b] This figure was obtained by informally asking a few verifiers. There are no published verification fees.
Source: Author.

Bibliography

Guan, D., Liu, Z., Geng, Y., Lindner, S. and Hubacek, K., 2012. The giga-tonne gap in China's carbon dioxide inventories. *Nature Climate Change* 2(9): 672–675.

IETA, 2013. The Chinese ETS Pilots: An IETA Analysis, November.

Ohshita, S., Price, L.K. and Zhu, T., 2011. *Target Allocation Methodology for China's Provinces: Energy Intensity in the 12th Five-Year Plan.* China Energy Group, Laurence Berkeley National Laboratory.

Shenzhen Municipality Legal System Office, 2013. Public Consultation for "Interim Administrative Measures for Carbon Emission Allowance Trading." October 29. http://fzj.sz.gov.cn:8080/cms/templates/fzb/fzb-Details.action?siteName=fzb&pageId=4442. Accessed July 2, 2014.

Shenzhen Municipality Market Supervision and Administration Bureau, 2012a. Specification with Guidance for Quantification and Reporting of the Organization's Greenhouse Gas Emissions. SZDB/Z 69.

2012b. Specification with Guidance for Verification of the Organization's Greenhouse Gas Emissions. SZDB/Z 70.

Shenzhen Municipality People's Congress Standing Committee, 2012. Provisions on Carbon Emission Management for the Special Economic Zone Shenzhen. October 30.

The State Council of the People's Republic of China, 2013. The State Council's Announcement Regarding the Publication of the Energy Development Policy Under the 15th 5-Year Plan. *Guofa*, 2. January 1.

Stutz, M., 2010. Carbon Footprint of a Typical Business Laptop From Dell. http://i.dell.com/sites/content/corporate/corp-comm/en/Documents/dell-laptop-carbon-footprint-whitepaper.pdf. Accessed July 2, 2014.

Tianya Forums. Energy Savings and Emission Reductions Thanks to 24/7 Forced Shutdowns 50 Days in a Row: All Enterprises Are on the Brink of Bankruptcy. Discussion on Tianya Forums: http://bbs.tianya.cn/post-develop-470284-1.shtml. Accessed July 2, 2014.

WRI, CAIT 2.0, 2014. Climate Analysis Indicators Tool: WRI's Climate Data Explorer. World Resources Institute, Washington, DC. http://cait2.wri.org. Accessed July 2, 2014.

Xinhuanet, 2013. NDRC Expert: China's Carbon Emissions May Peak Before 2025. August 12. http://news.xinhuanet.com/energy/2013-08/12/c_125151095.htm. Accessed July 2, 2014.

9 | Variant 4: coexistence of voluntary and mandatory frameworks at the company level – Carbon Disclosure Project, EU ETS and French legal requirements

ROMAIN MOREL AND IAN COCHRAN

9.1 Introduction

Some of the earliest greenhouse gas monitoring and reporting has been done by companies and corporations – whether public or private. These companies voluntarily piloted initial quantification and reporting at the corporate level to assess the contribution of their activities to climate change. In the 2000s, with the implementation of emission trading schemes and carbon taxes, the focus shifted to site-level, without necessarily an aggregation at corporate level. To date, little to no full, mandatory, MRV systems have been put into place for corporate reporting – particularly in terms of verification. However, the coexistence of multiple mandatory and voluntary frameworks that companies participate in has implications for the efficiency of the quantification conducted as well as the use of the information in the entities' internal "climate governance."

This chapter first briefly presents three of the main reporting frameworks to which multiple French companies participate in or are subject to.[1] France is a particularly interesting example as it is among the few countries – with the United Kingdom – to have made GHG monitoring and reporting mandatory at the corporate level. The second half of this chapter analyzes the impacts of this coexistence of frameworks on efficiencies and internal governance as well as the implications for a growing type of users of emissions performance data: investors.

---

[1] The fourth one, the EU ETS reporting framework, is described in Chapter 5.

9.2 French entities may be subject to up to four major mandatory or voluntary GHG emissions monitoring and reporting frameworks

In addition to the EU ETS (described in Chapter 5) which covers more than 1,300 French installations, French companies today participate in multiple GHG emission reporting systems. One of the earliest systems is the voluntary CDP Sustainability, formerly known as the Carbon Disclosure Project. In addition, GHG measurement and reporting has been included in statutory sustainable-development reporting requirements (including the Corporate Social and Environmental Responsibility and the mandatory development of Climate Action Plans).

Article 75, a dedicated GHG monitoring and reporting process

History

In 2009 and 2010, France passed the "Grenelle I" and "Grenelle II" laws. This legislation set a framework and implemented a number of objectives and priorities for public policies on environmental subjects. As part of the larger climate policy strategy, Article 75 of the Grenelle II law[2] requires greenhouse gas reporting for companies and government bodies. This information is to be used in the development of a Climate Action Plan to mitigate GHG emission.

Entities concerned

Entities concerned by this law are:

- private legal entities with more than 500 employees;[3]
- local governments with more than 50,000 inhabitants;
- public entities with more than 250 employees.

For private companies, the requirement applies at the legal entity level: no corporate consolidation of subsidiaries is required. To facilitate and harmonize reporting, the French environment ministry released a methodological guide (MEDDE, 2012). Reporting Scope 1 and Scope 2 emissions is mandatory for all entities, whereas Scope

[2] Law n° 2010–788 of July 12, 2010.
[3] 250 in overseas territories.

3 is only "recommended". For public entities, the reporting is limited to their assets (e.g., buildings) and jurisdictional competencies (e.g., wastewater treatment for cities).

GHG quantification is to be conducted at least every three years, with reporting of information required every third year. After the first reporting period, however, neither public nor private entities have fully complied with this requirement. By mid-2013, only half (49 percent) of covered private entities had communicated their GHG emission levels. Fewer public entities (28 percent) and local authorities (26 percent) had met the first deadline of December 31, 2012 (ADEME, 2013). In general, large companies complied more often than small and medium companies. Compliance also varied along sectoral lines: industry complies more often than services, with the exception of one specific service: transportation. The comparatively high level of reporting of transportation actors may be due to expected new sectoral regulation on carbon labeling of transport services.

Scope 3 emissions

The Environment and Energy Management Agency (ADEME) has released several sets of sectoral guidelines for Scope 3 emissions, elaborated together with representative organizations of the relevant sectors.

In the first reporting exercise, Scope 3 emissions were – at least partially – reported by less than half of private companies. On average, these companies account between four and six sources of emissions. The most reported sources of emissions are:

- upstream emissions from energy production (i.e., fugitive gas);
- emissions for the production of purchased products and services;
- fixed assets (amortization of emissions from the construction of buildings, roads, heavy machinery, etc.);
- waste treatment;
- upstream transport of goods;
- professional travel;
- employee commuting.

The most common rationale for not reporting Scope 3 emissions is the cost – in time or investment – of data collection and the fact that reporting Scope 3 emissions has not been perceived as a priority due to a lack of direct control over the sources (ADEME, 2014).

Verification

There is currently no sanction if a subject entity does not report its emissions. Further, there are no plans to require external verification of reported emissions. Nevertheless, 51 percent of reporting private entities used an external consultant to assess their carbon footprint. No specific information is available concerning the level of verification conducted.

Article 225, a broader reporting process on corporate social and environmental responsibility

History

Since 2001, France has required companies to report on their "Corporate Social and Environmental Responsibility" (CSER) as part of the "NRE" law.[4] Under this framework, listed companies are required to report on CSER on a yearly basis, including GHG emissions. This law has led to the publication of dedicated annual reports. This regulation was modified in 2010 by Article 225 of the "Grenelle 2" legislative package and the decrees specifying its implementation have been slowly released. In 2012, as part of this broader reporting framework, GHG emissions was made one of 42 mandatory indicators along with employment, training, equality, etc. (MJL, 2012). It is likely that this framework will further evolve with the transposition of the April 2013 European Commission directive on the publication of non-financial data for companies.

Entities concerned

CSER reporting required by Article 225 of the Grenelle 2 law expands to:

- companies[5] with listed stocks or bonds;
- companies with more than 500 employees and an annual income or assets worth more than €100 million.

When a given legal entity within a group fulfills these requirements alone, the data must be disclosed both at the group and at the legal

---

[4] «Nouvelles régulations économiques» or "New Economic regulations".
[5] Sociétés anonymes (SA), Sociétés en commandite par actions (SCA) and sociétés européennes (SE).

entity level. Studies on listed companies (indexes CAC40[6] and SBF120[7]) show that GHG emissions is one of the most reported CSER indicators. This high rate of reporting is mainly explained by the existence of other reporting frameworks such as Article 75 and the CDP (MEDDE and OREE, 2013). There are no data available on smaller companies given that they have had up to two additional years to comply with the reporting requirements.

While there is no official methodology, the perimeter of accounting and reporting has been defined: all consolidated and controlled entities, as defined by the relevant financial reporting regulation,[8] shall be accounted, no matter whether or not they fulfill the reporting threshold (MEDEF, 2012).

Scope 3 emissions

Reporting Scope 3 emissions is not mandatory under Article 225. No monitoring methodology is provided by the regulator for Scope 3. Only a small share of listed companies (15 percent) has reported Scope 3 emissions. Given that listed companies typically report more often and on a broader range of subjects than average, it can be hypothesized that potentially a smaller share of all companies may report Scope 3 emissions.

Verification

Within this reporting framework, the law defines verification as the external assessment of completeness (whether all issues are addressed) and "good faith" (whether information is comprehensive and coherent) (MJL, 2013). Compared to most other MRV frameworks on GHG emissions, this is minimal and imprecise. It does not refer to any specific methodology or norm for calculation of GHG emissions. The only reference, given by the accrediting entity, is the norm NF EN ISO/ CEI 17020 related to general conformity assessment.

---

[6] The CAC40 is a benchmark French stock market index of the 40 most significant values among the 100 highest market caps on the Euronext Paris stock exchange.

[7] A French stock market index based on the 120 most actively traded stocks listed in the Euronext Paris stock exchange.

[8] Financial regulations define "consolidated and controlled entities" on the basis of criteria such as the amount of shares owned by the holding and whether the holding has operational control over the entity.

The national decree formalizing the verification process was published in 2013 only with the accreditation process starting in June 2013 (MJL, 2013). Nevertheless, 73 percent of SBF120 companies have had their broader CSER declarations already verified – at least partially – for 2012. In most cases (87 percent), the companies that have verified their declaration chose one of their financial auditors to conduct the verification (Deloitte, 2013). Among them, one third had their CSER data verified for the first time in 2012. AMF[9] (2013) reports that of the 41 percent of companies that verified data, 91 percent were large companies. In the absence of specific guidance for verification (e.g., a methodology or a procedural norm such as ISO specifically on estimating GHG emissions), it is difficult to draw substantial conclusions from these figures, especially compared with other MRV processes studied in this book.

CDP Sustainability (former Carbon Disclosure Project), a global reporting process for major companies

History

CDP Sustainability (formerly known as the Carbon Disclosure Project) works with private companies and local governments on integrating climate change into their activities and governance. With a membership of over 700 institutional investors in 2013, the CDP has developed a voluntary reporting system to centralize standardized climate change, water and forest information from companies. These efforts are based in the CDP's belief that transparency on environmental risks – including greenhouse gas emissions – is an important step in fostering a systemic change in the global economy. First, the provision of disclosed GHG data – for example through different mainstream platforms such as Bloomberg Terminal – helps to ensure that the financial community has access to corporate climate change information necessary to drive investment flows towards low-carbon, sustainable projects and companies. Second, ensuring that companies are aware of and measuring their environmental risk is an important step to improving strategic management. Since its creation over a decade ago, the CDP has built an annual reporting platform used by thousands of

[9] The Autorité des Marchés Financiers (AMF) regulates participants and products in France's financial markets.

companies, whether medium-sized enterprises or large publicly traded corporations.

Entities concerned

CDP Sustainability does not place restrictions on which entities are eligible to use their platform to disclose their GHG emissions and larger climate strategy. Currently, CDP runs programs for corporations as well as for cities. Reporting includes both information on the company's annual greenhouse gas emissions, as well as a description of mitigation, adaptation and broad climate strategy of the company. The CDP allows corporate entities to choose their own perimeter for emission consolidation and reporting.[10] Nevertheless, entities are requested to be consistent in using the same perimeter throughout the disclosure reporting (CDP, 2013b).

Motivations/incentives for reporting

In each case, the decision to participate is voluntary. Nevertheless, on behalf of its member institutional investors,[11] the CDP annually invites the world's largest companies listed on the Global 500 (81 percent responding) to participate. In 2012, over 4,100 companies responded to its survey.[12] In France, companies making up 89 percent of the French stock market capitalization disclosed their GHG emissions and internal climate policy.

The CDP has identified a range of different reasons as to why it is in the interest of companies to report, including:

- answer shareholders' request to provide comparable and relevant climate data;
- identify greenhouse gas emission reduction opportunities;
- take a leadership position on understanding climate change risk;
- demonstrate how a company innovates in this area;
- communicate the climate change resilience of a company.

---

[10] The CDP reporting framework allows respondents to choose between financial control, operational control, equity share or a self-defined "Other" approach to consolidating emissions.

[11] In 2013, the CDP's signatory institutional investors represented over US$87 trillion in assets.

[12] Including 81% of the Global 500, 69% of the S&P 500 and 78% of the South Africa 100 companies: https://www.cdp.net/en-US/Programmes/Pages/CDP-Investors.aspx

The CDP places great emphasis on the mandate it holds on its member institutional investors to collect and transparently report these data. Over the past few years, the CDP has begun to work with a number of research, governmental and investor organizations to create the Carbon Disclosure Standards Board which is developing a *Climate Change Reporting Framework* to foster the integration of GHG and broader climate change reporting into annual financial reporting to facilitate investor access to this information (see Box 9.1).

The CDP issues a large number of reports on the information disclosed by companies. However, to date, little information has been available concerning differences in reporting between major national and international corporations versus smaller corporate entities involved in disclosure.

Scope 3 emissions

Institutions that choose to disclose are required to follow a reporting framework; however, they are free to use a large number of greenhouse gas quantification methodologies as well as in-house rules on perimeter of reporting.[13] The CDP nevertheless recognizes and advocates the WRI/WBCSD GHG Protocol as the principal source for methodological guidance. Entities are requested to indicate which quantification method has been used in their exercise.

The CDP requests that corporate actors report their Scope 3 emissions, indicating which subcategories are relevant to their business, and then disclosing and explaining any exclusion.[14] For the reporting of Scope 3 emissions, the CDP calls attention to the existence of the World Resources Institute and World Business Council for Sustainable

---

[13] "CDP makes no judgments on standards or methodologies applied by companies to produce their inventories. As such, it is impossible for CDP to explicitly accept/reject a specific calculation methodology. We expect that any tool used to calculate emissions for an inventory will follow the best practice and that it will adhere to good practice, and observe important aspects such as the accuracy and completeness principles of standards like the GHG Protocol".

CDP (2013b:86)

[14] Suggested Scope 3 subcategories include: Purchased goods and services; Capital goods; Fuel-and-energy-related activities (not included in Scope 1 or 2); Upstream transportation and distribution; Waste generated in operations; Business travel; Employee commuting; Upstream leased assets; Investments; Downstream transportation and distribution; Processing of sold products; Use of sold products; End of life treatment of sold products; Downstream leased assets; Franchises; Other (upstream); Other (downstream).

Development's Corporate Value Chain (Scope 3) Accounting and Reporting Standard as a supplement to the GHG Protocol Corporate Accounting and Reporting Standard. While this is used as the basis for its guidance, it does not specifically require, however, that institutions use this methodology.

The CDP has found that in practice Scope 3 emissions quantification and reporting remains limited. Further, the CDP indicates that instead of measuring carbon-intensive activities in their value chain, companies often focus mitigation activities on less significant emission sources (See Figure 9.1). As noted by the CDP in its 2013 *Global 500 Climate Change Report*, in 2012, "current reporting of indirect Scope 3 emissions does not reveal the full impact of companies' value chain" (CDP, 2013a: 7). While of the company reporting studies, 97% disclose Scope 1 and 2 emissions from their operations, only 53% quantify their broader "value chain" (including upstream and downstream emission sources). Further, the CDP indicates that instead of measuring carbon-intensive activities in their value chain, companies often focus mitigation activities on less significant emission sources (see Figure 9.1). For example, only 25% of companies report emission data for "use of sold products;" however, it is estimated that this represents up to 76% of Scope 3 emissions. Conversely, 72% of companies report business travel related emissions accounting for only an estimated 0.2% of total reported Scope 3 emissions (CDP, 2013a: 9). Finally, for financial companies, only 6% reported emissions from their investment activity as opposed to an 83% reporting rate on business travel. Further, in France in 2012, only 16% of companies quantified and disclosed more than half of their Scope 3 emissions.

The CDP does not elaborate on why different sectors are focused on over others. This appears directly linked to both the difficulties in gathering the necessary data for full Scope 3 reporting as well as the relative ease for companies to influence Scope 3 emissions (i.e., direct control over business travel versus limited ability to influence the carbon intensity of sourced upstream materials).

Verification

As part of its questionnaire, the CDP requests disclosing companies to indicate whether they have verified the emissions data reported.[15]

---

[15] Companies are given the option to declare the following concerning verification of each scope of emissions: No emissions data provided; No third

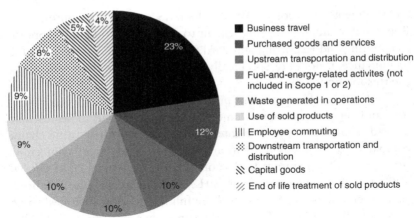

Figure 9.1 Ten most common Scope 3 categories (with emissions data) reported to CDP
Source: Based on CDP (2013a: 43).

While verification is not required to finalize disclosure for CDP purposes, the CDP nevertheless has taken steps to ensure that, when it occurs third-party verification activities undertaken by companies are broadly comparable. As such, CDP requires verification to be completed in accordance with one of the approximately 30 verification standards recognized by the CDP.[16] The CDP's criteria for third-party verification standards include:

- **Relevance:** The standard should specify that it relates to a third party audit or verification process; for a program-related standard, third party verification should be specified as part of the program compliance.
- **Competency:** The standard should include a statement regarding competency of verifiers; where it is a program and verification

party verification or assurance; No third party verification or assurance – regulatory CEMS required; Third party verification or assurance under way but not yet complete – first year it has taken place; Third party verification or assurance under way but not yet complete – last year's statement available; Third party verification or assurance complete.

[16] These include verification under the EU Emission Trading Scheme (EU ETS) Directive and the EU ETS related national implementation laws; the Tokyo Emission Trading Scheme; DNV Verisustain Protocol/Verification Protocol for Sustainability Reporting; the Climate Registry's General Verification Protocol (also known as California Climate Action Registry (CCAR)); etc. A full list of accepted verification standards is available on the CDP website at https://www.cdp.net/en-US/Respond/Pages/verification-standards.aspx

parties are stipulated, competency is assumed to be determined by the second party and therefore need not be explicit in the standard.

- **Independence:** The standard should contain a requirement that ensures that impartiality is maintained in cases where the same external organization compiles and verifies a responding company's inventory.
- **Terminology:** The standard should specify the meaning of any terms used for the level of the finding (e.g., limited assurance; reasonable assurance).
- **Methodology:** The standard should describe a methodology for the verification that includes the verification of the process and/or system controls and the data.
- **Availability:** The standard should be available for scrutiny.

(CDP, 2014)

Concisely, verification is focused on procedures rather than on the accuracy or comparability of the reported figures. As such, and similarly to article 225, CDP verification is very different from verification in most of the carbon pricing mechanisms described in this book.

Furthermore, the CDP has created the CDP Verification Partnership with partner organizations to facilitate the access of companies to third-party certification services.

Among the 403 Global 500 companies reporting in 2012, 270 (67 percent) reported having verification/assurance processes approved or under way for at least a portion of their emissions (CDP, 2013a: 43). It should, however, be noted that even if verification has occurred, this does not ensure that companies in similar market segments are using similar reporting perimeters. Further, information on whether each of the 270 companies had verified all emission data is not provided.

Each year, the CDP analyzes companies' responses to the questionnaire and scores them against two parallel schemes: disclosure and performance. The disclosure score assesses the completeness and quality of a company's response, while the performance score assesses the level of action, as reported by the company, on climate change mitigation, adaptation and transparency. This information is used to rank companies within two indexes: the Carbon Disclosure Leadership Index and the Carbon Performance Leadership Index.

The information reported by companies responding to the annual questionnaire is not required to be systematically verified. Nevertheless, the completeness of a company's response is "graded" on disclosure using a points system.[17] To achieve full points, companies must respond to all questions relevant to their business – and indicate why certain questions are not considered relevant/not calculated. Further, to be included in the Carbon Disclosure Leadership Index, companies must score maximum disclosure points for verification of Scope 1 and Scope 2 emissions. Points are linked to the percentage of emissions verified as well as reporting information on the type of verification or assurance used, the relevant standard and the submission of the verification statement as issued by the verifier (necessary to gain full points).

Box 9.1 Carbon Disclosure Standards Board's Climate Change Reporting Framework

CDP Sustainability has partnered with seven other business and environmental organizations to develop a voluntary reporting framework. This Climate Change Reporting Framework is designed to expand mainstream financial reporting to include climate change-related information. The framework has been developed to filter out for investors the information necessary to understand how climate change affects a company's financial performance.

This framework recognizes that value creation is correlated with disclosure of climate risk, greenhouse gas emissions and mitigation and adaptation activities. As such, the framework can assist corporate entities to understand how climate change can affect their performance. In turn, this information can be used to identify and address the actions to be taken to address the risks and opportunities.

Once disclosed as part of the larger financial reporting exercise, this information can assist investors to make informed decisions based on climate change-related opportunities and risks disclosed by a company. Further, the CDSB expects that analysts will be able to use disclosed climate-related information in determining impacts on future cash flow and ultimately company valuations.

Source: Based on www.cdsb.net/cdsb-reporting-framework.

---

[17] The CDP ranking methodology bases a significant percentage of the scores on verification: 9–13 percent of total points under the disclosure score and 15–17 percent of total possible points under the performance score. https://www.cdp.net/en-US/Respond/Pages/verification.aspx

9.3 MRV ID table

The MRV ID table is given in Table 9.1.

9.4 Four frameworks may be too many, even though they are flexible enough to be synergetic with one another

While the reporting frameworks presented above share many similarities and synergies, a few "incompatible" elements can be identified: reporting frequency, and to a lesser extent, the incentive to use French-specific emissions factors under Article 75. In addition, as explored in this section, it appears that most reporting systems and companies are converging on how they report Scopes 1 and 2 emissions. However, a number of differences remain concerning the perimeter of reporting as well as data consolidation and the need for further development of Scope 3 methods.

This section looks at the resulting differences, first identifying what inefficiencies have been noted by companies to result from them. Second, these issues are linked with the risk management and internal governance of the company to understand the feedback between GHG reporting and the use of the resulting information. The second half of this section will focus specifically on the case of Scope 3 emission reporting which remains a contentious topic for a number of private companies.

Convergence with Scope 1 and 2 emissions and synergies between frameworks

Race to the top

In terms of methodologies, the definition of scopes and the choice of perimeter, companies may be subject to "explicit" or "implicit" standard practices. "Explicit" standard practices are the specific methodologies, norms or choices of reported perimeters recommended or required by the organization in charge of organizing GHG reporting processes (such as the European Commission, ministries or public agencies for mandatory frameworks). "Implicit" standard practices are used when there is no explicit standard practice, and emerge with actors' interpretation of recommended guidelines and the practices of others.

Today, it appears that Scopes 1 and 2 emissions are increasingly easier to monitor and the methodologies used by different companies

Table 9.1 *MRV ID table*

	Article 225	Article 75	CDP disclosure
Type of reporting	Mandatory (no sanction but shareholder may request the report)	Mandatory (no sanction)	Voluntary
If voluntary: Motivations for reporting	Mandatory	Mandatory	Reputation and framed as a request from investors
Conditions for reporting	- Companies with listed stocks or bonds - Companies (SA, SCA, SCE) that have: - an income or a balance-sheet higher than €100m - more than 500 employees	- Private entities with more than 500 employees - Local authorities with more than 50k inhabitants - Public entities with more than 250 employees	No criteria for eligibility
Overall MRV costs	No data available	No data available	No data available. [a]€77,000 [17,000–363,000] per company per year for UK listed companies, including not only CDP but all relevant reporting frameworks (e.g., EU ETS, CRC, etc. when applicable) according to PWC and CDP (2007).

Reporting entity	Eligible legal entity by default and group under specific conditions with detailed information by entity	Legal entity (n°siren) (if a legal entity has several entities (n°siret) under one same n°siren, only one reporting)	Alignment on financial control boundary definition between the GHG Protocol and Climate Disclosure Standards Board. Companies using the Climate Change Reporting Framework (CCRF) should select financial control as their boundary in question 8.1
Minimum scope and incentives to expand the scope	Scope 1–2/None	Scope 1–2/None	Voluntary: Scopes 1, 2 and 3, reporting on all three scopes required to be included in the Climate Disclosure Leaders Index
Geographical scope	Same geographical scope as financially consolidated data	France only	Worldwide
Frequency of reporting	Annual	Every 3 years	Annual
Rules for measurement	None	Methodology based on ISO 14064-1. By default, emission factors shall come from the official database *Base Carbone*®. However, any documented emission factor is accepted. Official guidelines have been released.	Up to the reporting entity. Guidance based on WRI/WBCSD methodologies and protocols; however, a long list of other methods is accepted.

Table 9.1 (*cont.*)

	Article 225	Article 75	CDP disclosure
Uncertainty requirements and incentives to reduce uncertainty	No/None	The entity shall provide quantitative or qualitative considerations about uncertainty.	The reporting framework requests that reporting companies indicate the relative uncertainty around the emission levels reported. This estimate of uncertainty is divided between the different scopes.
Incentive for verification	Mandatory	None	CDP recommends verification; however, it is not required. Nevertheless, to be considered for their Leadership Indexes, companies must provide information on why verification did or did not occur, indicate the methodology used and provide the verifier's report if relevant.
Is requirements stringency adapted to the amount of emissions at stake (materiality)?	No, except for inclusion thresholds ("conditions for reporting").	No, except for inclusion thresholds ("conditions for reporting").	No
Verifying entity	Accredited by COFRAC	N/A	The CDP has developed a Partnership with verifiers to facilitate access to these services. Verification partners include: Bureau Veritas, LRQA, PricewaterhouseCoopers, SGS and TÜV NORD.

[a] These figures come from company surveys and were converted to euros using the 2010 average exchange rate of €1.17 per pound.

differ less and less. Gradually, as companies are compared with their peers – companies in the same sector, region and/or financial index – or tend to employ the same consulting firms for their reporting and verification, "implicit" standard practices emerge for comparable companies: similar methodologies and scopes end up being chosen by similar companies. Therefore, for most sectors and systems, accepted explicit and implicit standard practices are becoming widespread for Scopes 1 and 2 emissions. On the other hand the GHG emissions reported under Scope 3 do not show the same level of convergence.

For example, at the international level, the GHG Protocol is perceived as the reference for GHG quantification – explicitly identified as the recommended methodology to use by the CDP. While no official guidelines are in place, increasingly the use of other methodologies is seen to deviate from the common practice. To minimize errors of comparison between companies, actors may see using the implicit standard as less risky. The common use of the GHG Protocol helps in homogenizing reporting categories and the definition of scopes (reporting), and equally provides guidance to harmonize monitoring and quantification. However, as opposed to the exhaustive and directive Monitoring and Reporting Regulation attached to the EU ETS, the GHG Protocol provides only limited guidance for specific sources and industries. The GHG Protocol is more akin to the IPCC Good Practice Guidance for national GHG inventories insomuch as it is up to each corporation to interpret and adapt the guidelines to the available data, reporting perimeter, etc. As such, the reported emissions, especially under Scope 3 for which the guidance is the least detailed, may significantly differ from same-sector companies following the availability of data, technical choices made and the willingness to disclose what could be perceived as sensitive information on upstream emissions.

Furthermore, country-specific preferences for methodologies may differ from international practice on certain technical issues. For example, at the French level, the evaluation of the first reporting period of the Article 75 system demonstrated that a majority of companies use the French method "Bilan Carbone®" (57 percent).[18] Also, the suggested guidelines for Article 75 reporting refer to an official

---

[18] However, it is possible that smaller companies are overrepresented in this category.

French emission factors database – known as "*Base Carbone*" – with the request that the use of other emission factors should be justified and documented.

Therefore, a given company may be exposed to multiple explicit or implicit standard practices. The coordination of those practices at the company level can be challenging at first. In some cases, modifications to existing information systems may be required to make the marginal cost of monitoring relatively lower for each new framework. However, as the existing frameworks are very flexible in terms of monitoring method, the most demanding framework could become the baseline standard for all reporting exercises across the same reporting perimeter (race to the top). Therefore, it could be expected that the extra costs related to different new frameworks tend to decrease over time with the learning curve – e.g., information systems are improved to respond to more detailed reporting requirements.

On the other hand, some companies have voluntarily expanded the coverage of the most demanding framework, increasing the cost of MRV. For example, some companies reported using the EU ETS MRV guidelines in other regional areas than the EU.

Reporting perimeters: many synergies and a few incoherent requirements with higher impact in the first reporting years

Many synergies can be identified between reporting frameworks. For example, companies participating in CDP disclosure are generally subject simultaneously to the Article 225 system in France. Moreover, the perimeter of the analysis – the entire Group for example – is similar for both reporting frameworks. Small divergences on the integration of financially or operationally controlled subsidiaries may occur, with potentially detailed data on specific subsidiaries mandatory under Article 225. Nevertheless, the mandatory work undertaken under Article 225 could be used for reporting under CDP.

The synergies between the CDP and Article 225 exist as well in the verification process. Indeed, verification is meant to be mandatory under Article 225 and is enhanced by better scores under the CDP. As the scopes and methodologies are relatively similar, any verification process can be common to both reporting systems. Moreover, the practice shows that companies' financial auditors are usually designated as verifiers (Deloitte, 2013). For Article 225, the verifiers must be accredited by the COFRAC.[19] In early 2014 the "Haut Conseil du commissariat aux comptes" released the standard that frames the use of financial auditors as third-party verifiers for CSER (AGEFI, 2014).

However, synergies between Articles 75 and 225 are potentially lower, especially in stratified and international companies. Indeed, Article 75 aims to assess only emissions occurring on French territory and disaggregated by legal entity. The guidelines on carbon footprint analysis under Article 225 are less developed and detailed than for Article 75. More than two thirds of large companies (over 10,000 employees) assess this distinction by legal entity as "difficult" or "very difficult" to operate under Article 75 (ADEME, 2014). Therefore, the initial cost of reporting under Article 75 is potentially high compared with other frameworks but improvements in the reporting process and the information system shall substantially reduce it. The higher level of disaggregation and detail of Article 75 might help to improve the reporting under Article 225 and the CDP. The same could be said of the EU ETS. However, as the perimeter of Article 75 and the EU ETS are limited to France and the EU respectively, the related improvements may be limited to the French and European parts of Article 225 and CDP reporting.

Frequency and compliance: improving synergies between systems

The reporting cycles of the different systems analyzed vary. Reporting for the Article 75 requirement occurs every three years from date of entry into the system[20] and annually for Article 225, the ETS and the CDP disclosure. As such, added Article 75 reporting costs are potentially limited by the lower frequency of reporting and facilitated by similar, annual reporting exercises. However, as Article 75 tends to have more specific requirements, in particular regarding the disaggregation of emissions by entity, this difference in reporting frequency may create an incompatibility. Firms may indeed end up with two incompatible reporting procedures if it is more costly to report annually under Article 75 than to use two different reporting procedures: a

---

[19] *Comité Francais d'Accréditation.* French entity that provides accreditation to controlling entities on various topics. The decree on verification under Article 225 was released in June 2013 (MJL, 2013), so 2012 data were verified by non-accredited entities.

[20] NB: The frequency of reporting is currently under discussion as of mid-2014 and may be modified to be coherent with other reporting schemes, notably on energy efficiency.

simpler annual one for Article 225 and CDP and a more complex one every three years for Article 75.

A number of issues appear to affect an entity's compliance with the reporting frameworks. Currently, non-reporting entities are subject to sanctions only under the EU ETS. Nevertheless, those entities (in general large companies) that have already reported their GHG emissions tend to comply more frequently with other French reporting requirements. Unsurprisingly, the size of companies influences both their rate of compliance under the regulation and the methodologies they may choose. As mentioned above, listed companies have been obligated to conduct carbon footprint analysis since 2001 (Law "NRE"). The CDP started in 2002 and reinforced this need to assess carbon footprint, often targeting the largest listed companies on international and national exchanges. Some of these companies may also be subject to reporting under the EU ETS. When Articles 225 and 75 were passed in 2010, those companies with a history of reporting were better prepared and this can be seen as well in the rate of compliance increasing with the size of companies. This also explains why more time was given for smaller companies to comply. However, some listed companies have raised protest about the additional work requested by Article 75 (ADEME, 2014).

Thus, given that companies that have already been involved in existing systems tend to be more likely to comply with new reporting requirements, it seems necessary to ensure coherence between different reporting schemes. Indeed, different perimeters, required desegregation and frequency of reporting may lead to new added costs. The alignment of reporting schemes can facilitate companies' compliance and allow the exploitation of synergies between frameworks – even those not directly concerning GHG emissions. For example, it is still unknown whether future European regulations – especially the energy efficiency directive – on mandatory GHG and energy audits will further complicate the harmonization between regulations.

Internal coordination to respond to reporting requirements
As seen above, the level of reporting can vary significantly between frameworks. It is:

- at the installation level for the EU ETS;
- at the legal entity level for Article 75 and Article 225;
- at the group level for the CDP and Article 225.

Therefore, the same corporate entity or group may be willing to report at these three levels to comply with mandatory and mainstream voluntary frameworks. The reporting also occurs in different contexts: broader CSER and annual reports for Article 225; annual operational compliance for the EU ETS; specific mandatory GHG report for Article 75; and communication to investors for the CDP.

In practice, the degree of synergy and resource sharing is variable between entities (ADEME, 2013). In some cases, a single team at the corporate level is in charge of all these GHG reporting frameworks, whereas in others, multiple teams from the different entities concerned are providing their own response to these different reporting frameworks.

When the reporting entity is a group, a centralized reporting team can be implemented with the support of on-site teams to provide data. The information comes from a broad number of operational sources – different countries, branches, sites. For example, in the ETS, the contact can be common for different installations of the same company or different contacts per installation of the same group can be observed.

A lack of coordination between different reporting teams may lead them to require the same activity data at different times. This may be exacerbated by the use of different quantification methodologies and reporting perimeters (scopes, etc.) which in turn require different treatment of data.

Differing influences on company governance: case of Scope 3 reporting

Depending on the larger GHG reporting framework, companies pay a higher or lower level of attention to different parts of the GHG MRV process. For example, given that the CDP and Article 225 are directly linked with the investor communication, the reporting process is regulated as any other piece of financial communication. Therefore, communication and risk departments are usually involved in a validation process, but can equally be involved upstream in the definition of the monitoring process.

Comparability vs. information relevance trade-off: the risks of reporting with "alternative" methodologies, scopes and perimeters

The main risk for companies is reputational or "headline" risk. The incidence of "bad press" or communication may have financial implications, especially when investors are targets of the communication in question. For example, the CDP uses company reporting to rank disclosure on performance and transparency. In general, a good ranking can be perceived as an opportunity as investors are encouraged to invest in more transparent and efficient companies. However, a negative rank may discourage certain kinds of investors – notably Socially Responsible Investors (SRI) – and feed a communication campaign against the company.

Therefore, any divergence from the – explicit or implicit – standard practice, particularly in terms of the reporting perimeter, becomes a risk. It is important to note that a number of companies have expressed complaints about the CDP ranking process, particularly given the insufficient standardization of monitoring and reporting across competitors. Companies indeed have a lot of leeway in reporting: they set their own perimeter and also choose their own method to monitor activity data and emission factors. They can use this large margin of flexibility to their advantage. If the use of more rigorous methodologies or a broader definition of emission scopes by a company results in higher emission totals, the company runs the risk of appearing less efficient than its competitors. Conversely, if the methodological choices result in lower emissions than sector averages without a clear indication of how higher levels of efficiency were achieved, the company runs the risk of being accused of cherry-picking methodologies and scope to improve its results instead of implementing actions.

Today this may be most evident in the choice made in reporting Scope 3 emissions. The methodologies used for Scope 3 emissions are more complex and less standardized than methodologies on Scopes 1 and 2. As such, a company going beyond current sector practice in terms of reporting Scope 3 emissions would potentially be compared with companies reporting only a little more than emissions from Scopes 1 and 2. Thus, they could be seen in a negative light. Discussions both in France – in the case of the Article 75 and 225 frameworks – and internationally through CDP and the GHG Protocol more broadly remain contentious in terms of Scope 3 reporting.

Being prepared for more ambitious methodologies and scope is an asset: a business case for addressing Scope 3 emissions
In order to better anticipate future standards or to implement risk-adapted action plans, a company may choose to monitor Scope

3 emissions while the industry standard may focus only on Scopes 1 and 2. There is an implicit difference between a company measuring Scope 3 emissions, but choosing only to report publicly Scopes 1 and 2 emissions, versus being unable or unwilling to measure Scope 3 emissions altogether.

A single – but influential – actor within a sector may evolve the standard and then translate its readiness to a competitive advantage. For example, in France, the calculation of financed emissions – the main part of a bank's Scope 3 emissions – started in earnest between 2007 and 2008. The first steps were taken by the *Caisse d'Epargne Group* that decided to give environmental grades to the financial products it sold in order to anticipate an expected regulation on carbon labeling. Both NGOs and the French Environment Agency (ADEME) were involved in the development of the methodology applied. When a ranking of banks according to their financed emissions was released by NGOs in 2010 – and even though the carbon label regulation project was abandoned by the French government – *Caisse d'Epargne* was better prepared to answer external critics concerning its GHG performance.

Discussions on standardized methodologies to calculate financed emissions have gained speed with a number of initiatives launched in 2013–2014: at the international level UNEP-FI and the World Resources Institute as well as nationally in France through the ADEME, ORSE[21] and ABC.[22] As a result, as explicit and implicit standards evolve and take shape, not being ready to report Scope 3 emission levels can increasingly be perceived as a risk.

Ensuring usefulness: reporting seen as a burden rather than an opportunity

The complexity of the regulation may also influence the use of results internally. The first GHG footprint analysis made for financial communication gave a broader idea of the strengths and weaknesses of companies linked to GHG emissions. It enabled companies to start internal reflection on GHG and energy dependencies. However, Article 75 – especially its declination by legal entity and its restriction to

[21] *Observatoire de la Responsabilité Sociétale des Entreprise* – a French association whose membership is made up of economic and financial actors looking at sustainable development and CSER issues.

[22] *Association Bilan Carbone* – the association charged with the development and maintenance of the Bilan Carbone tool.

French domestic emissions – has been critiqued particularly by large companies as not being adapted to the design and implementation of an action plan at the business unit level (ADEME, 2014): several business units may be represented in the same legal entity while at the same time each business unit is active across several legal entities. In that case – a rather common one – Article 75 reporting is difficult to use when assessing the effectiveness of action plans at the business unit level. Another case of low relevance occurs when the action plan is implemented worldwide: a less disaggregated framework encompassing a larger geographical scope would then be more useful to reporters.

Whereas operational implications of the EU ETS or CDP reporting are rather obvious in terms of carbon costs or environmental communications, how to turn Article 75 reporting into an economic opportunity is unclear.

Nevertheless, multiple companies explicitly indicate that GHG monitoring informs their strategic decisions on the evolution of their operations and customers, notably linked with energy prices. When energy consumption is included in the core of their business models, companies already had implemented energy management for their production process (ADEME, 2013). In that case, a broader analysis, integrating for example the supply chain and the use of products, could be fed by quantified Scope 3 emissions. This reflection has been integrated by several building-sector actors. In these cases, energy prices and their evolution appear to have a direct impact on the value of the products they build and sell. Therefore, they are increasingly likely to integrate analysis on the use of building including heating and cooling systems, specific energy and transports, into the early planning stages.

9.5 Balancing internal management needs and an increasing range of use for external GHG data

GHG quantification and verification: integration with existing reporting and verification process

Until now, two mandatory frameworks require the verification of disclosed emissions in France: the EU ETS and Article 225. The EU ETS framework is very specific as only Scope 1 emissions are concerned and the perimeter of emissions sources is precisely defined. The objective is to obtain a high level of comparability and certainty as every ton of CO_2 reported plays into the competitiveness of the firm.

On the contrary, the verification process under Article 225 is mainly dedicated to verifying the existence and fairness of the monitoring and reporting processes rather than validating the comparability and certainty of the emission levels disclosed. It is integrated in a broader CSER reporting process. As such, the verification process requires fewer technical skills than for the EU ETS.[23] Moreover, being able to certify CSER information requires a clear overview of the whole company and of internal reporting processes.

Given this approach to verification, it is not surprising that the majority of French companies verifying their emissions use their existing financial auditor (see Section 9.1). Indeed, using another auditor would involve a learning curve to master the company's structure, thus increasing time and financial costs for the company itself. As such, it is less cumbersome for the current financial auditor to propose a cheaper package integrating accounting certification and CSR certification. However, in the case of smaller and less complex companies, the opportunity for CSER-specialized auditors appears to be greater as the competitive advantage of financial auditors may be lower.

Anticipating the use of data by external stakeholders to mitigate the risk

Data use by external stakeholders creates risks and opportunities
External stakeholders – observers, NGOs, financial and extra-financial analysts – use disclosed data on GHG emissions for different purposes. Investors were part of the first wave of entities advocating for expanding GHG reporting. Thus, the use of data by investors is one of the more developed external uses of data.

Given the origins of the CDP, its best-in-class approach using sectoral rankings of companies based on both GHG performance and transparency scores is similar to how socially responsible investment often occurs. The objective is to replicate the sectoral repartition of

---

[23] As verification under the EU ETS is more technical, concentrated on specific parts of companies and necessitates specifically accredited auditors, the auditor's job is closer to environmental certification. That can also be illustrated by sectoral accreditation instead of general accreditation.

a defined index and select only "best" companies in every sector to create an alternative investment portfolio. For investors, it is a way to implement socially responsible investments at relatively low cost, without significantly modifying investment perimeters.

This index-based approach has been used by several asset managers and investment index developers, such as NYSE Euronext (Low Carbon 100 Europe® Index) for example. The role of CDP in these initiatives remains important, if indirect. Analytic companies and extra-financial data providers such as Trucost, South Pole Carbon or Inrate use disclosed data from CDP as inputs in their analysis. Some of them may even quality-check disclosed data under the CDP. The disclosure of GHG data is then a business opportunity for external entities (2°ii, 2013).

Some analysts use GHG data not only to assess an environmental performance but to assess economic risks of these companies, especially in relation to energy and climate regulation. With the creation of the EU ETS, installation emissions are used to assess the present and future cost of purchasing allowances or credits. In that case, the use of GHG data is dedicated not only to an environmental purpose but for a better assessment of risk and a pure financial decision-making process.

NGOs and research centers may also use disclosure of GHG data to make their own ranking and advocating for better transparency and further action on mitigation. For disclosing companies, there is then a reputational risk of not – or poorly – reporting GHG emissions. Therefore, the internal process of monitoring and reporting GHG emissions may be critical to mitigate these risks.

For disclosing companies, the opportunity is to attract or retain investors. However, as seen above, the risk is both in being underrated for justified – or not – reasons and in releasing too detailed data that could be considered as industrial secrets.

On the other hand, with the use of GHG data by external entities having financial implications, a verification process of reporting entities' fairness becomes more and more essential. One can notice that this verification process is mandatory or much more developed for all reporting processes with economic implications (EU ETS and, although to a much lower extent, financial communication such as CDP and Article 225).

More generally, the increasing role of CSER data disclosure and regulations may have a growing impact on companies' governance.

Table 9.2 *Third-party use of GHG quantification data*

	Asset managers and index developers	Data providers	NGOs and research centers	State agencies
Use of disclosed data	- Picking best-in-class companies - Excluding less efficient companies - Improving risk assessment	- Use of disclosed data to provide database to analysts - Testing the quality of data	- Ranking of companies according to transparency and performance - Lobbying for further action	- Improving the knowledge on sectoral emissions - Improving the guidelines for monitoring and reporting
Risks for the reporting entity	- Decreasing its attractiveness to investors	- In case of poorly justified reporting, risk of seeing increased emissions in the database	- Reputational risk	- Not being prepared for more-restrictive regulation in the future - Not being prepared for new reporting guidelines
Opportunities for the reporting entity	- Having a competitive advantage to retain or attract investors	- The quality of reporting may be highlighted	- Ready positive communication campaign in case of good ranking	- Being a first mover and having competitive advantage when new regulations/guidelines are implemented

Source: Authors.

Therefore, the AMF (2013) explains that almost all CAC40 companies – and more generally a quarter of studied companies – have created a special committee composed of board members on extra-financial issues. Furthermore, the number of companies integrating CSER criteria in the variable remuneration of their management is increasing. Their analysis show that listed companies have integrated CSER deeper in their governance. This can be explained by both a more adapted structure and historically older solicitations. Listed companies may then be considered as being a step ahead.

9.6 Conclusions: the diversity of reporting frameworks leads to higher costs, risks and opportunities

Overlapping reporting schemes create many challenges both for authorities and reporting companies. Usually, the definition, the quantification and monitoring of Scope 1 and 2 emissions do not pose technical difficulties. However, the multiplication of reporting frameworks can lead to higher costs, especially for the first reporting exercises and when they require consolidation at the group level or deconsolidation at the legal entity level. Above all, frameworks that require reporting which do not match the operational realities of the company – such as disaggregated reporting when energy or environmental strategies are elaborated at the group level – decrease the usefulness of the regulation for reporting companies.

Scope 3 emissions can represent the lion's share of emissions and cannot be ignored in the implementation of a comprehensive risk/ opportunity analysis on energy-climate issues. However, due to more complex calculations and data needs, standardization of Scope 3 emissions quantification approaches is ongoing; this is despite the increasing number of sectoral methodological guides. Today – as opposed to Scope 1 and 2 emissions – there are neither implicit nor explicit standards for reporting scope 3 emissions. Nevertheless, a number of international and national efforts are currently under way to do so.

In general, verification of emissions occurs when there is an economic stake in reporting emissions. Currently in France, two verification processes may coexist at a company level: the EU ETS is focused on Scope 1 emissions, and implemented within the framework of a detailed set of guidelines aimed at ensuring the comparability and accuracy of emissions estimates. To date, the verification process of

CSER data is more focused on respecting procedures than on the comparability and certainty of the reported figures. The development of common standards for GHG monitoring and reporting could lead to increase the comparability, accuracy and precision of disclosed emissions. The development of standardized verification would, downstream, increase its enforcement at the same time.

Both explicit and implicit standards are arising; however, the relevance of each framework and the coherence between frameworks is still questionable. Coherent and relevant frameworks are nevertheless essential to allow companies to monitor GHG emissions at least cost and in a means pertinent for their operational needs. As managers of many of these different frameworks, national governments have a role in fostering this convergence. For example, the implementation of future European energy efficiency directives is an occasion to coordinate policies within a country but also between European countries. However, the risk of adding another layer of potentially irrelevant or incoherent regulation must be seriously assessed.

Bibliography

2°ii – 2° Investing Initiative, 2013. *From financed emissions to long-term investing metrics. State-of-the-art review of GHG emissions accounting for the financial sector.*

ADEME, 2013. *Premier colloque Bilan GES.* Symposium. www.colloque-bilanges.ademe.actesnumeriques.fr/. Accessed March 2014.

2014. *Evaluation de la première période réglementaire de l'article L. 229-25 du code de l'environnement (introduit par l'article 75 de la loi n°2010–788 du 12 juillet 2010).*

AGEFI, 2014. *Les auditeurs étendent leur champ de compétence à la RSE.* February 3, 2014.

AMF, 2013. *Rapport de l'AMF sur l'information publiée par les sociétés cotées en matière de responsabilité sociale, sociétale et environnementale.*

CDP, 2013a. *Global 500 Climate Change Report.* CDP Sustainability.

2013b. *Guidance for companies reporting on climate change on behalf of investors & supply chain members.* CDP Sustainability.

2014. *CDP Verification Standards.* https://www.cdp.net/en-US/Respond/Pages/verification-standards.aspx. Accessed March 2014.

Code de l'environnement, 2010. *Article L229-25 modifié par la loi n°2010-1563 du 16 décembre 2010 – art.17.*

Deloitte, 2013. *Reporting RSE selon l'article 225 de la loi «Grenelle 2». Bilan de la première année d'application.*

MEDDE, 2011. *Décret n° 2011–829 du 11 juillet 2011 relatif au bilan des émissions de gaz à effet de serre et au plan climat-énergie territorial.*
2012. *Méthode pour la réalisation des bilans d'émissions de Gaz à effet de serre conformément à l'article 75 de la loi n° 2010–788 du 12 juillet 2010 portant engagement national pour l'environnement (ENE).*
MEDDE and OREE, 2013. *Première année d'application de l'article 225 de la loi Grenelle 2.*
MEDEF, 2012. *Guide méthodologique. Reporting RSE. Les nouvelles dispositions légales et règlementaires.*
MJL, 2012. *Décret n° 2012–557 du 24 avril 2012 relatif aux obligations de transparence des entreprises en matière sociale et environnementale.*
2013. *Arrêté du 13 mai 2013 déterminant les modalités dans lesquelles l'organisme tiers indépendant conduit sa mission.*
PricewaterhouseCoopers and Carbon Disclosure Project, 2007. *Review of the Contribution of Reporting to GHG Emissions Reductions and Associated Costs and Benefits.* A research report completed for the UK Department for Environment, Food and Rural Affairs, 109pp.

10 | *Direct measurement in the EU ETS*

CHRIS DIMOPOULOS

10.1 Context

GHG emission data are critical to international efforts to mitigate anthropogenic influence on the planet. The EU ETS (Emission Trading System)[1] offers two methods for the determination of these emissions, a calculation and a direct measurement approach. Direct measurement is the monitoring of the mass emission of these compounds to air. The procedures, requirements and implications of each method have distinct differences. Chapter 5 emphasized the more commonly used "calculation approach"; in this chapter we discuss the direct measurement method or measurement-based approach as it is more commonly referred to in the MRR (Monitoring and Reporting Regulation)[2] of the EU ETS. Through its course we will answer some key questions:

- What are the main principles behind direct measurement?
- What are the selection criteria for direct measurement monitoring systems?
- What are the MRR requirements on direct measurement?
- What are the challenges of its implementation?
- What are the associated uncertainties?
- How does it compare against the calculation method?

The answers to these questions will allow the reader to understand the process behind the choice of a direct monitoring methodology and what needs to be considered in order for the method selected to be suitable to industry and individual installation characteristics. The direct measurement uncertainty requirements and if and how these can be adhered to, will also be discussed within the context of this chapter. Due to the nature of how the EU ETS operates the allowances from

---

[1] Directive 2003/87/EC of 13 October 2003.
[2] Commission Regulation 601/2012 of 21 June 2012.

each installation are surrendered and traded at an absolute value and with no uncertainty attached to them. However, in order to facilitate fair trade stakeholders within the scheme need to be confident that the traded allowances are comparable within specified limits. It is therefore essential that the initial reported GHG figures are determined with an uncertainty value associated with them and that this value is as low as practically possible depending on the size and emissions of each participating installation. The focus needs to be on continuously striving for progressively lower uncertainty values. In order for this to be achieved an understanding of the uncertainty influencing parameters and their control mechanisms is vital.

10.2 Direct measurement fundamentals

What are the main principles of direct measurement?

Direct measurement is one of the options available to emission trading scheme participants for quantifying their GHG emissions. In contrast to the calculation method that determines fuel or process input and calculation factors, the direct measurement approach measures exhaust gases from emission chimneys on industrial installations. These chimneys are commonly referred to as emission stacks or emission ducts. Some installations may have a large number of these stacks (e.g., oil refineries), or a limited number (e.g., power stations).

The actual measurements are carried out through CEMS (Continuous Emissions Monitoring Systems) or otherwise called AMS (Automated Measuring Systems), which are permanently installed on stacks. For the purpose of this chapter the term CEMS is going to be used as this is the term used in the MRR. These systems have the capability of providing 24-hour real-time data. However, as they have only got the capacity to measure a small proportion of the waste stream gas emitted to the atmosphere through each stack, it is fundamental that the sample analyzed is representative of all the GHG being released. The location therefore at which the sampling is carried out within the stack is significant.

CEMS are based on a number of different technologies and designs. They are divided into two main categories, extractive and in situ. Extractive systems continuously extract a sample from the stack gas and deliver it through a probe and sampling line into an analyzer.

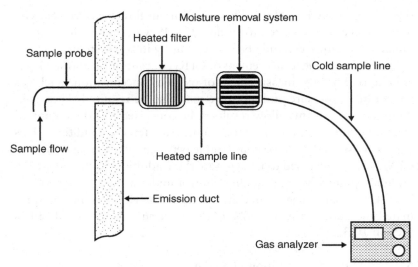

Figure 10.1 Extractive CEMS typical configuration
Source: NPL.

Figure 10.1 shows a typical configuration of an extractive system. Other variations do exist with fewer or additional components but the main principle remains the same. Sampling lines, probes and filters can be manufactured from a number of different materials depending on the targeted gas component and stack gas conditions. In situ systems on the other hand will execute the measurement within the stack either at a single point (point monitors) or across a length of the stack diameter (cross duct or path). Regardless of the type or design, all CEMS need to meet some key requirements in order for them to be able to generate valid results. The composition of the gas must remain the same while in the measuring system; gas entering each component of the system must be at appropriate conditions, e.g., temperature, pressure and flow, and the measuring system itself must be protected from any substance that may jeopardize its integrity and reliability such as corrosive gases or particulate matter.

CEMS that are used within the scope of trading schemes need to also be able to quantify an annual emission. In order for this to be achieved, the mass release of the GHG in question needs to be determined. This requires the measurement of both the concentration of the GHG and the stack gas volumetric flow. The concentration measurement is achieved by the concentration CEMS. The determination of the flow parameter is achieved by a continuous flow measurement system or sometimes referred to as flow CEMS. Continuous flow measurement by nature can only be carried out by in situ systems.

In addition to the measurement of GHG concentration and stack gas volumetric flow, the measurement of oxygen concentration, stack gas temperature, pressure and moisture may also be required. These peripheral measurements allow results to be converted and then reported at specific conditions, referred to as standard reference conditions. This allows emission data to be comparable between different installations. CEMS can be designed to incorporate these additional sensors. CEMS are underpinned by tight quality control under a European standard EN 14181 "Stationary source emissions – Quality assurance of automated measuring systems." EN 14181 is discussed in more detail in Section 10.3.

Measuring the concentration of a GHG

The gas analysis phase of a CEMS is where the concentration of the gas is actually quantified. It is an integral part of all CEMS regardless of whether they are extractive or in situ design. Gas analyzers operate under different principles and technologies which are ultimately dependent on the stack conditions and the gas component that is being measured. The inclusion of a number of different sensors within them allows for the detection of multiple gas components through one measurement system. Almost all CO_2 CEMS are based on infra-red (IR) technologies with Non-Dispersive IR (NDIR), Gas Filter Correlation (GFC), Differential Optical Absorption Spectroscopy (DOAS) and Fourier Transform Infra-Red (FTIR) being the most common. IR technologies are based on the unique absorption properties that all heteroatomic gaseous molecules such as CO_2 and N_2O display in the IR region. Homoatomic molecules on the other hand for example N_2, do not absorb any light in the IR region. We will use the measurement of CO_2 through the NDIR method as an example to describe in more detail the principle behind an IR-based CEMS.

In a simple non-dispersive IR analyzer, IR light is emitted from a heated element which is then passed through a filter which allows specific wavelengths, in this case the wavelengths where CO_2 absorbs light, to pass through it. The light is then split into two beams, one entering a cell with stack gas where some of its energy is lost due to the CO_2 present and one entering a reference cell that contains a

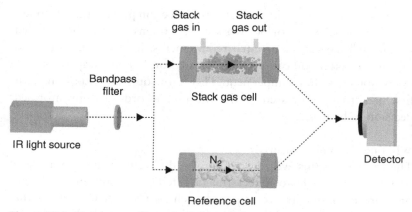

Figure 10.2 Simple non-dispersive infra-red detector
Source: NPL.

homoatomic gas, usually N_2, where no energy is lost. This energy difference between the two cells is proportional to the concentration of the CO_2 in the sample cell and is measured by a detector. Figure 10.2 shows a typical configuration of a simple non-dispersive infra-red detector.

Measuring the stack volumetric flow rate
Traditionally continuous stack flow measurement systems have not been popular in Europe; they predominantly have been used in the US for the trading of SO_2 under the 1993 US EPA Acid Rain Program. However, since the introduction of the EU ETS and as we progress through each phase of the scheme, continuous flow measurement systems are becoming increasingly commercially available in the European market. EN ISO 16911 "Manual and automatic determination of velocity and volume flow rate in ducts" describes the performance criteria and quality control of continuous flow measurement systems.

Selecting a fit-for-purpose CEMS

The selection process of a measurement system is fundamental in ensuring it is appropriate for its designated application and continues to be fit for purpose during the course of its lifetime. Certain criteria need to be met and the system's performance characteristics will have to be considered. It is critical during the selection process that the operator and the CEMS provider work closely to ensure that the installed system will meet its designated requirements. It is also important to remember that modifications after installation can be costly and sometimes not possible to implement. There are some key questions that first need to be addressed by the end user in order for an informed decision to be made.

What needs to be measured?
The answer to this will determine the different designs and types of CEMS available to detect the targeted gas component. If two or more components are required such as CO_2, N_2O and O_2 the focus needs to be on a system that will incorporate all the required sensors.

What is the expected range of the GHG concentration?
This requires at least an estimation of the maximum and minimum expected values during different modes of operation such as different loads, and in conditions that may create sudden spikes in the emissions. This will ensure that the CEMS selected will have suitable ranges to be able to produce continuous results with no missing data or gaps. The CEMS will need to have been certified for the specified ranges.

Could the emissions or process operating conditions change?
The operator needs to consider whether any change in the process conditions or any other significant changes in the future such as the installation of abatement on the emission source, may affect the emissions or the composition of the stack gas. If so an evaluation needs to be made on whether the emissions will still be within the certified range of the CEMS and on whether the CEMS will still be fit for purpose.

What normative documents does the CEMS need to adhere to?
For EU ETS participating installations, the first point of reference is the MRR. It specifies relevant standards that GHG CEMS need to comply with. MRR requirements for CEMS are discussed in detail in Section 10.3.

Will it meet the uncertainty requirements of the EU ETS?
The specifics of uncertainty requirements under the EU ETS and if and how they can be met are discussed in sections 10.3 and 10.4.

And finally what will the total cost be?
The operator needs to consider the lifespan cost of the instrument. The lifespan cost will include purchase and installation, calibration and maintenance, training of staff, and annual checks of the system which may have to be conducted by an external test house. For more information on CEMS costs refer to Section 10.5.

10.3 Direct measurement under the EU ETS

What is the scope?

Under Phase III of the EU ETS the list of GHGs regulated has been extended to include N_2O emissions from certain chemical processes and PFCs (perfluorocarbons) from aluminium smelting. It should be noted that N_2O generated from combustion is not reported under the EU ETS. Phase III also requires the measurement of all CO_2 that is transferred off an installation for CCS (carbon capture and storage) purposes. The methodologies that should be used for the measurement of GHGs from these activities are specified in the MRR. Needless to say the MRR also covers CO_2 measurement methodologies for installations and processes already being regulated since Phase II.

More specifically the MRR states that N_2O emissions should be determined through a measurement-based methodology (direct measurement). The same applies for all transferred CCS CO_2. PFCs from aluminium production on the other hand can only be measured through a calculation method. For all other CO_2 emission sources direct measurement is offered as an alternative to the calculation method as long as specific conditions are met. Adherence to these conditions allows any EU ETS installation, regardless of the category (A, B, C or low emitter) it falls under, to use a measurement-based methodology to quantify its CO_2 emissions. Certain exceptions do apply and are specified within the MRR. It should also be noted that when direct measurement is used, CO is considered as the molar equivalent of CO_2 and thus should also be measured within the stack and added to the CO_2 reported emissions. Any emissions arising from biomass can be

Table 10.1 N_2O *emitting installations*

Industrial sector	End product	Number of installations under EU ETS (2013)
Nitric acid production	Manufacture of synthetic fertilizer	19
Adipic acid production	Manufacture of nylon/ nylon fibres and other synthetic fibers	2
Glyoxal and glyoxylic acid production	Agrochemicals and pharmaceuticals	0
Caprolactam production	Production cycle of nylon materials	Not available*

N_2O emitting installations regulated under the EU ETS.
Note: *Caprolactam production is covered under Article 24 of the Directive which includes a number of other industrial processes so a specific number of caprolactam producing installations is not specified within the Commission database.

subtracted from the total annual CO_2 emissions. Currently the biomass fraction of the emissions is determined by analytic methods.

Direct measurement of N_2O emission sources

The main industry that is concerned with the measurement of N_2O emissions under the EU ETS is the synthetic fertilizer industry with nitric acid being a primary ingredient in the production of nitrogen-based fertilizer. There is only a small number of nitric acid producing sites throughout Europe and overall the number of N_2O emitting installations covered by the EU ETS (Table 10.1) is quite insignificant when compared to the ~12,000 CO_2 emitting installations.

Although the required monitoring approach is direct measurement there is still scope for calculation depending on site-specific characteristics. Following the measurement of the N_2O emissions the following equation should be applied for conversion into CO_2e as it is this figure that requires reporting to the relevant regulatory authority at the end of the year.

$$CO_2(e)[t] = N_2O_{annual}[t] \times GWP_{N_2O}$$

Equation 10.1

Where:

$$GWP_{N_2O} = 310$$

Direct measurement of transferred CO_2

The MRR has made provisions under Phase III for the subtraction from reported annual emissions of any CO_2 transferred out of an installation for CCS purposes. It has also allowed for any future innovations in regard to CO_2 capture technology to be incorporated within its scope. Currently the requirement is that CEMS shall be used for these measurements; however, in this case they are actually referred to as CMS (Continuous Monitoring Systems) as they are not measuring the emissions directly. Due to the potential of very high CO_2 concentrations being transported through these systems, the sourcing of fit-for-purpose certified CMS may prove challenging. In response the MRR has allowed for the measurement of "indirect CO_2," in other words measurement of all other gases within the gas stream and deduction of the CO_2 fraction by subtraction from the total. CMS need to follow any requirements that apply for CEMS, discussed later in this section, including EN 14181 specifications.

At the time of writing CCS is only being implemented at a very small scale in the EU through pilot plants and no EU ETS installation is known to transfer CO_2 off the plant for CCS. However, it has been included in the MRR in order to allow regulators to keep ahead of any developments and to be in a position to include installations if and when the technology becomes more widespread and available through increased national and EU funding and corporate investment.

Direct measurement of CO_2 emission sources

The MRR has recognized the increased confidence in CEMS measured emissions by introducing less stringent requirements for operators that choose direct CO_2 measurement as their preferred method. As it were, operators were required under Phase II to demonstrate "that using a CEMS achieves greater accuracy than the calculation approach using the most accurate tier approach" (Commission Decision [EU] No. 601/2012 – 2012). From Phase III onwards "greater accuracy" does not need to be demonstrated and, although emissions still need to be

Table 10.2 *Maximum permissible uncertainty for measurement-based methods*

	Tier 1	Tier 2	Tier 3	Tier 4
CO_2 Emission Sources	± 10%	± 7.5%	± 5%	± 2.5%
N_2O Emission Sources	± 10%	± 7.5%	± 5%	N/A
CO_2 Transfer	± 10%	± 7.5%	± 5%	± 2.5%

Note: The uncertainty needs to be reported at a 95% confidence interval.

corroborated through a calculation-based approach, this approach does not need to comply to any tiers. Tiers and respective maximum permissible uncertainties have been defined for CEMS as outlined in Table 10.2. An emission source is considered Tier 4 if it emits more than 5,000 tonnes of CO_2e per year or contributes more than 10 percent of the total annual emissions of the installation (Commission Decision [EU] No. 601/2012 – 2012). For all other emission sources, at least one tier lower than the highest tier is required. The requirements of Table 10.2 also apply to direct measurement of N_2O emission sources and transferred CO_2.

The uncertainties specified in Table 10.2 need to be compared to the average hourly emission uncertainty (see Equation 10.2) of the GHG being measured; this uncertainty is the combined uncertainty of concentration and flue gas volumetric flow rate (see Equation 10.3). This in fact is the most significant difference between assessing uncertainty for GHG CEMS and atmospheric pollutant CEMS. For atmospheric pollutants the parameter of interest is only the concentration of the gas, without taking into account the gas volumetric flow rate, and its uncertainty is assessed against Emission Limit Values (ELVs) specified in relevant EU Directives. As no ELVs exist for GHGs the average hourly emission is used instead. The specific procedure for determining the uncertainty of both the concentration and the volumetric flow rate is specified in ISO 14956 "Evaluation of the suitability of a measurement procedure by comparison with a required measurement uncertainty" and is based on performance characteristics of the individual CEMS.

The main normative document covering most if not all aspects of CEMS is EN 14181. The MRR requires all direct "measurements to be carried out applying methods based on EN 14181" (Commission Decision [EU] No. 601/2012 – 2012) and therefore follow the quality assurance procedures (QAL1, QAL2, QAL3) and the annual surveillance test (AST) specified within it. Although it was written primarily to address atmospheric pollutant CEMS and industrial sites that fall under the Industrial Emissions Directive (IED),[3] if its principles are adjusted accordingly, mainly to take into account the continuous flow measurement systems and their uncertainties, it can be applied to GHG mass emission measurement which is in fact what the MRR requires operators to do.

$$GHG\ emissions_{av\ hourly}(kg/h) =$$

$$\frac{\sum GHG\ concentration_{hourly}\left(\dfrac{g}{Nm^3}\right) \times flue\ gas\ flow\left(\dfrac{Nm^3}{h}\right)}{Hours\ of\ operation \times 1000}$$

Equation 10.2

Where:

GHG emissions$_{av\ hourly}$ = annual average hourly emissions in kg/h from the source;
GHG concentration$_{hourly}$ = hourly concentrations of emissions in g/Nm³ in the flue gas flow measured during operation;
Flue gas flow = flue gas flow in Nm³ for each hour.

$$U_{av\ hourly\ emissions} = \sqrt{u_{GHG\ concentration}^2 + u_{flue\ gas\ flow}^2}$$

Equation 10.3

Where:

$U_{av\ hourly\ emissions}$ = uncertainty of the annual average hourly emissions;
$u_{GHG\ concentration}$ = uncertainty of the hourly concentrations of emissions;
$u_{flue\ gas\ flow}$ = uncertainty of the hourly flue gas flow.

Direct measurement according to EN14181

EN 14181 specifies procedures for the quality assurance of CEMS. More specifically it designates what needs to be done in order for a CEMS to be fit for purpose and to generate reliable results throughout its lifetime. It also describes the procedure for the assessment of a CEMS measurement uncertainty capability. Although it should be the

---

[3] Directive 2010/75/EC of 24 November 2010.

first point of reference for any operator or interested party attempting to understand the requirements for GHG CEMS and how they fit within the scope of the EU ETS, there are a number of other standards that need to be followed or referred to. However, all of these are either directly mentioned within EN 14181 or somehow related to its requirements.

EN 14181 specifies three mandatory levels of quality assurance (QAL1, QAL2 and QAL3) that need to be met and an additional AST to be carried out, in order for its objectives to be met. Figure 10.3 displays an overview of the standard and its three quality assurance levels. The appendix to this chapter lists all the relevant standards with their full title and date of publication.

Quality assurance level 1 (QAL1)

QAL1 is a procedure that is carried out by the manufacturers of CEMS; however, operators need to ensure before purchase that an instrument has undergone QAL1 testing and certification.

The QAL1 procedure demonstrates that a CEMS is suitable for its purpose before its sale and installation, by conformance testing (sometimes known as "type approval"). This testing will indicate whether it can achieve the performance and uncertainty requirements specified in relevant EU Directives, in our case the MRR and Table 10.2 of this chapter. The QAL1 testing will ultimately ensure that the CEMS is certified and fit for purpose. Although referred to in EN 14181, the actual procedures for the testing and the uncertainty determination are actually described in EN 15267-3 and EN ISO 14956.

The uncertainty specified in the QAL1 certificate can act as the first point of reference from which to determine whether a CEMS will meet the uncertainty requirement of the MRR. However, the QAL1 uncertainty can only act as an indication and a further assessment needs to be carried out. This assessment needs to account for influencing parameters that may increase the uncertainty of the CEMS while in operation but also for the minimization of random errors over the course of a year as these errors are reduced with the increased number of measurements.

Quality assurance level 2 (QAL2)

QAL2 is the procedure for calibrating the CEMS following its installation. The actual installation of the CEMS can have a significant

Applying EN 14181

Purpose	Demonstration of fitness for pupose	Correct installation and calibration	Ongoing control
EN 14181	QAL 1 Quality Assurance Level 1	QAL 2 Quality Assurance Level 2	QAL 3 Quality Assurance Level 3 / AST Annual Surveillance Test
Frequency	Once	Every 3 or 5 years (or if required due to changes in plant or CEMS)	Frequent (QAL 3) Annually (AST)
Relevant standards	EN ISO 14956 EN 15267-3	EN ISO 16911-1 EN 15259 ISO 12039 EN ISO 21528 EN 14790 EN 14789	EN ISO 16911-1 EN 15259 ISO 12039 EN ISO 21528 EN 14790 EN 14789

Figure 10.3 Overview of EN 14181
Source: NPL.

impact on the success of this calibration and the CEMS' overall reliability, therefore the procedures of EN 15259, that describes how to select the location of the installation, also need to be followed. For continuous flow measurement systems as seen in Section 10.4, the location at which the measurement is made can mean the difference between results with high uncertainty or results with acceptable uncertainty. EN ISO 16911–2 describes the requirements needed for choosing the right location for a continuous flow measurement system.

The actual calibration involves calibrating the CEMS after it has been installed and is operational against an appropriate Standard Reference Method (SRM). This is done by carrying out SRM parallel measurements to the CEMS measurements and through this procedure deriving a calibration function. The SRM is deemed to provide the correct results within certain tolerances. The SRMs for the different GHGs can be seen in Figure 10.3 and are also listed in the appendix. The calibration process also verifies that the CEMS continues to meet the measurement uncertainty requirements, once installed. The QAL2 testing is carried out by an external laboratory that is certified under EN/ ISO/IEC 17025.

Quality assurance level 3 (QAL3)

QAL3 is the procedure for assessing, in an ongoing manner, the quality of the CEMS results and that it is still continuing to operate within the required uncertainty tolerances. This is done by checking the readings of the CEMS on a regular basis, by introducing known concentrations of compressed gases into the system in order to confirm that the results are consistent with those obtained during the QAL1 conformance tests. These checks are called zero and span checks. QAL3 checks are the responsibility of the operator.

Annual Surveillance Test (AST)

The AST is a procedure to evaluate the CEMS on a yearly basis to show that it continues to function correctly and that the calibration function remains valid by comparison with the results obtained in QAL2 and therefore the uncertainty is still within the specified limits. In some respects it is a shorter version of the QAL2, i.e., the SRM parallel measurements are less in number than the ones carried out during a QAL2. In that respect the AST is also carried out by an external laboratory, certified under EN/ISO/IEC 17025. If the AST shows that the calibration function is no longer valid the QAL2 needs to be repeated.

Continuous flow measurement according to EN ISO 16911

The publication of EN ISO 16911 has been partly as a response to the EU ETS requirements for direct measurement and should be used in conjunction with EN 14181. It incorporates or references relevant EN 14181 specifications and makes additions where deemed necessary. It also describes different methods that could be used as an SRM for stack flow measurement and a procedure for the calculation of flow based on energy consumption.

It should be noted that the MRR does allow for the flue gas flow to be determined through a calculation mass balance method instead of a continuous flow measurement system, in which case the MRR procedure for the calculation methodology needs to be followed.

10.4 Uncertainty influencing parameters in mass emission measurement

Now that the scope and uncertainty requirements for direct measurement under the MRR have been established, an assessment can be made as to whether these uncertainty targets can be met in practice. In order to accomplish this an understanding is needed of what the main influencing parameters are of each of the uncertainty components, i.e., flow and concentration, and in what way and how much each contributes to the final uncertainty value.

Flow measurement uncertainty

Flow measurement has often been the poor relation in emissions measurement and has been the least understood and most challenging of the two. It might be expected that measuring flow accurately from an emission duct would be relatively straightforward; unfortunately it is not. Traditionally it has been the biggest source of uncertainty in GHG measurement, which is one of the reasons why EU ETS installations have been largely apprehensive in using direct measurement as their preferred approach. This is what the power and cement industries state in their respective guidance documents on EU ETS monitoring methodologies: "accurate stack gas flow rate is fraught with difficulty" (Salway et al., JEP, 2011); "the low accuracy of volume flow measurement" (CSI, 2011). Both go on to say that this reason amongst others is why the calculation approach should be preferred for these two industries.

Studies on the uncertainty achieved by continuous flow measurement systems have been limited and those that have been carried out have produced variable results. For example studies carried out in the US by the Environmental Protection Agency (EPA) indicated that the uncertainty of continuous flow measurement systems can be less than ±5 percent. Another study, however, suggested that overestimations of mass emissions of SO_2 of up to 25 percent that had been identified in the US were due to systematic errors from the calibration of continuous flow measurement systems (Electric Power Research Institute, 1996). It has to be said that these errors were introduced as a result of limitations of the manual methods employed to calibrate the continuous flow measurement systems under a process similar to the EN14181 QAL2 procedure and therefore cannot be considered inherent uncertainties of the actual flow measurement systems. However, this just highlights the importance of identifying all sources of uncertainty and that errors in measurement can be introduced through a number of different routes.

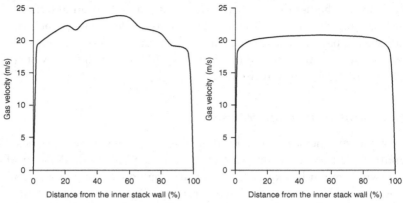

Figure 10.4 Stack gas flow profiles
Source: NPL.

In Europe it has been widely perceived that uncertainty of flow measurement systems can be in excess of ±15 percent especially if a non-uniform flow exists, the definition and principles of which are explained in the next paragraph. However, validation studies carried out in order to provide information for the formulation of ISO 16911 found that, if the performance criteria and location requirements specified within the standard are met, an uncertainty of at least ±4 percent, if not better, can be expected (EN ISO 16911, 2013). Moreover, as manufacturers are striving to meet EU ETS requirements, uncertainties of as low ±1.7 percent (Sira, MCERTS Certificate – MC130222/01, 2012) have been achieved at the QAL1 certification stage by newly designed instruments.

The main influence on the uncertainty of flow measurement is the flow profile of the gas within the stack at the cross section where the measurement is carried out. The flow profile is effectively the variation of the stack gas velocity across a line passing through the center of the stack. The velocity is actually an input in the flow equation and without it the volumetric flow rate cannot be calculated. A non-uniform flow profile displays asymmetry and fluctuations of the velocity across the stack gas and has a large influence on the uncertainty value. In that effect it may introduce systematic errors that if not taken into account may lead to the uncertainties of > ±15 percent already mentioned. Random errors are easier to control as they will be minimized with repeat measurements over the reporting year, a principle which applies to concentration measurements as well. Figure 10.4 illustrates what is called a fully developed profile (uniform) and a less developed and asymmetrical profile (non-uniform). The publication of EN ISO 16911 has addressed these issues by specifying requirements and conditions for measurement locations through pre-investigation surveys at the proposed installation location.

Concentration measurement uncertainty

Concentration measurement uncertainty is well understood and has been documented in normative and guidance documents in order for the requirements of the Large Combustion Plant (LPD)[4] and Waste Incineration (WID)[5] Directives now replaced with the IED to be fulfilled. Uncertainty of CO_2 CEMS usually ranges for certified instruments between typically ~±1 percent and ~±10 percent. Similar values are encountered for N_2O CEMS. ISO 14956 specifies the procedure for the determination of the uncertainty and EN 14181 the respective requirements and tolerances. The main uncertainty influencing parameters are the performance characteristics of the CEMS and the stack conditions at the location at which the measurement is carried out.

One thing to remember is that the uncertainty of peripheral measurements which may be required, such as O_2, moisture, pressure and temperature, will have to be considered and included in the uncertainty budget and will almost certainly increase the final uncertainty value.

Can the MRR tiers be achieved?

If we were to look at the most stringent uncertainty scenario under the MRR, i.e., Tier 4 (maximum permissible uncertainty of ±2.5%), we can determine by deduction from Equation 10.3 that the target value for each uncertainty component is ±1.76%, if we assign a hypothetical equal value on both uncertainty components. It has to be said that achieving this target value is certainly challenging. However, if instruments are selected carefully, operated according to the manufacturer's specifications and according to relevant standard requirements they

[4] Directive 2001/80/EC of 23 October 2001.
[5] Directive 2000/76/EC of 4 December 2000.

can potentially achieve mass emission uncertainties typically ranging from 1.5% to 2.5%, therefore meeting Tier 4 requirements.

Compliance with Tiers 1–3 should be more straightforward with the obvious prerequisite that the above conditions are still met. It is probable that as CEMS manufacturers respond to the MRR requirements more instruments will become available in the market which will be able to carry out measurements within the required uncertainty tolerances.

Ultimately it comes down to the ability of the manufacturer, operator and test house to identify, minimize and finally incorporate all significant random and systematic errors within an uncertainty budget, in order to be able to meet the MRR uncertainty requirements and more importantly ensure the CEMS generates accurate and reliable measurement results. The strict compliance with the requirements in the relevant normative documents described in this chapter is the first and most important step in achieving this.

10.5 Measurement vs. calculation

As a conclusion to this section and in order to fully appreciate and understand how direct measurement fits within the EU ETS framework it is useful to discuss the main differences between the two approaches available, calculation and direct measurement, and outline the advantages and disadvantages of each.

The exact number of installations opting for direct measurement for some or all of their emission sources under the EU ETS is difficult to establish. Apart from N_2O emission sources where a direct measurement approach is mandatory, it is difficult to know without access to monitoring plans – which in some member states are considered sensitive data and therefore not readily available – how many installations may be carrying out the direct measurement approach. What is certain is that its application is still very limited compared to the use of the calculation method.

There are a number of reasons for this, the main reason being that a lot of these installations will have already been implementing parts or the whole of the calculation approach before even joining the EU ETS. This will not have been necessarily to measure their emissions but for internal quality control and financial reasons. For example, the amount of coal purchased and consumed in a coal-fired power

Table 10.3 Direct measurement vs. calculation

	Measurement-based method	Calculation method
Cost	Advantages: • No analytic costs Disadvantages: • High capital costs: Purchase and installation: ~€30k–~€90k per stack • Ongoing costs: Service, training and maintenance yr: ~€8k–€30k per stack per year • AST and QAL2 costs	Advantages: • Low capital costs – metering systems may already be available Disadvantages: • Costly stock surveys • Potentially high analytic sampling costs depending on type of process and required frequency of analyses
Installation and calibration of CEMS/ metering systems	Advantages: • Accredited test houses (large number of them available) • EN 14181 Quality Assurance Controls Disadvantages: • Potential process interruptions during installation	Advantages: • Fuel supplier metering system can be used • Metering system may already be in place on installation • Metering devices may be under national legal metrological control Disadvantages: • Metering devices may need to be online for large part of the year making it difficult to calibrate them

Table 10.3 (*cont.*)

	Measurement-based method	Calculation method
Analysis of samples	Advantages: • Not required	Advantages: • May already be implemented for internal quality control reasons Disadvantages: • Difficult to obtain representative samples from varied fuel streams
Uncertainty of measurement	Advantages: • Uncertainty determined for annual emission of GHG Disadvantages: • Challenging to achieve low volumetric flow uncertainty • Determination of ancillary measurements uncertainty	Advantages: • Simplified approaches available Disadvantages: • Uncertainty determined just for activity data • Generic Emission factors with potentially high uncertainties may be used

station is an essential piece of information for the plant, not only for the obvious financial reasons but also for fuel management and other electricity output related calculations. So in fact most if not all of the metering systems required for the calculation of fuel consumption under the calculation method will already be in place at a plant like this and will not require any additional investment.

On the other hand the direct measurement approach requires a high capital investment for the purchase and installation of a CEMS. As an indication the purchase and installation of a GHG CEMS can cost in the range of ~€30k–~€90k per stack (Joint Research Centre, Institute for Prospective Technological Studies Sustainable Production and Consumption Unit European IPPC Bureau, 2013) depending on the type and number of sensors, so if we were to imagine an installation with a large number of emission sources like for example an oil refinery, it is quickly evident that in a situation like this direct measurement becomes too costly and impracticable to implement. The purchase of stand-by CEMS in order to provide continuous data when the main CEMS have malfunctioned or are non-operational for maintenance or any other reason is another cost that needs to be considered. Direct measurement is an easier and less costly option for installations with just one emission source especially if a CEMS for atmospheric pollutants is already installed on the stack and can be modified to incorporate the additional sensor for the GHG. An upgrade can cost in the range of ~€5k–~€15k (Joint Research Centre, Institute for Prospective Technological Studies Sustainable Production and Consumption Unit European IPPC Bureau, 2013). Table 10.3 outlines the main advantages and disadvantages of each method in terms of cost and other parameters.

Although direct measurement is not widely used within the EU ETS, there are industry examples where its use compared to the calculation method is a more viable option and in some cases may be preferred. The obvious example is the N_2O-emitting chemical industrial sectors listed in Table 10.1 where, as already mentioned, the use of direct measurement is mandatory. This is because direct measurement is not affected by the chemical reactions and their stoichiometric relationships when the N_2O is actually produced within the manufacturing process.

Another example where direct measurement is potentially a more suited option is for processes with high variability in their fuel stream, such as co-incineration plants. The use of the calculation method to quantify the CO_2 emissions from processes of this nature can be challenging. The fuel consumption can be measured by using different metering devices and should not pose a problem. However, the analytic determination of the carbon content of the fuels is not as straightforward. The MRR specifies for the determination of these parameters "the operator shall ensure that the derived samples are representative" (Commission Regulation [EU] No. 601/2012, 2012); however, obtaining a representative sample from a varied fuel stream will be both challenging and costly with the potential of high uncertainty. The frequency of laboratory analyses will have to be significantly increased and therefore inevitably the costs will increase; however, the representativeness of the sample may still be in question. With the use of a CEMS the measurement will be on the flue gas output from the chimney stack, therefore eliminating the need to know the input and composition of fuel into the process and avoiding the associated analytic uncertainty and costs. In this case the variability of the fuel stream does not have any effect on the uncertainty of the measurement results. It has to be mentioned, however, that in cases where there is a biomass fraction present in the fuel this may still need to be determined through an analytic method.

10.6 Conclusion: what method should be preferred?

In Europe generally the calculation method is considered more accurate and less challenging to use, although there have been indications lately, especially since the publication of EN 14181, that direct measurement is seen at least in some cases to have an equal or even better standing than the calculation approach. In the US on the other hand where there has been a lot more experience with mass emission measurements for the trading of SO_2 under the US EPA Acid Rain Program, direct measurement is seen to be preferable and consequently is a lot more widespread. Overall one could argue that there is no right or wrong answer as each approach has its own merits and shortcomings. Which one should be preferred is plant and process specific and dependent on individual installation characteristics. Ultimately the main things that need to be considered are the ability of the chosen method to meet the requirements of the MRR and the short-term and long-term costs of each method. There are a number of tools that will assist with this procedure, many of which have been described in this chapter, and include amongst others normative documents, certification documentation and industry and EU guidance.

The selection of the most appropriate method will effectively mean that the best trade-off is struck between the uncertainty of the emissions and the associated costs. When all is considered the integrity of the EU ETS can be kept intact only if measurements and calculations within its scope are as reliable and accurate as practically possible and this depends on all stakeholders involved from regulators down to plant operators and verifiers.

Appendix – Relevant international and European standards

EN 14181: 2004 – Stationary source emissions – Quality assurance of automated measuring systems

EN 15259: 2007 – Air quality – Measurement of stationary source emissions – Requirements for measurement sections and sites and for the measurement objective plan and report

EN ISO 14956: 2002 – Air quality – Evaluation of the suitability of a measurement procedure by comparison with a required measurement uncertainty

EN ISO 16911-2: 2013 – Stationary source emissions – Manual and automatic determination of velocity and volume flow rate in ducts – Part 2: Automated measuring systems

EN 15267-3: 2007 – Air quality – Certification of automated measuring systems – Part 3: Performance criteria and test procedures for automated measuring systems for monitoring emissions from stationary sources

EN/ ISO/IEC 17025: 2005 – General requirements for the competence of testing and calibration laboratories

Standard reference methods :

EN ISO 16911-1: 2013 – Stationary source emissions – Manual and automatic determination of velocity and volume flow rate in ducts – Part 1: Manual reference method

EN ISO 21258: 2010 – Stationary source emissions – Determination of the mass concentration of dinitrogen monoxide (N_2O) – Reference method: Non-dispersive infrared method

ISO 12039 – Stationary source emissions – Determination of carbon
   monoxide, carbon dioxide and oxygen – Performance characteristics and calibration of automated measuring systems
EN 15058: 2006 – Stationary source emissions – Determination of
   the mass concentration of carbon monoxide (CO) – Reference
   method: Non-dispersive infrared spectroscopy
EN 14789: 2005 – Stationary source emissions – Determination
   of volume concentration of oxygen (O_2) – Reference
   method – Paramagnetism
EN 14790: 2005 – Stationary source emissions – Determination of
   the water vapor in ducts

Bibliography

Cement Sustainability Initiative (CSI), 2011. CO_2 and Energy Accounting and
   Reporting Standard for the Cement Industry. www.wbcsdcement.org/
   pdf/tf1_co2%20protocol%20v3.pdf. Accessed April 25, 2013.
Commission Decision (EU) No. 2007/589/EC of 18 July 2007 establishing
   guidelines for the monitoring and reporting of greenhouse gas emis-
   sions pursuant to Directive 2003/87/EC of the European Parliament
   and of the Council.
Commission Regulation (EU) No. 601/2012 of 21 June 2012 on the moni-
   toring and reporting of greenhouse gas emissions pursuant to Directive
   2003/87/EC of the European Parliament and of the Council.
Directive 2000/76/EC of the European Parliament and of the Council of 4
   December 2000 on the incineration of waste.
Directive 2001/80/EC of the European Parliament and Council of 23
   October 2001 on the limitation of emissions of certain pollutants into
   the air from large combustion plants.
Directive 2010/75/EC of the European Parliament and Council of 24
   November 2010 on industrial emissions (integrated pollution preven-
   tion and control).
Department of Trade and Industry (DTI), 2004. Best practice Brochure –
   Cleaner Fossil Fuels Programme – Automated Measuring System
   Technologies.
Electric Power Research Institute, 1996. Flue Gas Flow Rate Measurement
   Errors – TR106698 – Interim Report.
EN 14181, 2004. Stationary source emissions – Quality assurance of auto-
   mated measuring systems.
EN ISO 16911, 2013. Manual and automatic determination of velocity and
   volume flow rate in ducts.

Environment Agency – Method Implementation Document (MID14181), 2012. EN 14181: Stationary source emissions – Quality assurance of automated measuring systems.

Environment Agency – RM-QG-01, 2011. Selecting continuous emission monitoring systems (CEMS) and the validity of MCERTS certificates. http://cdn.environment-agency.gov.uk/geho0112bvxk-e-e.pdf. Accessed April 26, 2013.

Environment Agency – Technical Guidance Note (TGN)M20, 2012. Quality assurance of continuous emission monitoring systems – application of EN 14181 and BS EN 13284-2.

European Commission – Directive 2003/87/EC of the European Parliament and of the Council of 13 October 2003 establishing a scheme for greenhouse gas emission allowance trading within the Community and amending Council Directive 96/61/EC.

European Commission – Draft Guidance Document – 2013 MRR Guidance on CEMS, MRR Guidance document No. 7, second draft of 11 October 2013.

European Commission – Guidance Document – The Monitoring and Reporting Regulation – General guidance for installations – MRR Guidance document No. 1, Version of 16 July 2012.

European Commission, 2013. Community transaction log – http://ec.europa. eu/environment/ets/oha.do;jsessionid=yvCrTv3V2m0k0LWcF227D8 npsL1MrkPtL9BqJ5QsxTwnYlj43c7P!-2056334981. Accessed May 2, 2013.

Evans, S., Deery, S. and Banda, J., 2009. How reliable are GHG combustion calculations and emission factors? Presented at the CEM 2009 Conference. www.renovaqualidadedoar.com.br/site/file/1_4%20How% 20Reliable%20are%20GHG%20Combustion%20Emission%20 Factors_v3.pdf. Accessed May 6, 2013.

Jernigan, J.R. – Thermo Fisher Scientific, Air Quality Instruments – An Overview of the CEMS Technologies and Equipment Installed by the Electric Utility Industry to Comply With the US EPA Part 75 Acid Rain Monitoring Program. www.thermo.com/eThermo/CMA/PDFs/Various/ File_2608.pdf. Accessed May 6, 2013.

Joint Research Centre – Institute for Prospective Technological Studies Sustainable Production and Consumption Unit European IPPC Bureau, 2013. Draft Reference Report on Monitoring of emissions from IED-installations – Annex A.5. Monitoring costs of emissions to air, October.

Mainhardt, H. – Intergovernmental Panel on Climate Change (IPPC), 2001. Good Practice Guidance and Uncertainty Management in National Greenhouse Gas Inventories – N_2O Emissions from Adipic Acid and

Nitric Acid Production. www.ipcc-nggip.iges.or.jp/public/gp/english/3_
Industry.pdf. Accessed May 3, 2013.

Salway, A.G., Eyres, D., Graham, D.P. and Quick, W. – Joint Environmental
Programme (JEP), 2011. Guidance for the Monitoring and Reporting
of CO_2 Emissions from Power Stations, EUETS Phase 2 Issue 2.

SIRA Certification Service – MCERTS Certificate – MC130222/01, June
2012. Product conformity certificate – Stack flow master system manufactured by ABB Ltd.

US Environmental Protection Agency (US EPA) – Clean Air Markets
Division, 2003. Part 75 CEMS Field Audit Manual.

PART III

MRV *at offset project scale*

11 | Trendsetter for projects: the Clean Development Mechanism

IGOR SHISHLOV

11.1 Context

The Clean Development Mechanism (CDM) in brief

The existing international climate regime set up by the Kyoto Protocol in 1997 imposed quantitative limits on greenhouse gas (GHG) emissions of developed countries and economies in transition that are included in Annex B to the Kyoto Protocol. These limits are enounced in countries' emissions quotas – Assigned Amount Units (AAU). The Kyoto Protocol (UN, 1998) incorporates four flexibility mechanisms that are supposed to help governments maximize the economic efficiency of achieving their commitments:

- *"Bubbling"* (article 4) permits a group of Annex B countries to redistribute their GHG emissions reduction commitments, as it was done by the European Union countries;
- *Joint Implementation* (article 6) permits Annex B countries to host emissions reduction projects that generate tradable Emission Reduction Units (ERU);
- *The Clean Development Mechanism* (article 12) permits developing (non-Annex B) countries to host emissions reduction projects that generate tradable Certified Emission Reductions (CERs);
- *International Emissions Trading* (article 17) permits Annex B countries to directly trade their Kyoto allowances (AAUs).

With over 6,500 registered projects and over 1.3 billion tCO_2e of GHG emissions reduced in developing countries as of June 2013 (UNEP Risoe, 2014), the CDM is the largest carbon offset scheme in the world. According to the CDM Policy Dialogue report (UNFCCC, 2012), the CDM raised over US\$215 billion in mostly private investments in climate change mitigation over ten years. This figure is 10–20 times higher than the value of 1.3 billion tons CO_2e of carbon assets

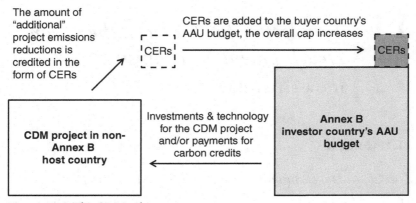

Figure 11.1 The CDM scheme
Source: Shishlov and Bellassen (2012).

generated. Indeed, the leverage effect of carbon finance enables raising private investments in climate-friendly projects that may significantly exceed revenues from the sale of carbon credits (Shishlov and
Bellassen, 2013).

Being an offsetting mechanism, the CDM represents an environmental "zero-sum" game, whereby emissions reductions generated
in developing countries can be used for compliance by developed
countries and individual companies (Figure 11.1). Therefore, in order
to ensure that the overall magnitude of GHG abatement does not
decrease, emissions reductions under the CDM have to be "real, measurable and additional to any that would occur in the absence of the
certified project activity" (UN, 1998).

Thus, unless included in a positive list of project types deemed
automatically additional, a CDM project has to prove that the project scenario is different from what would have happened otherwise,
which is often referred to as the "baseline scenario." Most demonstra-
tions follow the additionality tool developed by the CDM Executive
Board – an algorithm consisting of three or four steps: identification of
alternatives to the project activity, investment analysis and/or barrier
analysis and, finally, common practice analysis.

- *Barrier analysis* involves the identification of barriers – such as
  investment, technological or "prevailing practice" (when the project
  is "first of its kind"), etc. – that would impede the implementation
  of a project without its registration under the CDM scheme.

- *Investment analysis* aims at proving that a project is less attractive than the alternative investment options. If the CER sale is the only source of revenue for the project – e.g., destruction of industrial gases in the chemical industry – a simple cost analysis showing that the project generates additional costs is sufficient. In case a project generates revenues other than from the sale of CERs – e.g., generation of electricity from renewable energy sources or fuel savings due to the improved energy efficiency – investment comparison or a benchmark analysis is warranted.
- *Common practice analysis* mandates an analysis of the whole sector in order to identify whether a proposed project is a "common practice" in the industry. The advantage of this approach is that it is more objective, since it does not include judgments with regard to motivation for launching a project. However, it is very difficult to define what exactly constitutes a "common practice."

Project-by-project additionality demonstration, as required under the CDM, proved to be cumbersome in some sectors. For example, the additionality of certain project types, such as large hydro power plants, has been questioned (Schneider, 2009). The CDM Executive Board recognized this issue, and the ongoing reform of the mechanism is therefore aimed *inter alia* at standardization of additionality demonstration.

The CDM regulatory structure and legislation hierarchy

The governance structure of the CDM includes four main governing bodies (Figure 11.2).

- *The CDM Executive Board (CDM EB)* supervises the CDM. It is the main governing body responsible for all technical elements of the mechanism: the validation of methodologies, the accreditation of auditors, the registration of projects and the issuance of CERs. The Executive Board has ten members and ten alternate members representing different regions and is supported by the staff from the UNFCCC. The CDM EB is supported by several structures:
  - *the UNFCCC Secretariat* provides administrative and procedural support to the Board;
  - *the Methodologies Panel* (Meth Panel) is responsible for reviewing and providing recommendations on methodologies and methodological changes;

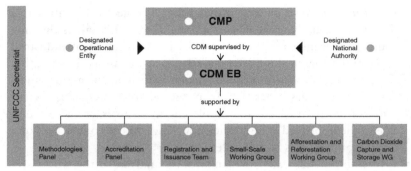

Figure 11.2 The CDM governance structure
Source: UNFCCC (2013a).

- *the Accreditation Panel (CDM AP)* is responsible for accrediting auditors;
- *Registration and Issuance Team (RIT)* assists the Board in reviewing requests for project registration and CER issuance;
- *Afforestation & Reforestation Working Group (A/R WG)* assists the Board with matters related to afforestation and reforestation projects;
- *The working group on proposed methodologies and project categories for small-scale CDM project activities (SSC-WG)* assists the Board with reviewing proposed methodologies and new project categories for small-scale[1] CDM projects;
- *Carbon Dioxide Capture and Storage Working group (CCS WG)* assists the Board with matters related to carbon capture and storage (CCS) projects;
- *CDM Assessment Teams (CDM AT)* are ad hoc groups that assess entities applying for accreditation supporting the Accreditation Panel.

- *The Conference of the Parties to the UNFCCC serving as the meeting of the Parties (CMP)* to the Kyoto Protocol takes the political decisions and annually provides political guidance to the CDM EB. These decisions include the work plan of the CDM EB, the types of projects allowed, etc.

---

[1] Less than 15 MW capacity for energy projects, less than 15 GWh per year for energy efficiency projects or less than 15 ktCO$_2$e of emissions reductions per year for other projects.

- *Designated Operational Entities (DOE)* are independent auditors accredited by the Executive Board (and confirmed by the CMP) that perform two functions: validating that a proposed CDM project initially complies with all CDM requirements – that is its relevant methodology – and verifying the pursued implementation of the project and of its requirements – that is the actual GHG emissions reductions.
- *Designated National Authorities (DNA)* are the official interlocutors, most often a part of a ministry, of the UNFCCC in the countries that have ratified the Kyoto Protocol. The DNA of a host country issues the Letter of Approval (LoA) which is necessary for the registration of a CDM project. The DNA of a host country also plays a key role in assessing the sustainable development benefits of a CDM project as well as defining standardized baselines for all or part of its jurisdiction. An LoA from a DNA of an Annex B country is also necessary for the transfer of CERs (note that the latter LoA is not required for registration of a CDM project).

While the Kyoto Protocol set out general principles of flexibility mechanisms, technical details and procedures were further elaborated through subsequent climate negotiations. The most notable package of rules was established at the seventh Conference of the Parties (COP7) to the UNFCCC (UNFCCC, 2002) in Marrakesh in 2001 (often referred to as the "Marrakech Accords") and confirmed at the first Conference of the Parties serving as the meeting of the Parties (CMP1) to the Kyoto Protocol in Montreal in 2005 (UNFCCC, 2006). COP7 established inter alia Modalities and Procedures for the implementation of the CDM (17/CP.7) marking the official birth of the mechanism. The legislative hierarchy of the CDM includes six levels – from CMP decisions to various supporting documents of the CDM Executive Board (Figure 11.3). Overarching requirements for monitoring, reporting and verification, with which sector-specific methodologies must comply, are defined by the following documents:

- *Modalities and procedures for a clean development mechanism* (Decision 3/CMP.1) for general requirements for baseline and monitoring methodologies;
- *CDM Project Standard* (CDM-EB65-A05-STAN) for project design requirements including principles of monitoring;

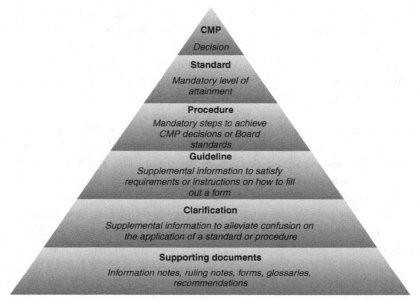

Figure 11.3 The CDM legislation hierarchy
Source: UNFCCC (2013a).

- *CDM Project Cycle Procedure* (CDM-EB65-A32-PROC) for procedures for submission and publishing monitoring reports;
- *CDM Validation and Verification Standard* (CDM-EB65-A04-STAN) for procedures of validation and verification;
- *Standard for sampling and surveys for the CDM* (CDM-EB69-A04);
- *Guidelines for completing the proposed new baseline and monitoring methodology form* (CDM-EB66-A25-GUID);
- *Guidelines for Completing the Monitoring Report Form* (CDM-EB54-A34);
- Other *guidelines, clarifications and supporting documents* published by the CDM EB.

Throughout its more than ten-year history, the CDM has followed a "learning-by-doing" approach, whereby the transparency of the framework made it possible to identify loopholes and spur reforms that have been ongoing since the inception of the CDM. The latest reforms have mainly focused on the standardization of additionality demonstration and baseline setting as well as streamlining the procedures and

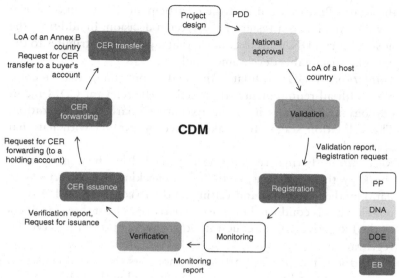

Figure 11.4 The CDM project cycle
Source: Shishlov and Bellassen (2012).

giving more opportunities to underrepresented countries and sectors (Shishlov and Bellassen, 2012). Several important regulatory changes related to monitoring, reporting and verification procedures have been initiated recently and will be discussed later.

The CDM project cycle

The CDM project cycle (Figure 11.4) consists of several main stages that involve four key stakeholders – project participants (PP), designated national authorities (DNA), designated operational entities (DOE), the CDM Executive Board (EB) – as well as different types of documentation.

- *Project design.* The project participant submits the Project Design Document (PDD) following a template developed by the Executive Board. A PDD mainly follows an approved methodology to demonstrate that the project complies with the CDM requirements.
- *National approval.* DNAs of countries participating in a project issue Letters of Approval (LoA), confirming that they have ratified

the Kyoto Protocol and that their participation in the mechanism is voluntary, i.e., is a result of a sovereign decision. In addition, the host country's DNA has to confirm that a project contributes to the national sustainable development policy.

- *Validation.* A DOE validates the PDD, confirming that it complies with all requirements stipulated by the relevant CDM methodology and submits it to the Executive Board for registration. The validation stage often takes place in parallel with national approval.
- *Registration.* Formal registration is preceded by the completeness check by the Secretariat, vetting (i.e., checking the correctness of data) by the Secretariat and vetting by the Executive Board. A thorough review is conducted in case one party or at least three members of the Executive Board request it, otherwise the project proceeds to registration.
- *Monitoring.* The project participant monitors the actual emissions reductions according to the methodology used in the PDD.
- *Verification.* A different DOE provides a written certification of emissions reductions after conducting an ex-post review confirming that the emissions reductions took place in the amount claimed by the monitoring report. The DOE then submits the verification report together with a request for CER issuance to the Executive Board.
- *CER issuance.* Similar to the registration, issuance of CERs is preceded by completeness check by the Secretariat, vetting by the Secretariat and vetting by the Executive Board. A party or at least three members of the Executive Board may request a review. The CERs are then issued to the pending account of the Executive Board of the CDM registry.
- *CER forwarding.* The project participant submits a request for CER forwarding to the Executive Board. The CDM registry administrator then forwards CERs to the respective holding accounts. 98 percent of CERs go to project participants while 2 percent go to the adaptation fund that finances measures related to adaptation to the negative effects of climate change in developing countries.
- *CER transfer.* An LoA of an Annex B country is necessary for the transfer of CERs to the national registry of this country, i.e., to a buyer's account.

Geography and typology of CDM projects

The CER supply is highly concentrated with 90 percent of all issued credits coming from four largest CDM countries: China, India, South Korea and Brazil, while African countries account for less than 3 percent (Figure 11.5a). Such a concentrated distribution of CDM projects does not come as a big surprise though: at the dawn of the CDM, ex-ante studies already predicted that the largest developing countries such as China, India and Brazil would become the CDM "stars." These countries possess the key factors influencing the CDM attractiveness of the host countries – high levels of GHG emissions, strong institutional capacity and favorable investment climate (Jung, 2006). Ex-post studies (Dinar et al., 2008; Flues, 2010; Winkelman and Moore, 2011) confirmed that the geographical distribution of CDM projects is mainly determined by absolute GHG emissions and relative emissions intensity, overall investment climate and the level of international cooperation between countries.

From the sectoral perspective the CDM has also been rather concentrated – over half of all CERs issued by July 1st, 2013, originated from projects focused on reducing emissions of industrial gases – HFC-23 and N_2O (Figure 11.5b). This dominance can be explained by the earlier start of HFC-23 and N_2O projects, as well as their high returns on investments. Besides, the large size of these projects – the ten biggest projects, all focused on destruction of industrial gases, have issued 37 percent of all CERs – enables them to benefit from the economy of scale and submit their monitoring reports more often, while smaller projects might tend to wait until a large number of emissions reductions is accumulated in order to reduce transaction costs. The second largest sector after industrial gas destruction is renewable energy, especially hydro and wind power. These project types are attractive due to additional revenues that stem from the sale of electricity to the grid. Other important sectors in the CDM are energy efficiency, waste and fuel-switching.

The diversity of CDM project types – over 200 approved methodologies – reflects the low-cost abatement search function of the mechanism. The bottom-up framework coupled with market-based approach made it possible to mobilize private sector investments in climate change mitigation and to foster technological innovation and

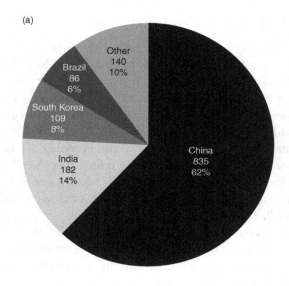

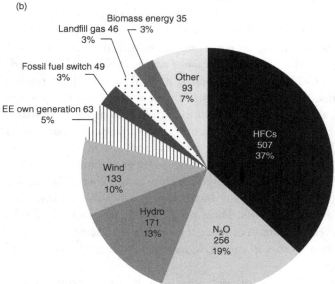

Figure 11.5 Geographical and sectoral distribution of CER issuance as of July 2013 (Mt CO_2e)
Source: CDC Climat Research based on UNEP Risoe (2014).

technology transfer in developing countries. The latter function of the CDM, however, has received mixed evaluations, as the potential for technology transfer largely depends on the project type (Shishlov and Bellassen, 2012).

11.2 Monitoring

The object of monitoring

Being one of the mechanisms under the Kyoto Protocol, the CDM may include projects aimed at reducing emissions of any of the GHGs covered by the UNFCCC, namely carbon dioxide (CO_2), methane (CH_4), nitrous oxide (N_2O), perfluorocarbons (PFCs), hydrofluorocarbons (HFCs) and sulfur hexafluoride (SF_6). The seventh GHG – nitrogen trifluoride (NF_3) – was included in December 2011 and will be monitored during the second Kyoto commitment period (2013–2020). It may therefore also be covered by the CDM. In total the CDM projects cover 15 sectors as classified by the CDM Methodology Booklet as of November 2012 (UNFCCC, 2013b):

1. Energy industries (renewable/nonrenewable sources)
2. Energy distribution
3. Energy demand
4. Manufacturing industries
5. Chemical industries
6. Construction
7. Transport
8. Mining/mineral production
9. Metal production
10. Fugitive emissions from fuel (solid, oil and gas)
11. Fugitive emissions from production and consumption of halocarbons and SF_6
12. Solvent use
13. Waste handling and disposal
14. Land-use, land-use change and forestry (LULUCF)
15. Agriculture

Unlike national inventories or cap-and-trade schemes, which require monitoring absolute levels of GHG emissions at a territorial or site scale, the object of MRV in carbon offset projects is *emissions reductions*. This means that a project developer has to monitor not only realized emissions within the project boundary, but also the hypothetical emissions that would have occurred in the absence of a project, which is usually referred to as a baseline. Since CERs are issued against emissions reductions realized by a project, the issue of monitoring is closely linked to the question of the baseline setting. This is why all CDM methodologies include rules for both baseline setting and monitoring. Another important feature of MRV for the CDM is that it requires calculation of emissions not only within the project boundary, but also within the boundary of emissions indirectly affected by a project – so-called *leakage*.

Methodologies form the cornerstone of monitoring

The sectors listed above vary significantly in terms of monitoring approaches depending on the nature of GHG emissions, which explains the need for specific methodologies that reflect the peculiarities of different project types and subtypes. Methodologies are designed in a bottom-up manner: stakeholders, usually project developers, come up with a project idea and propose a methodology to monitor its emissions reductions. The methodology must contain all the elements required by the Guidelines for completing the proposed new baseline and monitoring methodology form (CDM-EB66-A25-GUID) most importantly:

- a definition of a project boundary;
- an identification of a baseline scenario;
- a description of the additionality assessment procedure;
- a description of how baseline, project and leakage emissions shall be monitored;
- a list of all data that shall be collected (activity data and emission factors);
- the equations to calculate emissions reductions.

The draft methodology is submitted by the project developer to the UNFCCC Secretariat. After a completeness check, the Secretariat, normally assisted by external experts, drafts a recommendation for consideration by the Meth Panel. On this basis, the Meth Panel then issues a recommendation to the EB who takes a decision on the methodology (Figure 11.6). Small-scale methodologies are assessed by the

Figure 11.6 Procedure for approval of new methodologies
Source: Michaelowa and Michaelowa (2013).

SSC-WG, while afforestation/reforestation methodologies are assessed by the A/R WG.

Historically, the bottom-up approach to development of methodologies resulted in multiple project-specific methodologies not tailored to be applied across all projects of the same type. In light of this constraint, the CDM Executive Board attempted to consolidate methodologies to create a concise list of broadly applicable approaches and eliminate inconsistencies among them. As of June 2013 the CDM Methodologies Booklet (UNFCCC, 2013b) included 201 active methodologies including 91 large-scale methodologies (AM), 21 large-scale consolidated methodologies (ACM), 85 small-scale methodologies (AMS) and 4 afforestation/reforestation methodologies (UNEP Risoe, 2014). Large-scale, small-scale and A/R methodologies may have different monitoring requirements. The diversity of CDM projects in terms of sectors, sizes and types of gases results in a variety of monitoring approaches – from direct flow measurement (e.g., landfill gas) to sampling and modeling (e.g., forestry).

One of the CDM reforms introduced in 2009 was the Programs of Activities (PoAs), a framework that allows implementing an unlimited number of CDM program activities (CPAs) under one registered PoA. This modality enables the use of small-scale methodologies that are not available in the regular CDM. Small-scale replicable projects (often with scattered emissions) under PoA also benefit from reduced transaction costs, which makes them more attractive for investors.

Monitoring procedure

General guiding principles of monitoring are set up by the CDM Project Standard (CDM-EB65-A05-STAN):

- relevance
- completeness
- consistency

- accuracy and conservativeness
- transparency.

According to the CDM Modalities and Procedures (Decision 3/ CMP.1), Project Design Documentation must include a monitoring plan that provides for:

a) the collection and archiving of all relevant data necessary for estimating or measuring anthropogenic emissions by sources of greenhouse gases occurring within the project boundary during the crediting period;

b) the collection and archiving of all relevant data necessary for determining the baseline of anthropogenic emissions by sources of greenhouse gases within the project boundary during the crediting period;

c) the identification of all potential sources of, and the collection and archiving of data on, increased anthropogenic emissions by sources of greenhouse gases outside the project boundary that are significant and reasonably attributable to the project activity during the crediting period;

d) the collection and archiving of information relevant to the assessment of environmental impact of a project;

e) quality assurance and control procedures for the monitoring process;

f) procedures for the periodic calculation of the reductions of anthropogenic emissions by sources by the proposed CDM project activity, and for leakage effects.

The CDM thus requires the monitoring of baseline emissions, actual project emissions and leakage. The amount of emissions reductions eligible for carbon crediting is then calculated by "subtracting the actual anthropogenic emissions by sources from baseline emissions and adjusting for leakage" (Decision 3/CMP.1).

The general principle of calculating GHG emissions can be described as a product of activity data and emission factor (see Chapter 1, Section 1.3).

Monitoring frequency

The *crediting period* is the maximal time period over which an offset project may obtain carbon credits, and hence needs to be monitored. For a CDM project, it is limited to seven years with a possibility to renew up to two times or to ten years non-renewable (CDM-EB65-A05-STAN). To provide some certainty to project developers, the version of the methodology in place at the beginning of a *crediting period* applies all over. Hence, renewing a crediting period may mean adapting to a new version of the methodology, in addition to other requirements associated with *crediting period* renewal such as re-demonstrating additionality.

Regarding the frequency of actual monitoring, the CDM Project Standard (CDM-EB65-A05-STAN) provides a certain amount of room for maneuver depending on the variability of data and the frequency of reporting:

- Variables that impact the GHG emission reductions continuously (e.g., quantity of the fuel inputs, amount of heat or electricity produced, gas captured, etc.) shall be measured continuously and recorded at an appropriate time interval (e.g., monthly for a *monitoring period* of six months or more; weekly if the *monitoring period* is less than six months; daily if the *monitoring period* is one month or less). For default values (such as an IPCC value), where the value is confirmed ex-post, the most recent value shall be applied.
- Data elements that are generally constant (e.g., emission factors, calorific value, system efficiencies) shall be measured or calculated at least once a year, unless other specifications are provided in the selected methodology.

Pre-implementation costs

Upfront transaction costs borne by CDM project developers include PDD development, validation costs (internal and DOE), UNFCCC registration fees and the cost of installing the monitoring system. These costs vary considerably depending on the project size and type and may range from €37,000 for small-hydro projects to €434,000 for very large adipic acid N_2O projects. The cost of monitoring equipment may range from zero – in case there is no additional CDM-specific equipment to be installed – to €15,000 (Warnecke et al., 2013). Validation costs may also vary depending on the size and nature of a project.

PoAs provide a framework for bundling several similar project activities, thus reducing costs of registering each activity. For example, a PoA focused on efficient cooking stoves becomes less costly than a classic CDM as of the second activity, while more complex project types may take 3–5 activities to justify the use of the PoA framework (Beaurain and Schmidt-Traub, 2010).

Periodic monitoring costs

The project developer is responsible for carrying out all monitoring activities, which is usually done either "in-house" using the developer's own resources or by a hired specialist consulting firm. This choice may significantly affect the actual monitoring costs: it was reported that the cost of the external consulting firm can exceed €1,000 per man-day, while internal costs may be considerably lower (Guigon et al., 2009). Monitoring costs may thus decrease over time thanks to the learning curve and the potential switch to in-house monitoring. The estimates of periodic monitoring costs usually fall in the range €3,000–18,000 (Table 11.1).

For the cost overview of this chapter (MRV ID Table 11.4) and detailed cost calculations (e.g., Table 11.5), the CDM Market Support Study (Warnecke et al., 2013) is retained as the most reliable for three main reasons. First, the data in this study are collected from a sample of DOEs and project developers in sectors, most represented in the CDM. Second, cost estimates of the study are consistent with previous research (Table 11.1). Finally, it is the latest study available to our knowledge.

Monitoring costs may also vary drastically depending on the project type. For example, in the case of transportation projects monitoring costs may be as high as €144,000 due to the requirements to conduct multiple surveys of passengers (Replogle and Bakker, 2011). Besides the absolute figures, the relative importance of monitoring costs in the cost structure of a CDM project depends on the abatement cost, and hence the type of a project. More specific estimations of monitoring costs in different project types will be provided in case studies (see Chapters 12–14).

Throughout the decade-long history of the CDM, the Executive Board has implemented multiple reforms to streamline the administrative procedures, to expand the mechanism into new sectoral and geographical scopes and to improve procedures for setting baselines and demonstrating additionality. Many of these changes are directly

Table 11.1 *Periodic monitoring costs in CDM projects*

Cost estimate	Source
€10,000	Michaelowa and Stronzik (2002)
€9,600*	Krey (2005)
€5,000	Guigon et al. (2009)
€1,500–5,000 for projects <50 kCER/year	Warnecke et al. (2013)
€3,000–10,000 for projects >50 kCER/year	Warnecke et al. (2013)
€5,000–18,000 for N₂O projects	Warnecke et al. (2013)

* Converted from US dollars into euros using the average annual (respective publication year) exchange rate.

related to monitoring – methodology consolidation, the introduction of the standard for sampling and surveys and the materiality standard, tools to calculate baselines, etc. – while others focused on simplifying reporting and verification procedures (Shishlov and Bellassen, 2012).

Treatment of uncertainty

With regard to data uncertainty, project developers have to "reduce bias and uncertainties as far as is practical/cost-effective, or otherwise use conservative assumptions, values and procedures to ensure that GHG emission reductions by sources or GHG removals by sinks are not over-estimated" (CDM-EB65-A05-STAN). The same principle is applied to baselines: "the establishment of a baseline is considered conservative if the resulting projection of the baseline does not lead to an overestimation of emission reductions attributable to the CDM project activity" (CDM-EB66-A25-GUID).

At the same time, there is no overall data certainty requirement in monitoring guidelines (some requirements appear in specific methodologies though). Only the sampling error of activity data is subject to such a requirement. A monitoring plan shall include *inter alia* uncertainty levels of variables (CDM-EB65-A05-STAN). More specifically, "project proponents shall use 90/10 confidence/precision [that is a 90 percent confidence that the estimate falls within 10 percent of the actual value], as estimated with the criteria for reliability of sampling efforts for small-scale project activities and 95/10 for large-scale project activities" (CDM-EB69-A4). The choice of upper/lower bounds shall ensure conservativeness of emissions reduction estimation. To our knowledge, there is no reference to uncertainty for other data sources than surveys and samples in the CDM rules.

Even for the assessment of uncertainty, the requirements are rather light. This assessment is not required for activity data, and for default values, uncertainty should be described, but not necessarily quantified. In case there is no country – or project – specific information regarding default parameters (e.g., emission factors) available, the IPCC default values may be used (CDM-EB25). Methodologies have to "describe the uncertainty of key parameters and, where possible, provide an uncertainty range at 95% confidence level for key parameters for the calculation of emission reductions" (CDM-EB66-A25-GUID).

The overarching CDM guidelines, thus, do not include clear provisions regarding the possible trade-off between monitoring cost and uncertainty, for example by scaling the amount of carbon crediting to the stringency of monitoring. The conservativeness principle for baseline setting and monitoring does not refer to a "buffer" proportional to uncertainty, while the sampling requirements only provide a threshold (90/10 or 95/5) and not an incentive that decreases with sampling error. Nevertheless, some methodologies, e.g., in the forestry sector (AR-ACM0003 and AR-AM0014) provide for a discount factor based on sampling error (see Chapter 13).

The CDM Executive Board acknowledged that the rules regarding treatment of uncertainty apply only to selected variables and are not consistent across methodologies. At its 39th meeting in 2008 the Executive Board requested the Methodology Panel to work on the guidelines regarding treatment of uncertainty including the issue "flexibility to choose the level of uncertainty" (CDM-EB39). Until recently, this topic was not prioritized and was not further developed. The CMP7 that took place in Durban in 2011 reopened the issue and requested the Executive Board to "address the issue of uncertainties of measurements in baseline and monitoring methodologies, so that these types of uncertainties do not need to be considered in addressing materiality" (9/CMP.7). As of 2012 the Executive Board has been working on developing a new standard (or amending the existing ones) to address the issue of monitoring uncertainty in a systematic way. Interestingly, the new rules "should provide flexibility in optimizing measurement instrumentation based on cost-benefit considerations" (CDM-EB73-AA-A04).

The first draft standard on uncertainty of measures was proposed by the Executive Board in May 2013 and included *inter alia* provisions for discounting carbon credits based on monitoring uncertainty: "if the overall measurement uncertainty exceeds five per cent, the aggregated emission reductions shall be discounted adjusted by the calculated overall uncertainty" (CDM-EB73-AA-A04). The draft also proposed specific formulas for calculating the overall monitoring uncertainty of a project.

Differences with other major offset standards on monitoring

Unlike the CDM, several voluntary offset standards provide guidelines regarding treatment of emissions reduction uncertainty. Notably, the Verified Carbon Standard (VCS) – the standard currently certifying most carbon credits purchased for other purposes than complying with a carbon pricing regulation (e.g., branding a company or a product as *carbon neutral*) – explicitly incorporates the issue of monitoring uncertainty in its two main documents:

- the VCS Program Guide stipulates that "all GHG emission reductions and removals must be quantifiable using recognized measurement tools (**including adjustments for uncertainty** and leakage) against a credible emissions baseline" (VCS, 2012a);
- the VCS Standard stipulates that methodologies have to clearly explain uncertainties related to assumptions, parameters and procedures and how they are addressed. Besides, 90 or 95 percent confidence interval of parameters has to be estimated: "where a methodology applies a 90 percent confidence interval and the width of the confidence interval exceeds 20 percent of the estimated value or where a methodology applies a 95 percent confidence interval and the width of the confidence interval exceeds 30 percent of the estimated value, an appropriate confidence deduction shall be applied" (VCS, 2012b).

Uncertainty of carbon stocks is of particular concern in forestry projects. The Forestry Carbon Sequestration Project Protocol developed by Chicago Climate Exchange (CCX), another offset standard, addresses this issue through discounting. Moreover, CCX provides an explicit incentive to apply more accurate monitoring, as "no discount will be applied for instances when in-field inventories are conducted on an annual basis." It is also stipulated that for forestry projects "in order to encourage high-quality inventories, smaller discounts are applied to projects with a higher degree of accuracy for a given level of precision" (CCX, 2009). Another CCX methodology – for Avoided Emissions from Organic Waste Disposal – applies a default discount factor of 0.9 to baseline emissions to account for uncertainties.

The Program Manual of the Climate Action Reserve (CAR) includes a provision to apply for a deviation from approved monitoring and measurement approaches, as long as it does not "diverge significantly from the approved methodology." In that case however, the Reserve retains the right to "impose additional constraints and/or discount factors on the proposed monitoring or measuring methods" (CAR, 2011). There is thus a legal window for the regulator to apply discounting for monitoring uncertainty.

The Japanese Verified Emission Reduction (J-VER) scheme relies on extremely standardized procedures. Notably, the additionality demonstration under J-VER is based on a "positive list" of methodologies rather than project-by-project additionality demonstration. The monitoring process itself is also significantly simplified with a wide use of conservative default values to calculate emissions reductions (IGES, 2013c).

Apart from carbon offsetting, some other policies may provide for a trade-off between monitoring and incentives. For example, Vine and Sathaye (2000) noted that the US Environmental Protection Agency's Conservation Verification Protocols provide an incentive for more rigorous monitoring of energy efficiency improvements, whereby developers adopting more stringent monitoring with inspections are eligible for higher rewards, while those using default values can only claim a part of energy savings.

Differences with the EU ETS

The different nature of the CDM and the EU ETS systems by default affects the MRV approaches regarding the scope of monitoring and management of methodologies (Table 11.2).

At the same time there are certain differences that are not directly linked to the nature of the two mechanisms. A recent study

Table 11.2 *Comparison of monitoring approaches in the CDM and the EU ETS*

	CDM	EU ETS
Monitoring scope	Project activities	Installations
MRV methodology invention procedure	Bottom-up	Top-down
MRV methodology update process	Continuously	Fixed for trading periods
MRV methodology documentation	Distributed	Concentrated

Source: Warnecke (2014).

demonstrated that although MRV under the CDM is often perceived as being more relaxed than that of the EU ETS, in reality monitoring requirements under the CDM are often more stringent and less flexible (Warnecke, 2014).

For example, a given CDM methodology clearly specifies whether a calculation-based or measurement-based monitoring approach is to be used. Conversely, the EU ETS offers installations an option to choose between calculation and direct measurement of emissions, although the latter is rarely used in practice.

Both systems embrace the principle of conservativeness, however in the CDM it is explicitly laid out only for surveys and samples, while other data sources are dealt with only in sector-specific methodologies and/or tools. At the same time the treatment of monitoring uncertainty is clearly regulated under the EU ETS through maximum uncertainty thresholds in a tier-based approach (see Chapter 5).

11.3 Reporting

Monitoring report

In order to apply for CER issuance, the project proponent has to prepare a monitoring report according to the CDM Project Standard and submit it to the auditor – Designated Operational Entity (DOE) – for verification.

The monitoring report must include all data, parameters and other information required by a given methodology. Besides the information on baseline emissions, project emissions and leakage, the monitoring report must include the following elements (CDM-EB65-A05-STAN):

a) the operational and management structure to be put in place to implement the monitoring plan;
b) provisions to ensure that data monitored and required for verification and issuance be kept and archived electronically for two years after the end of the crediting period or the last issuance of CERs, whichever occurs later;
c) definition of responsibilities and institutional arrangements for data collection and archiving;
d) quality assurance and quality control (QA/QC) procedures;
e) uncertainty levels associated with methods and measuring instruments to be used for various parameters and variables;
f) specifications of the calibration frequency for the measuring equipments. In cases where neither the selected methodology, nor the Board's guidance specify any requirements for calibration frequency for measuring equipments, project participants shall ensure that the equipments are calibrated either in accordance with the local/national standards, or as per the manufacturer's specifications. If local/national standards or the manufacturer's specifications are not available, international standards may be used.

Reporting procedure

The monitoring report has to be prepared in English as the working language of the Executive Board (CDM-EB54-A34). The DOE shall make the monitoring report publicly available through a dedicated interface on the UNFCCC CDM website no later than 14 days before undertaking the site visit for the verification (CDM-EB65-A32-PROC). On average the monitoring report is made public 70 days after the end of the respective monitoring period (IGES, 2013a), which represents the time necessary for a project developer to prepare the report.

The duration of monitoring periods, i.e., the frequency of submission of monitoring reports, is not predefined. The economic rationale suggests that larger projects that benefit from the economies of scale may be willing to submit their reports more often in order to benefit from a faster revenue flow. Conversely, smaller projects would normally be willing to wait until a large enough amount of emissions reductions has been accumulated before submitting a report in order to reduce transaction costs per CER. This rationale indeed corresponds to current practice, as proven by Cormier and Bellassen (2013): project size is the most influential factor on monitoring duration. As of June 2013 the average duration of 5,922 monitoring periods for large-scale projects was 322 days, while the average duration of 2,314 monitoring periods for small-scale projects was 508 days (IGES, 2013a).

If no monitoring reports have been published within two years after the registration of a project, the project proponent shall update the status of its implementation through a dedicated interface on the CDM website. According to the CDM Project Procedure, in that case the proponent has to indicate one of the following statuses (CDM-EB65-A32-PROC):

a) The project is under implementation, but has not reached the stage of monitoring. In this case the project proponent shall provide an update of the status at 180-day intervals thereafter;
b) The project has not yet been implemented, but is still planned to be implemented. In this case the project proponent shall also provide an update of the status at 180-day intervals thereafter;
c) The project has been implemented, but the project participants have not yet decided to proceed with the request for issuance stage;
d) The implementation of the project has been cancelled;
e) Any other reason for not having submitted a monitoring report.

The freedom of choice of reporting frequency implicitly offers project proponents the opportunity to reduce transaction costs per CER through economies of scale, which can be especially significant for small-scale projects.

Reporting costs

The cost of preparing periodic monitoring reports is usually included in the cost of periodic monitoring activity. It is usually negligible, although may increase in the case of scattered projects. For example, Beaurain and Schmidt-Traub (2010) estimated reporting costs for PoAs in the range of €10,000–15,000. Project developers may also reduce relative reporting costs per CER by reducing the reporting frequency.

Differences with other major offset standards on reporting

Most carbon offset standards, including the CDM, the VCS and the Gold Standard, explicitly require project developers to prepare monitoring reports. Other standards, such as CAR, do not require monitoring reports as such, but oblige project developers to set up a record-keeping system (IETA, 2011).

11.4 Verification

Verification procedure

According to the CDM Modalities and Procedures "verification is the periodic independent review and ex-post determination by the designated operational entity (DOE) of the monitored reductions in anthropogenic emissions by sources of greenhouse gases that have occurred as a result of a registered CDM project activity during the verification period" (Decision 3/CMP.1). Note that in order to minimize the potential conflict of interests the DOE conducting verification has to be different from the DOE that validated the CDM project during the registration phase. However, upon request the Executive Board may allow the same DOE to perform both validation and verification. The simplified procedure for small-scale projects also allows the same DOE to perform both validation and verification (Shishlov and Bellassen, 2012).

In order to issue CERs, a CDM project must obtain a written certification from a DOE confirming that in a given monitoring period a project achieved a verified amount of emission reductions, which would not have taken place in the absence of the project activity. DOEs are independent auditors that tend to be large international auditing firms such as TÜV SÜD, Bureau Veritas, Deloitte, etc. although accreditation is usually specifically granted to one or several franchises. As part of the verification procedure a DOE shall perform the following tasks (Decision 3/CMP.1):

a) determine whether the project documentation provided complies with the requirements of the registered PDD and relevant provisions of the CMP;
b) conduct on-site inspections, as appropriate;
c) if appropriate, use additional data from other sources;

d) review monitoring results and verify that the monitoring methodologies have been applied correctly and their documentation is complete and transparent;

e) recommend to the project participants appropriate changes to the monitoring methodology for any future crediting period, if necessary;

f) determine emission reductions that would not have occurred in the absence of the CDM project activity;

g) identify and inform the project participants of any concerns relating to the conformity of the actual project activity and its operation with the registered PDD;

h) provide a verification report to the project participants, the Parties involved and the Executive Board. The report shall be made publicly available.

The verification report has to include the assessment of a project with regard to (CDM-EB65-A04-STAN):

• compliance of the implementation of a project with a registered PDD;
• compliance of the monitoring plan with the applicable methodology;
• compliance of the monitoring activities with the registered monitoring plan;
• compliance with the calibration frequency of measuring equipment;
• assessment of data and calculation of emission reductions.

If a DOE finds issues related to implementation and/or monitoring of a project activity that could "impair the capacity of the registered project activity to achieve emission reductions or influence the monitoring and reporting of emission reductions," it may request corrective actions. In doing so, the DOE must abide by the materiality standards of the CDM. A piece of information is considered material if its omission or misstatement may lead to an overestimation of emissions reductions by more than a given threshold, which depends on the project size (CDM-EB-69-A06):

a) 0.5 percent of the emission reductions or removals for project activities achieving a total emission reduction or removal of equal to or more than 500,000 tons of carbon dioxide equivalent per year;

b) 1 percent of the emission reductions or removals for project activities achieving a total emission reduction or removal

between 300,000 and 500,000 tons of carbon dioxide equivalent per year;

c) 2 percent of the emission reductions or removals for large-scale
project activities achieving a total emission reduction or removal
of 300,000 tons of carbon dioxide equivalent per year or less;

d) 5 percent of the emission reductions or removals for small-scale
project activities other than project activities covered under sub-
paragraph (e) below;

e) 10 percent of the emission reductions or removals for the type of
project activities referred to as micro-scale project activities, i.e.,
renewable energy projects of up to 5 MW and energy efficiency
projects of up to 20 GWh of energy savings per year (Decision 9/
CMP.7).

The stringency of verification is thus adapted to the importance
of information at stake via the materiality standard. Note that the
materiality provisions under the EU ETS are less gradual than those of
the CDM. Although emissions reductions are necessarily smaller than
emissions, one may nevertheless compare the materiality provisions
under both schemes as the most common CDM projects – industrial
gas and renewables – bring emissions down to zero, and therefore
equate project emissions reductions to baseline emissions. For large-
scale installations/projects (>500 $ktCO_2e$ per year) the materiality
threshold is 2% under the EU ETS and 0.5% under the CDM. For
installations with annual emissions <500 $ktCO_2e$ per year the materiality threshold is 5% under the EU ETS, while in the CDM it ranges
from 1% for projects with annual emissions reductions between 300
and 500 $ktCO_2e$ to 5% for small-scale (<60 $ktCO_2e$) and 10% for
micro-scale (<20 $ktCO_2e$) projects.

Depending on the nature and importance of an issue – e.g.,
material vs. non-material error – the DOE can request the project proponent to correct these issues using one of the three options
(CDM-EB65-A04-STAN):

• *Corrective action request (CAR)* is raised if: non-compliance with
the monitoring plan or the respective methodology is found, modifications to the implementation and monitoring the project activity
have not been documented, mistakes in assumptions, data or calculations that impact the quantity of emission reductions have been
made, or the Forward action requests (FAR, see below) from the

previous monitoring period have not been addressed. All CARs have to be resolved before requesting the issuance of CERs.

- *Clarification request (CR)* is raised if the information provided by a project proponent is insufficient or not clear enough to determine whether the CDM requirements have been met. All CRs have to be resolved before requesting the issuance of CERs.
- *Forward action request (FAR)* is raised if corrective actions or adjustments in implementation or monitoring of the project activity are required during the subsequent monitoring period. A FAR would typically be raised if a non-material error is found by the DOE.

All CARs, CLs and FARs have to be reflected in the verification report.

Request for CER issuance

After the DOE verifies the emission reductions in a given monitoring period, it requests CER issuance using the CDM project issuance request form. The DOE has to provide the UNFCCC Secretariat with all supporting documents included in the completeness checklist, namely:

- monitoring report;
- spreadsheet with emission reductions calculation;
- verification report;
- certification report;
- signed request for issuance of CERs.

If a DOE has not submitted an issuance request within 180 days after the publication of the monitoring report, it shall update the status of the verification activity through a dedicated interface on the CDM website. According to the CDM Project Procedure, in that case a DOE has to indicate one of the following statuses (CDM-EB65-A32-PROC):

a) The verification contract has been terminated. In this case the DOE shall also provide a reason for the termination to the Board through the Secretariat on a confidential basis.
b) The DOE has issued a negative verification opinion.
c) The DOE has raised one or more CARs or CRs, for which no response has been received from the project participants or the coordinating/managing entity. In this case the DOE shall also

provide a summary of the issues raised and update or reconfirm the status of the verification activities at 90-day intervals thereafter.

d) The DOE is performing verification activities and it has not yet sent any corrective action or clarification requests to the project participants or the coordinating/managing entity. In this case the DOE shall also provide an explanation on the length of time taken and update or reconfirm the status of the verification activities at 90-day intervals thereafter.

The Secretariat shall maintain a publicly available list of all submitted requests for issuance on the UNFCCC CDM website. The Secretariat shall also make publicly available the schedule for processing the requests for issuance, including the expected date of commencement. The Secretariat has to conduct the completeness check within 7 days after the receipt of the request for CER issuance. After that, the Secretariat has to conduct the information and reporting check within 23 days after the completeness check.

Unless a Party involved in the project and/or any member of the Board requests a review of the request for issuance within 28 days after the date of publication of the request for issuance for the project activity or 42 days of receipt of request for issuance for the PoA, respectively, the Board shall instruct the registry operator to issue CERs.

Upon the positive conclusion of completeness and information and reporting checks, the Secretariat shall publish the request for issuance on the UNFCCC website, which is then deemed received by the Executive Board for consideration. Within 14 days after publication of the request, the Secretariat shall prepare a summary note of the request for the Executive Board.

Request for review

A Party involved in the project and/or any member of the Board may request a review of the request for issuance within 28 days after the date of publication of the request for issuance for the project activity or 42 days of receipt of request for issuance for the PoA, respectively (CDM-EB65-A32-PROC). This has to be done using the CDM issuance request review form providing *inter alia* reasons for requesting a review. The review commences if a Party – through its DNA – or at least three members of the Board requested it. The Secretariat has to fix a date for the review commencement and notify project participants and the DOE.

Two independent assessments – by the Secretariat and by the Registration and Issuance Team (RIT) – have to be carried out within 14 days of the commencement of the review according to the Procedure for Review of Requests for Issuance of CERs (CDM-EB-64-A04). Both assessments have to take into account responses received from project participants and the DOE. The assessments have to be concluded with a decision to approve or to reject the issuance request:

- If both the Secretariat and the RIT come to the same conclusion, this decision becomes final within 20 days unless a member of the Executive Board raises an objection. If a member of the Board raises an objection, the issue has to be taken to the next Board meeting.
- If the conclusions of the Secretariat and the RIT are different, the Executive Board has to take the final decision at its next meeting.

For each issue raised in the request for review, project participants and the DOE have to respond with either a revision of respective documents or an explanation why the revision is not required. These responses have to be provided no later than 28 days after the request for review notification. Project participants or the DOE may request one telephone call with the Secretariat to clarify the issues identified in the request for review.

CER issuance

If the Secretariat does not receive a request for review from a Party or at least three members of the Board or if the Board approves the issuance request after a review, the CDM registry administrator shall proceed with issuance of the respective amount of CERs to the pending account. The project proponent may then request a CER transfer to the credit buyer's account using the "Certified emission reductions forwarding request form." A letter of approval from an Annex B country is required in order to effectuate the CER transfer.

Direct costs of verification

The cost of the periodic verification has been estimated in the range of €5,000–30,000 (Table 11.3). Project participants may reduce

Table 11.3 *Periodic verification costs in CDM projects*

Cost estimate	Source
€8,000	Michaelowa and Stronzik (2002)
€3,200–14,400*	Krey (2005)
€3,650–18,250*	UNEP (2007)
€5,000–6,000	Guigon et al. (2009)
€10,000–15,000	Beaurain and Schmidt-Traub (2010)
€3,760–18,800*	IGES (2013b)
€5,000–15,000 for projects <50 kCER/year	Warnecke et al. (2013)
€15,000–30,000 for projects >50 kCER/year	Warnecke et al. (2013)
€25,000 for N_2O projects	Warnecke et al. (2013)

* Converted from US dollars into euros using the average annual (respective publication year) exchange rate.

verification costs per CER by increasing the duration of monitoring periods and decreasing the frequency of reporting.

Periodic verification costs may also vary depending on the nature of a project. For example it is estimated that verification costs for PoAs can be significantly higher and reach €40,000 (IGES, 2013b).

Additional costs borne by project proponents are related to the UNFCCC fees and the internal time consumed in dealings with the DOE. UNFCCC fees amount to €0.08–0.15 per CER in addition to the 2 percent of the issued CERs, which go to the climate change adaptation fund.

Indirect costs from the DOE accreditation procedure

Getting and keeping accredited is a rather demanding process for the DOE, and may constitute a significant part of the fee the DOE then demands from project developers.

According to the Procedure for accrediting operational entities by the Executive Board (CDM-EB56-A02) the accreditation process comprises the following steps (Figure 11.7):

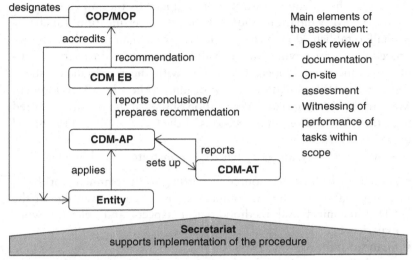

Figure 11.7 DOE accreditation procedure
Source: CDM Rulebook.

a) an application for accreditation by an entity;
b) a completeness check of the application documentation by the Secretariat;
c) consideration of the application by the CDM Accreditation Panel;
d) a desk review by the CDM Assessment Team of the documentation provided by the entity;
e) on-site assessment by the CDM Assessment Team at the central office of the entity and/or at any other site where the CDM functions are to be undertaken;
f) a recommendation on accreditation or rejection of application by the CDM Accreditation Panel to the Board;
g) a decision by the Board on accreditation or rejection of application of the entity;
h) recommendation for designation to the CMP by the Board.

After the Board decides to accredit an entity and recommends it for designation, the entity is allowed to carry out sector-specific validation and/or verification/certification functions on a provisional basis until a decision of the CMP on its designation.

A DOE shall demonstrate its commitment to the implementation of the CDM validation and/or verification/certification functions. It shall establish, document, implement and maintain documented procedures for carrying out its validation and/or verification/certification functions competently, in line with the requirements specified in the CDM Modalities and Procedures, the Clean Development Mechanism Validation and Verification Standard (hereinafter referred to as the VVS) and relevant decisions of the COP/MOP and the Board (CDM-EB67-A05).

More specifically, an entity has to demonstrate the following:

- sufficiency of human resources according to the planned workload;
- managerial and technical competence, including knowledge of the CDM technical and methodological aspects and relevant work experience;
- financial stability;
- established procedures for validation/verification and information management.

Accreditation costs

According to the Procedure for accrediting operational entities by the Executive Board (CDM-EB56-A02), accreditation fees are as follows:

- The non-reimbursable application fee is €11,300.[2] Entities from non-Annex B Parties may have the possibility of paying 50 percent of the non-reimbursable fee when they apply for accreditation, provided that they state their inability to pay the full fee at application, bearing in mind that they need to meet the standards as contained in paragraphs 1 (c) and (d) of Appendix A to the CDM M&P.[3] The remaining 50 percent of the fee should be paid at a later stage once and if the entity is accredited and designated and starts operation.
- Fee and costs associated with an on-site assessment of the premises of a would-be DOE: the entity shall pay for the following cost items (dates, schedules and accommodation arrangements to be coordinated through the Secretariat): (a) Business class airfare for each assessment team member; (b) Applicable UN daily subsistence

[2] US$15,000 (conversion using the average annual exchange rate of the year of the document).
[3] It is nevertheless likely that the financial stability of an entity applying for such a delay may be questioned.

allowance for the CDM-AT. In addition, the AE shall pay a fee to cover the cost for the work provided by the CDM-AT members. The Secretariat shall provide the would-be DOE with the payment instructions and pre-filled receipts indicating the number of the CDM-AT members and the days of intervention.

In addition a DOE bears the following costs after accreditation:

- costs associated with performance assessment, which has to be conducted by a CDM Assessment Team after commencement of validation/verification activity by a DOE;
- costs associated with regular on-site surveillance, which has to be conducted at least once every three years by the Accreditation Panel taking a minimum of four person-days;
- costs associated with application for extension of the accreditation for additional sectoral scope(s);
- costs associated with changes notified by the DOE, such as the change of company ownership or its legal status;
- costs of "spot-checks" (see below);
- costs of an appeal against rejected accreditation or suspension.

The level of the fee per person is set by the Executive Board and is currently €300 per person-day.

DOE suspension

The Board may conduct a spot-check of a DOE at any time. Spot-checks can be triggered *inter alia* by a recommendation from the Accreditation Panel or based on information received from a third party. The reason for a spot-check shall remain confidential. The Board may then decide to suspend totally or partially the accreditation of a DOE based on the recommendation of the CDM Accreditation Panel or other review processes conducted by the Board, including the provisions of the policy framework to address non-compliance by designated operational entities (CDM-EB56-A02).

There have been several suspensions undertaken by the Executive Board, including the temporary suspension of the biggest auditor TÜV SÜD in 2010. Suspension was recommended by the CDM Accreditation panel and was triggered by two faults:

- the DOE gave positive validation to projects, over which it had additionality concerns;

• the personnel qualification criteria were not met, namely there was a lack of technical sector-specific work experience.

Differences with other major offset standards on verification

All major carbon offset standards require some form of verification of emission reductions. Unlike the CDM, VCS allows the same auditor for validation and verification. Interestingly, most carbon offset standards are in some way or another free-riding on the CDM. Most of them derived part of their procedures and methodologies from the CDM. The VCS even accepts automatically all CDM methodologies. But the accreditation process is probably the mostly important element of this free-riding. Indeed, many standards such as the Gold Standard are content with CDM-accredited auditors without further inquiries, thus avoiding these auditors and themselves a costly process. The VCS only recently started to accredit auditors based on another standard than the CDM-AP,[4] and still grants automatic accreditation to DOEs: only one-fourth of VCS accredited reviewers are not DOEs, most of them located in countries that have not ratified the Kyoto Protocol such as the US and Canada.

11.5 What practitioners say about it

Is there an incentive to reduce the uncertainty of monitoring in the CDM?

The CDM has many implicit incentives to reduce the uncertainty which may arise from any lack of data or non-compliance with the guidelines (i.e., availability of calibration reports for every single meter). These uncertainties are always "punished" by the DOE with a deduction of the number of CERs that can be issued based on the principle of conservativeness. In some methodologies, such incentives are also made very explicit through options to apply a simple yet conservative approach (default factors) versus a complex yet less uncertain approach. These incentives translate directly into financial incentives since the compliance with CDM rules would lead to higher CER

---

[4] The VCS does not accredit auditors by itself but recognizes the accreditations provided by the CDM-AP and the International Accreditation Forum (IAF) member body such as the American National Standards Institute (ANSI) for ISO14065 scope.

revenues by avoiding deductions in the issuance volume through conservative discounts in the case of non-compliance.

Patrick Bürgi and Sophie Tison, South Pole Carbon

From a project developer's perspective, ensuring timely verification is extremely important and there is a strong incentive to reduce uncertainty where it can streamline issuance. However, there is not necessarily an incentive to innovate as adherence to methodology is paramount.

Samuel Bryan, NEXUS Carbon for Development

What is the most important thing about MRV in the CDM?

Conservativeness and completeness of data are the most important things in the CDM. The CDM provides also very specific guidance for a very large number of project types, which is unprecedented in other market-based instruments (in terms of the amount and level of depth of monitoring methodologies). The checks and balances created under the CDM through its established standards, methodologies, tools and guidance as well as the accreditation system for DOEs and the quality assurance process at UNFCCC level are other important aspects of MRV under the CDM, which are quite unique.

Patrick Bürgi and Sophie Tison, South Pole Carbon

Independent third party evaluation gives value to the results of MRV, so this is crucial. The CDM is an evolving body of rules subject to interpretation so the most important thing becomes to ensure that the methodology and precedents are followed. Therefore a transparent process is also important.

Samuel Bryan, NEXUS Carbon for Development

In projects focused on efficient cooking stoves distribution, checking on all appliances would not be feasible economically and time wise. Therefore, it is crucial to ensure that targeted population, determination of cluster (if existing) and sample sizes are sufficient to ensure that the precision of the sample means are 90/10 to estimate emissions reductions.

Milena Begovic, EcoAct

What is the first thing you would change in the MRV procedures in the CDM?

MRV procedures in the CDM should be streamlined in order to lower transaction costs and allow more projects to be monitored and verified. Default values, standardized approaches can, for example, be used together with some conservativeness factors in order to simplify the rules without compromising environmental integrity. A better reflection of the materiality concept in the CDM rules would also help to streamline the rules and lower the transaction costs. Last but not least, a re-enforcement of DOE responsibilities and autonomy through a strict accreditation, training and quality assurance system as opposed to a constant duplication of work and responsibilities between DOEs and the UNFCCC Secretariat would also represent a big step forward.

Patrick Bürgi and Sophie Tison, South Pole Carbon

Streamlining procedures to ensure timely verification is important. Although this is an important balance between rigor and efficiency that needs to be reached, currently it takes 6–9 months to achieve issuance and this is too long.

Samuel Bryan, NEXUS Carbon for Development

In the monitoring section of the PDD, the maximum uncertainty tolerated by the DOE is very uneven from one document to another. Therefore, there is a need to improve uniformity and provide further simplification of the monitoring and sampling procedures.

Milena Begovic, EcoAct

11.6 MRV ID table

Table 11.4 *MRV ID table*

Context
Regulators — *The Conference of the Parties serving as the meeting of the Parties (CMP)*: political decisions and annual guidance of the CDM EB.
— *The CDM Executive Board (CDM EB)*: validation of methodologies, accreditation of auditors, registration of projects and issuance of CERs. The CDM EB takes most decisions pertaining to MRV, with the exception of highly political decisions which require CMP approval.
— *Designated Operational Entities (DOE)*: validation of CDM projects and verification of GHG emissions reductions.

Table 11.4 (*cont.*)

	- *Designated National Authorities (DNA):* issuance of the Letter of Approval (LoA) for a CDM project by the host country.
Type and level of incentive to comply	For projects proponents: - Positive incentives ("carrots"): issuance of CERs (timeliness and quantity) - Negative incentives ("sticks"): non-compliance with monitoring requirements may trigger a request for CER issuance review and possible ultimate non-issuance of CERs For DOEs: - Positive incentives ("carrots"): fees for successful CER issuance - Negative incentives ("sticks"): suspension or withdrawal of accreditation, i.e., temporary or permanent loss of business
Entities concerned	*Project proponents*: -6,755 projects registered as of May 2013 (UNEP Risoe, 2014) -1,491 project proponents (UNEP Risoe, 2014) -90% private domestic investors (Philp, 2013) - Estimated €167 billion (UNFCCC, 2012) to €230 billion (UNEP Risoe, 2014) investments[a] *DOEs*: -42 accredited auditors as of May 2013 (UNFCCC, 2013a) *Consultants*: -550 CDM consultants (UNEP Risoe, 2014)
Sectors concerned	All, except nuclear energy, soil carbon sequestration, forest management and avoided deforestation. Reforestation is allowed.
Gases concerned	All Kyoto Protocol gases (CO_2, CH_4, N_2O, HFC-23, PFC, SF_6, plus NF_3 as of 2013).
Overall MRV costs	Periodic MRV costs per project per year: €23,000 (€6,500–40,000) Periodic MRV costs per ton CO_2e: €0.32 (€0.05–1.03) Total MRV costs (including PDD elaboration, validation, UNFCCC fees and periodic MRV) per project per year: €55,000 (€12,300–132,600)

Table 11.4 (*cont.*)

Total MRV costs (including PDD elaboration, validation, UNFCCC fees and periodic MRV) per ton CO_2e: €0.57 (€0.21–1.58) (calculated based on data from Warnecke et al. (2013), see Table 11.5

	Monitoring
Rules	Most importantly, the methodology relevant to the project subtype, but also: - *Modalities and procedures for a clean development mechanism* (Decision 3/CMP.1, Annex) on general requirements for baseline and monitoring methodologies; - *CDM Project Standard* (CDM-EB65-A05-STAN) on establishing and applying monitoring methodologies; - *All guidelines, clarifications and supported documents published by the CDM EB.*
Other reference documents	- CDM Methodology Booklet fourth edition (CDM-EB69) - Standard for sampling and surveys for the CDM (CDM-EB69-A4) - IPCC Fourth Assessment Report: Climate Change 2007 (2007) for global warming potentials of GHGs - *IPCC Guidelines for National Greenhouse Gas Inventories* (1996 and 2006) for default values and parameters calculation - *Good Practice Guidance and Uncertainty Management in National Greenhouse Gas Inventories* (2001) for statistical approaches used in monitoring
Uncertainty requirements	- Project proponents shall reduce bias and improve precision as far as is practical/cost-effective, or otherwise use conservative assumptions, values and procedures to ensure that GHG emission reductions by sources or GHG removals by sinks are not over-estimated (CDM-EB65-A05-STAN).

Table 11.4 (*cont.*)

	- There is no overall uncertainty requirement, but there are requirements for some emission factors and activity data in some methodologies, and there is an overarching requirement for sampling error (see below).
Achieved precision range	Depends on the project type.
Cost range	Periodic monitoring costs per project per year: €5,500 (€1,500–10,000) Periodic monitoring costs per ton CO_2e: €0.08 (€0.01–0.33) (based on data from Warnecke et al. (2013), see Table 11.5)
Scope	- Scope 3: direct and indirect emissions and leakage. - Operational emissions, i.e., corresponding to the emissions of an activity which may include one or several entities (most projects). - Project-related emissions, i.e., mostly site-specific.
Frequency	- Variables that continuously affect the amount of GHG emissions (reductions), such as the quantity of fuel input or the amount of gas captured, have to be measured constantly (daily to monthly). - Variables that remain largely unchanged, e.g., emissions factors, have to be measured or calculated at least once a year (CDM-EB65-A05-STAN). Exceptions may be accepted on case-by-case basis during the review of methodologies.
Source for activity data	Measurements, estimates, sampling and surveys. Sometimes default values may be used for activity data, e.g., for the intensity of use of compact fluorescent lamps in the methodology for demand-side energy efficiency (AMS II.J).

Table 11.4 (*cont.*)

Uncertainty range for activity data	- Project proponents (PPs) shall use 90/10 confidence/ uncertainty as the criteria for reliability of sampling efforts for small-scale project activities and 95/10 for large-scale project activities (CDM-EB69-A4). There are, however, exceptions in some methodologies. - The monitoring plan shall include *inter alia* uncertainty levels, methods and the associated accuracy level of measuring instruments to be used for various parameters and variables (CDM-EB65-A05-STAN).
Source for emission factors	DNAs, IPCC Guidelines on National GHG Inventories, peer-reviewed literature, measurements, surveys, etc.
Uncertainty range for emission factors	- In case there is no country- or project-specific information regarding default parameters (e.g., emission factors) available, the IPCC default values may be used (CDM-EB25). - Methodologies have to "describe the uncertainty of key parameters and, where possible, provide an uncertainty range at 95% confidence level for key parameters for the calculation of emission reductions" (CDM-EB66-A25-GUID). - Methodology developers are also encouraged to refer to Chapter 6 of the IPCC Good Practice Guidance and Uncertainty Management in National Greenhouse Gas Inventories for more Guidance on analysis of uncertainty (EB41-A12).
Direct measurement	Sometimes, depending on a project type (e.g., the amount of methane captured in landfill projects is directly measured with a gas meter).
Incentives to reduce uncertainty	There is no explicit incentive to reduce uncertainty in the overarching guidelines. However, there is an implicit incentive to improve precision through the choice of methodology: sometimes, two methodologies coexist for similar project types, thus allowing project proponents to choose a more stringent monitoring methodology, which allows claiming more CERs (Shishlov and Bellassen, 2014).

Table 11.4 (*cont.*)

	In addition, some methodologies use adjustment factors or discount factors to address the uncertainty of measurements in a conservative manner (CDM-EB68-A10): - Many methodologies and tools allow using IPCC default values. In a number of cases these default values are adjusted for their uncertainty, i.e., a conservative bound of the uncertainty interval is chosen; - Similarly, many methodologies define default values in a conservative manner, thereby addressing the uncertainty associated with the use of default values; - Some methodologies adjust historical data to address significant uncertainties. For example, in the case of retrofit or replacement projects, ACM0002 for renewable energy generation deducts a standard deviation from the average historical electricity generation to adjust for the uncertainty associated with intermittent electricity generation patterns.
Is requirements stringency adapted to the amount of emissions at stake (materiality)?	Mostly no. The only exception is monitoring frequency which is adapted to reporting frequency and hence, indirectly, to the amount of emissions at stake.
Reporting	
Rules	Most importantly, the methodology relevant to the project subtype, but also: - *CDM Project Cycle Procedure* (CDM-EB65-A32-PROC) on procedures for submitting and publishing monitoring reports; - and the other documents already listed in the *monitoring* section.
Other reference documents	- Guidelines for completing the monitoring report form (CDM-EB54-A34-GUID) - Materiality standard under the clean development mechanism (Decision 9/CMP.7)

Table 11.4 (*cont.*)

Format	According to the CDM Project Standard (CDM-EB65-A05-STAN) project proponents have to use the latest version of the monitoring report form applicable to the project activity, taking into account the grace period of the form if it has been revised.
Level of source disaggregation	- Disaggregation of monitoring methodologies down to project subtype. - Disaggregation of emissions down to single source. - Some methodologies allow to aggregate sources to the site level, e.g., for buildings AM0091: "Energy efficiency technologies and fuel switching in new buildings."
Frequency	- Up to the project proponent: the length of a monitoring period – i.e., the interval between two reporting events – can span from ten days to ten years. - The average duration of monitoring periods is 322 days for large-scale projects and 508 days for small-scale projects (IGES, 2013a). - If a project does not submit a monitoring report within two years after registration, the proponent has to provide explanations through a dedicated online interface (CDM-EB65-A32-PROC).
Timeline	- The monitoring report must be made publicly available by the DOE 14 days prior to undertaking the site visit for the verification (CDM-EB65-A05-STAN). - On average the monitoring report is made public 70 days after the end of the respective monitoring period (IGES, 2013a).
Language	English
Is requirements stringency adapted to the amount of emissions at stake (materiality)?	Yes, through the choice offered to the project proponent regarding reporting frequency and the concept of materiality (see verification).

Table 11.4 (*cont.*)

Cost range	Usually negligible and included in periodic monitoring costs. PoAs may be an exception: although they save transaction costs compared to the project approach through the pooling of project "instances," they create a specific reporting challenge for the aggregation of data. One study provides a separate estimate for PoAs in the range of €10,000–15,000 (Beaurain and Schmidt-Traub, 2010).
Verification	
Rules	Most importantly, the methodology relevant to the project subtype and the Project Design Document, but also: - the *CDM Validation and Verification Standard* (CDM-EB65-A04-STAN) for procedures of validation and verification; - and the other documents already listed in the *reporting* section.
Other reference documents	- Clean development mechanism accreditation standard for operational entities (CDM-EB67-A05) - Procedure for accrediting operational entities by the Executive Board (CDM-EB56-A02) - Performance monitoring of designated operational entities (CDM-EB73-A14) - Guideline on the application of materiality in verification (CDM-EB-69-A06) - Procedure for Review of Requests for Issuance of CERs (CDM-EB-64-A04)
Format	No specified format although the verification report must include all elements mentioned in the *verification* section.
Frequency	Verification occurs at each reporting event (submission of monitoring report).
Timeline	On average it takes: -70 days from the end of a monitoring period to the publication of a monitoring report; -185 days from the publication of a monitoring report to the request for issuance by a DOE; -84 days from the request for issuance to the issuance of CERs (IGES, 2013a).

Table 11.4 (*cont.*)

Language	English
Accredited entities for verification	*Designated Operational Entities* (DOE) accredited by the CDM Executive Board and designated by the COP/MOP.
Control of accredited entities	The Board may decide to suspend totally or partially the accreditation of a DOE based on the recommendation of the CDM-AP or other review processes conducted by the Board (see the *verification* section and CDM-EB56-A02).
Cost of accreditation	According to the Procedure for accrediting operational entities by the Executive Board (CDM-EB56-A02), accreditation fees are as follows: - non-reimbursable application fee is €11,300; - fee and costs associated with an on-site assessment of the premises of an AE/DOE; - other costs related to performance assessment, reaccreditation, change of scope of a DOE, etc.
Support of accredited entities	- The Executive Board provides DOEs with feedback based on their assessment. - The Executive Board established a DOE forum to enhance communication between the Board and DOEs.
Is requirements stringency adapted to the amount of emissions at stake (materiality)?	Yes, substantially. Both through the materiality decision and through the verification frequency which is set by the project proponent himself.
Cost range	Periodic verification costs per project per year: €17,500 (€5,000–30,000) Periodic verification costs per ton CO_2e: €0.24 (€0.04–0.70) (based on data from Warnecke et al. (2013), Table 11.5)

[a] Converted from US dollars into euros using the average annual (respective publication year) exchange rate.

Appendix – Transaction costs for CDM projects

Table 11.5 *Transaction costs for CDM projects*

	ktCO$_2$e/year	Upfront TC MC/yr low	high	MC/t CO$_2$e low	high	VC/yr low	high	VC/tCO$_2$e low	high	M&V/yr low	high	M&V/tCO$_2$e low	high	Issuance fee	Total TC/tC low	high	Total TC/tCO$_2$e low	high
Biomass energy	79	56	177	5	10	0.06	0.13	15	29	0.19	0.37	20	39	0.25	0.49	11	39	64	0.49	0.81
Coal mine/bed methane	510	133	274	5	10	0.01	0.02	20	30	0.04	0.06	25	40	0.05	0.08	78	107	133	0.21	0.26
EE households	26	44	169	1.5	5	0.06	0.19	7.5	15	0.29	0.58	9	20	0.35	0.77	1.5	15	35	0.58	1.33
EE own generation	197	69	103	3	10	0.02	0.05	15	27	0.08	0.14	18	37	0.09	0.19	30	51	75	0.26	0.38
Fossil fuel switch	491	119	145	3	10	0.01	0.02	20	25	0.04	0.05	23	35	0.05	0.07	75	103	118	0.21	0.24
Hydro large-scale	208	70	96	3	10	0.01	0.05	15	15	0.07	0.07	18	25	0.09	0.12	31	54	75	0.26	0.36
Hydro small-scale	29	37	67	1.5	5	0.05	0.17	7.5	11.5	0.26	0.40	9	16.5	0.31	0.57	1.5	15	26	0.51	0.90
Landfill gas	160	69	185	5	10	0.03	0.06	20	28	0.13	0.18	25	38	0.16	0.24	24	53	72	0.33	0.45

Table 11.5 (cont.)

	ktCO2e/ year	Upfront TC low	high	MC/yr low	high	MC/t CO2e low	high	VC/yr low	high	VC/tCO2e low	high	M&V/yr low	high	M&V/tCO2e low	high	Issuance fee	Total TC/tC low	high	Total TC/tCO2e low	high
Methane avoidance	59	53	174	5	10	0.08	0.17	15	29	0.25	0.49	20	39	0.34	0.66	8	32	59	0.54	1.00
N2O nitric acid	289	109	205	5	18	0.02	0.06	25	25	0.09	0.09	30	43	0.10	0.15	44	78	98	0.27	0.34
N2O adipic acid	7294	338	434	5	18	0.00	0.00	25	25	0.00	0.00	30	43	0.00	0.01	1,137	1,167	1,167	0.16	0.16
Wind large-scale	120	57	82	3	10	0.03	0.08	15	22	0.13	0.18	18	32	0.15	0.27	18	40	59	0.33	0.49
Wind small-scale	15	40	64	1.5	5	0.10	0.33	7.5	10.5	0.50	0.70	9	15.5	0.60	1.03	0.5	14	24	0.92	1.58
Solar	30	38	69	1.5	5	0.05	0.17	5	10.5	0.17	0.35	6.5	15.5	0.22	0.52	2	12	27	0.41	0.91
Average (excluding N2O)	160	65	134	3	8	0.04	0.12	14	21	0.18	0.30	17	29	0.22	0.42	23	45	64	0.42	0.73
Average	679	88	160	3	10	0.04	0.11	15	22	0.16	0.26	19	31	0.20	0.37	104	127	145	0.39	0.66

Notes: TC – transaction costs. MC – monitoring costs. VC – verification costs. Costs are either expressed in k€ (per project) or in € (per tCO2e). The average excluding N2O projects is likely more representative as these projects are very large and very few (about 20 projects in more than 6,000 CDM projects).

Warnecke et al. (2013) assumes a frequency of verification events of one year for projects larger than 50 ktCO2e/yr and two years for smaller projects. The study spreads upfront costs over 7–10 years depending on project types to calculate average annual total costs (last two columns).

Source: Adapted from Warnecke et al. (2013).

Bibliography

Beaurain, F. and Schmidt-Traub, G., 2010. *Developing CDM Programmes of Activities: A Guidebook*. South Pole Carbon Asset Management Ltd, Zurich, 75pp.

CAR, 2011. *Program Manual*. Climate Action Reserve, Los Angeles, 42pp.

CCX, 2009. Forestry Carbon Sequestration Project Protocol. Chicago Climate Exchange, Inc., 70pp.

Cormier, A. and Bellassen, V., 2013. The risks of CDM projects: how did only 30% of expected credits come through? *Energy Policy* 54 (March): 173–183.

Dinar, A., Rahman, S.M., Larson, D. and Ambrosi, P., 2008. Factors affecting levels of international cooperation in carbon abatement projects. Policy Research Working Paper No. 4786. World Bank, 38pp.

Flues, F., 2010. Who hosts the Clean Development Mechanism?: Determinants of CDM project distribution. Working Paper No. 53. Center for Comparative and International Studies (ETH Zurich and University of Zurich), 41pp.

Guigon, P., Bellassen, V. and Ambrosi, P., 2009. Voluntary carbon markets: what the standards say... Working Paper No. 4, Mission Climat. Caisse des Depots. Paris, 46pp.

IETA, 2011. Monitoring, Reporting and Verification (MRV) Considerations for Offset Projects. International Emissions Trading Association, 16pp.

IGES, 2013a. CDM Project Database. Institute for Global Environmental Strategies. http://pub.iges.or.jp/modules/envirolib/view.php?docid=968. Accessed October 2013.

IGES, 2013b. One Hundred Questions & Answers about MRV in Developing Countries. v.1.2. Institute for Global Environmental Strategies, 135pp.

IGES, 2013c. Measurement, reporting, and verification (MRV) for low carbon development: learning from experience in Asia. Policy Report. Edited by: K. Koakutsu, K. Usui, A. Watarai, Y. Takagi. Institute for Global Environmental Strategies, 149pp.

Jung, M., 2006. Host country attractiveness for CDM non-sink projects. *Energy Policy* 34(15): 2173–2184.

Krey, M., 2005. Transaction costs of unilateral CDM projects in India – results from an empirical survey. *Energy Policy* 33(18): 2385–2397.

Michaelowa, A. and Michaelowa, K., 2013. Bureaucratic influence when secretariats grow: the example of the UNFCCC. CIS Working Paper No. 80. University of Zurich, Switzerland, 31pp.

Michaelowa, A. and Stronzik, M., 2002. Transaction costs of the Kyoto mechanisms. HWWA Discussion Paper, No. 175, 36pp.

Philp, L., 2013. Stranded Costs on the Demise of the Clean Development Mechanism. CO_2 Spain, 12pp. www.co2spain.com/strandedcosts.php. Accessed April 2014.

Replogle, M. and Bakker, S., 2011. Can the Clean Development Mechanism be made more effective for the transportation sector? Report to the UNFCCC Practitioner Workshop on the Improvement of CDM Methodologies for Transportation. Bonn, Germany.

Schneider, L., 2009. Assessing the additionality of CDM projects: practical experiences and lessons learned. *Climate Policy* 9(3) (May 1): 242–254.

Shishlov, I. and Bellassen, V., 2012. 10 lessons from 10 years of the CDM. Climate Report No. 37. CDC Climat Research, Paris, 39pp.

2013. Unlocking private investments in energy efficiency through carbon finance. Climate Brief No. 27. CDC Climat Research, Paris, 5pp.

2014. Review of monitoring uncertainty requirements in the CDM. Working Paper No. 16. CDC Climat Research, Paris, 33pp.

UN, 1998. Kyoto Protocol to the United Nations Framework Convention on Climate Change, 20pp.

UNEP, 2007. Guidebook to Financing CDM Projects. United Nations Environment Programme, 104pp.

UNEP Risoe, 2014. CDM/JI Pipeline Databases. United Nations Environment Programme. www.cdmpipeline.org/. Accessed April 2014.

UNFCCC, 2002. Report of the Conference of the Parties on Its Seventh Session, Held at Marrakesh from 29 October to 10 November 2001. UNFCCC, 72pp.

UNFCCC, 2006. Report of the Conference of the Parties Serving as the Meeting of the Parties to the Kyoto Protocol on Its First Session, Held at Montreal from 28 November to 10 December 2005. UNFCCC, 100pp.

UNFCCC, 2012. Synthesis Report of the Call for Input on the CDM Policy Dialogue. UNFCCC, 28pp.

UNFCCC, 2013a. Official CDM website. https://cdm.unfccc.int/. Accessed October 2013.

UNFCCC, 2013b. CDM Methodology Booklet – Fifth Edition. Accessed April 2014.

VCS, 2012a. VCS Program Guide. Version 3. Verified Carbon Standard, 21pp. www.v-c-s.org/sites/v-c-s.org/files/VCS%20Program%20Guide%2C%20v3.5.pdf. Accessed October 2013.

VCS, 2012b. VCS Standard. Version 3. Verified Carbon Standard, 50pp. www.v-c-s.org/sites/v-c-s.org/files/VCS%20Standard%2C%20v3.4.pdf. Accessed October 2013.

Vine, E.L. and Sathaye, J.A., 2000. The monitoring, evaluation, reporting, verification, and certification of energy-efficiency projects. *Mitigation and Adaptation Strategies for Global Change* 5(2): 189–216.

Warnecke, C., 2014. Can CDM monitoring requirements be reduced while maintaining environmental integrity? *Climate Policy*: 1–24.

Warnecke, C., Klein, N., Perroy, R. and Tippmann, R., 2013. CDM Market Support Study. KFW. www.jiko-bmub.de/files/basisinformationen/application/pdf/kfw_cdm_market_support_study.pdf.

Winkelman, A.G. and Moore, M.R., 2011. Explaining the differential distribution of Clean Development Mechanism projects across host countries. *Energy Policy* 39(3): 1132–1143.

12 | Case study 1: monitoring requirements for projects reducing N_2O emissions from fertilizer use across standards

CLAUDINE FOUCHEROT

12.1 Context

Agriculture is the fourth largest sector in terms of global anthropogenic greenhouse gas emissions (GHG). It accounts for 14 percent of global emissions, i.e., 6.6 $GtCO_2e$/year (Bernstein et al., 2007). Three types of gas are involved: nitrous oxide (N_2O), methane (CH_4) and to a lesser extent carbon dioxide (CO_2). In fact, agriculture is the largest sector when it comes to emitting gases other than carbon dioxide, and accounts for 60 percent and 50 percent of global N_2O and CH_4 emissions respectively.

N_2O agricultural emissions correspond to cropland and pasture N_2O emissions linked to the use of organic and mineral nitrogen fertilizers. It results from microbial processes of nitrification and denitrification which occur in soils. Cropland and pasture account for almost 40 percent of agricultural emissions worldwide. This figure only accounts for "within farm" emissions. Upstream emissions, from the manufacture and transport of agricultural inputs, are not included. N_2O and CO_2 emissions due to nitrogen fertilizer production would add about 20 percent to the 2.3 $GtCO_2e$/year from cropland and pasture (Figure 12.1). One of the Clean Development Mechanism (CDM) methodologies is precisely focused on these upstream emissions.

One way of reducing nitrous oxide emissions is to limit the use of nitrogen fertilizers (sustainable use of fertilizers, planting legumes, avoiding bare soils, changing the kinds of nitrogen fertilizers used, etc.). Water management also has an impact on the denitrification process, which can be defined as an alternative breathing mechanism: for example, soil drainage enables improved aeration, and therefore reduces denitrification and the associated N_2O emissions. However, it is difficult to estimate its impact on N_2O emissions.

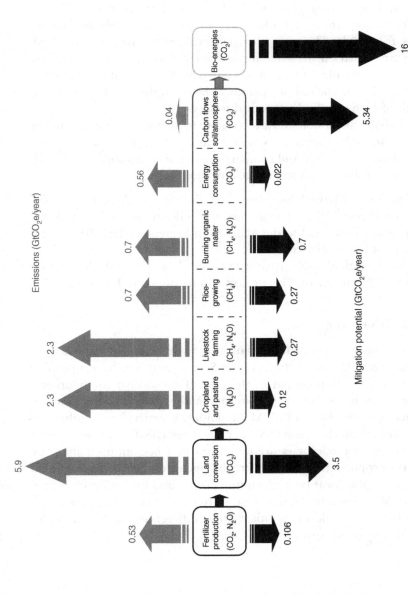

Figure 12.1 Agricultural emissions and mitigation potential worldwide
Source: Foucherot and Bellassen (2011).

As of September 2013, seven methodologies are available across all carbon offset standards to assess N_2O emissions reductions from cropland agricultural projects (Table 12.1). Three of them (1 VCS, 1 ACR, 1 CAR) are almost identical and cover N_2O emissions reductions from reduced use of nitrogen fertilizer on agricultural crops. They are based on the same methodology developed by the Electric Power Research Institute and Michigan State University (MSU-EPRI Methodology). The minor differences between them came about as a result of each standard's approval process.

All these methodologies are related to nitrogen fertilization but scopes are quite different as well as monitoring procedures. In this case study, we analyze and compare the two methodologies for which there is at least one project in the pipeline:

- MSU-EPRI Methodology (which is declined in three methodologies – VCS/ACR/CAR). Only one small pilot project has been developed and submitted to the ACR. As of September 1st, 2013, it still had not been registered.
- InVivo Methodology (JI) because it leads to the first GHG offset project in this sector. This project was registered in January 2012.

12.2 Monitoring

As previously mentioned, the main way to decrease N_2O emissions is to limit the use of nitrogen fertilizer. Several practices have a positive impact on fertilization but in the case of the InVivo Methodology, legumes inclusion in crop rotation is the only eligible practice. Concerning the MSU-EPRI Methodology, practices must adhere to the appropriate Best Management Practices (BMPs) of the region.[1] Moreover, methodologies are developed in a bottom-up manner by project proponents. Thus, their requirements and content depend on the geographic location of the initial project and its regulatory framework. More specifically, they tend to rely on pre-existing data which vary from one region to another. These differences result in different monitoring processes.

---

[1] Choice of fertilizer, rate of fertilizer application, frequency of application, application technique, etc.

Table 12.1 *Approved methodologies for reduced N$_2$O emissions from fertilizer use across standards*

Standard	Methodology	Date of methodology validation	Number of projects in the pipeline	Number of projects registered
Clean Development Mechanism (CDM)	AMS-III.A./Version 02: Offsetting of synthetic nitrogen fertilizers by inoculant application in legumes-grass rotations on acidic soils on existing cropland. This methodology is not strictly about N$_2$O agricultural emissions since offset credits are generated by CO$_2$ emissions reductions from synthetic nitrogen fertilizer production.	July 2009	0	0
CDM	AMS-III.BF/Version 1.0: Reduction of N$_2$O emissions from use of Nitrogen Use Efficient (NUE) seeds that require less fertilizer application.	November 2012	0	0
Joint Implementation (JI)	*Méthodologie spécifique aux projets de réduction des émissions de N$_2$O dues à la dénitrification des sols agricoles par l'insertion de légumineuse dans les rotations agricoles.* This methodology accounts for N$_2$O emissions reductions from the use of legumes in crop rotations.	April 2011	1	1
American Carbon Registry (ACR)	Methodology for Quantifying Nitrous Oxide (N$_2$O) Emissions Reductions through Reduced Use of Nitrogen Fertilizer on Agricultural Crops *(from MSU-EPRI Methodology).*	July 2012	1	0

Table 12.1 (*cont.*)

Standard	Methodology	Date of methodology validation	Number of projects in the pipeline	Number of projects registered
ACR	N_2O Emissions Reductions through Changes in Fertilizer Management.	November 2010	0	0
Verified Carbon Standard (VCS)	VM0022: Quantifying N_2O Emissions Reductions in Agricultural Crops through Nitrogen Fertilizer Rate Reduction, v1.1 *(from MSU-EPRI Methodology).*	March 2013	0	0
Climate Action Reserve (CAR)	Nitrogen management: This methodology covers N_2O emissions reductions from reduced use of nitrogen fertilizer on agricultural crops *(from MSU-EPRI Methodology).*	January 2013	0	0

In Vivo methodology: legumes inclusion in crop rotations

Calculation based on crop areas and region-specific emission factors

Through their symbiotic metabolism, legumes are able to fix nitrogen from the air and do not need nitrogen fertilizer application.

N_2O emissions reductions (N_2O_{red}) are calculated based on the area of each crop and region-specific emission factors for each crop:

$$N_2O_{red(i)} = \sum_{k=1} A_{ki} \left(Baseline\right) \times EF_{ki} - \sum_{k=1} A_{ki} \left(Project\right) \times EF_{ki}$$

Equation 12.1

with: $N_2O_{red(i)}$ = *emission reductions in region i in* tCO_2e, *i = region i;* A_k = *Area of the crop k in ha;* EF_k = *Emission factor of the crop k in* $tCO_2e\ ha^{-1}$

and $EF_{k\ =\ non\text{-}legume}$ = N_k(synthetic) × EF(synthetic) + N_k(organic) × EF(organic) + N_k(crop residues) × EF(crop residues)

$EF_{k\ =\ legume}$ = 71.8 g of $N–N_2O$/ha/yr

with N = nitrogen fertilizer application rates or nitrogen amount from crop residues (this information is from national surveys); EF(synthetic) (organic)(crop residues) = Emission factor for direct and indirect N_2O *emissions from N inputs (same as used in the national inventory).*

Monitoring of baseline emissions

For the **monitoring of baseline emissions**, five variables must therefore be collected:

- **Crop areas by region (A_{ki}):** data come from annual statistics published on the French Ministry of Agriculture website. An average value based on the three years before project implementation is used for the baseline.
- **Amount of synthetic N fertilizer ($N_k$synthetic):** it is the regional average synthetic N fertilizer application rate used on each crop. Data come from national statistics available on the French Ministry of Agriculture website. Results of the last survey (2011) are used to determine the baseline. These surveys are conducted every five years.
- **Amount of organic N fertilizer ($N_k$organic):** it is the regional average organic N fertilizer application rate used on each crop. These

Table 12.2 *Amount of N from crop residues*

Crops	Amount of N from crop residues (kg/ha)
Sugar beet	90.00
Potato	40.00
Cereals (barley, wheat, oats, corn, etc.)	31.30
Oilseed	29.70
Fodder beet	140.00

data are not available on the French Ministry of Agriculture website. They come from famers' or cooperatives' records. When data are not available, the application rate is assumed to be equal to zero (conservative approach). In any case, the most recent data should be used.

- **Amount of N from crop residues ($N_k$crop residues):** the default values as in the national GHG inventory are used (Table 12.2). And EF crop residues = $0.0125 \times N_k$crop residues.
- **Emission factors for direct and indirect N_2O emissions from N inputs and non-legume crop residues ($EF_{synthetic}$, $E_{organic}$, $EF_{crop\ residues}$):** the values used are the same as in the national GHG inventory.

Monitoring of actual project emissions

The only additional data monitored during the project are crop areas. These activity data are derived from the reports filed by farmers under the Common Agricultural Policy.

Emissions factors are assumed to be the same before and during the project. $EF_{legumes}$ is lower than for other crops since legumes do not need N fertilizer application: the higher the area cropped with legumes, the higher the amount of emissions reductions.

MSU-EPRI methodology

This methodology uses directly the link between N fertilizer application rates and N_2O emissions. The less the farmer uses N fertilizer the more N_2O emissions are reduced. Nevertheless, in the CAR Methodology, yield is monitored to control that reduced fertilizer use is offset by better management rather than simply leading to reduced yield.

Thus, contrary to the InVivo Methodology, the amount of nitrogen fertilizer used during the project is monitored. In VCS and ACR methodologies (resulting from MSU-EPRI Methodology) synthetic and organic fertilizers are taken into account to calculate emissions reductions whereas in the CAR Methodology, only synthetic fertilizers are monitored. However, none of these three methodologies take into account N_2O emissions due to crop residues (see Table 12.3).

Monitoring of baseline emissions

- **Amount of N fertilizer:** Two methods can be used to determine the baseline N fertilizer rate. The first method uses site-specific management records (N fertilizer purchase and application rate, manure application rate and manure N content) and the second one uses county-level records. With this method, N fertilizer rates are calculated using regional recommendations based on yield goal estimates and crop yield data at regional level. This second method is used when N fertilizer rate for a specific crop cannot be established from project proponent records. It is not eligible in the CAR Methodology. Both methods require data from at least the previous five years (monoculture) or six years (three cycles of a two-crop rotation, or two cycles of a three-crop rotation).
- **Crop area:** these data also come from project proponent records that are filed under farm-related programs such as state and federal BMPs (Best Management Practices).
- **Emission factors for direct and indirect N_2O emissions from N inputs:** two different emission factors can be used depending on the geographic location: (1) projects located in the US North Central Region must use a specific emission factor from empirical research on producer fields throughout Michigan; and (2) projects that are not located in this region must use the emission factor from the 2006 *IPCC Guidelines for National Greenhouse Gas Inventories*. In the ACR Methodology, project proponents can propose their own project-specific emissions factor as long as they demonstrate, based on empirical data published in peer-reviewed scientific journals, that this new and specific emission factor is conservative.

Monitoring of actual project emissions

Amounts of N fertilizer used must be monitored on a yearly basis. Crop areas must also be monitored although only once per crediting period. These activity data are derived from farmer records that are filed and verified under farm-related programs such as state and federal BMPs (Best Management Practices).

With the CAR Methodology, project proponents must also collect the following data: crop yield to make sure that there is no leakage due to yield; planting and harvesting dates to determin to which crediting period shall the emission reductions be assigned; fertilizer application method and placement; type of equipment used for fertilizer application; and whether irrigation was used (see Table 12.3). These project activity data are used to corroborate field management assertions. They must also implement a Corn Stalk Nitrate Test (CSNT)[2] for each eligible corn[3] crop prior to the end of the reporting period. Test results are used to detect excessive N use. An excessive N concentration does not necessarily mean that the farmer has not reduced the N fertilizer rate as there are many factors which influence N concentration, but verification bodies use these results to prioritize selection of fields for site visit (see Verification).

Monitoring of leakage

In VCS and ACR versions of the MSU-EPRI Methodology, leakage is assumed to be equal to zero since: (1) land has been maintained in crop production for five or six years prior to project implementation; (2) crop production pursuance, using business as usual management practices, is the most realistic scenario in the absence of a project; and (3) no crop yield reductions are expected due to project implementation. This last expectation may not be realized as the amount of fertilizer use is often correlated with yield. This is why, in the CAR version of the MSU-EPRI Methodology, offset credit deductions are applied if yields decline significantly in the project area.

---

[2] One CSNT sample shall be comprised of 15 segments taken from corn stalks across the project field. It must be sent to a qualified laboratory for analysis.
[3] Only emissions reductions related to the corn cultivation cycle shall be credited under the CAR methodology. However, additional quantification methods for N application rate reductions may be added in future versions of the protocol covering additional crop systems.

Table 12.3 *Comparison between methodologies*

	InVivo methodology	MSU-EPRI methodology		
		VCS	ACR	CAR
Standard	JI	VCS	ACR	CAR
Geographic location	France	US	Global	US North Central Region
N management practice	Legumes inclusion in crop rotations	Must adhere to the appropriate Best Management Practices of the region with respect to fertilizer timing, placement and formulation		
Source of N	- Synthetic and organic fertilizer - Crop residues	Synthetic and organic fertilizer		Only synthetic fertilizer
GHG boundary	N_2O direct and indirect			
Activity data or direct measurement?	Activity data			
Activity data monitored	- Crop areas	- Amount of fertilizer; - N content of fertilizer; - Crop areas - Evidence for similar expected yield as baseline	- Amount of fertilizer; - N content of fertilizer; - Crop areas	- Amount of fertilizer; - N content of fertilizer; - Crop areas - Planting and harvest dates - Crop yield - Application method - Crop N content
Stakeholder in charge of monitoring	Farmers			

Table 12.3 (cont.)

	InVivo methodology	MSU-EPRI methodology
Sources for activity data	Common Agricultural Policy reporting for crop areas Regional statistics for baseline crop areas and fertilizer use	Project proponent records kept for existing state or federal programs such as BMPs
Frequency	Annual	Each crediting period for crop areas and annual for the other activity data
Sources for emission factors	National GHG inventory for most emission factors Field experiments for the emission factor of legume crop residues	- IPCC default emission factor if more specific EF are not available - Research reports in the US North Central Region Project-specific value based on empirical data published in peer-reviewed journals Research reports: all projects are located in the US North Central Region

Monitoring frequency and crediting period

Activity data have to be monitored and reported every year regardless of the methodology except for crop area under the MSU-EPRI Methodology which shall be monitored only once per crediting period.

The crediting period is the maximal time period over which an offset project may obtain carbon credits that is therefore monitored. For JI projects, this period has to be negotiated with the host country but is limited to seven years with a possibility to renew it up to two times or to ten years non-renewable. The first crediting period of the only offset project covering N_2O agricultural emissions, which is a JI offset project, was one year and four months (from September 1st, 2011 until December 31st, 2012). In principle, the project is eligible for a second one although whether it does apply for one and obtain it is uncertain given the current regulatory and market uncertainties related to JI projects.

For ACR projects, the crediting period is also limited to seven years but there is no limit to the allowed number of project crediting period renewals. Offset projects that lead to N fertilizer rate reductions must be implemented for at least one year.

For CAR projects, the crediting period is defined as five eligible crop years, which may occur over a period of up to ten years (in the case of monoculture, the crediting period is five years, while for a two-field crop rotation it is ten years. For three-field crop rotation, the crediting period is limited to ten years). The crediting period may be renewed once.

Concerning the VCS, the crediting period shall be a maximum of ten years which may be renewed at most twice. This is an exception to the rules generally applying to ALM (Agricultural Land Management) projects (a minimum of 20 years up to a maximum of 100 years, renewable four times within the overall 100 years limit).

Monitoring uncertainty

ACR and VCS methodology

The ACR and VCS Standard specify that methodologies should include information and procedures for estimating uncertainty concerning the baseline and project scenario. In the VCS and ACR version of the MSU-EPRI Methodology, activity data uncertainty is assumed to be equal to zero when they come from project proponent records. However, using county-level records to calculate baseline emissions increases activity data uncertainty as it is not site specific data. This approach is however conservative by design as the organic N fertilizer rate is not taken into account, which reduces the baseline value from which N rate reductions can be made.

When a project takes place in the US NCR, the uncertainty associated with N_2O emissions reductions brought about by a reduction in the N rate between the baseline period and the project period is calculated using the following equation:

$$UNC = [1 - \{0.63 \times exp(-40 \times [N_{proj}]^2)\}] \times 100 \qquad \text{Equation 12.2}$$

Where:

UNC: uncertainty in N_2O emissions reductions associated with a reduction in N rate (%) for a 95% confidence interval. This uncertainty only covers the N_2O emission rate per ton of N applied: it does not include the – likely negligible – uncertainty associated with the amount of N applied and the crop area.

This equation was fitted on bootstrapped values from field experiments:[4]

N_{proj}: project N fertilizer applied (Mg N ha^{-1} yr^{-1})

Then, conservativeness factors specified in the CDM Methodology Panel guidance on addressing uncertainty in its Thirty Second Meeting Report, Annex 14 (see Table 12.4), are used to calculate credit award deductions as a result of uncertainty.

Thus, where uncertainty in emissions reductions is less than 15 percent, no deduction is be applied.

Concerning projects which are not located in the US NCR, the project proponent shall demonstrate that the use of the IPCC Tier 1 emissions factor is conservative for calculating N_2O emissions at the project site.

---

[4] 480 values have been used (32 values for 15 pairs of N fertilizer reductions: 0; 45; 90; 135; 180; 225 kg N ha^{-1} yr^{-1}). For each pair a random sample of 32 baseline values was taken and replaced with a random sample of 32 project values to compute a mean reduction. This process was repeated 100,000 times and the overall standard error of the means was calculated.

Table 12.4 *Conservativeness factors and uncertainty deduction for N₂O emissions reductions based upon uncertainty at 95% confidence level*

Uncertainty range at 95% confidence level of project emissions reductions (UNC)	Conservativeness factor	Uncertainty deduction
UNC < 15%	1.000	0.000
15% < UNC ≤ 30%	0.943	0.057
30% < UNC ≤ 50%	0.893	0.107
50% < UNC ≤ 100%	0.836	0.164

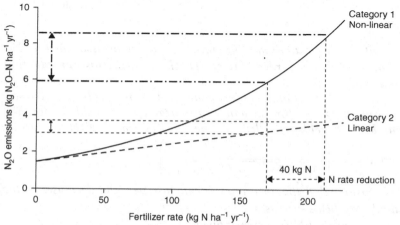

Figure 12.2 Comparison between non-variable and variable EF to calculate N₂O emissions reductions in the MSU-EPRI methodology
Source: American Carbon Registry (2012).

There is therefore no incentive to reduce uncertainty beyond the 15 percent threshold.

Under the ACR, project proponents can use a linear approach, with a non-variable Emission Factor (IPCC default), or a non-linear approach, with a variable EF (for the North Central Region of the United States). The non-linear approach is more accurate and often results in larger N₂O emission reductions than calculated using the linear approach as IPCC EF is conservative: for the same reduction of 40 kgN ha⁻¹ yr⁻¹, using the IPCC EF yields a much lower reduction of emissions, and hence a much lower amount of carbon credits (see Figure 12.2). This is an important incentive, together with the discount factor, to reduce uncertainty by proposing a new, project-specific, emission factor.

CAR methodology
The CAR methodology uses modified, but similar uncertainty equation based on a project's geographic location (again, geographic location is limited to the US NCR):

If the project is located in Michigan:

$$UNC_f = (UAF) \times (100 - 63 \times \exp(-40 \times 10^{-6} \times [N_{proj}]^2)$$

- If the project is not located in Michigan:

$$UNC_f = (UAF) \times (100 - 63 \times \exp(-40 \times 10^{-6} \times [N_{proj}]^2 + 15)$$

Equation 12.3

Where:
UNC_f = *Uncertainty in N_2O emission reductions associated with a reduction in N rate for field f relative to the average emission reduction value (%);*
UAF = *Uncertainty adjustment factor to scale μ_f (conservativeness factor for structural uncertainty for field f) for the number of fields enrolled in the project, in a given reporting*

$$period = 1 + \left(\frac{32}{\sqrt{(number\ of\ field\ enrolled)}} \right)$$

It ensures that the uncertainty deduction per field decreases as the number of fields increases.
N_{proj} = *project N fertilizer applied*
The conservativeness factor is then calculated as follows:

If $UNC_f < 15$, then $\mu_f = 1$ and
if $UNC_f \geq 15$, then $\mu_f = \exp(-UNC_f/300)$

Equation 12.4

JI methodology
Uncertainty assessment is not required in this methodology.

Monitoring costs

Methodologies have been developed in view of activity data that are already available. As previously mentioned, they are derived from farmer records that are used for compliance with farm-related programs or policy, which minimizes costs despite the diffuse nature of these projects. These data are collected by an aggregator who has the responsibility to develop and submit an aggregate report. One can therefore assume that monitoring costs are not significantly higher than the cross-sectoral estimates provided in Chapter 11. For the JI project, these costs are estimated at €20,000 by the project proponent (Choquet, 2014), including upfront costs and first year monitoring costs.

12.3 Reporting

For all methodologies, an annual monitoring report is required. The aggregator is in charge of the preparation of the report, allowing economies of scale. They must prepare the monitoring report according to the guidelines of the relevant standard (see Chapter 11).

The CAR has specific rules for the reporting of agricultural N_2O projects: project emissions reductions must be quantified, reported and verified on an annual basis. The reporting period does not have to start on January 1st: the period must be the most appropriate period based on the cultivation cycles and start date of fields. However, this crediting period must be uniformly defined for every field of a same aggregated project even if individual fields may have cultivation cycles that start on different dates. Moreover, only emission reductions from a complete cultivation cycle can undergo verification. This means that emission reductions from a complete cultivation cycle should be verified at once, and only emission reductions occurring during an aggregate's fixed reporting period are credited during that reporting period. Thus the following pro-rata rule is applied:

The aggregator must divide total emission reductions from the reporting period by 365 days to calculate the average daily emission reductions associated with a given field and multiply by the total days of the cultivation cycle falling within reporting period currently undergoing verification. The remaining emission reductions from the complete cultivation cycle should be verified along with the field's total emission reductions from this cultivation cycle, but shall be credited under the subsequent aggregated reporting period.

Reporting costs are probably higher in this subsector than the cross-sectoral project average due to the necessity to aggregate numerous farm-level monitoring data. Indeed, the necessary aggregation is similar to the aggregation of the CDM Program of activities distributing efficient cookstoves to rural households. The monitoring reports of these programs are estimated to cost 50–100 percent higher than those of more straightforward programs or standard CDM projects (Beaurain and Schmidt-Traub, 2010).

12.4 Verification

General requirements

Generally, aggregators are in charge of coordinating every aspect of the verification process. Indeed, they have to select the auditor, to assist project participants in preparing documents for the verification and to facilitate the verification process, coordinating the exchanges with the auditor. Each standard has a list of accredited verification bodies by sector which has to follow verification guidelines (see Chapter 11).

In all standards, auditors are accredited for a specific set of sectors for which they can prove that they have either internal or externally secured expertise, in addition to their general expertise in project audit. In the CAR for example, only ISO-accredited verification bodies with lead verifiers trained by the Reserve are eligible to verify nitrogen management project reports. All verification bodies must include a Certified Professional Agronomist or Certified Crop Advisor in the team, who must be present for all site verification visits.

Specificities under the CAR

The CAR Methodology is the only one to establish a minimum site and desktop verification frequency depending on project size and number of participants. The verification body must establish the verification schedule using a combination of risk-based and random sampling. The risk-based approach is informed by CNST results: fields for which the CNST is found to be most inconsistent with the reported amount of fertilizer applied are prioritized for a site visit. In any case, each field must undergo a minimum of one site visit verification per crediting period.

For example, for small projects (less than 20 fields), a minimum of 20 percent of the fields shall be verified *in situ* in a given verification event. As previously mentioned, fields are selected by a risk-based approach and then randomly, until 20 percent has been reached. For large and multi-participant projects, a minimum of 5 percent of the total number of eligible fields must be visited. However, the number of site visits is unlikely to exceed these minima as they tend to be more expensive, and each site visit only saves half a desk verification. Indeed, the following equation is used to calculate the number of desk verifications:

$$D = \frac{n - S}{2} \qquad \text{Equation 12.5}$$

Where, n = number of fields in the aggregate; S = number of site visits and D = number of desk verifications.

Auditors must make sure that the project is eligible for the CAR, recalculate emission reductions and produce a risk assessment.[5] To this end, they must verify a few items listed in the methodology which sometimes requires their professional judgments (e.g., verify accuracy of project start date for all verified fields based on operational records; verify that the project does not include irrigated corn cropping systems and, if irrigation was used, verify that emergency irrigation was justifiable, etc.).

In case of successful verification of each field in the sample, the project will be credited for the given crediting period. In case of issues, the

---

[5] There are 11 Risk Assessment Verification Items, such as: verify that appropriate training was provided to personnel assigned to GHG reporting duties; verify that appropriate monitoring data are measured or referenced accurately, etc.

error shall be corrected if possible. However, if no corrective action is possible no credit is issued for this field and the verification body must verify an additional field managed by the same participant. If this additional verification is also unsuccessful, no credits shall be issued for any of the fields managed by the project participant. In addition, the verification body has to use its professional judgment to determine if it is necessary to sample additional project participants for site visit verification. This provides a very strong incentive not to have more than one disfunctioning field per participant.

Error is considered relevant if the difference between the project proponent's and the verification body's assessments of emissions reductions is greater than 5 percent. Then, if the aggregated percent error (total errors for the sampled fields) is less than 5 percent, CRT issuance is equal to the amount reported by the aggregator. If it is greater than 5 percent, CRT issuance is reduced by the total amount of aggregated percent error rate.

The additional MRV requirements of the CAR Methodology make it more costly than its VCS or ACR counterpart, but no cost assessment has been made yet.

12.5 Conclusion

Methodologies are designed in a bottom-up manner. Thus, their approach and content depend on the geographic location and regulatory framework applying to the first project on which they are used. More specifically, they depend on data availability (e.g., data already reported in an existing regulatory framework such as the Common Agricultural Policy) which varies from one region to another.

One of the main features of the agricultural sector is the diffuse nature of its emissions. Several agricultural producers must aggregate their reductions with fellow farmers to create an offset project. Verification of these large amounts of data cannot be comprehensive. A risk-based sampling is implemented.

These two factors (the use of existing data, sample verification) allow MRV costs to be reduced.

12.6 MRV ID table

Table 12.5 *MRV ID table*

	JI (track 1) in France	VCS	CAR	ACR
		Context		
Regulator	- *Designated Focal Point (DFPs):* establishes the general procedure and guidelines, approves methodologies, projects and credit issuance requests. - *Accredited independent entity (AIE):* independent auditor accredited by the JISC who makes a recommendation on whether the project and its documentation abide by the general procedure and the relevant methodology. CDM-accredited auditors are also accepted.	- *The VCS Board:* establishes the general procedure and guidelines. - *Validation/Verification Bodies (VVB):* two accredited VVBs assess the methodology, one VVB decides on whether the project and its documentation abide by the general procedure and the relevant methodology.	- *The CAR board:* Adoption of methodologies in public sessions; - *Verification Bodies accredited by the American National Standards Institute (ANSI):* decides on whether the project and its documentation abide by the general procedure and the relevant methodology.	- *The ACR staff:* Adoption of methodologies after scientific peer review process (three reviewers: one lead and two secondary); - *ARB (California Air Resources Board) approved verification bodies:* decides on whether the project and its documentation abide by the general procedure and the relevant methodology.
Methodologies	*Méthodologie spécifique aux projets de réduction des émissions de N_2O dues à la dénitrification des sols agricoles par l'insertion de légumineuses dans les rotations agricoles.* This methodology is about N_2O emissions reductions due to legumes inclusion in crop rotations.	Quantifying N_2O Emissions Reductions in Agricultural Crops through Nitrogen Fertilizer Rate Reduction (VM0022; version 1.0)	Nitrogen Management Project Protocol (version 1.1)	Methodology for Quantifying Nitrous Oxide (N_2O) Emissions Reductions from Reduced Use of Nitrogen Fertilizer on Agricultural Crops (Version 1).

Table 12.5 (*cont.*)

	JI (track 1) in France	VCS	CAR	ACR
Type and level of incentive to comply	**For projects proponents:** - Positive incentives ("carrots"): issuance of ERUs (timeliness and quantity); - Negative incentives ("sticks"): ERU discounting due to high monitoring uncertainty. **For AIEs:** - Positive incentives ("Carrots"): fees for successful CER issuance; - Negative incentives ("sticks"): suspension or withdrawal of accreditation, i.e., temporary or permanent loss of business.	**For projects proponents:** - Positive incentives ("carrots"): issuance of VCUs (timeliness and quantity); - Negative incentives ("sticks"): VCU discounting due to high monitoring uncertainty (some methodologies use adjustment factors or discount factors to address the uncertainty of measurements in a conservative manner).	Same as VCS	Same as VCS
Entities concerned	Methodology developers: InVivo, CDC Climat, CITEPA Project proponents: InVivo is the aggregator, 11 agricultural cooperatives are involved in this PoA (Program of Activities)	Methodology developers: EPRI (Electric Power Research Institute) and MSU (Michigan State University)	Same as VCS	Same as VCS

	N$_2$O emissions from fertilizer use	N$_2$O emissions from fertilizer use	N$_2$O emissions from fertilizer use	N$_2$O emissions from fertilizer use
Sectors concerned	N$_2$O	N$_2$O	N$_2$O	N$_2$O
Gases concerned	€20,000 per year, including upfront costs.	Likely similar to JI. No specific assessment available.	Likely similar to JI. No specific assessment available.	Likely similar to JI. No specific assessment available.
Overall MRV costs				
	Monitoring			
Rules	Methodology PDD (JI PoA-DD)	Methodology (VM0022; version 1.0)	Methodology	Methodology
Other reference documents	- JI guidelines - Procedures for programs of activities under the verification procedure under the Joint Implementation Supervisory Committee - national guidelines and procedures for approving JI projects - Guidance on criteria for baseline setting and monitoring (version 03) - IPCC Fourth Assessment Report: Climate Change 2007 (2007) for global warming potentials of GHGs - 2006 IPCC Guidelines for national GHG inventories - The peer-reviewed literature	- VCS Program Guide, v3.4 - VCS Standard, v3.3 - Monitoring Report, v3.2 - IPCC Fourth Assessment Report: Climate Change 2007 (2007) for global warming potentials of GHGs - 2006 IPCC Guidelines for national GHG inventories - The peer-reviewed literature	- Climate Action Reserve Program Manual - IPCC Fourth Assessment Report: Climate Change 2007 (2007) for global warming potentials of GHGs - 2006 IPCC Guidelines for national GHG inventories - The peer-reviewed literature	- American Carbon Registry Standard v2.1 - IPCC Fourth Assessment Report: Climate Change 2007 (2007) for global warming potentials of GHGs - 2006 IPCC Guidelines for national GHG inventories - The peer-reviewed literature

Table 12.5 (*cont.*)

	JI (track 1) in France	VCS	CAR	ACR
Required uncertainty	No explicit requirements.	Uncertainty in N_2O emissions reductions associated with a reduction in N rate (%) (UNC) must be below 15% at 95% confidence level. If greater than 15%, an uncertainty deduction is used (see Section 12.2).	Same as VCS	Same as VCS
Achieved precision range	Not available: no uncertainty assessment required.	Not applicable: no project implemented yet.	Not applicable: no project implemented yet.	Not applicable: no project implemented yet.
Cost range	€10,000 per year.	Likely similar to JI.	Likely similar to JI.	Likely similar to JI.
Scope	Direct and indirect N_2O emissions are measured (The special boundary includes the project site where fertilizer is directly applied as well as any additional soils and waters where byproducts of the fertilizer N input are re-deposited). Upstream emissions related to manufacture and transport are not included.	- Same as JI	Same as JI	Same as JI

Frequency	Yearly	Yearly	Yearly	Yearly
Source for activity data	- Common Agricultural Policy reporting: crop area - Cultural practices survey which occurred every five years: amount of synthetic N fertilizer	Project proponent records or country-level data (only for the baseline determination if site-specific management records are not available): amount of fertilizer, crop area, crop yield	Field measurements (Corn Stalk Nitrate Test), Project proponent records or country level data (amount of fertilizer, application method, placement method crop area, crop yield, planting and harvest dates, dates when emergency irrigation is used, type of system, justification for use).	Project proponent records or country-level data (amount of fertilizer, crop area, crop yield).
Uncertainty range for activity data	No explicit requirements.	No explicit requirements.	No explicit requirements.	No explicit requirements.
Source for emission factors	National GHG inventory	- 2006 IPCC Guidelines for national GHG inventories (IPCC Tier 1) - Empirical research on producer field throughout Michigan (IPCC Tier 2)	Empirical research on producer field throughout Michigan (IPCC Tier 2).	Same as VCS but a project-specific emission factor is allowed if justified based on empirical, peer-reviewed articles.
Uncertainty range for emission factors	No explicit requirements.	Credits discounted above 15%.	Same as VCS.	Same as VCS.

Table 12.5 (*cont.*)

	JI (track 1) in France	VCS	CAR	ACR
Direct measurement	None	None	None	None
Incentive to reduce uncertainty	None	Credit discounting above 15% uncertainty on emissions reductions from fertilizer application (see Section 12.2).	Same as VCS	- Credit discounting above 15% uncertainty on emissions reductions from fertilizer application (see Section 12.2). - Project proponents can propose a project-specific emissions factor as long as they can demonstrate by using empirical data published in peer-reviewed scientific journals that this EF is conservative. Otherwise, they must use the IPCC linear default which is likely conservative in the US context (see Section 12.2).

	National guidelines on JI projects ("projets domestiques CO$_2$")	VCS Program Guide, v3.4 / VCS Standard, v3.3 / Monitoring Report, v3.2	Climate Action Reserve Program Manual	American Carbon Registry Standard v2.1
Is requirements stringency adapted to the amount of emissions at stake (materiality)?	No. Requirements stringency is the same regardless of project size.	No. Requirements stringency is the same regardless of project size.	To the contrary: an uncertainty adjustment factor (UAF) makes requirements more stringent for projects with fewer fields involved (see Section 12.2).	No. Requirements stringency is the same regardless of project size.
Reporting				
Rules	National guidelines on JI projects ("projets domestiques CO$_2$")	VCS Program Guide, v3.4 VCS Standard, v3.3 Monitoring Report, v3.2	Climate Action Reserve Program Manual	American Carbon Registry Standard v2.1
Other reference documents	No other relevant document.	No other relevant document.	No other relevant document.	No other relevant document.
Format	No specified format.	Following the format of Monitoring Report, v3.2	Following the format indicated in the methodology (Part 7, Climate Action Reserve, 2013).	No specified format.
Level of source disaggregation	Disaggregation down to field level.	Disaggregation down to field level.	Disaggregation down to field level.	Disaggregation down to field level.
Frequency	Up to the project proponent.	Up to the project proponent: at least every ten years.	Yearly or every two years for single field projects.	Up to the project proponent: at least every five years.

Table 12.5 (*cont.*)

	JI (track 1) in France	VCS	CAR	ACR
Timeline	Not specified.	Not specified.	The monitoring report must be submitted within 12 months of the end of each crediting period.	Not specified.
Language	French	English	English	English
Is requirements stringency adapted to the amount of emissions at stake (materiality)?	No. Requirements stringency is the same regardless of project size.	No. Requirements stringency is the same regardless of project size.	No. Requirements stringency is the same regardless of project size.	No. Requirements stringency is the same regardless of project size.
Cost range	Included in "monitoring costs."	Likely similar to JI.	Likely similar to JI.	Likely similar to JI.
		Verification		
Rules	JI Guidelines	VCS Program Guide, v3.4 VCS Standard, v3.3 Verification Report, v3.2 Validation and Verification Manual	- Climate Action Reserve Program Manual - Climate Action Reserve Verification Program Manual - Climate Action Reserve Nitrogen Management Project Protocol	- American Carbon Registry Standard v2.1 - American Carbon Registry Guidelines 2012

Other reference documents	No other relevant document.	No other relevant document.	No other relevant document.	No other relevant document.
Format	No specified format.	Following the format of the Verification Report, v3.2 available on the VCS website.	No specified format.	No specified format.
Frequency	Verification takes places at every reporting event, that is after the publication of the monitoring report.	Verification takes places at every reporting event, that is after the publication of the monitoring report.	Verification takes places at every reporting event, that is after the publication of the monitoring report.	ACR requires: - A desk-based verification audit at each request for issuance of new ERTs; - A full verification including field visit at the first verification and again at least every five years.
Timeline	No specified timeline.	No specified timeline.	No specified timeline.	No specified timeline.
Language	French	English	English	English
Accredited entities for verification	7 accredited independent entities (AIEs) and 24 *Designated Operational Entities* (DOE) for agricultural scope.	Named validation and verification bodies (VVB): 22 entities accredited by the VCS for agricultural scope. These are either accredited under ISO for VCS validation, mostly smaller structures, or accredited under the CDM.	ISO-accredited verification bodies with lead verifiers trained by the reserve are the only ones which can be eligible to verify nitrogen management project report. All verification bodies must include a Certified	Five entities are specifically accredited by the ACR for nitrogen management projects. In addition, ACR automatically accredits auditors already accredited under the CDM or JI.

Table 12.5 (*cont.*)

	JI (track 1) in France	VCS	CAR	ACR
			Professional Agronomist or Certified Crop Advisor in the team, who must be present for all site verification visits. Three entities are accredited by the CAR for nitrogen management projects.	
Control of accredited entities	The Board may decide to suspend totally or partially the accreditation of a DOE based on the recommendation of the CDM-AP or other review processes conducted by the Board (see Chapter 11 and CDM-EB56-A02).	Accredited V/VBs shall undergo surveillance during the first and second years after the year of their initial accreditation or reaccreditation. ANSI may decide to conduct surveillance visits out of sequence and without prior notice or with short notice if a complaint is received regarding the performance of the V/VB.	CAR may conduct a performance review of its auditors, or oversee a verification activity anytime. Lead verifiers within each accredited company must repass CAR exams every three years.	Not specified.

Cost of accreditation	According to the Procedure for accrediting operational entities by the Executive Board (CDM-EB56-A02), accreditation fees are as follows: - Non-reimbursable application fee is US$15,000; - Fee and costs associated with an on-site assessment of the premises of an AE/DOE; - Other costs related to performance assessment, reaccreditation, change of scope of a DOE, etc.	Temporary accreditation: Non-refundable fee of €6,500 for seven sectoral scopes, plus €1,000 for each additional sectoral scope thereafter. VVBs pay an annual fee to maintain accreditation depending on their gross annual revenues (US$1,500 if they are below US$375,000, 0.4% of their revenue if revenues are above US$375,000 and below US$13.75m and US$55,000 for revenues above US$13.75m). Assessment and surveillance fees are US$1,250 per day per assessor plus expenses.	The costs of accreditation are determined by the accreditation body and generally include an initial non-refundable application fee, an assessment fee for the surveillance performed by the assessors, a sector scope extension fee, and annual accreditation fee allowing the verification body to use the accreditation body's symbol of accreditation, known as the "mark." There is also an additional fee to extend the scope of accreditation, which is collected when verification bodies seek eligibility to perform verifications for new sectors.	Application fee: US$2,000 Scope expansion fee: US$500

Table 12.5 (*cont.*)

	JI (track 1) in France	VCS	CAR	ACR
Support provided to accredited entities	No specific support provided.	No specific support provided.	No specific support provided.	No specific support provided.
Is requirements stringency adapted to the amount of emissions at stake (materiality)?	No. To the contrary, the sampling requirements lower the costs for larger projects.	Yes: the acceptance threshold (materiality) concerning all errors, omissions and false statements is higher for smaller projects: • 5% for projects under 300,000 tCO_2/year; • 1% for projects over 300,000 tCO_2/year (large projects).	Somewhat: project developers may choose a two-year verification period for single-field projects. In addition, the materiality threshold varies between 1% and 5% of emissions reductions, and is more lenient (5%) with smaller projects. The sampling requirements during verification being proportional to project size, the resulting uncertainty requirement is more stringent for smaller projects (see Section 12.4).	
Cost range	€20,000 per verification.	No data.	No data.	No data.

Bibliography

American Carbon Registry, 2012. *Methodology for quantifying nitrous oxide (N₂O) emissions reductions from reduced use of nitrogen fertilizer on agricultural crops.*

Beaurain, F. and Schmidt-Traub, G., 2010. *Developing CDM Programmes of Activities: a Guidebook.* South Pole Carbon Asset Management Ltd, Zurich.

Bernstein, L., Bosch, P., Canziani, O., Chen, Z., et al., 2007. IPCC, 2007: climate change 2007: synthesis report. Contribution of working groups I, II and III to the Fourth Assessment Report of the Intergovernmental Panel on Climate Change. Intergovernmental Panel on Climate Change, Geneva.

Choquet, P.-L., 2014. Personal communication.

Climate Action Reserve, 2013. *Nitrogen Management, Project Protocol.*

Foucherot, C. and Bellassen, V., 2011. Carbon Offset Projects in the Agricultural Sector (Climate Report No. 31). CDC Climat Research, Paris.

Guigon, P., Bellassen, V. and Ambrosi, P., 2009. Voluntary carbon markets: what the standards say... (Working Paper, Mission Climat). Caisse des Depots.

InVivo, 2011a. *Dossier Descriptif de Projet programmatique, Programme InVivo (JPoA-DD).*

2011b. *Méthodologie spécifique aux projets de réduction des émissions de N₂O dues à la dénitrification des sols agricoles par l'insertion de légumineuses dans les rotations agricoles.*

Krey, M., 2005. Transaction costs of unilateral CDM projects in India – results from an empirical survey. *Energy Policy* 33: 2385–2397.

Michaelowa, A. and Stronzik, M., 2002. Transaction costs of the Kyoto mechanisms (HWWA Discussion Paper, No. 175).

Michigan State University (MSU), Electric Power Research Institute (EPRI), 2012. *ACR Methodology, Methodology for Quantifying Nitrous Oxide (N₂O) Emissions Reductions from Reduced Use of Nitrogen Fertilizer on Agricultural Crops.*

2013. *VCS Methodology VM0022, Quantifying N₂O Emissions Reductions in Agricultural Crops through Nitrogen Fertilizer Rate Reduction.*

The Earth Partners, 2013. *VCS Moule VMD0029, Estimation of Emissions of Non-CO₂ GHGs from Soils.*

UNEP, 2007. *Guidebook to Financing CDM Projects.* United Nations Environment Programme, Denmark.

UNFCCC, 2009. *AMS-III.A, Offsetting of synthetic nitrogen fertilizers by inoculant application in legumes-grass rotation on acidic soils on existing cropland.*

    2012. *AMS-III.BF, Reduction of N$_2$O emissions from use of Nitrogen Use Efficient (NUE) seeds that require less fertilizer application.*

Verified Carbon Standard, 2012. *VCS Standard, VCS Version 3.*

13 | Case study 2: monitoring requirements for reforestation and improved forest management projects across standards

MARIANA DEHEZA

13.1 Context

On the voluntary carbon market, 26% of all the carbon credits that were exchanged in 2012 came from forestry projects, with 9% from projects reducing emissions from deforestation and forest degradation (REDD) and 17% from reforestation and improved forest management (IFM) projects (Peters-Stanley et al., 2013). REDD projects, which take a territorial approach to MRV, are treated in a specific case study of part I variant 2 (see Chapter 4). This case study focuses on the MRV procedures and their associated uncertainty for forestry projects across two certification standards: the CDM and the VCS. These two standards were chosen because they are the two most used among certification standards for forestry projects (Peters-Stanley and Hamilton 2012). In 2011, 60% of all transacted forestry credits in both the voluntary and the compliance market were certified by the CDM or the VCS.

The Verified Carbon Standard (VCS) is one of the most widely used standards in the voluntary market, with 55 percent of transacted credits (56 $MtCO_2e$) according to Peters-Stanley et al. (2013). This standard was founded by The Climate Group, International Emissions Trading Association (IETA), The World Economic Forum and the World Business Council for Sustainable Development (WBCSD) in 2005.

As of May 2013, 1,005 projects have been registered under this standard and issued more than 120 million verified carbon units (VCU). Within those, 73 are forestry projects, with an estimated capacity of generating 27 MVCUs per year.[1] VCS also constitutes the most popular standard for forestry projects, with 28 percent of all forestry projects transacted worldwide (Peters-Stanley and Hamilton 2012).

---

[1] Calculated from the VCS project database as of May 2013.

Any methodology accepted by the CDM can be used in the VCS. Protocols – or methodologies – developed by the Climate Action Reserve (CAR) are also accepted, except for the CAR forest protocol. No VCS-specific AR methodology has been developed as project proponents opted to use the CDM methodologies. Together, the CDM and the VCS have validated nine reforestation or IFM methodologies (Table 13.1).

13.2 Monitoring in the CDM for reforestation projects and VCS IFM projects

Which emissions are monitored?

Possible sources of emissions/sequestration
Monitoring reforestation or improved forest management projects amounts to counting carbon sequestration – or emissions – in the newly planted forest or improved forest and the emissions related to forestry operations (transportation, plowing, seeding, thinning, etc.). Carbon sequestration/emissions can occur in six compartments or carbon pools (IPCC, 2006), although, depending on the methodology, not all six necessarily need to be monitored:

- **Above-ground biomass:** including stems, branches and the foliage of trees as well as non-woody vegetation and shrubs.
- **Below-ground biomass:** including living roots.
- **Deadwood:** including non-living biomass such as standing or lying on the ground stumps or buried dead roots.
- **Litter:** non-living biomass with a diameter less than a certain threshold defined in the methodologies. It also includes decomposing lying deadwood.
- **Soil organic carbon:** including all soil components derived from plants and animals.
- **Harvested wood products.**

Similarly, depending on the methodology, not all emissions related to forestry operations need to be monitored.

Along with carbon sequestration and emissions other components of a forestry carbon project are also monitored:

- project boundary (e.g., GPS coordinates of the reforested plots);
- project implementation (e.g., the implementation of planned project activities);

Table 13.1 *Active carbon accounting methodologies for reforestation (AR) and improved forest management (IFM) methodologies in the CDM and the VCS as of January 2014*

Standard	Project type	Methodology	Number of projects registered
CDM	AR	CDM – AR-ACM0003 – Large-scale Methodology: Afforestation and reforestation of lands except wetlands	28 in the CDM 25 in the VCS
CDM	AR	CDM – AR-AM0014 – A/R Large-scale Methodology Afforestation and reforestation of degraded mangrove habitats	0 in the CDM
CDM	AR	CDM – AR-AMS0003 Simplified baseline and monitoring methodology for small-scale CDM afforestation and reforestation project activities implemented on wetlands	1 in the CDM
CDM	AR	CDM – AR-AMS0007 Simplified baseline and monitoring methodology for small-scale CDM afforestation and reforestation project activities implemented on lands other than wetlands	23 in the CDM 20 in the VCS
VCS	IFM	VM0003 Methodology for Improved Forest Management through Extension of Rotation Age	1 in the VCS
VCS	IFM	VM0005 Methodology for Improved Forest Management: Low Productive to High Productive Forests	0 in the VCS
VCS	IFM	VM0010 Methodology for Improved Forest Management: Conversion from Logged to Protected Forest	4 in the VCS
VCS	IFM	VM0011 Methodology for Calculating GHG Benefits from Preventing Planned Degradation	1 in the VCS
VCS	IFM	VM0012 Improved Forest Management in Temperate and Boreal Forests (LtPF)	2 in the VCS

- leakage (e.g., emissions from increased harvest indirectly driven by an IFM project which decreases harvest locally).

The CDM focuses on above-ground and below-ground biomass
Under the general guidelines of the CDM, all five carbon pools must be accounted for, unless "transparent and verifiable information" proves that a pool will not decrease compared to the baseline scenario (CDM-EB66-A25-GUID). Most forestry-related emissions are considered *de minimis* according to CDM EB decisions, and therefore not monitored, with the notable exception of CH_4 and N_2O emissions from biomass burning (Table 13.2). Note that CO_2 emissions from biomass burning are *de facto* accounted for by tracking the carbon content of the relevant pools.

In practice, "transparent and verifiable information" that a given pool does not decrease can be provided for all five pools in most cases, so project developers have the choice on whether counting them. Calmel et al. (2011) point out that the cost of accounting for a given pool is usually weighed against the expected impact on additional carbon sales in order to make this choice. As a result, the most generic CDM reforestation methodology (AR-ACM0003) only requires accounting for above-ground and below-ground biomass. The methodology specific to wetlands (AMS0003) requires the accounting of all pools except litter, probably due to the importance of soil carbon in wetlands.

IFM methodologies pay a specific attention to harvested wood products
In the case of IFM VCS projects, soil carbon and litter are not accounted for as they are deemed unlikely to decrease. Similarly to the CDM, the VCS allows the exclusion of other pools such as deadwood or below-ground biomass if they are expected to increase in the project scenario. A particular treatment is given to the wood products pool for this type of project: most methodologies require that this pool be accounted as it may decrease due to project activity. Some methodologies (VM0005 and VM0011) even recommend considering this pool as zero in the project scenario in order to maintain conservative estimates and simplify the accounting.

Table 13.2 *Compulsory and optional accounting in reforestation and improved forest management projects*

	Carbon pools (compulsory)	Carbon pools (optional)	Carbon pools (not accounted for)	Other emission sources accounted for	Emission sources considered *de minimis*
CDM (reforestation methodologies)	All (unless the pool does not decrease)	Pools which do not decrease	None	CH_4 and N_2O from biomass burning	Emissions from forestry operations Materiality standard (Decision 9/CMP.7). Emissions below a certain threshold do not need to be accounted
VCS (Improved Forest Management methodologies)	Above-ground biomass Below-ground biomass (VM0005 and VM0012) Deadwood (all except VM003) Wood products (all except VM0003)	Deadwood and wood products for VM0003 Belowground biomass (VM0005)	Litter and soil carbon (all) Below-ground biomass (VM0005) Above-ground non-tree biomass (all except VM003)	CH_4 from biomass burning as part of forest management (VM0003 and VM0010) CH_4, CO_2, N_2O from combustion of fossil fuels in vehicles and machinery (VM0005, VM0011)	N_2O from biomass burning (VM0003 and VM0005) CO_2, CH_4, N_2O from fossil fuels combustion conservatively excluded as emissions are likely greater in the baseline (VM0010 and VM0012)

Possible leakage: displacement of agricultural activities, activity shifting within the same company and market effect

As stated in Chapter 11, MRV for the CDM also requires the calculation of emissions or removals not only within the project boundary, but also the calculation of emissions indirectly affected by a project, most commonly referred to as "leakage." In the case of reforestation projects all CDM methodologies require the calculation of leakage due to the displacement of pre-project agricultural activities considered to be significant.[2]

In the case of the VCS, IFM project developers should prove that there is no leakage within their operations – i.e., on other lands they manage/operate outside the boundary of the VCS activity. Therefore, there may be no leakage due to activity shifting within the company. Methodologies VM0003, VM005 and VM0010 also provide for the determination of leakage due to market effect when harvest is reduced due to project implementation. In this case, leakage is equal to the net emissions from timber harvest activities in the baseline scenario multiplied by an appropriate leakage discount factor. These leakage discount factors are determined in regard to the effect of the IFM project activity on harvesting levels; for example, if a rotation extension of 5–10 years is planned by the project a 10 percent discount factor is applied. For the leakage factor associated with the market effect, VM0012 allows project developers to refer to the latest available version of the CAR's market leakage formula.

Stratification and sampling: two key underlying components which drive uncertainty and costs

Stratification of the project area into relatively homogeneous units can either increase the measuring precision without unduly increasing the

---

[2] Displacement of agricultural activities is considered to be insignificant if at least one of the following conditions applies: 1) the total area subjected to pre-project grazing activities to be displaced is less than 5 percent of the area of the entire A/R CDM project activity, or less than 50 ha; 2) the total number of animals expected to be displaced is not more than 40 Livestock Standard Unit (LSU); 3) the supplementary agricultural activities or LSUs above this threshold are displaced to areas identified as degraded or degrading lands or to areas (such as existing grasslands or tree plantations) with the carrying capacity that allows for accommodation of the displaced animals during the entire displacement period.

cost, or reduce the cost without reducing measuring precision because of the lower variance within each homogeneous unit. All CDM and VCS methodologies available for reforestation and IFM projects indicate that if the project area is not homogeneous in terms of biomass distribution, stratification should be carried out. Methodologies indicate the criteria to be applied in order to define the different strata which include: vegetation types, planting date and management plans, soil types, natural impacts altering the pattern of biomass distribution, etc.

When performing stratification, the differences among various strata should be easily identifiable. The area of a stratum should not be less than 10 percent of the total area to be sampled. No further detail on what is considered a homogeneous stratum such as a quantitative threshold for variance is provided in the methodologies. This is left to the professional judgment of the auditor. In any case, a faulty stratification increases the uncertainty estimate, and the project proponent is therefore incentivized to come up with a robust stratification (see the section on sampling error). Different strata are determined as a function of soil type, age of the plantations and species.

Given that biomass distribution can change during the project lifetime, stratification is reviewed by the auditor at every verification event and can be changed by the project proponent if needed. For example, if part of an existing stratum is flooded between two verification events, the flooded zone will likely grow more slowly. In this case, the stratum needs to be split into two new strata, flooded and not flooded.

Carbon stocks in the different carbon pools are estimated based on permanent sample plots. Following stratification applied to non-homogeneous project areas, project developers pursue their monitoring procedure by determining the sample size (Figure 13.1). This sample size depends on the uncertainty level required by each methodology. The number of plots is estimated in the Project Design Document (PDD) and a tool exists for this purpose in the CDM. The VCS allows project developers to use the same tool for IFM projects.

Once the number of sample plots has been determined, their location needs to be chosen inside each stratum. They can be randomly or systematically distributed, but the choice must be specified in the PDD. Most methodologies use systematic distribution of plots which means that plots are located usually in the form of a grid following a regular distribution pattern. Plot size according to methodologies should be

Figure 13.1 Field monitoring procedure
Source: Author.

between 100 and 1,000 m² and their shape can be rectangular, square or circular. Data are then collected and measurements are made during each monitored period. Specific information on sampling design applied in three reforestation projects is further detailed in Table 13.4.

Monitoring plans

The PDD needs to include a monitoring plan that provides for collection of all relevant data necessary for:

a) verification that the applicability conditions to each methodology apply;
b) verification of changes in carbon stocks in selected pools;
c) verification of project and leakage emissions.

The procedure is similar for VCS IFM projects. Monitoring plans for reforestation and IFM projects contain a detailed list of parameters to be monitored including their description, their monitoring procedure and further comments. They generally include:

a) the monitoring of forest establishment and management operation (e.g., invoices for the purchase of seedlings, operational documents describing the type of operation practiced and its results, etc.) if required for compliance with the applicability conditions of each methodology;
b) information on how geographic coordinates of the project boundary are established, recorded and archived;
c) the description of the sampling method to be applied including sample size, type of measurements to be made in each sampling plot and the method chosen to determine the location of sample plots;
d) the schedule of measurement events;
e) the procedures for project implementation (forest management operations) and monitoring including the procedures for training the monitoring personnel, the equipment used in inventories as well as their maintenance, the procedures for handling records and storing information;

f) a list of the quality control (QC) and quality assurance (QA) procedures undertaken for data monitored that usually include independent re-measurement of a percentage (5–10 percent) of sample plots to confirm that measurement and data recording were done properly. A full re-measurement of all tree sample plots is required if the discrepancy between the original and the revised calculated carbon stocks is larger than 10 percent.

Monitoring in practice: teamwork coordinated by the project proponent

As of May 2013, ten reforestation projects had already issued credits through the CDM and had therefore produced a monitoring report. To assess the practical arrangement pertaining to monitoring, three of them were analyzed in more detail, together with two VCS IFM projects which have already issued credits (Table 13.3).

For most of these projects, the project developer itself is in charge of monitoring. Universities and research institutes often collaborate in mapping, photo-interpretation and modeling tasks. When there are multiple project developers, such as the Indian agroforestry project, monitoring teams are organized among project participants and tasks are distributed according to their field of expertise. Exceptionally, for the Chilean project, monitoring has been subcontracted to a consultancy firm specialized in forest inventories.

In the case of the Canadian project certified by the VCS, Nature Conservancy Canada (the project proponent) is also in charge of monitoring, though the monitoring report was prepared by an external consultancy firm 3GreenTree Ecosystem Services.

Which supporting evidence for the baseline scenario?

The baseline scenario is determined with the help of a specific tool developed for all CDM reforestation projects: "Combined tool to identify the baseline scenario and demonstrate additionality in A/R CDM project activities."[3] First all alternative land-use scenarios considered

---

[3] http://cdm.unfccc.int/methodologies/ARmethodologies/tools/ar-am-tool-02-v1
.pdf

Table 13.3 *Description of three CDM reforestation projects and two VCS improved forest management projects*

Ref.	Title	Host country	Methodology	Length of crediting period (yrs)	Average annual credit issuance as of May 2013 (tCO$_2$e/yr)	Date of registration	Monitoring periods
4957	Securitization and carbon sinks project	Chile	AR-AM005 replaced by AR-ACM0003	30	40, 537	01/03/ 2012	01/31/2003 – 09/30/2012
4653	Kachung Forest Project: Afforestation on Degraded Lands	Uganda	AR-AM004 replaced by AR-ACM0003	20	4, 960	04/04/2011	10/01/2006 – 11/22/2012
4531	Improving Rural Livelihoods Through Carbon Sequestration By Adopting Environment Friendly Technology based Agroforestry Practices	India	AR-AM004 replaced by AR-ACM0003	30	11, 105	02/28/ 2011	06/25/2004-08/31/2011
607	Darkwoods Forest Carbon Project	Canada	VM0012	100	308, 656	01/23/2013	04/01/2008-12/31/2010
872	Afognak Forest Carbon Project	United States	VM0012	30	56, 745	07/27/2012	01/01/2006-12/31/2011

Source: Author from UNEP Risoe (2013) and VCS project database.

realistic and credible in regard to relevant national and/or sectoral policies have to be identified. Land-use records, field surveys, data and feedback of stakeholders are inputs for this process.

Various data and parameters are needed in order to apply this tool and usually include:

- invoices proving the starting date of the project activity;
- letters of support coming from different stakeholders as well as contracts and agreements stating the intention to claim carbon credits following project implementation;
- information in order to identify credible alternative land-use scenarios gathered on field surveillance to be carried out by the project proponent as well as available studies on relevant national and sectoral policies. This information may include data collected from forest and agriculture censuses, the list of current laws and regulations, etc.

COP16 in Cancun provided for a possibility for host countries' DNAs to submit standardized baselines concerning all or part of the country for consideration by the Executive Board (UNFCCC, 2011). Following the decisions of COP16, the Executive Board adopted the Guidelines for the Establishment of Sector Specific Standardized Baselines (EB62), streamlining the procedure for submitting and using standardized baselines. Concerning the reforestation sector, specific guidelines have been adopted in EB70. These guidelines mention that proposed standardized baselines may, depending upon availability of data, include estimated values of baseline carbon stocks and baseline net GHG removals by sinks in the above-ground and below-ground carbon pools, on a per hectare basis. Proposed values may be reported by strata within the identified areas of land. Where the values are based on sample-based estimation, the associated uncertainty estimated at a 90 percent confidence level should not be more than 10 percent. Where the uncertainty is larger than 10 percent, the values must be demonstrated to be conservative estimates (CDM-EB70-A10-GUID).

In the case of IFM projects certified by the VCS, the project developers need to provide evidence that the project proponent meets the applicability conditions outlined for this baseline scenario in each methodology. For instance methodology VM0005 requires the baseline to be a logged-over natural Evergreen Tropical Rainforest with no or insignificant regrowth and this needs to be proven in order to apply this methodology for the accounting of GHG emissions and absorptions.

The CDM does not require reviewing the baseline after project registration, unless the crediting period is renewed (every 20 years). To the contrary, the Verified Carbon standard (VCS) requires a re-evaluation of the baseline scenario every 10 years even if no crediting period renewal is expected.

Monitoring frequency: mostly five years

As mentioned in Chapter 11, the crediting period is the maximal time period over which an offset project may obtain carbon credits that is therefore monitored. For CDM projects in other sectors, this period is limited to 7 years with a possibility to renew up to two times or to 10 years non-renewable (CDM-EB65-A05-STAN). For reforestation projects certified by the CDM, this period is extended, and limited to 20 years which may be renewed at most two times or 30 years non-renewable. In the case of renewal, the auditor has to determine and to inform the Executive Board if the original baseline is still valid or has been updated (Decision 5/CMP.1).

For all AFOLU projects certified by the VCS, the project crediting period shall be a minimum of 20 years up to a maximum of 100 years, which may be renewed at most four times with a total project crediting period not to exceed 100 years.

Regarding monitoring frequency, there are no specific requirements and carbon stocks therefore tend to be monitored just before a verification event. In practice, this tends to be every five years.

In the CDM AR methodologies, leakage monitoring is only required for the first five years of the project activity.

Sampling error, most often the only explicit uncertainty requirement

CDM uncertainty requirements
Activity data: focus on the sampling error of tree biomass
For CDM reforestation methodologies, sampling error is the only source of error considered in the computation of uncertainty, referred to as the *maximum allowable relative margin of error*. The other

Table 13.4 *Trade-off between monitoring uncertainty and carbon revenues for CDM reforestation projects*

Relative margin of error	Deduction rate (DR)
Less than or equal to 10%	0%
Greater than 10% but less than or equal to 30%	6%
Greater than 30% but less than or equal to 50%	12%
Greater than 50% but less than or equal to 100%	21%
Greater than 100%	37%

Source: AR-TOOL14.

possible sources of error, such as the carbon density of wood, measurement errors or allometric factors,[4] are neglected (see Section 13.7).

Uncertainty requirements depend on the scale of the project. For small-scale projects (methodologies AR-AMS0003 and AR-AMS0007), the only uncertainty requirement concerns the estimated tree biomass: it must be within ±10 percent at 90 percent confidence level.

For large-scale projects, uncertainty may exceed ±10 percent at the expense of the amount of credits issued. Deductions range between 6 percent and 37 percent depending on the relative margin of error (see Table 13.4). The method choice allows for a first trade-off between monitoring cost and uncertainty: the *stock change method* is less demanding in terms of monitoring, as trees need not be marked, but the relative error of the more demanding *increment method* is diminished by a factor of $\sqrt{2}$ for the same number of sample plots compared to the *stock change method*. Other possible trade-offs can be made through stratification and sample size: the more effort is put into these, the lower the uncertainty, and hence the more credits are received. More details on uncertainty requirements are presented in the appendix.

Emissions factors: no requirement beyond uncertainty assessment
In case there is no country- or project-specific information regarding default parameters (e.g., emission factors) available, the IPCC default

---

[4] Allometric factors are commonly used to estimate whole tree biomass, including branches and roots, by extrapolating easily measurable parts such as the trunk.

values may be used (CDM-EB25). The only requirement regarding the uncertainty of emission factors comes from the general CDM guidelines and consists in assessing the uncertainty. Methodologies have to "describe the uncertainty of key parameters and, where possible, provide an uncertainty range at 95% confidence level for key parameters for the calculation of emission reductions" (CDM-EB66-A25-GUID). Methodology developers are also encouraged to refer to Chapter 6 of the IPCC Good Practice Guidance and Uncertainty Management in National Greenhouse Gas Inventories for more guidance on analysis of uncertainty (EB41-A12).

More detailed information on how the monitoring has been performed in each of the analyzed CDM reforestation projects is available in Table 13.5.

VCS uncertainty requirements

On a general basis, the VCS demands that, where applicable, methodology elements provide a means to estimate a 90% or 95% confidence interval. Where a methodology applies a 90% confidence interval and the width of the confidence interval exceeds 20% of the estimated value or where a methodology applies a 95% confidence interval and the width of the confidence interval exceeds 30% of the estimated value, an appropriate confidence deduction shall be applied. In practice, VCS methodologies tend to make the same simplification as their CDM counterparts, namely that sampling error is the only source of uncertainty. Some, however, such as VM012, include other sources of uncertainty.

The methods used for estimating uncertainty shall be based on recognized statistical approaches such as those described in the IPCC Good Practice Guidance and Uncertainty Management in National Greenhouse Gas Inventories. Confidence deductions shall be applied using conservative factors such as those specified in the CDM Meth Panel guidance on addressing uncertainty in its Thirty Second Meeting Report, Annex 14 (see Chapter 11).

The VCS specifies that in the case where methodologies apply complex models, these models must:

• prove that they have been reviewed and tested by a recognized organization or an appropriate peer-reviewed journal;

- assess all plausible sources of model uncertainty, such as structural uncertainty or parameter uncertainty, using recognized statistical approaches such as those described in the 2006 IPCC Guidelines for National Greenhouse Gas Inventories;
- apply conservative factors to discount for model uncertainty.

If a methodology uses data collected directly from primary sources, the data shall comply with relevant and appropriate standards, where available, for data collection and analysis, and be audited at an appropriate frequency by an appropriately qualified, independent organization. Secondary sources can either be peer-reviewed publications or appropriately qualified and independent organizations or government agencies.

If proxies are used, it shall be demonstrated that they are strongly correlated with the value of interest and that they can serve as an equivalent or better method (e.g., in terms of reliability, consistency or practicality) to determine the value of interest than direct measurement of the value itself.

Deduction factors also apply and depend on each methodology; detailed information can be found in the appendix.

The number of sample plots drives monitoring costs

Monitoring costs

Operational monitoring costs for afforestation projects depend not only on the size of the project. Monitoring costs are subject to both fixed and variable costs as generalized by Cacho et al. (2004) (Equation 13.1).

$$m_t = \frac{\alpha_m + \beta_m \cdot n}{A} \qquad \text{Equation 13.1}$$

Where:

m_t = Monitoring costs

α_m = Fixed costs including the costs of transporting monitoring teams into project areas

β_m = Variable costs vary in direct proportion to the number of plots (n) installed in order to perform the monitoring. They include salaries, transportation costs between the plots, data entry and analysis costs.

A = Total project area in hectares

Table 13.5 *Monitoring details of three CDM reforestation projects*

Ref.	Size	Sampling design	Monitoring intervals	Monitored variables	Quality control and quality assurance	Uncertainty achieved and overall emission reductions
4957	2,917 hectares	9 strata (species, plantation date, and site class) 42 permanent sample plots (PSP) Stock change method Sample size: 400 m²	9 years for the first monitoring period. In addition to monitoring the living biomass at successive monitoring intervals, disturbances will be recorded, if any, at the time of occurrence.	**Project boundary:** monitored using GPS and verified through field surveys *(periodically)* **Forestry inventory data** *(collected in the field every five years inside the PSP applied to a BEF)* • DBH • Height • Number of trees/ha • Commercial volume/ha with and without bark • Total area of all sample plots in stratum i/ha • Area of stratum **Disturbances** *(at the time of occurrence)* • Total burned area/ha • Total pest-affected area/ha **Emissions** *(every five years using surveys and field observations)* • Carbon emissions from extractions and burning fires **Leakage:** not monitored as considered zero since no displacement of agricultural and livestock activities happens because of the project.	**Forest inventory data:** each team will re-measure the standing above-ground biomass in at least one in ten plots measured by another team. Once the data is processed it will be compared and validated by *Growth Simulation Outputs* for specific site indexes. **Afforested area of each site:** in order to guarantee the mapping quality updated aerial photographs and restitution procedures will be applied to control the accuracy of the updated maps.	During the first monitoring period: 8.5% sampling error for a 90% confidence level in the estimation of total carbon sequestered by plantations Net GHG removals by sinks: 40,537 tCO$_2$e/yr during the period between January 31, 2003 and September 30, 2012

| 4653 | 2,099 hectares | 2 strata (grass and shrub land, and cropland) 51 permanent sample plots Stock change method Sample size: 200–400 m² | 6 years for the first monitoring period Variable-specific frequency for mortality and management activities | **Planted area and survival rate:** mortality assessment is performed one month after planting and 1 year after planting for each planted area. If mortality is higher than 50% in a continuous subportion of one of these planted area, this area is replanted and is mapped as a different stratum *(first 3 years)*. **Forestry management activities** *(recorded at event occurrence including their level of advancement and the area covered)*: including area of pruning, area of thinning, area of harvest, area replanted following harvesting, area affected by diseases and pests, area burnt by fire. **Project boundary and area of each stratum:** monitored using GPS and verified through field surveys *(yearly for the project boundary and every years for each stratum)* **Forestry inventory data** *(collected in the field every five years inside the PSP applied to a BEF)*
• DBH
• tree height
Volume of fuel-wood supply gathered in the project area *(estimated yearly through inventory data)* **Leakage:** *estimation of the leakage resulting from the conversion for cropland applying the associated tool* | 10–20% of plots randomly selected and re-measured | 9% according to the verification report (the value from the original monitoring report was found to be erroneous by the auditor) Net GHG removals by sinks: 4,959 tCO$_2$e/yr during the period October 1, 2006 to November 22, 2012 |

Table 13.5 (cont.)

Ref.	Size	Sampling design	Monitoring intervals	Monitored variables	Quality control and quality assurance	Uncertainty achieved and overall emission reductions
4531	1,608 hectares	5 strata (based on species and districts) 100 permanent sample plots (only 77 would be necessary to reach the 90% threshold, but more are used to buffer against plot losses or other risks) Stock change method Sample size: 256 m² (16 m*16 m)	7 years for the first monitoring period Variable-specific frequency for mortality and management activities	**Planted area and survival rate:** the initial survival rate of planted trees is assessed three months after planting, and re-planting shall be conducted if the survival rate is lower than 90% of the initial planting density. Planting in gaps is performed during year 2 and year 3. Final survival checking is conducted three years after the planting **Forestry management activities** (*recorded at event occurrence including their level of advancement and the area covered*): including area of pruning, area of thinning, area of harvest, area replanted following harvesting, area affected by diseases and pests, area burnt by fire **Project boundary and area of each stratum:** monitored using GPS and verified through field surveys (*yearly for the project boundary and every five years for each stratum*)	To minimize the possible errors in the process of data entry, the entry of both field data and laboratory data will be reviewed by an independent expert team and compared with independent data to ensure that the data is realistic.	During the first monitoring period 9.28 % sampling error for a 90% confidence level was achieved in the estimation of total carbon sequestered by plantations Net GHG removals by sinks: 11,106 tCO$_2$e/yr during the period between 06/25/2004 and 08/31/2011

Forestry inventory data *(collected in the field every five years inside the PSP applied to a BEF)*

- DBH
- tree height
- total number of PSP in stratum
- total size of all strata
- sample plot area
- number of trees in sample plots

Leakage: *estimation of the leakage resulting from the conversion for grazing land applying the associated tool (the following parameters are measured yearly)*

- number of animals present in project area

Source: Author based on project design documents, monitoring and verification reports.

Table 13.6 *Monitoring details of two VCS improved forest management projects*

Ref.	Size	Sampling design	Monitoring intervals	Monitored variables	Quality control and quality assurance	Precision achieved and overall emission reductions
607	54,792 ha	17 strata 20 permanent sample plots Project may deploy variations of size and shape of the sample plots as plot network integrates biodiversity monitoring	3 years for the first monitoring period Project activities, natural disturbances updated annually	**Forestry inventory data** (*collected in the field at least every five years inside the PSP*) • Area of forest land • sample plot area • DBH • tree height • mean tree age **Forestry management activities** (*recorded at event occurrence including their level of advancement and the area covered*): including area of pruning, area of thinning, area of harvest, road construction, area replanted following harvesting, area affected by diseases and pests, area burnt by fire **Leakage:** *estimation of the leakage resulting from activity shifting and market leakage (measured yearly)* • updating the timber harvest level of other properties of the project developer • market leakage calculations achieved using harvest levels and ex-post activities data	10% of plots were re-measured	During the first monitoring period 10% sampling error for a 90% confidence level was achieved in the estimation of total carbon sequestration Net GHG removals by sinks: 308,656 tCO_2e/yr during the period between 04/01/2008 and 12/31/2010

872	3,326.5 ha	3 strata 22 permanent sample plots where plot size (radius = 4 m, 14 m or 20 m) was determined based upon the DBH range of the trees within the plots such that a minimum of 40 trees were measured in each plot	6 years for the first monitoring period Inventory data will be updated annually or at each monitoring period, including the results of project activities, natural disturbances, and other changes to the inventory	**Forestry inventory data** (*collected in the field at least every five years inside the PSP*) • sample plot area • DBH • tree height • mean tree age • mortality rates • harvesting rates • total mass of dead organic matter • lying deadwood Annual monitoring of: • area of forest land (remote sensing and GIS) **Leakage:** *estimation of the leakage resulting from activity shifting and market leakage (measured yearly)* • updating the timber harvest level of other properties of the project developer • market leakage calculations achieved using harvest levels and ex-post activities data	FORECAST model was applied and field monitoring was used to evaluate the output from the model 10% of plots were re-measured	Inventory error (EI) = 11.9% and a model error (EM) = of 3.5% led to an uncertainty factor of 6.9% deducted from reported emission reductions Net GHG removals by sinks: 56,746 tCO_2e/yr during the period between 01/01/2006 and 12/31/2011

Source: Author based on project design documents, monitoring and verification reports.

Upfront monitoring costs such as material purchasing, setting up a database, training costs, remote sensing purchase are considered by Cacho et al. (2004) as establishment costs (E).

Project developers apply different strategies to balance monitoring costs and uncertainty. A key driver of monitoring costs is the number of sample plots that are installed in the project area (see Equation 13.1), leading to the following strategies:

- *Stratification:* a well-designed stratification reduces the number of sample plots without reducing precision.
- *Allocating a higher number of sample plots than what is calculated:* some projects, such as the Indian reforestation project, add supplementary plots in order to insure against the loss of sample plots in the monitoring period. As pointed out by Vallejo et al. (2011), reforestation projects often evolve over the crediting period and it is probable that changes in stratification will occur, potentially requiring additional sampling plots.

Chenost and Gardette (2010) have also estimated the costs of monitoring. Their estimation indicates a cost ranging between €10 and €20 per hectare for reforestation projects. However, there are no details on whether these cost ranges include establishment costs or not.

Applying the model presented in Cacho et al. (2004) to our list of projects under the assumptions applied by the same authors of a fixed cost of €3,750 and a variable cost of €375/plot gives a range of €20,000–40,000 (Table 13.7). The resulting numbers only provide a broad idea: cost and productivity of labor may drastically change the figures across countries.

These costs are in line with the range provided by Chenost and Gardette (2010) with the exception of project 4531 which has intentionally applied more sample plots than what was needed in order to achieve the required level of precision. Verification reports indicate that none of the project developers used the possibility to accept a discount on credits as they have all achieved the required precision.

Nevertheless Pearson et al. (2013) report much higher monitoring costs for three reforestation projects registered under the CDM and the VCS which appear to include establishment costs as well as field measurements (Table 13.8).

The authors point out that the project in South America had higher relative transaction costs, though they do not explain the reasons for

Table 13.7 *Monitoring cost of three CDM reforestation projects*

Ref.	Title	Size (ha)	Number of sample plots	Cost (€/ha)	Cost (€/tCO$_2$)	Total cost (€)
4957	Securitization and carbon sinks project	2,917	42 PSP	6.68	0.05	215,858
4653	Kachung Forest Project: Afforestation on Degraded Lands	2,099	51 PSP	10.90	0.73	209,900
4531	Improving Rural Livelihoods Through Carbon Sequestration By Adopting Environment Friendly Technology based Agroforestry Practices	1,608	100 PSP	25.65	0.23	144,720

Source: Author's calculations based on Cacho et al. (2004).

Table 13.8 *Monitoring cost of three CDM and VCS reforestation projects[a]*

Title	Size (ha)	Standard	Monitoring costs (€)	Cost (€/ha)
Reforestation Project in East Africa	2,213	CDM	181,818	86.62
Reforestation Project in East Africa	10,815	VCS	453,725	41.95
Reforestation Project in South America	918	VCS	217,816	237.27

[a] As Pearson et al. (2013) present their costs in US$, a 1.32 US$/€ exchange rate is used.
Source: Pearson et al. (2013).

such high costs in comparison to other projects. These very high figures are an exception when compared with other sources (Chenost and Gardette, 2010; Martel, 2013; Torres, 2013; UNFCCC, 2009). This is why we put the per project values of Table 13.7 as the most reliable in the MRV ID table at the end of this chapter. For average per tCO_2 values we calculate the average of two out of the three projects depicted in Table 13.7: the second project is excluded due to its surprisingly low sequestration rate (see Table 13.5).

Overall MRV costs
In order to perform the calculations of the range of overall per tonne MRV costs that appear in the MRV ID table we add to the costs of monitoring, the following costs of reporting and verification and apply them to our example projects:

- €5,500 [4,000–7,000] per year for upfront costs (costs of PDD development and validation, based on the smaller projects of Chapter 3.1 and spread over ten years);
- €3,000 [2,000–4,000] per year for verification based on Chapter 3.1 and assuming one verification every five years;
- €0.14 per tCO_2 issuance fee and adaptation tax (assuming a price of 3 €/tCO_2 for the latter).

13.3 Reporting

In order to apply for the issuance of credits, the project developer needs to prepare a monitoring report according to the CDM Project Standard or the VCS Standard (see Chapter 11). For CDM projects, the monitoring plan must include details on the data and parameters monitored in order to calculate baseline and project emissions and removals and leakage. These details include the recording frequency, the source of data and measurement procedures including all the data collected in the field using the permanent sample plots.

In the case of the VCS the structure of the monitoring report is quite similar to that of the CDM. One of the major differences is that an explicit subsection has to be included showing the calculation of the uncertainty factor.

13.4 Verification: what are auditors looking for?

The verification procedure detailed in Chapter 3.1 for the CDM is very similar to the one applied to VCS projects. In both standards, the auditor shall confirm that specific requirements pertaining to forestry projects have been followed (Table 13.9). For the VCS, these specific requirements include a permanence risk assessment that is a quantified risk that the planned carbon sequestration is lost before the end of the crediting period. This risk assessment determines the project's contribution to the AFOLU buffer pool specific to forestry projects.

At the first verification, the DOE, in accordance with paragraph 34(d) of the CDM modalities and procedures for afforestation and reforestation project activities, shall confirm those areas of land for which the control over reforestation project has been established by the project participants since validation. Also as a part of the first verification report, the DOE shall confirm that the boundary of the reforestation project geographically delineates exclusively the reforestation project under the control of the project participants.

Since forestry projects strongly rely on sampling practices, the CDM and the VCS Validation and Verification Manual encourage the use of adapted tools in order to choose the appropriate testing method as well as their own professional judgment. These tools include the Standard for Sampling and Surveys for CDM Project Activities and Program of Activities (PoAs), the IPCC 2006 Guidelines for National Greenhouse

Table 13.9 *Specific validation requirements for CDM reforestation projects*

Means of validation and verification applied by the DOE	Reporting requirements
Validation requirement 1 – Project boundary: the DOE shall confirm whether the PDD contains a description of the project boundary.	
Document review and/or interviews, determine whether the project participants control reforestation activities for all areas of land planned for A/R project activity. The DOE shall confirm that project participants at least possess the exclusive right, defined in a way acceptable under the legal system of the host Party, to perform the A/R activity with the aim of achieving net anthropogenic GHG removals by sinks. If the total number of documents to be reviewed and persons/entities to be interviewed is higher than ten, then the DOE may apply a sampling approach.	The DOE shall describe the documentation assessed and/or oral statements delivered by persons interviewed (if any) and determine their acceptability under the legal system of the host Party. If the DOE has applied a sampling approach, it shall also describe how many sites have been assessed and how these sites were selected.
Verification requirement 2 – Selection of carbon pools: the DOE shall determine whether the carbon pools to be considered in the proposed A/R project activity were selected in accordance with the requirements of the selected methodology.	
The DOE shall confirm that information has been provided to justify the exclusion of certain carbon pools if the methodology allows for such an option. In doing so, the DOE shall confirm that all documents referred to in the PDD are correctly quoted and interpreted. If relevant, the DOE shall cross-check the information provided in the PDD with other available information from public sources or local experts.	If the methodology allows for the option to exclude certain pools and this option is selected by project participants, the DOE shall provide a statement as to whether the selection of carbon pools complies with the selected methodology, and whether the exclusion is justified.
Verification requirement 3 – Eligibility of land: The DOE shall confirm whether the PDD contains a description of the project boundary.	

Table 13.9 (*cont.*)

Means of validation and verification applied by the DOE	Reporting requirements
Based on a review of information that reliably discriminates between forest and non-forest land according to the particular thresholds adopted by the host Party (exemplary sources are listed in the above-mentioned procedures) and a site visit.	The DOE shall describe how the validation of the eligibility of the land has been performed, by detailing the data sources assessed and by describing its observations during the site visit. The DOE shall provide a statement as to whether the entire land within the project boundary is eligible for a proposed A/R project activity.

Verification requirement 4 – Approach proposed to address non-permanence: the DOE shall confirm that the project participants specified the approach selected to mitigate the non-permanence risk.

The DOE shall review the PDD to ensure an approach to address non-permanence is selected according to the relevant provisions of the modalities and procedures for afforestation and reforestation project activities.	The DOE shall confirm whether the approach selected by the project participants to address non-permanence has been specified in the PDD.

Verification requirement 5 – Timing of management activities, including harvesting cycles, and verifications: the DOE shall determine whether the PDD describes the planned management activities, including harvesting cycles, and verifications such that a systematic coincidence of verification and peaks in carbon stocks would be avoided.

The DOE shall review the forest management plan and the monitoring plan for the proposed A/R project activity to confirm that a systematic coincidence of verification and peaks in carbon stocks is avoided.	The DOE shall describe how the project participants have ensured that a systematic coincidence of verification and peaks in carbon stocks would be avoided.

Verification requirement 6 – Socio-economic and environmental impacts, including impacts on biodiversity and natural ecosystems: the DOE shall validate the documentation received from the project participants on its analysis of the socio-economic and environmental impacts, including impacts on biodiversity and natural ecosystems, and impacts outside the project boundary of the proposed afforestation or reforestation project activity under the CDM.

Table 13.9 (*cont.*)

Means of validation and verification applied by the DOE	Reporting requirements
The DOE shall confirm the above requirement by means of a document review and/or using local official sources and expertise. If the above-mentioned analysis leads to the conclusion that a negative impact that may be considered significant by the project participants or the host Party has been detected, then the DOE shall determine whether a socio-economic impact assessment and/or an environmental impact assessment has been undertaken in accordance with relevant host Party regulations, and the outcome of such impact assessment is summarized in the PDD.	The DOE shall confirm whether the project participants have undertaken an analysis of the socio-economic and environmental impacts and, if required by the host Party, a socio-economic impact assessment and/or an environmental impact assessment in accordance with relevant host Party regulations. The DOE shall also note whether the outcome of such impact assessment has been summarized in the PDD and whether a description of the planned monitoring and remedial measures to address the negative impacts has been included in the PDD.

Source: Author.

Gas Inventories and the IPCC 2003 Good Practice Guidelines for Land Use, Land-Use Change and Forestry.

For instance, in projects with a large number of permanent sample plots, the auditors re-visit the location of a number of randomly selected inventory plots and perform checks and re-measurements in order to verify the monitored values.

As pointed out in Chapter 3.1, the balance between auditing costs and revenues from carbon credits drives verification frequency. Among the CDM and VCS projects we have analyzed we observe that monitoring periods range from five to ten years. However, in terms of data measured in the field, five-year intervals are commonly applied as observed in Table 13.5. Both standards include strong incentives to verify carbon sequestration at least every five years: temporary credits delivered under the CDM become outdated after five years, and the VCS applies a release of buffer credits from the AFOLU pooled buffer account at each reassessment of the non-permanence risk analysis at every verification event.

In terms of verification costs, Chenost and Gardette (2010) estimate a cost range of €20,000–50,000 incurred by project developers.

13.5 Conclusion

Most often, for forestry carbon projects the only uncertainty requirement regards sampling error, which is driven by the quality of stratification and by the number of sample plots. Stratification and the number of sample plots are also key drivers of monitoring costs. The methodology generally allows the balancing of uncertainty and monitoring costs by discounting the number of credits when uncertainty is higher than 10 percent. But project proponents do not seem to use this possibility as they always manage to reduce uncertainty below this threshold.

CDM and VCS MRV requirements are mostly similar for forestry projects. The few differences include: permanence (risk assessment required by the VCS due to the non-temporary nature of VCS credits), uncertainty scope (larger than sampling error for some VCS methodologies) and harvested wood products (not monitored under the CDM).

13.6 MRV ID table

Detailed definitions of the items of this table are provided in the appendix.

Appendix – Determination of monitoring uncertainty

CDM *reforestation projects*

CDM rules do not include any generic uncertainty requirement. Uncertainty requirements are methodology-specific. For reforestation projects, uncertainty requirements depend on the scale of the project. For small projects (AR-AR-AMS0003 and AMS0007), the only uncertainty requirement is that the maximum relative margin of error – sampling error – for estimating tree biomass should not exceed the ±10 percent with a confidence level of 90 percent.

For large-scale projects (AR-ACM0003, AR-AM0014), uncertainty requirements are those contained in the AR-TOOL14: they are also

Table 13.10 *MRV ID table*

	Context	
	CDM	VCS
Regulator	- *The CDM Executive Board (CDM EB)*: validation of methodologies, accreditation of auditors, registration of projects and issuance of tCERs and lCERs (CDM forestry credits). The CDM EB takes most decisions pertaining to MRV, with the exception of highly political decisions which require CMP approval. - *Designated Operational Entities (DOE)*: validation of CDM projects and verification of GHG emissions reductions and absorptions. - *Designated National Authorities (DNA)*: issuance of the Letter of Approval (LoA) for a CDM project by the host country.	- *The VCS Association (VCSA)* is responsible for the management, the review and establishes the rules and requirements that operationalize the VCS. The VCSA is also responsible for the methodology approval process. - *Steering and Advisory Committees and Technical Working Groups* are set up on an ad hoc basis to draft VCS requirements and to assist in the development of the VCS program.
Type and level of incentive to comply	**For projects proponents:** - Positive incentives ("carrots"): issuance of CERs (timeliness and quantity) - Negative incentives ("sticks"): CER discounting due to high monitoring uncertainty **For DOEs:** - Positive incentives ("carrots"): fees for successful CER issuance - Negative incentives ("sticks"): suspension or withdrawal of accreditation, i.e., temporary or permanent loss of business	**For projects proponents:** - Positive incentives ("carrots"): issuance of VCUs (timeliness and quantity) - Negative incentives ("sticks"): VCU discounting due to high monitoring uncertainty **For DOEs:** - Positive incentives ("carrots"): fees for successful VCS issuance - Negative incentives ("sticks"): suspension or withdrawal of accreditation, i.e., temporary or permanent loss of business

Entities concerned	*Project proponents:* - 44 reforestation projects registered as of May 2013 (UNEP Risoe, 2013) with 42 project developers (private entities, associations, NGOs, carbon funds and research institutes) *DOEs:* - 18 accredited auditors as of May 2013 (UNFCCC website) for projects in the forestry sector *Consultants:* - 550 CDM consultants (UNEP Risoe, 2013)	*Project proponents:* - 45 reforestation and 8 IFM projects registered as of January 2014 (VCS website) - *Validation and Verification bodies (VVB):* - 22 accredited VVBs as of May 2013 for projects in the forestry sector (VCS website)
Sectors concerned	Reforestation projects (AR)	Reforestation (AR) Improved Forest Management (IFM) – our focus in this chapter REDD projects (not treated in this chapter) and considered to be a jurisdictional approach and treated in Chapter 1.3
Gases concerned	CO_2, CH_4, N_2O	CO_2, CH_4, N_2O
Overall MRV costs	0.8 [0.3–1.4] €/tCO_2 17,000 [11,000–21,000] €/project/yr	Likely similar to CDM reforestation projects

Table 13.10 (*cont.*)

	Monitoring	
	CDM	VCS
Rules	- *Modalities and procedures for afforestation and reforestation project activities under the CDM* (Decision 5/CMP.1, Annex, paragraph 12) on general requirements for baseline and monitoring methodologies - *CDM Project Standard (CDM-EB65-A05-STAN)* on establishing and applying monitoring methodologies - All guidelines, clarifications and supported documents published by the CDM EB - Four active methodologies specific to the forestry sector (large and small scale) • *CDM – AR-ACM0003 – Large-scale Methodology: Afforestation and reforestation of lands except wetlands* • *CDM – AR-AM0014 – A/R Large-scale Methodology Afforestation and reforestation of degraded mangrove habitats* • *CDM – AR-AMS0003 Simplified baseline and monitoring methodology for small-scale CDM afforestation and reforestation project activities implemented on wetlands* • *CDM – AR-AMS0007 Simplified baseline and monitoring methodology for small-scale CDM afforestation and reforestation project activities implemented on lands other than wetlands*	- *VCS Program Guide, v3.4* - *VCS Standard, v3.3* - *AFOLU Requirements, v3.3* - *Program Fee Schedule, v3.3* - *Registration & Issuance Process, v3.4* - *Methodology Approval Process, v3.4* - *AFOLU Non-Permanence Risk Tool, v3.2 Monitoring Report, v3.2* - Methodologies for improved forest management projects: • *VM0003 Methodology for Improved Forest Management through Extension of Rotation Age* • *VM0005 Methodology for Improved Forest Management: Low Productive to High Productive Forests* • *VM0010 Methodology for Improved Forest Management: Conversion from Logged to Protected Forest* • *VM0011 Methodology for Calculating GHG Benefits from Preventing Planned Degradation* • *VM0012 Improved Forest Management in Temperate and Boreal Forests (LtPF)*

	- Three associated tools:
	  • *Estimation of carbon stocks and change in carbon stocks of trees and shrubs in A/R CDM project activities (AR-TOOL14/CDM-EB70)*
	  • *Estimation of the increase in GHG emissions attributable to displacement of pre-project agricultural activities in A/R CDM project activity for estimating carbon leakage*
	  • *Calculation of the number of sample plots for measurements within A/R CDM project activities*	

Other reference documents	- CDM Methodology Booklet fourth edition (CDM-EB69) - Standard for sampling and surveys for the CDM (CDM-EB69-A4) - IPCC Fourth Assessment Report: Climate Change 2007 (2007) for global warming potentials of GHGs - IPCC Guidelines for National Greenhouse Gas Inventories (1996 and 2006) - Good Practice Guidance for Land Use, Land-Use Change and Forestry (2003) for statistical approaches used in monitoring - Standard for sampling and surveys for CDM project activities and program of activities (CDM-EB-69-A04)	- IPCC Fourth Assessment Report: Climate Change 2007 (2007) for global warming potentials of GHGs - IPCC Guidelines for National Greenhouse Gas Inventories (1996 and 2006) - Good Practice Guidance for Land Use, Land-Use Change and Forestry (2003) for statistical approaches used in monitoring - Peer-reviewed literature
Uncertainty requirements	No overall requirement, only on activity data	No overall requirement, only on activity data
Achieved uncertainty range	1%–9% for sampling error on tree biomass based on three projects	10–12% for sampling error 3.5% for model error
Cost range	0.14 [0.05–0.23] €/tCO$_2$e €5,500 [4,000–8,000] per project per year (assuming that monitoring is undertaken once every five years)	Likely similar to CDM reforestation projects

Table 13.10 (cont.)

Scope	- Scope 1: upstream (e.g., fertilizer manufacture) and downstream (e.g., substitution effect of harvested wood) are not accounted - Territorial scope corresponding to the emissions inside the project perimeter	- Scope 1: upstream (e.g., fertilizer manufacture) and downstream (e.g., substitution effect of harvested wood) are not accounted - Territorial scope corresponding to the emissions inside the project perimeter
Frequency	At least every five years	At least every five years
Source for activity data	Field measurements (such as DBH, height, number of trees, etc.), surveys and default values according to each methodology	Field measurements (such as DBH, height, number of trees, etc.), surveys and default values according to each methodology
Uncertainty range for activity data	$\pm 10\%$ at 90% confidence interval for sampling error of tree biomass (see appendix for details)	The requirements relate to the sampling error on carbon stock in tree biomass and range from $\pm 5\%$ of the estimate at a 95% confidence level to $\pm 10\%$ of the estimate at a 90% confidence level. In another, uncertainty from leakage emissions is added to the uncertainty on tree biomass in the overall uncertainty level (see appendix for details).
Source for emission factors	DNAs, IPCC Guidelines on National GHG Inventories, peer-reviewed literature, measurements, surveys (such as carbon fraction or biomass expansion factors [BEF] and wood density)	DNAs, IPCC Guidelines on National GHG Inventories, peer-reviewed literature, measurements, surveys (such as carbon fraction or biomass expansion factors (BEF) and wood density)

	CDM	VCS
Uncertainty for emission factors	No specific requirement beyond assessing the uncertainty of emission factors	In one VCS methodology, there is also a constraint on "model" error, that is error from allometric equations
Direct measurement	No direct measurement of CO_2 fluxes or other greenhouse gases in the existing methodologies	No direct measurement of CO_2 fluxes or other greenhouse gases in the existing methodologies
Incentive to reduce uncertainty	Avoid an eventual deduction of credits if the relative sampling error on tree biomass is above 10%	Avoid an eventual deduction of credits if the required precision level is not reached
Is requirements stringency adapted to the amount of emissions at stake (materiality)?	No. Requirements stringency is the same no matter the size of the project.	No. Requirements stringency is the same no matter the size of the project.
Reporting		
	CDM	VCS
Rules	Most importantly, the methodology relevant to AR projects, but also: - *CDM Project Cycle Procedure* (CDM-EB65-A32-PROC) on procedures for submitting and publishing monitoring reports; and the other documents already listed in the *monitoring* section	- *VCS Program Guide, v3.4* - *VCS Standard, v3.3* - *AFOLU Requirements, v3.3* • Monitoring Report, *v3.2*

Table 13.10 (*cont.*)

Other reference documents	- Guidelines for completing the monitoring report form (CDM-EB54-A34-GUID) - Materiality standard under the clean development mechanism (Decision 9/CMP.7)
Format	Project proponents have to use the latest version of the monitoring report form applicable to the project activity, taking into account the grace period of the form if it has been revised	Following the format of Monitoring Report, v3.2
Level of source disaggregation	Disaggregation down to single carbon pools and sources of emissions	Disaggregation down to single carbon pools and sources of emissions
Frequency	Up to the project proponent: the length of a monitoring period – i.e., the interval between two reporting events – frequently every five years	At least every ten years (preceding verification), it often takes place every five years
Timeline	On average for AR projects the monitoring report is made public 15 months before credits are issued (IGES 2013a)	On average for registered VCS IFM projects the monitoring report is made public four/five months before credits are issued (calculated from data extracted from the VCS project database)
Language	English	English
Is demand stringency adapted to the amount of emissions at stake (materiality)?	Yes, through the choice offered to the project proponent regarding reporting frequency and the concept of materiality (see "Verification")	See "Monitoring"

	Verification	
	CDM	VCS
Cost range	0.32 [0.1–0.64] €/tCO$_2$e €5,500 [4,000–7,000] per project per year These costs include all monitoring and reporting costs other than those related to actual measurements	Likely similar to the CDM
Rules	Most importantly, the CDM Validation and Verification Standard (CDM-EB65-A04-STAN) for procedures of validation and verification	Validation and Verification Manual
Other reference documents	- Clean development mechanism accreditation standard for operational entities (CDM-EB67-A05) - Procedure for accrediting operational entities by the Executive Board (CDM-EB56-A02) - Performance monitoring of designated operational entities (CDM-EB73-A14) - Guideline on the application of materiality in verification (CDM-EB-69-A06) - Procedure for Review of Requests for Issuance of CERs (CDM-EB-64-A04) - Standard for sampling and surveys for CDM project activities and program of activities (CDM-EB-69-A04)	- VCS Program Guide, v3.4 - VCS Standard, v3.3 - AFOLU Requirements, v3.3
Format	No specified format although the verification report must include all elements mentioned in Chapter 11	Following the format of the Verification Report, v3.2 available on the VCS website

Table 13.10 (*cont.*)

Frequency	Verification takes places at every reporting event, that is, after the publication of the monitoring report	Verification takes places at every reporting event, that is after the publication of the monitoring report
Timeline	Depends on the project and the DOE (among the five projects reviewed in this chapter between one and six months)	Depends on the project and the VVB (among the three projects reviewed in this chapter between two weeks and two months)
Language	English	English
Accredited entities for verification	DOEs: 18 organizations accredited by the CDM Executive Board and designated by the COP/MOP for the AFOLU sector. Mostly franchises of international audit companies such as Ernst & Young and Tüv Sud.	Validation and verification bodies (VVB), that is entities which are either accredited by the CDM or under ISO VCS: 22 entities
Control of accredited entities	The Board may decide to suspend totally or partially the accreditation of a DOE based on the recommendation of the CDM-AP or other review processes conducted by the Board (see Chapter 11 and CDM-EB56-A02)	Accredited V/VBs shall undergo surveillance during the first and second years after the year of their initial accreditation or reaccreditation. ANSI may decide to conduct surveillance visits out of sequence and without prior notice or with short notice if a complaint is received regarding the performance of the V/VB.
Cost of accreditation	According to the Procedure for accrediting operational entities by the Executive Board (CDM-EB56-A02), accreditation fees are as follows:	Temporary accreditation: non-refundable fee of €6,500 for seven sectoral scopes, plus €1,000 for each additional sectoral scope thereafter.

	- Non-reimbursable application fee is €10,800 - Fee and costs associated with an on-site assessment of the premises of an AE/DOE - Other costs related to performance assessment, reaccreditation, change of scope of a DOE, etc.	VVBs pay an annual fee to maintain accreditation depending on their gross annual revenues (€1,175 if they are below €294,000, 0.4% of their revenue if revenues are above €294,000 and below €10.8m and €43,175 for revenues above €10.8m) Assessment and surveillance fees are €980 per day per assessor plus travel expenses.
Support of accredited entities	- The Executive Board provides DOEs with feedback based on their assessment - The Executive Board established a DOE forum to enhance communication between the Board and DOEs	None
Is requirements stringency adapted to the amount of emissions at stake (materiality)?	Yes: the acceptance threshold (materiality) concerning all errors, omissions and false statements is higher for smaller projects: 0.5–10% depending on project size (see Chapter 11)	Yes: the acceptance threshold (materiality) concerning all errors, omissions and false statements is higher for smaller projects: • 5% for projects under 300,000 tCO_2/year • 1% for projects over 300,000 tCO_2/year (big projects)
Cost range	0.31 [0.2–0.5] €/tCO_2e €8,100 [4,500–12,500] per project per year These costs include verification, issuance fee and CER tax	Likely similar to the CDM: on the one hand, accreditation is less costly for auditors, who may then charge smaller fees, but on the other hand, the VCS requires an additional desk review by a second auditor and a permanence risk assessment.

Source: Author.

based on the sampling error for the estimation of tree biomass but the error may exceed ±10 percent at the expense of a discount on the credits issued.

Their definition depends on the method chosen for the estimation of ex-ante and ex-post carbon stocks in the baseline and project scenario method:

- *The stock change method:* applicable for ex-ante and ex-post estimation of tree biomass. The change in carbon stock in trees between two successive points of time is calculated as the difference between the two estimated stocks. This method does not require permanent sample plots with marked trees. The relative error of the mean tree biomass is defined by:

$$RE_{max} = u_{b_{TREE,t}} = \frac{t_{VAL} * s_{b_{TREE,t}}}{b_{TREE,t}}$$

Where:

t_{VAL} = student t-value for a confidence level of 90 percent and n–M degrees of freedom (where n is total number of sample plots within the project boundary, and M is the total number of tree biomass estimation strata);

$s_{b_{TREE,t}}$ = standard deviation of mean tree biomass per hectare;

RE_{max} = maximum relative error;

$u_{b_{TREE,t}}$ = uncertainty of tree biomass carbon per hectare;

$b_{TREE,t}$ = average biomass per hectare.

- *The increment method:* sampling plots are permanent and trees must be tracked by a unique identifier, which allows the estimation of the increment in biomass of each tree between two measurements. The change in biomass of individual trees is monitored and evaluated over time. The maximum relative error is estimated as follows:

$$RE_{max} = \frac{u_{\Delta b_{TREE,t}}}{\sqrt{2}} = \frac{\dfrac{t_{VAL} * s_{\Delta b_{TREE,t}}}{\Delta b_{TREE,(t1,t2)}}}{\sqrt{2}}$$

Where:

$u_{\Delta b_{TREE,t}}$ = uncertainty of the change in tree biomass carbon per hectare between time t1 and time t2 (in percent);

t_{VAL} = student t-value for a confidence level of 90 percent and n-M degrees of freedom where n is total number of sample plots within the project boundary, and M is the total number of tree biomass estimation strata;

$s_{\Delta b_{TREE,t}}$ = standard deviation of mean biomass increment per hectare;

$\Delta b_{TREE,t}$ = mean biomass increment per hectare.

Greater sampling error is tolerated for the increment method than the stock change method (through the $\sqrt{2}$ coefficient). In both cases if relative error is greater than 10 percent, the project developer must either install additional sample plots and thus increase monitoring costs or accept a deduction in the number of credits issued. The deductions vary between 6 percent and 37 percent depending on the error margin reached (see Table 13.4).

VCS improved forest management projects

VCS rules do not include any generic uncertainty requirement. Uncertainty requirements are methodology-specific.

For most methodologies (VM005, VM011, VM003, VM010), the requirements relate to carbon stock in tree biomass and range from ±5% of the estimate at a 95% confidence level from ±10% of the estimate at a 90% confidence level.

In VM012, the requirement is applied to both the sampling error and the "model" error, that is the error associated with allometry. If this error is lower than 10% at a 90% confidence interval, the uncertainty factor (ε_p) is 1.5%. If it exceeds 10%, the uncertainty factor is 1.5% + ε_p −10%.

In all cases, if the precision is not reached, the project manager must accept a deduction on the number of credits issued. This deduction depends on the methodology.

For instance for methodologies VM0003 and VM0005, total uncertainty from sampling on tree biomass ($C_{IFM-ERROR}$) equals:

$$C_{\text{IFM-ERROR}} = \sqrt{\text{Uncertainty}_{\text{BSL}}{}^2 + \text{Uncertainty}_{\text{P}}{}^2}$$

where $\text{Uncertainty}_{\text{BSL}}$ = baseline uncertainty and $\text{Uncertainty}_{\text{P}}$ = project scenario uncertainty. Then, total uncertainty is compared to the project's net carbon sequestration (C_{IFM}):

- if $C_{\text{IFM-ERROR}} \leq 10\%$ of C_{IFM} no deduction applies;
- if $C_{\text{IFM-ERROR}} > 10\%$ of C_{IFM} a discounted value of C_{IFM} should be applied as follows:

$$C_{\text{IFM-MOD}} = \frac{100 - C_{\text{IFM-ERROR}}}{100} * C_{\text{IFM}}$$

For methodology VM0010, total uncertainty from sampling on tree biomass ($C_{\text{IFM-ERROR}}$) is computed in the same manner, though deduction differs as follows:

- if $C_{\text{IFM-ERROR}} \leq 15\%$ of C_{IFM} no deduction applies;
- If $C_{\text{IFM-ERROR}} > 15\%$ of C_{IFM} a discounted value of C_{FIM} should be applied as follows:

$$C_{\text{IFM-MOD}} = C_{\text{IFM}} * \left(1 - C_{\text{IFM-ERROR}}\right)$$

For methodology VM0011, uncertainty includes both sampling error on tree biomass in the baseline and in the project scenario, but also the error associated with leakage assessment:[5]

$$\sigma_{IFM\text{-}LtPF,t} = \sqrt{\left(\sigma_{baseline,t}\right)^2 + \left(\sigma_{project,t}\right)^2 + \left(\sigma_{leakage,t}\right)^2}$$

The relative uncertainty is then calculated, relative to annual net anthropogenic GHG emission reductions ($C'_{IFM\text{-}LtPF,t}$):

$$U_{IFM\text{-}LtPF,t} = \frac{\sigma_{IFM\text{-}LtPF,t}}{C'_{IFM\text{-}LtPF,t}} * 100$$

---

[5] The uncertainty associated with leakage takes into account uncertainty in the estimation of emissions due to activity shifting, illegal harvesting, natural disturbances, implementation of the shifted baseline activity and market effects.

Relative uncertainty is then compared to the net anthropogenic greenhouse removals by sinks (C_{IFM}):

- If $U_{IFM\text{-}LtPF,t} \leq 10\%$ no deduction applies.
- If $U_{IFM\text{-}LtPF,t} > 10\%$ eventual credits are deducted as follows:

$$CC_{IFM\text{-}LtPF,t} = \frac{100 - \left(U_{IFM\text{-}LtPF,t} - 10\right)}{100} * C'_{IFM\text{-}LtPF,t}$$

Bibliography

Beaurain, F. and Schmidt-Traub, G., 2010. *Developing CDM Programmes of Activities: a Guidebook*. South Pole Carbon Asset Management Ltd, Zurich.

Cacho, O., Wise, R. and MacDicken, K., 2004. Carbon monitoring costs and their effect on incentives to sequester carbon through forestry. *Mitigation and Adaptation Strategies for Global Change* 9(3): 273–293.

Calmel, M., Martinet, A., et al., 2011. *REDD+ at Project Scale: Evaluation and Development Guide*. ONFI, Paris.

Chenost, C. and Gardette, Y.M., 2010. *Bringing Forest Carbon Projects to the Market*. UNEP, Paris.

Guigon, P., Bellassen, V. and Ambrosi, P., 2009. Voluntary carbon markets: what the standards say... (Working Paper, Mission Climat). Caisse des Depots.

IPCC, 2006. *2006 IPCC Guidelines for National Greenhouse Gas Inventories*. Chapter 4: Agriculture, Forestry and Other Land Uses (AFOLU). IGES, Hayama, Japan.

Krey, M., 2005. Transaction costs of unilateral CDM projects in India – results from an empirical survey. *Energy Policy* 33: 2385–2397.

Martel, S., 2013. Évaluation préliminaire des coûts de suivi pour un projet en métropole, Oral presentation in the 6th meeting of the Forest Carbon and Wood Club.

Michaelowa, A. and Stronzik, M., 2002. Transaction costs of the Kyoto mechanisms (HWWA Discussion Paper, No. 175).

Pearson, T., Brown, S., Sohngen, B., Henman, J. and Ohrel, S., 2013. Transaction costs for carbon sequestration projects in the tropical forest sector. *Mitigation and Adaptation Strategies for Global Change* (May): 1–14.

Peters-Stanley, M. and Hamilton, K. 2012. *Developing Dimension: State of the Voluntary Carbon Markets 2012*. Forest Trends' Ecosystem Marketplace, Washington, DC.

Peters-Stanley, M., Gonzales, G. and Yin, D., 2013. *Covering New Ground: State of the Forest Carbon Markets 2013*. Forest Trends' Ecosystem Marketplace, Washington, DC.

Torres, D., 2013. Les méthodes et coûts du suivi pratiqués dans les pays en développement, Oral presentation in the 6th meeting of the Forest Carbon and Wood Club.

UNEP, 2007. *Guidebook to Financing CDM Projects*. United Nations Environment Programme, Denmark.

UNEP Risoe, 2013. CDM Pipeline. http://cdmpipeline.org/. Accessed May 4, 2013.

UNFCCC, 2009. Cost of implementing methodologies and monitoring systems relating to estimates of emissions from deforestation and forest degradation, the assessment of carbon stocks and greenhouse gas emissions from changes in forest cover, and the enhancement of forest carbon stocks. Technical paper.

2011. Guidelines for the establishment of sector specific standardized baselines, EB 62 Report Annex 8. UNFCCC.

Vallejo, A., Reddy, R.C. and van der Linden, M., 2011. *Manual for Monitoring of CDM Afforestation and Reforestation Projects – Part I – Standard Operational Procedures*. Carbon Finance Unit, World Bank, Washington, DC.

14 | *Case study 3: monitoring requirements for fugitive emissions from fuels in the CDM*

ALEXANDRA BARKER AND
RODERICK ROBINSON

14.1 Fugitive emissions scale and scope

Fugitive emissions are uncontrolled releases from leaking equipment (assumed to be sealed), uncontrolled but routine venting or emissions to air from other uncontrolled sources. Although they are unmonitored releases they are not necessarily unintentional, for example compressor stations may have planned but unmonitored releases. In this chapter the term fugitive emissions follows the definition in the Revised 1996 IPCC Guidelines, "an intentional or unintentional release of gases from anthropogenic activities excluding the combustion of fuels" (IPCC, 1997). Fugitive emissions are significant sources from the mineral oil refining and natural gas industry due to the large number of components which are potential sources at each facility. Emissions tend to occur from production, distribution and storage processes. There can be numerous leak sources throughout a single plant and this diffuse nature makes them difficult to detect and quantify. This chapter will focus on component leaks within the scope of above-ground equipment.

For CDM project activities there is an interest in mitigating or reducing greenhouse gas emissions and hence this case study will focus on the detection and quantification of fugitive methane emissions. However, it should be noted that many of the methodologies are based on techniques developed in the oil and gas industry to detect hydrocarbon emissions. Fugitives and combustion account for 19 percent of reported methane emissions in Europe (Global Methane Initiative, 2013). Methane is the primary constituent of natural gas, with the potential to be emitted to the atmosphere during production, processing, storage, transmission and distribution (UNEP/WMO, 2011).

Offset projects based on the capture of fugitive methane are attractive to project developers: there are currently ten CDM methodologies (see Table 14.3 in the appendix) relevant to fugitive emissions from fuels (mining, oil wells, gas flaring in power plants, equipment leaks and low carbon electricity). As of December 31st, 2013, 215 projects using these methodologies had registered under the scope of this sector (2.6 percent of all registered CDM projects) (UNFCCC, 2013a). As of June 2012, US$2,013 million had been invested in fugitive-based project activities (UNFCCC, 2012). One explanation for this success is that these projects generate high numbers of certified emission reductions (CERs) due to the global warming potential of methane being 28 times[1] that of carbon dioxide, indicating it is more powerful in heat-trapping over a 100-year time period (IPCC AR5, 2013).

According to petroleum guidance from pollutant inventories (SPRI Petroleum Guidance, 2013), fugitive emissions account for 20–50 percent of total volatile organic compound (VOC) emissions from refineries. Fugitive emissions tend to be related to the equipment or its maintenance within a plant; a typical refinery contains over 300,000 connections, each one a potential leak source (SPRI Petroleum Guidance, 2013). Leaks from pressurized components such as compressors, valves, pumps and connectors are a primary source of refinery emissions (EPA, 2007). Factors contributing to leaking components include equipment design, quality of the seal and the frequency of maintenance. Loss of component tightness can result in leakages; valves account for 50–60 percent of fugitive emissions (EC, 2006).

Specifically relating to methane fugitive emissions, detecting and repairing gas leaks from dispersed, unplanned point sources or "leaks" has recently been recognized as an important monitoring procedure within gas producing facilities to maximize the climate benefit of using natural gas by further reducing greenhouse gas emissions (C2ES, 2013).

Fugitive emissions from industrial installations have environmental impacts on the atmosphere, water and soil; this, in addition to waste production and use of energy by industry, has led to the development of EU legislation which controls the actions of CDM project activities (see Table 14.4 in the appendix). Fugitive emissions are currently regulated by a number of mechanisms. For example, fugitive emissions from the oil and gas sector are quantified within national emissions inventories under the Kyoto Protocol; UN inventories are

---

[1] Most CERs were issued based on global warming potential of 21 which was the reference value in the CDM before 2013. It is currently set to 28.

required to report national greenhouse gas emissions such as methane (EU Directive 2002/358/EC). Gas production, processing and oil refineries are also required to report annual emission estimates of fugitive methane under the European Pollutant Release and Transfer Register (E-PRTR) (Directive 2006/166/EC). In Europe the Industrial Emissions Directive (IED) (Directive 2010/75/EU) (replaced the IPCC Directive 2008/1/EC) which calls upon Best Available Techniques reference documents (BREF)[2] includes regulations on fugitive emissions. The BREF for the Refining of Mineral Oil and Gas recognizes Best Available Techniques (BAT) for fugitive emissions as important, and identifies techniques for quantifying them. In order to meet the requirements, CEN, the European Committee for Standardisation, is developing standard methods.

Other reasons to select the fugitive emissions sector as a case study are the recent expansion of natural gas production, the high percentage of GHG emissions of methane that venting and fugitive emissions account for, and the relative lack of experience with regard to studies on fugitive emissions (EPA, 2007). The recent expansion of the gas industry particularly in North America is owed to technological advances enabling extraction of unconventional sources such as shale gas which constitutes a large and new gas supply. Increasing shale gas production and use is important, and fugitive emissions from the processes associated with it are not fully understood. According to the environmental strategies report by Glancy (2013), shale gas extraction produces higher fugitive emissions than conventional gas sources. It is also an area where there is significant scope for novel methodologies to be implemented by projects to improve current practice. Natural gas produces significant emissions and yet is the least carbon intensive of fossil fuels, but in order to fully benefit from the increased use of natural gas over more carbon-intensive fuels such as oil and coal, fugitive emissions need to be addressed (C2ES, 2013).

14.2 General principles of fugitive emission methodologies

There are three-tier IPCC method approaches to monitoring fugitive emissions in the oil and gas industry as indicated in Figure 14.1:

---

[2] http://eippcb.jrc.ec.europa.eu/reference/

Tier 1:   widely applied and easy-to-use default emission factors, which
          provide relatively crude estimates
Tier 2:   calculations based on activity data and country-specific emis-
          sion factors
Tier 3:   bottom-up approach in which component-level emission fac-
          tors are applied within leak detection and repair (LDAR)
          programs or direct measurement identifies leaking compo-
          nents and subsequent maintenance is carried out (IPCC,
          2006, 2014).

As the approaches progress from Tier 1 to Tier 3 the emissions reported
become less reliant on generic assumptions and more representative of
facility-specific emissions.

This case study will focus upon CDM methodologies relevant to
fugitive emissions from fuels (solid oil and gas) (sector 10 in 2006 IPCC
Guidelines for National Greenhouse Gas Inventories, Chapter 4).

In a CDM project, the project participant is responsible for developing a monitoring strategy in line with the approved methodology.
Monitoring programs for fugitive emissions are currently based on
EPA Reference Test Method 21, "Determination of Volatile Organic
Compound Leaks" (40 CFR Part 60). This method is also referred
to by the IPCC Good Practice Guidance (IPCC, 2000). The procedure identifies measurement methods and correlation equations to
estimate fugitive emissions leak rates (kg/h) for when potential leaks
may be occurring from inaccessible equipment. It specifies the necessary requirements when collecting screening data in order to estimate
emissions (EPA, 1995). The operation of screening devices (i.e. instruments with analyzers to detect leaks from process equipment), their
specifications and performance criteria are outlined in Method 21
(API, 2009; EPA, 2007). A similar methodology has been standardized in Europe by CEN as EN 15446, "Fugitive and diffuse emissions
of common concern to industry sectors. Measurement of fugitive
emission of vapours generating from equipment and piping leaks."

There are ten CDM methodologies relevant to fugitive emissions
(see Table 14.3 in the appendix) and these refer to the approaches in
the 2006 IPCC Guidelines for National Greenhouse Gas Inventories.
These guidelines propose a three-tier approach (introduced in
Figure 14.1) to estimate fugitive emissions from the oil and gas industry (IPCC, 2000, 2006).

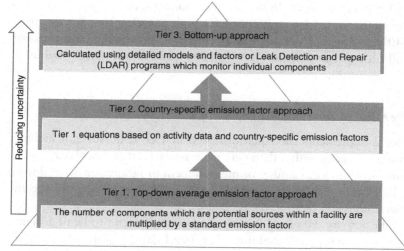

Figure 14.1 Progression of methods from Tier 1 to Tier 3 for the detection and quantification of fugitive emissions in the oil and gas industry

Tier 1: Top-down average emission factor approach

The simplest method of calculating fugitive emissions uses a correlation equation which requires activity data (gas throughputs) and a default (national level) emission factor (IPCC, 2000):

$$Project\ emissions = Activity\ data \times Emission\ factor$$

Emission factors are generally those submitted and accepted by the IPCC Emission Factor Database (EFDB) (IPCC, 2014). In the oil and gas sector many of these emission factors are based on API (American Petroleum Industry) figures which were derived from the initial GRI/EPA (1996) study, and most of which originate from research carried out in North America. It should be noted that emission factors within the EFDB have primarily been developed to enable the compilation of large-scale (national) emissions inventories, and as such they tend to work well as average factors, but may not have the finesse to reflect small-scale differences between facilities.

IPCC emission factors for developing countries used in the Tier 1 approach have been developed from a combination of the 1996 Revised IPCC Guidelines, the limited measurement data available and expert judgment. In developing countries, these emission factors for methane fugitive emissions have high uncertainties. For example, −40 to +250 percent for gas production, processing, transmission and storage, and from −20 to +500 percent for gas distribution (IPCC, 2006).

Tier 2: Country-specific emission factor approach

Tier 2 implements the equations used in Tier 1; however, it includes country-specific rather than default emission factors. Local data can be sourced from local studies or measurement programs, or derived from a Tier 3 approach by back-calculating to produce more country-specific Tier 2 emission factors (IPCC, 2006).

The activity data used in the calculation also tend to be of a higher temporal and spatial resolution than Tier 1 data, as well as being more disaggregated to provide a country-specific emission calculation.

Tier 3: Bottom-up approach

This detailed technology-based approach provides site-specific emission estimates by assessing individual sources of emissions, but this requires a range of detailed activity data including production statistics, infrastructure data including design practices and processes, equipment leaks, and reported emissions from process venting as well as accidental releases and damages (IPCC, 2000). Process infrastructure data, detailed production accounting data, and measurements are combined to provide a total fugitive emissions estimate for the facility.

The source-specific approach relies on bottom-up estimates: component-specific estimates or field measurements are scaled up to take into account the components over the whole plant. This often includes Leak Detection and Repair (LDAR) programs. LDAR is an industry best practice that allows facilities to control emissions from leaks by knowing when to repair or replace leaking components. In addition it has both an economic value as well as being a "duty of care" safety procedure due to the explosiveness of large methane leaks. Yet, LDAR programs seldom quantify the leaks. They often employ only two fundamental steps: (1) locate the source of leaks, and (2) repair the leak (see Figure 14.2). Measuring leak sources at large industrial facilities can be difficult. EPA method 21 provides a crude estimation of leak rates from leak screening data (measurement of concentration) and correlation tables. Measurement of fugitive emissions can use direct (e.g., Hi-Flow sampler or bagging techniques) or indirect techniques (e.g., optical gas imaging); the former is used in the measurement of accessible components and the latter for the remote measurement of inaccessible components (see Table 14.1 for more details on the advantages of both direct and indirect methods).

The Tier 3 approach can use emission factors; however, these are produced from component-level data unlike emission factors used in Tier 1 and 2 methods. Tier 3 emission factors are often available from the American Petroleum Institute (2004) and the EPA based on calculation at the component level using equipment and operating parameters and updated using recent measurement data (Chambers et al., 2008; IPCC, 2006).

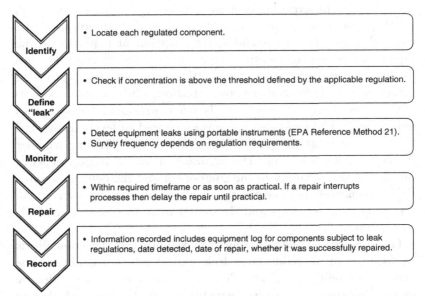

Figure 14.2 Five steps within a Leak Detection and Repair (LDAR) program
Source: Adapted from EPA (2007).

Monitoring strategy

Emission factors continue to be widely used in the monitoring procedures of many CDM project activities due to the costs and technical capability required for direct measurement, as well as the inability of the economically viable techniques to capture the variability of emission rates from short-term measurements. However, this is not the case for project activities under CDM methodology AM0023 – which applies to refineries, compressors and distribution systems – as measurement techniques within the gas industry are well-developed. Monitoring fugitive emissions involves two processes: finding the leaks and quantifying the leaks.

Methods of leak detection
The most common practice for leak detection is to survey components within a facility with a portable analyzer. EPA Reference Method 21 refers to this technique as "sniffing" (EPA, 2007). Intensive surveys sampling every potential leak point must be manually carried out using hand-held screening devices such as organic vapor analyzers (OVA), toxic vapor analyzers (TVA) or acoustic emission detectors (see Table 14.5 in the appendix). The instrument is placed on the piping component to measure the ambient methane concentration in the vicinity of the component; OVAs and TVAs use a probe to detect areas of high methane concentration, whilst acoustic screening devices detect acoustic signals when pressurized gas escapes from a leak. The measured value is compared to levels recognized by state and local air quality organizations to determine whether the component is leaking. The accuracy of leak detection depends on the speed, proximity to the component and the detector's sensitivity. A relatively poor correlation has been identified between these screening measurements and the actual mass emissions rate (EPA, 1995, 2003).

Less time-consuming techniques can optimize leak detection efforts by focusing on detecting large leak sources which account for the majority of refinery emission flux; more efficient and cost-effective monitoring strategies can be carried out more frequently (Epperson et al., 2007). For example optical gas imaging (OGI) is an advanced method of leak detection that enables a wider area to be rapidly imaged. Enhanced or "smart" LDAR programs have been developed around these OGI techniques to improve the operation of LDAR programs. The most common of these techniques currently used is passive infrared spectral imaging at a wavelength which produces a real-time video image of the methane gas plume in its field of vision (EPA, 2007). Components can be surveyed from a safe distance and without interrupting processes within the facility. The portable infrared cameras effectively identify the presence of leaks from inaccessible components; however, they have a minimum leak rate that they can detect (typically 0.8g CH_4/hr). The imaging is dependent on a number of factors including the user's skills, and it does not quantify mass emissions (FLIR, 2013). This technique could therefore be combined with techniques that can quantify emission rates such as a Fourier Transform Infrared Spectroscopy (FTIR) system or Differential Absorption Light detection and ranging (DIAL) to quantify mass concentrations (see Table 14.5 in the appendix).

Methods of leak quantification
Traditionally the quantification of leaks has involved correlation factors to convert concentration measurements to emission rates; however, direct methods are now available for measurement of emission fluxes from leaking components, for example bagging techniques and Hi-Flow samplers (as used in the CDM methodology AM0023).

The bagging technique is a simple method in which a leak is enclosed by a bag. Flow rate from leaking components is calculated from the methane concentration and flow (EPA, 2003). Similarly Hi-Flow samplers quantify leak emissions rates from specific components. A vacuum sampling hose captures leak emissions in addition to some ambient gas. The leak rate is calculated from the flow rate and the "additional" methane concentration in the sample once the sample is "corrected" for the background concentration (EPA, 2003).

Indirect measurements are an alternative to direct measurements of flow rates and gas concentrations at the source (see Table 14.1). Indirect measurements use a theoretical or empirical model to calculate total site emissions based on methane concentration at a representative point for the refinery, process activity and meteorological data. Indirect methods can be used for an initial estimation of total emissions, then screening can identify the main sources, and direct methods can determine emissions from these individual sources (IPCC, 2000).

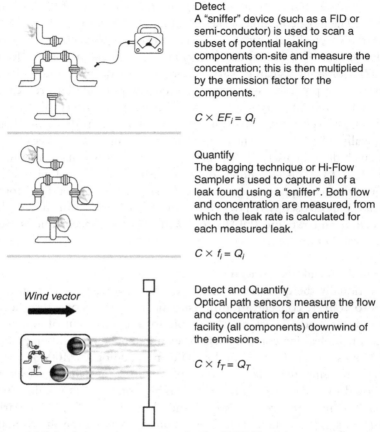

Detect
A "sniffer" device (such as a FID or semi-conductor) is used to scan a subset of potential leaking components on-site and measure the concentration; this is then multiplied by the emission factor for the components.

$$C \times EF_i = Q_i$$

Quantify
The bagging technique or Hi-Flow Sampler is used to capture all of a leak found using a "sniffer". Both flow and concentration are measured, from which the leak rate is calculated for each measured leak.

$$C \times f_i = Q_i$$

Wind vector

Detect and Quantify
Optical path sensors measure the flow and concentration for an entire facility (all components) downwind of the emissions.

$$C \times f_T = Q_T$$

Figure 14.3 Leak measurement scenarios for IPCC Tier 3 bottom-up approach

Recent advances in monitoring methods for the quantification of all sources of fugitive emissions are developing the bottom-up approach by moving towards screening methods with indirect measurements that use modern remote optical techniques. Site-wide emissions are considered rather than measuring leaks from a limited number of components which are directly measured as in the detection and quantification methods (Figure 14.3). For example full-site screening and emissions quantification can be carried out in a single step using Open-Path Fourier Transform Infrared Spectroscopy (OP-FTIR) (Figure 14.3, "remote optical technique") or Differential Absorption Light Detection and Ranging (DIAL) (Figure 14.4).

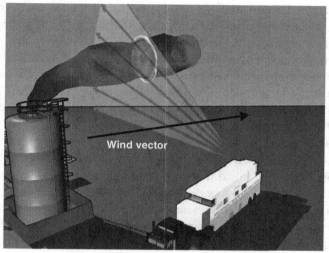

Figure 14.4 Measurement of methane plumes using Differential Absorption Lidar (DIAL)

OP-FTIR systems measure the average concentration of gases over the path measured. They speciate as well as quantify chemicals. This method can both locate emission "hotspots" and quantify the emission rates (EPA, 2006a). Emissions rates can be determined from open-path techniques using EPA Other Test Method (OTM) 10, "Optical Remote Sensing for Emission Characterization from Non-point Sources." A plume map is produced from the beam geometry, path length, wind speed and direction, and methane concentrations measured by the FTIR. The integrated concentration is then combined with wind speed to estimate emission rate (EPA, 2006b).

DIAL is a laser-based optical method which provides an improved evaluation of all sources of fugitive emissions in comparison to the single site average estimations resulting from the Tier 1 emission factor approach. Methane absorbs the laser's signal in the infrared (IR) wavelength, and the backscatter signal is collected. DIAL can remotely measure the concentration profile of methane in the atmosphere over a radius of up to 1 km and produces a two-dimensional contour of concentrations. This spectral concentration data is combined with wind data to calculate a flux and apportion emissions to different areas of a plant, identifying "hotspots." Previous DIAL studies have produced time-weighted mean average emissions with an estimated error of +5 to –15 percent of actual emissions at the time of measurement (Chambers et al., 2008; Robinson et al., 2011). Additionally, unlike direct measurement, this indirect approach is not significantly affected by complex wind turbulence caused by the industrial site as it is capable of measuring far enough downwind of the source (Chambers et al., 2008). However, DIAL has a limited ability with regard to identifying individual components which require repair. DIAL does not allow for source apportionment to individual components and therefore is less useful within LDAR programs to identify leaks to repair, although hotspots can be identified from plume mapping. DIAL measurements could therefore be used to validate an LDAR program, ensuring emission measurements are representative of an entire site and leaks are not "missed." However, confirmation measurements can be difficult and expensive on large, complex sources (IPCC, 2000).

Uncertainty in three-tier approaches

Under the CDM, quality control and assurances should be documented including an assessment of the uncertainties and deviations associated with the monitoring strategy implemented (IPCC, 2000). Uncertainties should be estimated for all parameters (e.g., activity data and emission factors) used in the calculation of baseline or project emissions; however, the calculation of emissions from emission factors does not consider their associated uncertainties, rather an average emission factor is used. Uncertainty estimates tend to be based on measurement data, literature, expert judgment and the recommendations of the IPCC (API, 2009). Chapter 2 of the IPCC Good Practice Guidance and Uncertainty Management in National Greenhouse Gas Inventories (2000) details the methods of assessing uncertainty. The difference between observed and true fugitive emissions data includes the errors associated with the method of estimation (IPCC, 2000).

Sources of uncertainty (IPCC, 2000) are:

- measurement errors
- uncertainties in emission factors
- application of emission factors
- use of statistics
- lack of representativeness of data

- applicability of models
- expert judgment.

Tier 1: average emission factor approach (IPCC, 2000)

According to CDM guidelines, default values (e.g., emission factors) can be used for parameters where no project-specific information is available. Where limited measurement data are available to develop emission factors for specific regions in developing countries, expert knowledge has been applied and emission factors developed for a different region. However, factors developed for other regions can be successfully applied where the practice of emission control and the equipment used are similar, though regional differences can reduce the accuracy of results (IPCC, 2006). Many commonly used emission factors were developed by the American Petroleum Industry based on research in the US despite carbon offset projects frequently being based in developing nations. These API (2009) emission factors can be based on a limited dataset; for example, fugitive methane equipment leaks specifically from refineries were derived from a study conducted at only two refineries.

Emission factors for processes within gas systems are often expressed as a range indicating uncertainty and variability. Uncertainty surrounding emission factors depends on the quality of the emission factor, the pollutants of interest and the source (i.e., component type). High quality emission factors can have an error of ±25 percent whilst low quality factors can have uncertainties of a magnitude more than ten times that (IPCC, 2000). The uncertainty in the calculation of fugitive emissions is reduced when appropriate emission factors are regularly reviewed and updated and then selected based on recent measurement data, technological development and the impact of new regulations.

While emission factors may be representative of the average for industry, they may over-or underestimate emissions for a specific site. For example emission factors may overestimate refineries' contribution to fugitive emissions by excluding emission reductions achieved through LDAR programs. Conversely, studies comparing Tier 1 estimates with actual measurements of the plants in Europe and Canada (Tier 3) have indicated that emission factors for fugitives emitted from refinery and gas operations are underestimated by around 10–20 times. Factors causing a significant risk of underestimation include unforeseen emission sources and the assumption that all equipment operates as designed (EPA, 2006a). This under-reading of baseline emissions results in an underestimation and therefore conservative estimation of emission reductions.

The only activity data used in the Tier 1 approach are system throughputs. However, fugitive equipment leaks within gas distribution and transmission systems tend not to be proportional to the system throughputs; thus it introduces uncertainty into the calculation of emissions. Further disaggregation of the gas industry into subcategories (gas production, processing, transmission, storage and distribution systems) would enable production data to be related to a more appropriate variable; for example, for the distribution and transmission systems this may be length of pipeline (IPCC, 2000).

Tier 2: country-specific emission factor approach

Uncertainties within the Tier 2 approach are very similar to those identified above in the Tier 1 approach; however, the use of a country-specific factor should ensure greater confidence in emission estimates reported using the Tier 2 approach. Emission factors are still based on a limited dataset; however, studies which led to their development were conducted in the same country and therefore likely to have more similarities to the project activity the factor is now being applied to. Variables such as geographic location, weather conditions and financial status are usually less variable within a country than between countries.

Tier 3: bottom-up approach

Measurement of fugitive emissions is inherently difficult due to their heterogeneous nature. The set-up, calibration and use of monitoring equipment can introduce errors within LDAR programs. However, the Tier 3 approach has become widely accepted as the least uncertain. Direct measurement provides the greatest potential accuracy of measuring simple point source emissions, although nearby sources can interfere with direct measurement techniques such as Hi-Flow samplers. When using indirect measurement techniques such as OGI it is important to identify the maximum leak location as methane leaked from a component disperses and is diluted by surrounding air. Remote sensing of gas facilities can improve the quantitative accuracy of emissions monitoring by taking account of total site emissions in a lumped-analysis of large complex sources, including those in inaccessible areas (IPCC, 2000).

It is also difficult to measure fugitive emissions over long timescales and usually measurements are taken over several days to give a "snapshot" of plant emissions in time (Chambers et al., 2006). The extrapolation of these measurements to produce a time-weighted annual emissions estimate introduces uncertainty; however, research conducted in Europe suggests this is an appropriate method (EPA, 2006a). Although routine measurements are generally prohibitively costly, more regular surveys could improve monitoring accuracies as leaks are detected and accounted for closer to the actual leak start time. Additionally increasing the number of components measured within a refinery can improve the estimation of leak rate. Similarly emission factors which are developed from local scale measurement data may over-or underestimate fugitive emissions where data are not representative of a site or there is difficulty in accessing emission sources (EPA, 2006a; Robinson et al., 2011).

The lack of available and continuous activity data poses a challenge for calculating baseline and project emissions using the Tier 1, 2 or 3 approaches. Activity data (e.g., amount of refined oil produced) are correlated with proxy data (e.g., hours of operation of the facility) to fill in knowledge gaps. These gap-filling techniques are associated with high levels of uncertainty as the assumption produces errors from missed sources (IPCC, 2006). Acquiring local scale activity data can reduce the uncertainty associated with these assumptions.

Quality control and quality assurance

Quality control (QC) and quality assurance (QA) minimize uncertainties. QC procedures are the routine checks to measure and control the quality of the reported emissions, ensuring correct and complete data with no inconsistencies are reported, as well as identifying and addressing errors and omissions. After QC the completed inventory is reviewed by a third party (or employees not involved in the development of the emissions inventory); this is known as QA. QA/QC procedures address sources of uncertainty such as double or miscounting, by ensuring appropriate sampling, measurement and estimation procedures are carried out (IPCC, 2000).

14.3 CDM methodology AM0023

CDM project activities tend to take a production-based approach in regard to scope, only taking responsibility for direct emissions from their projects (Scope 1). When quantifying greenhouse gas emissions from baseline and project activities, methodologies often focus on one type of emission: in the case of method AM0023: "Leak detection and repair in gas production, processing, transmission, storage and distribution systems and in refinery facilities," only methane emissions are accounted for in the calculations. Methane is one of the biggest sources of fugitive emissions in the oil and gas industry and the main gas emitted through leaks, whilst carbon dioxide and nitrous oxide concentrations in natural gas are very low. This method detects and repairs natural gas and refinery gas leaks in above-ground process equipment to avoid emissions of methane (IPCC, 2000).

AM0023 was the first methodology approved within the gas sector (Quality Tonnes, 2013). There are currently 14 registered CDM projects using this methodology, all of which currently apply Approach 2 to calculate project emissions. These projects have avoided the emission of 8 million tCO_2e, that is 0.56 percent of cumulated avoided emissions in the CDM (UNFCCC, 2013b); emission reductions per project so far range from 160,000 to 1,300,000 tCO_2e.

Calculation of emission reductions

As for all CDM projects (see Chapter 11), emission reductions from CDM methodology AM0023 are calculated as the difference between the estimated baseline emissions and project emissions. In Approach 2, the associated uncertainty is included within the calculation of emissions.

$$ER = BE - PE$$

$$BE = M_{BE} - U_{M_{BE}}$$

$$PE = M_{PE} + U_{M_{PE}}$$

Where:

ER = Emissions reductions, the difference between baseline emissions and project emissions, after having accounted for leakage;

BE = Baseline emissions, the quantity of methane emitted through leaks from components which were detected and repaired during the first year of the crediting period. The crediting period is the maximum period over which an offset project can obtain carbon credits. This period begins from when the first leak is successfully repaired as part of the project activity.

PE = Project emissions, the leaks from components whereby a repair has ceased to function, or a new leak has occurred which was not previously detected in a survey;

M_{BE} = Estimated baseline emissions;

M_{PE} = Estimated project emissions;

$U_{M_{BE}}$ = Uncertainty of estimated baseline emissions;

$U_{M_{PE}}$ = Uncertainty of estimated project emissions.

Project proponents following CDM methodology AM0023 can choose between two approaches to calculate baseline and project emissions (Figure 14.5).

1. Where emission flux is not directly quantified, emissions are calculated using emission factors or algorithms (Figure 14.5: Approach 1). Leaks are detected using fast response semi-conductor sensors such as electronic gas detectors, organic vapor analyzers or toxic vapor analyzers, acoustic leak detection, or optical gas imaging instruments and the concentration of methane in the gas measured (see techniques in Table 14.5 in the appendix). The concentration is then multiplied by a default emission factor, for example at the equipment level of on-shore natural gas production, the emission factor $2.66E^{-05}$ tonne CH_4/hr is used per kilometer of gathering pipeline (API, 2009). Such estimates from all detected leaks are then summed up to constitute the baseline. Whilst this approach involves direct measurement of concentration to detect leaks, the use of default factors makes this a Tier 1 approach.

2. If a project developer opts for the direct measurement approach (Figure 14.5: Approach 2), leak flow rates are calculated based on measurements of flow rate of the sampled stream and the methane concentration of the flow (UNFCCC, 2013b). Leak rates are then summed up into annual estimates of fugitive emissions from a refinery process plant. Leak flow rates are measured using bagging techniques, Hi-Flow samplers, or a calibrated bag (UNFCCC, 2011). This is a Tier 3 appoach as direct measurement is carried out to quantify emissions.

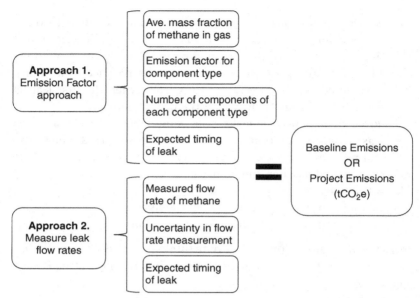

Figure 14.5 Two approaches to calculate baseline and project emissions in CDM methodology AM0023

Information about components and leaks, in addition to maintenance (and replacement) schedules, are recorded in a database of all project activity data which is continuously updated (UNFCCC, 2013b).

Uncertainty in the two approaches of CDM methodology AM0023

CDM methodologies have to "describe the uncertainty of key parameters and, where possible, provide an uncertainty range at 95% confidence level for key parameters for the calculation of emission reductions" (UNFCCC, 2011).

For projects using emission factors (Approach 1 in methodology AM0023), uncertainty is not included in the calculation of emission reductions. There is therefore no systematic incentive to use a less uncertain emission factor or to upgrade to Approach 2 unless the project developer knows that the use of the default emission factor results in systematically underestimated emissions reductions. The general principle of conservativeness applies to emission factors in that when two different emission factors are considered equally relevant, the more conservative is used.

For projects using Approach 2, the uncertainty of the flow rate measurement is included in the calculation of emissions reductions: the estimate of baseline emissions uses the lower end of the uncertainty range at 95 percent confidence interval, whilst project emissions from leaks use values from the upper end of the uncertainty range. As a large number of measurements are potentially involved, the uncertainty range of baseline and project emissions can be calculated using combined uncertainties of all measurements of each (IPCC, 2006). There is therefore a driver to reduce uncertainty in Approach 2 as it is subtracted from emission reductions claimed, and hence influences the amount of carbon credits delivered to the project developer; there is an embedded incentive to reduce uncertainty associated with, for example, gas flow measurement. However, in many project implementations the reported uncertainties determined for the total of all the component leak rate measurements are typically small. This is because they typically refer to the IPCC Good Practice Guidance and Uncertainty Management in National Greenhouse Gas Inventories (IPCC, 2000) which assumes random uncorrelated uncertainty sources. Any systematic uncertainties caused by consistent errors across all measurements, such as an error in calibration, would invalidate this assumption and lead to bigger uncertainties and therefore need to be considered within the project design.

As a result, projects using Approach 2 have an incentive to reduce uncertainty – at least the uncertainty due to methane flow rate from an identified leak. However, those using Approach 1 neither have an incentive to reduce uncertainty, nor to "upgrade" to Approach 2. In addition, the choice offered to project developers between the two approaches may foster strategic behavior: a project developer knowing that their leaks tend to be smaller than the default value will use Approach 1 even if they have the capability to conduct direct emission measurements.

14.4 Cost of monitoring

LDAR programs cost €30,000–67,000 per refinery per year

Project developers using CDM methodology AM0023 currently all implement a monitoring strategy which calculates emission reductions from direct measurement of flow rates and gas concentrations at the source (Figure 14.5: Approach 2), despite the lower cost incurred by the emission factor approach; traditional "sniffing" techniques for detection and quantification are time-consuming for experienced personnel and require specialist equipment (Chambers et al., 2008).

A high spatial and temporal resolution of routine measurements within an LDAR strategy will deliver more accurate, up-to-date datasets, but are not feasible due to the costs associated with monitoring dispersed sources (IPCC, 2000). According to research by Carbon Limits (2014), a quarterly survey frequency is reasonable for LDAR programs but is likely to result in LDAR costs higher than the associated benefits from recovered gas and carbon credits. Meanwhile annual and semi-annual surveys produce negative abatement costs due to the value of carbon saved outweighing the cost of less frequent surveys.

Fugitive leaks result in lost product and therefore profit; generally the value of saving a gas is greater than the cost of leak repair (once it has been located) (Carbon Limits, 2014). The EPA calculated an approximate value of US$1,370 per ton for product lost due to equipment leaks (EPA, 1992). Properly implementing leak detection and repair programs can maximize safety, efficiency and profitability by boosting productivity. In addition to this it can help prevent violation of the emissions rules existing in some countries[3] thus avoiding penalties and improving regional air quality (EPA, 2007). Improvements in the emissions monitoring method within CDM methodology AM0023 lead to more leak detection and subsequent repair of leaks. Hence, the economic incentives for improving monitoring are two-fold:

---

[3] In most cases, a system put in place to comply with existing emissions rules would not be eligible for CDM certification.

1. Minimize the loss of methane, a valuable product;
2. Maximize the amount of carbon credits obtained, as those are proportional to the number of leaks detected and repaired; 1 tonne of methane is worth 25 carbon credits.

Accordingly, in addition to the direct incentive to decrease the uncertainty of the emission flux measurement, there is an indirect incentive to increase the number of leaks detected. Recent technological developments have resulted in instruments which can remotely detect and quantify a larger number of fugitive emission sources, in comparison to the time-consuming efforts that were involved in the traditional screening method, whereby components within a gas facility had to be measured individually. Remote optical techniques are able to identify emission "hotspots" so that more detailed LDAR surveys using "sniffer" devices can be conducted in these areas to develop a cost-effective monitoring strategy and find more leaks to be repaired within monitoring programs.

During an initial survey gas facilities have high leak abatement potential and thus a low survey and repair cost per metric ton of CO_2e abatement as more leaks are found. However, the initial LDAR survey tends to cost the most as carrying out leak repairs reduces the number of components which are likely to be leaking in following surveys (Carbon Limits, 2014). For large facilities this initial screening survey using "sniffing" devices tends to cost US$10–50 per component measured; however, the following surveys of an ongoing screening program cost approximately US$1 per component; these costs include monitoring instruments and labor costs (Dumdei et al., 2009).

Bagging tends to cost over US$500 per component bagged, in addition to the screening costs for the remaining components. Under methodology AM0023, using bagging techniques as in Approach 2 is therefore economically advantageous if the leaking methane is valued at more than US$500 per component (Carbon Limits, 2014).

Hydrocarbon monitors such as Flame Ionization Detectors (FIDs) used within LDAR programs cost approximately US$5,000, whilst smart LDAR programs incur a higher capital cost as infrared cameras tend to cost US$20,000–50,000 (Dumdei et al., 2009). Despite these high instrument costs, and the additional training required, smart LDAR costs are roughly one third of those incurred by LDAR programs. Smart LDAR does not require scaffolding or man-lifts, and it is focused on the detection and repair of large leaks; LDAR programs can cost approximately €67,000 with the biggest cost being the leak repair (40 percent of the total cost), whilst smart LDAR based on OGI tends to cost €30,000 with the biggest cost (almost 59 percent) being inventory management (Wilwerding, 2012).[4] Smart LDAR reduces methane at low cost due to its ability to conduct rapid surveys. A cost-effective monitoring program could therefore include regular OGI surveys with infrequent LDAR surveys using analyzers.

Of 600 gas plants (excluding compressor stations) surveyed within the Carbon Limits (2014) study of emission reduction projects, 221 gas plants benefitted economically from an LDAR program. The average survey value to the facility owners was almost US$10,000. Despite 60 percent of the gas plants experiencing an economic loss from conducting an LDAR program, they still produced a net benefit when the cost of reducing methane was considered, as may be required to meet emission requirements and avoid penalties. Therefore although LDAR program incurred a cost for project developers, there was a negative abatement cost per metric ton of CO_2e reduced by the programs. Compressor stations, surveyed separately, showed similar results. Of 565 compressor stations surveyed, LDAR programs were economically advantageous for roughly 30 percent. The average survey value at compressor stations was almost US$3,500. Carbon Limits (2014) have therefore identified that the value of gas saved frequently outweighs the cost of surveys and repairs.

MRV costs for CDM projects on fugitive emissions

No estimate is provided for the MRV costs in fugitive emissions projects in Chapter 11. These costs are estimated here to be around €167,000 [161,000–172,000] per year and 0.22 [0.21–0.23] €/tCO_2e (Table 14.2).

This estimate derives from the following steps:

- the costs of developing a monitoring plan amounts to 7% of project upfront MRV costs (Guigon et al., 2009) and upfront MRV costs amount to 58% of total project MRV costs on average (see Chapter 11);

[4] The 2010 average exchange rate of 0.785 €/US$ is used to convert the original figures into euros.

- the costs of implementing a monitoring plan amounts to 19–41%[5] of project recurring MRV costs (Guigon et al., 2009) and recurring MRV costs amount to 42% of total project MRV costs on average (see Chapter 11);
- the costs of developing and implementing a monitoring plan are removed from the MRV costs provided in Chapter 11 for the closest project type in terms of size, namely coal mine methane, and the aforementioned €67,000 costs of most commonly implemented LDAR programs are added in their stead. Per tCO_2e costs are obtained by dividing by 762,000 tCO_2e average yearly emissions reductions from CDM projects using the AM0023 methodology.

14.5 Discussion

Locating fugitive equipment leaks in a chemical plant can improve safety, increase productivity and ensure regulatory compliance whilst maximizing operational efficiency. Determining a monitoring strategy, however, is a complex task. A monitoring strategy for fugitive emissions should monitor a number of sources, have high temporal resolution and be mobile (IPCC, 2000). However, the decision asto which monitoring technique is best to implement within a project activity is based on the cost–uncertainty trade-off; the Approach 1 emission factor (IPCC Tier 1) approach tends to incur the lowest capital cost; however, Approach 2 (IPCC Tier 3) based on site-specific measurement tends to report emissions more accurately.

There is an uncertainty surrounding the calculation of emission reductions from both approaches outlined within CDM methodology AM0023. Uncertainty is not included in the calculation of emission reductions in Approach 1. Conversely Approach 2 explicitly states uncertainty associated with direct measurements of flow rate and this value is deducted from the emission reductions claimed. Therefore whilst in Approach 2 there is an incentive to reduce the uncertainty value to improve the accuracy of emissions reporting, in Approach 1 there is no incentive. This would suggest that the simpler Approach 1

---

[5] Assuming that CERs are worth 10 €/tCO_2e and calculating the range from large-scale (50 $ktCO_2e$/yr) to small-scale (5 $ktCO_2e$/yr) projects. The estimate is largely insensitive to the price assumption since it only affects the cost of the 2 percent tax on CERs which itself represents a minor part of the total MRV costs.

with its lower monitoring accuracy would be the favorable approach for project developers. Even though refineries implementing LDAR programs do not have a direct incentive to directly measure leak flow rate, they often do so in order to obtain a more precise estimate of how much gas they recover, and therefore to judge whether the program is worth its costs. This may explain why Approach 2 is applied more widely than Approach 1, despite the lack of direct incentive to apply it.

LDAR surveys are considered the current practice which project developers tend to undertake most often. The study conducted by Carbon Limits (2014) indicates that the value of gas saved in carrying out an LDAR program frequently outweighs the monitoring and repair costs. Monitoring strategies should therefore focus on improving the implementation of current LDAR programs to control emissions from leaks as improper implementation has previously been seen as a cause of inaccurate emissions reporting (Wilwerding, 2012). In all cases, increasing leak detection and repair improves safety, increases productivity, ensures regulatory compliance and increases the credits obtained in proportion to the amount of methane emissions avoided.

Recently more complex facilities have introduced more monitoring points and therefore enhanced the need for combined monitoring programs which provide a balance between direct and indirect measurements to achieve the optimum emissions detection and quantification, at a reasonable cost to the project developer. Advances in optical and laser technology for gas leak detection are finding more leaks and much faster than the traditional "sniffer" devices (Brown, 2011). Indirect measurement techniques can be used to identify areas of high leakage emissions such as compressor stations, and estimate total emissions so that a focused measurement strategy using "sniffers" (direct measurement) can then target these "'hotspot" areas of fugitive emission (IPCC, 2000; Quality Tonnes, 2013). Open-path techniques are therefore becoming more appealing to project developers as they minimize the use of labor-intensive surveys and focus quantification efforts on large leaks; less than 1 percent of potential leak sources contribute to over 90 percent of fugitive emissions in refineries (API, 1997). In addition, these remote techniques also provide the advantage of being able to conduct on-site measurement of inaccessible components.

A topic for further research is the advancements in reducing leakage. A research focus should be on the development of improved leak identification so that more leaks can be addressed. Open-path techniques have begun to find more leaks than traditional "sniffer" surveys alone were able to. Improved understanding and more accurate measurement of fugitive emissions from the natural gas industry could identify cost-effective emission reduction opportunities and reduce product loss.

Appendix

Table 14.1 *Advantages (✓) and disadvantages (✗) of direct vs. indirect methods used within the Tier 3 bottom-up approach*

Direct	Indirect
✓ Accurate, disaggregated results	✓ All emissions measured (no missed sources)
✓ Fast, low cost for a few simple point sources	✓ Fast, low cost for large complex sources
✓ Sensitive	✓ Off-site measurements
✓ Easier to assess uncertainties	✓ For a variety of sources
✓ Easy to operate	✓ Safely determine emissions (from difficult to access sources)
✓ Data reduction	✓ Low maintenance cost
✓ Isolate and measure emissions	✓ Faster maintenance surveys
✗ Slow maintenance surveys	✗ High initial equipment cost
✗ Only measure accessible emission sources	✗ May be dependent on meteorological conditions
✗ Measure selected individual sources, not total site emissions so sources not included in the survey may be missed	✗ Other sources interfere
	✗ Detection sensitivity lower than direct measurement (emissions measured downwind are diffuse)
	✗ Requires greater expertise
	✗ Large potential errors
	✗ Individual sources not known as emissions are aggregated

Source: IPCC (2000).

Table 14.2 *MRV ID table*

Context	
Regulator	UNFCCC CDM Executive Board (guided by the Conference of the Parties): validate methodologies, register projects and issue credits. Designated Operational Entities: accredited to conduct validation and verification of CDM projects.
Type and level of incentive to comply	• Positive incentives ("carrots"): issuance of CERs (timeliness and quantity) • Negative incentives ("sticks"): non-compliance with monitoring requirements may trigger a request for CER issuance review and possible ultimate non-issuance of CERs
Entities concerned	Project proponents: • 10 CDM methodologies relevant to fugitive emissions from fuels • 222 registered projects using fugitive methodologies as of March 2014 (2.6% of all registered CDM projects) (UNFCCC, 2013a) DOEs: • 25 accredited auditors for validation and verification as of March 2014 Consultants
Sectors concerned	Fugitive emissions from fuels (solid, oil and gas)
Gases concerned	CH_4 & CO_2
Overall MRV costs	€167,000 [161,000–172,000] per project per year 0.22 [0.21–0.23] €/tCO_2e
Monitoring	
Rules	Guidance relating to the clean development mechanism (Decision 3/CMP.9) Modalities and procedures for a clean development mechanism (Decision 3/CMP.1) Ten methodologies under Scope 10, fugitives from fuels:

Table 14.2 (*cont.*)

- AM0074: New grid connected power plants using permeate gas previously flared and/or vented
- AM0064: Capture and utilization or destruction of mine methane (excluding coal mines) or non-mine methane
- ACM0008: Consolidated methodology for coal bed methane, coal mine methane and ventilation air methane capture and use for power (electrical or motive) and heat and/or destruction through flaring or flameless oxidation
- AM0023: Leak detection and repair in gas production, processing, transmission, storage and distribution systems and in refinery facilities
- AM0043: Leak reduction from a natural gas distribution grid by replacing old cast iron pipes or steel pipes without cathodic protection with polyethylene pipes
- AMS-III.W: Methane capture and destruction in non-hydrocarbon mining activities
- AMS-III.BI: Flare gas recovery in gas treating facilities
- AM0009: Recovery and utilization of gas from oil wells that would otherwise be flared or vented
- AM0037: Flare (or vent) reduction and utilization of gas from oil wells as a feedstock
- AM0077: Recovery of gas from oil wells that would otherwise be vented or flared and its delivery to specific end-users

Eight associated tools:
- Tool for the demonstration and assessment of additionality
- Combined tool to identify the baseline scenario and demonstrate additionality
- Tool to calculate project or leakage CO_2 emissions from fossil fuel combustion

Table 14.2 (*cont.*)

	• Tool to calculate baseline, project and/or leakage emissions from electricity consumption • Tool to calculate the emission factor for an electricity system • Tool to determine the baseline efficiency of thermal or electric energy generation systems • Project emissions from flaring • Assessment of the validity of the original/current baseline and update of the baseline at the renewal of the crediting period
Other reference documents	• IPCC 2006 Guidelines for National Greenhouse Gas Inventories • IPCC Fifth Assessment Report: Climate Change 2013 • ISO 11771 Air quality (determines emission factors) • EN 15446 Fugitive and diffuse emissions (measures fugitive emission from equipment leaks) • Emission Factor Database (IPCC, 2014) • CDM Methodology Booklet Fourth Edition • CDM Methodology Tools • IPCC Good Practice Guidance and Uncertainty Management in National Greenhouse Gas Inventories (2000)
Uncertainty requirements	None beyond the description of uncertainty, as in all CDM projects (UNFCCC, 2011).
Achieved uncertainty range	The uncertainty varies depending on the project activity and the monitoring method undertaken. For example, from −40 to +250% for gas production, processing, transmission and storage using a Tier 1 approach in developing countries, down to −15 to +5% using DIAL methods (see Section 14.2).
Cost range	LDAR programs tend to cost around €67,000 per year and per facility whilst smart LDAR programs cost approximately €30,000 (see Section 14.4).

Table 14.2 (*cont.*)

Scope	Scope 3: direct and indirect emissions and leakage
Frequency	No specified frequency for monitoring (project developer decides duration), it can be weeks or years, though it does need to be stated in the monitoring plan.
Source for activity data	Field measurements from representative surveys and default values.
Uncertainty range for activity data	No specific requirement. When Approach 2 is used, a precision of ±10% is usually reached on gas flow.
Source for emission factors	Emission factors can come from peer-reviewed papers, though are often from IPCC Guidelines on National GHG Inventories and found in the Emission Factor Database (EFDB).
Uncertainty range for emission factors	No specific requirement.
Direct measurement	Mandatory for methane concentration of the gas. Allowed (Approach 2) but not mandatory (Approach 1) for gas flow.
Incentives to reduce uncertainty	Restricted to the measurement of gas flow in Approach 2. No incentive to reduce uncertainty in Approach 1.
Is requirements stringency adapted to the amount of emissions at stake (materiality)?	No
Reporting	
Rules	• Rules outlined in the ten methodologies relevant to fugitives from fuels • CDM Project Cycle Procedure (CDM-EB65-A32-PROC) (outlines procedures for submitting and publishing monitoring reports)

Table 14.2 (*cont.*)

Other reference documents	Guideline Completing the monitoring report form (CDM-EB54-A34-GUID)
Format	The more recent version of the monitoring report form applicable to the project activity must be used.
Level of source disaggregation	Disaggregation can be down to the component level, for example fugitive leakage from valves on a refinery. Alternatively it can be at the site level.
Frequency	Up to the project proponent. Typically between 4 and 11 months, with an average 7 months.
Timeline	The monitoring report must be made publicly available by the DOE 14 days prior to undertaking the site visit for the verification (CDM-EB65-A05-STAN). On average the monitoring report is made public 70 days after the end of the respective monitoring period (IGES, 2013).
Language	English
Is requirements stringency adapted to the amount of emissions at stake (materiality)?	To some extent: although the requirements are the same for all projects, the frequency is up to the project developer to decide. As a result, smaller projects report less often.
Cost range	Usually negligible and included in periodic monitoring costs (see Chapter 3.1).
Verification	
Rules	CDM Validation and Verification Standard (CDM-EB65-A04-STAN)
Other reference documents	Standard for sampling and surveys for CDM project activities and program of activities (CDM-EB69-A04).
Format	No format is stipulated.
Frequency	Up to the project proponent: verification is undertaken following the submission of each monitoring report.

Table 14.2 (*cont.*)

Timeline	See Chapter 11.
Language	English
Accredited entities for verification	DOEs: 25 organizations accredited by the CDM Executive Board.
Control of accredited entities	The performance of DOEs is checked via regular on-site surveillance (EB56-A02-B.7) and spot-checking (EB56-A02-B.8). The Executive Board can recommend the suspension or withdrawal of an entity's designation to the COP/MOP if the DOE no longer meets the accreditation standards.
Cost of accreditation	Procedure for accrediting operational entities by the Executive Board of the Clean Development Mechanism (CDM-EB56-A02): • Non-reimbursable application fee US$15,000 • Fee and costs associated with an on-site assessment of the premises of an AE/DOE • Costs associated with performance assessment • Costs associated with regular surveillance • Costs associated with application for extension of the accreditation for additional sectoral scope(s) • Costs associated with changes notified by the AE/DOE • Cost of "spot-checks" • Cost of appeals
Support of accredited entities	• AE/DOE Forum set up by the Executive Board to enhance communication between the EB and DOEs and provide guidance on decisions and clarification on specific issues • EB to provide constructive feedback to DOEs, communicating its observations to DOEs through the Secretary of the Board • EB meets with DOEs and applicant entities at regular intervals to exchange views and experiences

Table 14.2 (*cont.*)

Is requirements stringency adapted to the amount of emissions at stake (materiality)?	Yes: there is a materiality threshold which decreases with project size (from 10% to 0.5%). In addition, verification frequency is decided by the project proponent (see Reporting).
Cost range	No specific data for fugitive emissions. Periodic verification costs per project per year: €17,500 (5,000–30,000) Periodic verification costs per ton CO_2e: €0.24 (0.04–0.70) (see Chapter 3.1)

Table 14.3 *Effects of CDM projects on fugitive emissions from fuels (UNFCCC, 2013c)*

Category		GHG destruction		Date of method validation	GHG offset	Effect
Small-scale	Waste gas/ energy recovery	AMS-III.BI	Flare gas recovery in gas treating facilities – Version 1.0	October 2013	CO_2 reduced	
	Mining activities	AMS-III.W	Methane capture and destruction in non-hydrocarbon mining activities – Version 2.0	December 2011	CH_4 stopped	GHG destruction
Large-scale		ACM0008 consolidated	Consolidated methodology for coal bed methane, coal mine methane and ventilation air methane capture and use for power (electrical or motive) and heat and/or destruction through flaring or flameless oxidation – Version 7.0	August 2010	CH_4 stopped	
		AM0064	Capture and utilization or destruction of mine methane (excluding coal mines) or non-mine methane – Version 3.0.0	March 2012	CH_4 stopped	
	Pipe replacement	AM0043	Leak reduction from a natural gas distribution grid by replacing old cast iron pipes or steel pipes without cathodic protection with polyethylene pipes – Version 2.0	November 2007	CH_4 stopped	GHG emission avoidance

Table 14.3 (cont.)

Compressors and distribution systems	AM0023	Leak detection and repair in gas production, processing, transmission, storage and in refinery facilities – Version 4.0.0	September 2011	CH_4 stopped	
Oil production	AM0037	Flare (or vent) reduction and utilization of gas from oil wells as a feedstock – Version 2.1	March 2008	CO_2	Fuel/ feedstock switch
	AM0009	Recovery and utilization of gas from oil wells that would otherwise be flared or vented – Version 6.0.0	July 2012	CO_2 reduced	Displacement of a more GHG-intensive output
	AM0077	Recovery of gas from oil wells that would otherwise be vented or flared and its delivery to specific end-users – Version 1.0	February 2009	CO_2 reduced	
Low carbon electricity	AM0074	AM0074: Methodology for new grid connected power plants using permeate gas previously flared and/or vented – Version 3.0.0	May 2012	CO_2 reduced GHG removal by sinks	

Table 14.4 *Standards which address fugitive emissions*

Geographical application	Regulation	Implications
European	Directive 1996/62/EC Ambient air quality assessment and management	Ambient air quality must be monitored
	Directive 1996/61/EC Integrated pollution prevention and control	Individual facilities carrying out activities mentioned in Annex I (e.g., petroleum product processing) will report emissions
	Directive 2002/358/EC Approval, on behalf of the European Community, of the Kyoto Protocol to the United Nations Framework Convention on Climate Change and the joint fulfillment of commitments thereunder	Acceptance of the Kyoto Protocol. Member States are responsible for their commitments to the agreed quantified emission reductions – States to reduce their aggregated greenhouse gas emissions by 8% below 1990 levels, during 2008 to 2012.
	Directive 2006/166/EC Establishment of a European Pollutant Release and Transfer Register and amending Council Directives 91/689/EEC and 96/61/EC	Pollutant release and transfer registers (PRTRs), a database reporting information on releases of pollutants and off-site transfers of pollutants and waste. To be used for comparisons and future decisions in environmental matters. Tracks trends to show progress in pollution reduction and demonstrate monitoring compliance.
	Directive 2007/589/EC Establishing guidelines for the monitoring and reporting of greenhouse gas emissions pursuant to Directive 2003/87/EC of the European Parliament and of the Council	Guidelines for the monitoring and reporting of greenhouse gas emissions for the operation of the emission allowance trading scheme – to assist operators to achieve the highest standard of emission monitoring. Clarifies monitoring plan and uncertainty requirements.

Table 14.5 *Advantages (✓) and disadvantages (✗) of equipment used in monitoring fugitive emissions*

Equipment	Advantages	Disadvantages
Detect Leaks		
Organic vapor analyzers and toxic vapor analyzers:		
Hydrocarbon monitors e.g., flame ionization detectors (FID)	✓ sensitive to small gas concentrations	✗ slow detection (single points are tested) ✗ labor intensive ✗ operator dependency results in missed leaks ✗ background level of a gas limits the sniffing sensitivity (minimum measurable leak rate) ✗ instrument must be in contact with component
Acoustic monitoring (EPA, 2003):		
Acoustic emission detectors	✓ no interference with equipment's operation ✓ provide relative indication of leak size	✗ labor intensive ✗ lots needed for extended pipeline ✗ difficult to distinguish small leaks from background noise
Thermal monitoring:		
Thermal imaging (Kulp et al., 1998; Weil, 1993)	✓ cover a large area ✓ can be used from ground, vehicle, aircraft or satellite platforms thus long pipelines assessed	✗ detecting small temperature differences requires expensive imagers ✗ not effective if temperature of natural gas and surroundings are equal ✗ high capital cost imaging equipment ✗ spectral resolution not good enough for compound resolution

Table 14.5 (*cont.*)

Equipment	Advantages	Disadvantages
Optical Gas Imaging (OGI) (EPA, 2003): Infrared cameras	✓ high spatial coverage ✓ less time-consuming ✓ less labor intensive ✓ no need to visit and manually measure leak points ✓ point or area source survey ✓ no interference with equipment's operation	✗ low sensitivity (focus is on large leaks) ✗ relies on operators' skill increasing the risk of false negatives (not detecting leaks)
On-site measurement of leak emission rates		
Organic vapor analyzers and toxic vapor analyzers:		
Hydrocarbon monitors e.g., flame ionization detectors (FID)	✓ portable instruments	✗ low spatial coverage thus time-consuming and expensive to assess long pipelines ✗ requires frequent calibration ✗ instrument must be in contact with component
Bagging techniques (EPA, 2003):		
Bagging	✓ direct measure of concentration	✗ low spatial coverage ✗ time-consuming ✗ instrument must be in contact with component

Table 14.5 (*cont.*)

Equipment	Advantages	Disadvantages
Flow monitoring:		
Flow-through flow meters	✓ low capital cost ✓ no interference with equipment's operation	✗ does not pinpoint leak's location ✗ numerous false alarms
High volume or Hi-Flow samplers (Lott et al., 1996)	✓ complete emissions capture prevent interference from other nearby sources	✗ instrument must be in contact with component affected by upwind pollution
Open-path monitoring:		
Tunable Diode Laser Absorption Spectroscopy (TDLAS) (Hanson et al., 1980)	✓ temperature difference between gas and surroundings not required ✓ high spatial coverage	✗ high capital cost of implementation ✗ numerous false alarms ✗ skilled operator required
Fourier Transform Infrared Spectroscopy (FTIR) (Griffiths and De Haseth, 2007; EPA, 2011)	✓ temperature difference between gas and surroundings not required ✓ high spatial coverage	✗ high capital cost of implementation ✗ numerous false alarms ✗ skilled operator required ✗ small field-of-view
Remote sensing:		
Differential Absorption Lidar (DIAL)	✓ produces time-weighted mean average of emissions ✓ identifies leak "hotspots" ✓ quantifies emissions up to a 1 km radius ✓ representation of gas flux	✗ high capital cost ✗ influenced by downwind terrain ✗ component point source not identified

Bibliography

American Petroleum Institute (API), 1997. Analysis of Refinery Screening Data (API Publication No. 310), American Petroleum Institute, Washington, DC.

 2004. *Smart Leak Detection and Repair (LDAR) for Control of Fugitive Emissions*. www.ihs.com/. Accessed April 3, 2013.

 2006. API Manual of Petroleum Measurement Standards, Chapter 14.

 2009. *Compendium of Greenhouse Gas Emissions Methodologies for the Oil and Gas Industry*. Washington, DC. www.api.org/ehs/climate/new/upload/2004_COMPENDIUM.pdf. Accessed May 3, 2013.

Brown, T.G., 2011. *Innovative Technologies to Detect and Measure Leaks*. International Gas Union Research Conference 2011. USA.

Carbon Limits, 2014. Quantifying Cost-effectiveness of Systematic Leak Detection and Repair Programs Using Infrared Cameras. The Clean Air Task Force. www.catf.us/resources/publications/view/198. Accessed August 2, 2013.

Centre for Climate and Energy Solutions (C2ES). www.c2es.org/technology/factsheet/natural-gas. Accessed August 2, 2013.

Chambers, A., Strosher, M., Wootton, T., Moncrieff, J. and McCready, P., 2006. *DIAL Measurements of Fugitive Emissions from Natural Gas Plants and the Comparison with Emission Factor Estimates*. Environmental Protection Agency. 15th International Emission Inventory Conference, New Orleans, May 15–18.

Chambers, A., Wootton, T., Moncrieff, J. and McCready, P., 2008. Direct measurement of fugitive emissions of hydrocarbons from a refinery. *Journal of the Air & Waste Management Association* 58(8): 1047–1056.

Dumdei, B., Dunn, J., Melvin, E. and Hahs, R., 2009. *Operations and Maintenance of Natural Gas Transmission and Distribution Systems Emission Reductions Projects*. URS Corporation, Chicago.

Energy Information Administration (EIA), 2013. Levelized Cost of New Generation Resources in the Annual Energy Outlook 2013. Independent Statistics and Analysis, U.S. Energy Information Administration. www.eia.gov/forecasts/aeo/pdf/electricity_generation.pdf. Accessed June 3, 2013.

Environmental Protection Agency (EPA), 1992. Hazardous Air Pollutant Emissions From Process Units in the Synthetic Organic Chemical Manufacturing Industry – Background Information for Proposed Standards, Vol. 1C – Model Emission Sources. Emission Standards Division, US EPA, Office of Air and Radiation, Office of Air Quality Planning and Standards, Research Triangle Park, NC. November.

1995. 1995 Protocol for Equipment Leak Emission Estimates; EPA-453/R-95-017; US EPA; Office of Air and Radiation, Office of Air Quality Planning and Standards, Research Triangle Park, NC.

2003. *Lessons Learned From Natural Gas STAR Partners*. Directed Inspection and Maintenance at Gas Processing Plants and Booster Stations. US EPA, Washington, DC. https://www.globalmethane.org/documents/m2mtool/docs/ll_dimgasproc.pdf. Accessed May 9, 2013.

2006a. VOC Fugitive Losses: New Monitors, Emissions Losses, and Potential Policy Gaps. *International Workshop*. US EPA.

2006b. Optical Remote Sensing for Emission Characterization from Non-point Sources. FINAL ORS Protocol. Technology Transfer Network Emission Measurement Center. US EPA.

2007. Leak Detection and Repair Compliance Assistance Guidance – A Best Practices Guide. US EPA, Washington, DC. www.epa.gov/compliance/resources/publications/assistance/ldarguide.pdf. Accessed May 9, 2013.

2011. EPA Handbook: Optical Remote Sensing for Measurement and Monitoring of Emissions Flux. US EPA. Research Triangle, NC. www.epa.gov/ttnemc01/guidlnd/gd-052.pdf. Accessed May 9, 2013.

Epperson, D., Lev-On, M., Taback, H., Siegell, J. and Ritter, K., 2007. Equivalent leak definitions for smart LDAR (leak detection and repair) when using optical imaging technology. *Journal of the Air and Waste Management Association* 57(9): 1050–1060.

European Commission, 2006. Integrated Pollution Prevention and Control. Reference Document on Best Available Techniques on Emissions from Storage. July. http://eippcb.jrc.ec.europa.eu/reference/BREF/esb_bref_0706.pdf. Accessed April 12, 2013.

Forward-looking infrared imaging systems (FLIR). Thermal Imaging for Oil & Petrochemical. FLIR Systems. www.flir.com/thermography/americas/us/view/?id=49559. Accessed March 3, 2013.

Gas Research Institute and Environmental Protection Agency (GRI/EPA), 1996. Methane Emissions from the Natural Gas Industry, Vols 1–15, Final Report by Harrison, M.R., Shires, T.M., Wessels, J.K. and Cowgill, R.M.

Glancy, R.P., 2013. *Quantifying Fugitive Emission Factors from Unconventional Natural Gas Production Using IPCC Methodologies.* IGES, Hayama, Japan.

Global Methane Initiative, 2013. European Commission Global Methane Reduction Actions. Ref. Ares(2013)2843722. www.globalmethane.org/documents/EC_GMI_reduction_actions.pdf. Accessed March 14, 2013.

Griffiths, P.R and De Haseth, J.A, 2007. Fourier Transform Infrared Spectrometry (2nd Edn.) *Chemical Analysis*, Vol. 83. John Wiley & Sons, Chichester, UK.

Guigon, P., Bellassen, V. and Ambrosi, P., 2009. Voluntary carbon markets: what the standards say... (Working Paper No. 2009-4). CDC Climat Research, Paris.

Hanson, R.K., Varghese, P.L., Schoenunga, S.M. and Falcone, P.K., 1980. Absorption spectroscopy of combustion gases using a tunable IR diode laser. *Laser Probes for Combustion Chemistry*, D.R. Crosley (Ed.), ACS Symposium, Series 134, American Chemical Society, Washington, DC.

IEA, 2008. Energy Technology Perspectives 2008: Scenarios and Strategies to 2050. OECD Publishing. Paris. www.iea.org/techno/etp/etp_2008_exec_sum_english.pdf. Accessed March 4, 2013.

IGES, 2013. CDM Project Database. Institute for Global Environmental Strategies.

Intergovernmental Panel on Climate Change (IPCC), 1997. *Revised 1996 IPCC Guidelines for National Greenhouse Inventories*. Houghton, J.T., Meira Filho, L.G., Lim, B., Tréanton, K., Mamaty, I., Bonduki, Y., Griggs, D.J. and Callander, B.A. (Eds.). IPCC/OECD/IEA, Paris.

2000. IPCC Good Practice Guidance and Uncertainty Management in National Greenhouse Gas Inventories. *Fugitive Emissions from Oil and Natural Gas Activities*. Energy Sector. www.ipcc-nggip.iges.or.jp/public/gp/english/. Accessed March 4, 2013.

2006. IPCC Guidelines for National Greenhouse Gas Inventories. Vol 2, Chap 4. Carras, J.J., Franklin, P. M., Hu, Y., Singh, A.K., Tailakov, O.V., Picard, D., Ahmed, A.F.M., Gjerald, E., Nordrum, S. and Yesserkepova, I.

2007. IPCC Fourth Assessment Report, Working Group 1, Chap 2. Changes in Atmospheric Constituents and in Radiative Forcing, Table 2.14, p. 212. Cambridge University Press, Cambridge and New York.

2013. IPCC Fifth Assessment Report, Working Group I. Climate Change 2013: The Physical Science Basis. Final Draft Underlying Scientific-Technical Assessment.

2014. Emission Factor Database (EFDB). IPCC National Greenhouse Gas Inventories Programme. www.ipcc-nggip.iges.or.jp/EFDB/main.php. Accessed March 6, 2013.

Kulp, T.J., Powers, P.E. and Kennedy, R., 1998. Remote imaging of controlled gas releases using active and passive infrared imaging systems. *Proceedings of Infrared Technology and Applications* XXIII, SPIE Vol. 3061: 269–278.

Lott, R.A., Howard, T. and Web, M., 1996. *Estimating Fugitive Emissions: Problems and Solutions.* Presented at the Fugitive Emissions Symposium. Las Vegas, NV, August 15–16, p. 22.

Quality Tonnes. *QT's Approved CDM Methodologies, AM0023* (Reducing Gas Leaks in Pipeline Compressor Stations). www.qualitytonnes.com/methodologies4.htm. Accessed August 2, 2013.

Robinson, R., Gardiner, T., Innocenti, F., Woods, P. and Coleman, M., 2011. Infrared Differential Absorption Lidar (DIAL) measurements of hydrocarbon emissions. *Journal of Environmental Monitoring* 13.

RTI International, 2011. Emissions Estimation Protocol for Petroleum Refineries. www.epa.gov/ttn/chief/efpac/protocol/Emission_Estimation_Protocol_for_Petroleum_Refinerie_052011.pdf. Accessed August 2, 2013.

Scottish Pollutant Release Inventory Reporting (SPRI), 2013. Petroleum Activities Guidance Note 2013. www.sepa.org.uk/. Accessed August 2, 2013.

Shishlov, I. and Bellassen, V., 2012. 10 lessons from 10 years of the CDM (No. 37), Climate Report. CDC Climat Research, Paris.

United Kingdom Accreditation Service, 2012. M3003: the Expression of Uncertainty and Confidence in Measurement. Eds 3. United Kingdom Accreditation Service Middlesex, UK.

United Nations Framework Convention on Climate Change (UNFCCC), 1998. Kyoto Protocol to the United Nations Framework Convention on Climate Change.

2011. Approved baseline and monitoring methodology AM0023: Leak detection and repair in gas production, processing, transmission, storage and distribution systems and in refinery facilities. Clean Development Mechanism. http://cdm.unfccc.int/filestorage/L/V/8/LV8NU1GYWTK06COJPDIXQ35FR2MA47/EB63_repan14_AM0023_ver04.0.0.pdf?t=VTl8bXNqemo5fDCVM-mA_wKnFXslNdhFQKfT. Accessed June 3, 2013.

2012. Benefits of the Clean Development Mechanism. G.A. Kirkman, S. Seres, E. Haites and R. Spalding-Fecher, United Nations Framework Convention on Climate Change (UNFCCC). http://cdm.unfccc.int/about/dev_ben/about/dev_ben/ABC_2012.pdf. Accessed July 12, 2013.

2013a. *Project activities,* Data as of: December 31, 2013. CDM Insights. http://cdm.unfccc.int/Statistics/Public/CDMinsights/index.html. Accessed July 12, 2013.

2013b. *Project Search: Fugitive emissions from fuels (solid, oil and gas).* Clean Development Mechanism. http://cdm.unfccc.int/Projects/proj-search.html. Accessed August 2, 2013.

2013c. *Methodologies linked to sectoral scopes.* Clean Development Mechanism. http://cdm.unfccc.int/DOE/scopes.html. Accessed August 2, 2013.

United Nations Environment Programme and World Meteorological Organization (UNEP/WMO), 2011. Integrated Assessment of Black Carbon and Tropospheric Ozone. UNEP/WMO. ISBN: 92 -807-3141-6.

Wilwerding, J., 2012. LDAR Programs: friend or foe? HaaenSage Engineering. www.valve-world.net. Accessed August 9, 2013.

15 | Synthesis

VALENTIN BELLASSEN, NICOLAS STEPHAN,
MARION AFRIAT, EMILIE ALBEROLA,
ALEXANDRA BARKER, JEAN-PIERRE CHANG,
CASPAR CHIQUET, IAN COCHRAN, MARIANA
DEHEZA, CHRIS DIMOPOULOS, CLAUDINE
FOUCHEROT, GUILLAUME JACQUIER, ROMAIN
MOREL, RODERICK ROBINSON AND IGOR
SHISHLOV

This chapter brings together all the previous ones. Based on the detailed presentation and analysis of the MRV requirements of so many different carbon pricing and management mechanisms – hereafter "carbon pricing mechanisms," it synthesizes and compares how they answered to the five cross-cutting questions identified in the general introduction to the book:

- What are the MRV requirements?
- What are the costs for entities to meet these requirements?
- Is a flexible trade-off between requirements and costs allowed?
- Is requirements stringency adapted to the amount of emissions at stake (materiality)?
- What is the balance between comparability and information relevance?

15.1 MRV requirements across schemes

The first cross-cutting question – what are the MRV requirements? – is too large to be answered in a synthetic way. This section thus focuses on two components of this question that have a major impact on MRV costs: requirements pertaining to third-party verification and those pertaining to monitoring uncertainty.

Verification requirements are broadly similar across the board

Most carbon pricing mechanisms impose a verification of the reports by an independent third party. Verification requirements are broadly similar across carbon pricing mechanisms:

- the third party must be accredited by a regulator for GHG emissions audits and this accreditation tends to be sector-specific;
- the third party must assess whether the methods used and the reporting format comply with the relevant guidelines;
- the third party must assess the accuracy, i.e., the absence of bias, of the reported figures;
- the regulator is allowed to question the opinion of the auditor, but seldom does so;
- the third party tends to be paid directly by the verified entity.[1] Although this creates a potential conflict of interest, the risk of losing the accreditation is a much stronger incentive and keeps auditors from being complacent with their client (Cormier and Bellassen, 2013).

Some details may differ (Table 15.1). Verification frequency is one example: it tends to be annual for most entities at site/company scale whereas it is variable – up to the project proponent – at project scale. The emphasis put on individuals vs. firms also varies across schemes: UNFCCC accredited reviewers act in their own name, and so do auditors in California and Australia. Under the EU ETS[2] and the CDM, however, it is firms rather than individuals which are accredited, although one of the key criteria to obtain accreditation is of course to secure individual competence either internally or through long-term subcontracting.

The only schemes which stray away from these general observations are the schemes with little financial stakes: subnational inventories[3] and company-level footprints.[4] The latter are nevertheless often verified: verification is incited under the Carbon Disclosure Projects – verified respondents get a higher score within their transparency

---

[1] Random verification of a few entities only – as is the case for small projects under the Gold Standard and for small installations under the Australian Carbon Pricing Mechanism – is an exception: the auditor is then paid by the regulator. The verification of national GHG inventories under the UNFCCC is also not directly paid for by the countries under review.
[2] Member States have some leeway on the accreditation procedures for EU ETS verification. As a result, and although most countries accredit firms, some accredit individuals.
[3] Conducted under the EU covenant of mayors, the GHG Protocol or the Bilan Carbone Territorial.
[4] Conducted under the Carbon Disclosure Project or French regulatory framework (Grenelle I).

Table 15.1 *Verification requirements across carbon pricing mechanisms and management schemes*

Legend for the fourth column caracterizing the type of requirements.

		Standard or regulation	None	Focused on reporting procedures rather than reported figures	Variable frequency, accredited third party	Annual frequency, accredited third party	Verification requirements
Jurisdiction	National inventories	United Nations Framework Convention on Climate Change (UNFCCC)				■	Annual, performed by a team of UNFCCC accredited experts with the support of the UNFCCC Secretariat.
	Subnational inventories	GHG Protocol/Covenant of mayors/ Bilan Carbone Territorial	■				None. However, strongly recommended by all reporting guidelines and protocols.
	Jurisdictional REDD+	Verified Carbon Standard (VCS)			■		Variable frequency, performed by a UNFCCC or ISO accredited firm.
Site/ company	EU ETS	Monitoring and Reporting Regulation (MRR)/Verification Regulation (VR)				■	Annual, performed by a firm accredited by the relevant national authority.
	Waste sector in the Australian CPM	National Greenhouse and Energy Reporting Act (NGER)			■		Annual for large emitters, performed by a team of experts accredited by the national authority. Variable for others (sample-based, paid by the regulator).
	Imported electricity in the Californian ETS	Mandatory reporting of greenhouse gas emissions regulation (MRR)				■	All electricity importers must be annually verified no matter their size. However, in-depth verifications are only conducted once per compliance period (a few years), unless a specific risk is identified.

	Shenzhen ETS	Specification with guidance for quantification and reporting of the organization's greenhouse gas emissions (SZDB/Z 69)	Annual, performed by a firm accredited by the relevant authority (DRC).
Company-level footprint		French Grenelle II law –Article 75	None.
		French Grenelle II law – Article 225	Annual. Limited to completeness of information and "fairness." No detailed set of guidelines to verify the reports against.
		Carbon Disclosure Project (CDP)	None. 67% of companies voluntarily have their footprint verified, but even then the verification tends to be limited to "internal consistency." Verification increases the company's overall transparency score.
Offset project	Projects	Clean Development Mechanism (CDM)	Variable frequency, performed by a UNFCCC accredited firm.
	Agricultural N_2O projects	Climate Action Reserve (CAR)/VCS/ American Carbon Registry (ACR)	Variable frequency, performed by a UNFCCC or ISO accredited firm.
		Joint Implementation (JI) – France	Variable frequency, performed by a UNFCCC or EU ETS accredited firm.
	Reforestation projects	CDM	Variable frequency, performed by a UNFCCC accredited firm.
	Forest management VCS projects		Variable frequency, performed by a UNFCCC or ISO accredited firm.
	Fugitive projects	CDM	Variable frequency, performed by a UNFCCC accredited firm.

rating – and it is even mandatory for some companies under the French Grenelle II law (Article 225). Yet these verifications are peculiar: what matters are the reporting procedures of the company – do they ensure the internal consistency and "fairness" of the reported figures – rather than the accuracy and precision of the reported figures. In addition, the requirements on the expertise of the third party on GHG emissions is rather limited in these schemes: indeed, companies tend to use their financial auditors, which saves time as they are already familiar with the company structure and its accounts.

Requirements on monitoring uncertainty are seldom comprehensive

Sources of monitoring uncertainty are multiple. When calculation methods are used, there are as many sources of uncertainty as there are variables and parameters used in the calculation. Methods exist to combine the uncertainty from all sources in order to produce a comprehensive estimate (see for example GHG Protocol or IPCC GPG). Yet, carbon pricing mechanisms seldom set a requirement on the overall uncertainty of a given source. The case of direct measurement in the EU ETS is a notable exception. The EU ETS and a few offset project methodologies get close, as quantitative requirements are set on most sources of uncertainty – activity data and emission factors – involved in the calculation method. Most schemes also require a minimum calibration frequency when instruments are used. This frequency is often borrowed from existing national or international standards. The impact of calibration requirements on the actual uncertainty may be significant but is difficult to quantify across sectors and schemes (Warnecke, 2014).

However, the majority of carbon pricing mechanisms only set quantitative requirements on a few sources of uncertainty (Table 15.2). When financial stakes are low, that is, when mechanisms are primarily about accounting and tracking rather than directly pricing carbon, as in most jurisdictional schemes or for company-level footprint, the requirements are either qualitative – e.g., using a context-specific emission factor for major sources – or non-existent. Hence, most carbon pricing mechanisms and management schemes only exert partial control over the uncertainty that is reported.

15.2 Incentives to reduce monitoring uncertainty tend to be partial and indirect

Conservativeness: gap between principle and practice

MRV concepts and principles are often presented without significant attention to how they are applied in practice. *Conservativeness* is probably the most notable example and it perfectly illustrates this gap between theory and practice.

Conservativeness means that when the data are uncertain, a conservative value should be used so that emissions are not underestimated. This principle is often interpreted as an incentive to reduce monitoring uncertainty, often by adding one or two standard deviations to the estimate. If it were so, *conservativeness* would indeed provide an implicit incentive to reduce uncertainty.

But in practice, most of the rules in carbon pricing mechanisms do not discourage the use of default values or the uncertainty of the monitoring method (Table 15.3). For example, the UNFCCC guidelines for national GHG inventories allow for any type of uncertainty range, provided that the estimate is not biased. The EU ETS limits the uncertainty of some elements but does not reward further uncertainty reduction as long as the threshold is met.

The CDM Executive Board has yet to clarify and systematize its application of the conservativeness principle, except in the case of surveys and samples. Although some CDM tools and methodologies are already awarding fewer credits in proportion to reported uncertainty, this is not systematic. Many CDM methodologies provide an implicit incentive to reduce uncertainty by using conservative default values (Warnecke, 2014). Yet, these incentives remain limited for three reasons:

- In most cases, this conservativeness only concerns one or two parameters whereas the number of parameters involved in the calculation often exceeds ten (Chapters 13 and 14). These parameters were possibly chosen during the validation of the methodology as the most influential ones based on expert judgment. But this leaves out many sources of uncertainty whose importance has not been assessed in a systematic manner.
- Conservativeness is only applied to the most uncertain option out of three or four possible monitoring methods (e.g., UNFCCC, 2008).

Table 15.2 *Type of uncertainty requirements across carbon pricing mechanisms and management schemes*

Legend for column "type of requirements".

None	Qualitative (e.g., key categories should use a country-specific emission factor)	Quantitative, covering a few sources of uncertainty (e.g., sampling error shall be no greater than 10%)		Quantitative, covering most sources of uncertainty (e.g., total uncertainty shall be no greater than 2.5–10%)

For details on acronyms, please refer to Table 15.1.

		Standard or regulation	Formal requirements
Jurisdiction	National inventories	UNFCCC	Key categories must use at least Tier 2. General objective to reduce uncertainty over the long run.
	Subnational inventories	GHG Protocol/Covenant of mayors/Bilan Carbone Territorial	None.
	Jurisdictional REDD+	VCS	Accuracy of land classification must be at least 75%. If activity-based accounting (only baseline is monitored at jurisdictional level), a deduction is applied if the uncertainty of emissions factor exceeds 30%. If land-based accounting (full jurisdictional MRV), a deduction is applied if the total uncertainty of baseline emissions exceeds 50%. IPCC default emission factors (Tier 1) can only be used for sources representing less than 15% of total carbon stocks.

Site/company		
EU ETS	MRR	Uncertainty on activity data must be below 1.5–15%, depending on the the size of the emission source. Uncertainty requirements on emission factors may be qualitative (e.g., mandatory use of a given value) or quantitative (e.g., 1% for the carbon content of fuels, minimum frequency for fuel sampling, etc.). Overall uncertainty must be below 2.5–10% if a direct measurement approach is used.
Waste sector in the Australian CPM	NGER	No explicit requirements beyond a qualitative objective to minimize uncertainty. However, the relevant Australian or international measurement standards must be applied when facility-specific emission factors are used.
Imported electricity in the Californian ETS	MRR	Overall uncertainty of electricity meters at facility level must be lower than 5%. Otherwise, no requirements on the source of emissions itself beyond the proof of origin (NERC e-tag) and the requirements applied in the jurisdiction where electricity is produced (e.g., US EPA GHG Reporting Rule).
Shenzhen ETS	SZDB/Z 69	None yet specified. In addition, the use of default factors is always allowed, and therefore likely to be largely used since it is cheaper both *per se* and because it fits well with the existing reporting on energy use.
Company-level footprint	CDP/Grenelle II Article 225 & 75	None.

Table 15.2 (cont.)

Offset project	Projects	
	CDM	No explicit requirement in the overarching guidelines except for sampling and survey for which uncertainty must be below 10%. Subsector-specific calculation tools and methodologies may introduce either qualitative – through the mandatory use of a given method or meter – or quantitative requirements but none is systematic.
Agricultural N_2O projects	CAR/VCS/ACR	A deduction is applied if the uncertainty associated with the emission factor exceeds 15%. For activity data, projects rely on data reported and verified under other existing regulations which set their own requirements (e.g., federal or state BMP programs).
	JI – France	For activity data, projects rely on data reported and verified under the Common Agricultural Policy which sets its own requirements.
Reforestation projects	CDM	Depends on methodologies: either a fixed 10% maximum or a deduction based on the sampling error on tree biomass.
Forest management projects	VCS	In some methodologies, the overall uncertainty – including model errors such as allometry – is considered in the deduction factor. In others, the approach is similar to reforestation projects under the CDM and limited to sampling error.
Fugitive projects	CDM	If gas flow rate is measured (approach 2), a deduction is applied based on the uncertainty of gas flow rate measurement.

- An alternative method to the conservative default value is not systematically offered in the methodology. When this happens, a project proponent wishing to be rewarded for further reducing uncertainty will have to appeal to the Methodology Panel to revise the methodology. The resources – time and technical – necessary to undertake such a step represent a significant barrier.

Conservativeness is not a panacea

Nevertheless, there may be good reasons not to be conservative when monitoring emissions. One is that conservativeness gives a competitive advantage to larger installations or entities where economies of scale make it economically feasible to use fewer default values and more precise monitoring methods (see Section 15.3). In the EU ETS, this would exacerbate the distortion created by MRV costs and likely explains why the regulator has abstained from embedding conservativeness in the Monitoring and Reporting Regulation (MRR). In California, the default emission factor applied to imported electricity is rather generous: it corresponds to a clean gas power plant. This is the very contrary of being conservative, but it was likely necessary to avoid judicial proceedings from neighboring states for breaching the constitutional right to free interstate commerce (Cosbey et al., 2012). The EU faced a similar dilemma when setting an emission factor for oil produced from Canadian tar sands under the Fuel Quality Directive (Kokoni and Skea, 2014). In offset schemes, however, the risk of adverse selection offers a strong argument in favor of conservativeness.

Should there always be an incentive to reduce uncertainty?

Although generally rare, incentives to reduce monitoring uncertainty are embedded in a few carbon pricing mechanisms (Table 15.3). Some offset project methodologies for example discount the amount of credits issued in proportion to the overall monitoring uncertainty (e.g., VCS VM012 on improved forest management) or in proportion to the uncertainty of one component of the estimate (e.g., leak flow rate in CDM AM0023 on fugitive emissions).

These provisions may make sense in offset schemes which are vulnerable to adverse selection (Millard-Ball, 2013): project proponents who benefit from the error – because their monitored emissions reductions are by chance above the true value – are more likely to join than those whose emissions reductions are underestimated. This selection bias eventually produces an overestimate in the aggregated total, despite the random nature of each individual error.

However, economic theory and literature do not provide unconditional support for incentives to reduce uncertainty (Shishlov and Bellassen, 2014). In general, uncertainties tend to balance out rapidly with an increasing number of emission sources and therefore tend to be of little concern. Exceptions may emerge in specific cases of information asymmetry or when a scheme encompasses only a few large sources.

Indeed, the regulator should in theory worry more about bias than about precision. And in many configurations reducing the reported uncertainty does not reduce the risk of bias. To reduce the risk of bias, the *expert judgment* of independent and competent auditors remains the most suited approach.

In practice, there is no clear consensus among regulators on the importance of monitoring uncertainty. The European Commission cites the large uncertainty of waste emissions as one of the main reasons to keep the waste sector outside the EU ETS (European Commission, 2006) whereas it did not visibly hinder Australia from including it in its carbon pricing mechanism. Based on economic theory and the existing literature on this topic alone, it is not possible to clearly determine "who made the best choice."

15.3 MRV costs: large economies of scale

Economies of scale are the dominant feature of MRV costs, at least when these costs are compared on a *per ton of* CO_2e basis. These economies have an automatic component: the division of a given cost by a larger denominator; and an intended one: regulation, mandatorily applied to a large number of sources and entities, must not impose too heavy a burden on the complying entities as these cannot opt out.

MRV costs decrease with the comprehensiveness of the perimeter

The larger and the more comprehensive a scheme, the lower the MRV costs. Jurisdictional schemes tend to cover all sources within

Table 15.3 *Incentives to reduce monitoring uncertainty across carbon pricing mechanisms and management schemes*

Legend for column "type of requirements".

None	Qualitative (e.g., general principle of "continuous improvement")	Indirect (e.g., through a conservative emission factor) and quantitative, but covering only a few sources of uncertainty	Direct (e.g, deduction factor) and quantitative, covering most sources of uncertainty

For details on acronyms, please refer to Table 15.1.

		Standard or regulation	Requirements
Jurisdiction	National inventories	UNFCCC	Key categories must use at least Tier 2. General objective to reduce uncertainty over the long run.
	Subnational inventories	GHG Protocol/Covenant of Mayors/Bilan Carbone Territorial	None.
	Jurisdictional REDD+	VCS	If activity-based accounting (only baseline is monitored at jurisdictional level), a deduction is applied if the uncertainty of emissions factor exceeds 30%. If land-based accounting (full jurisdictional MRV), a deduction is applied if the total uncertainty of baseline emissions exceeds 50%. IPCC default emission factors (Tier 1) can only be used for sources representing less than 15% of total carbon stocks.
Site/company	EU ETS	MRR	None once the mandatory threshold is met. A principle of "continuous improvement" is nevertheless embedded in the MRR.

Table 15.3 (*cont.*)

Waste sector in the Australian CPM	NGER	Incentive to upgrade to method 2 when methane capture is higher than 75%.
Imported electricity in the Californian ETS	MRR	None, unless the source is cleaner than the emission factor for unspecified sources, in which case there is an incentive to upgrade to "specified source." Inversely, there is an incentive to maintain a high uncertainty "unspecified" status if the source is dirtier than the default emission factor.
Shenzhen ETS	SZDB/Z 69	None yet specified. On the contrary, the use of uncertain default factors is always allowed, and therefore likely to be largely used since it is cheaper both *per se* and because it fits well with the existing reporting on energy use.
Company-level footprint	CDP/Grenelle II Articles 75 & 225	None.
Offset project Projects	CDM	None in the overarching guidelines except for sampling and surveys for which the more conservative uncertainty bound must be used. Subsector-specific methodologies may introduce either explicit – deduction proportional to uncertainty – or implicit – choice between a conservative default value and a more precise and more costly monitoring method – but none is systematic.
Agricultural N₂O projects	CAR/VCS	A deduction is applied if the uncertainty associated with the emission factor exceeds 15%.

	ACR	A deduction is applied if the uncertainty associated with the emission factor exceeds 15%. Project proponent is allowed to come up with a project-specific emission factor. The conservative default emission factor provides an incentive to do so.
	JI – France	None.
Reforestation projects	CDM	In some methodologies, a deduction is applied based on the sampling error on tree biomass.
Forest management projects	VCS	In one methodology, the overall uncertainty – including model errors such as allometry – is considered in the deduction factor. In the others, the deduction is applied only based on sampling error.
Fugitive projects	CDM	If gas flow rate is measured (approach 2), a deduction is applied based on the uncertainty of gas flow rate measurement.

a jurisdiction which adds up to a large amount of GHG emissions. As a result, they exhibit much lower MRV costs than other schemes per tCO_2e.

However, even when the amount of emissions per entity is comparable, for example between cap-and-trade schemes and offset schemes, comprehensiveness pushes MRV costs down (Figure 15.1; Table 15.4). Indeed, company/site scale schemes tend to be mandatory and therefore to cover all entities that meet the inclusion thresholds (e.g., more than 20 MW for combustion installations under the EU ETS). As such, they must be especially careful with the costs they impose on regulated entities as these may distort the market (e.g., by putting higher costs on smaller entities) or even put unbearable burden on some firms (Warnecke, 2014). Conversely, offset schemes in which participation is voluntary cannot bankrupt participating companies through MRV costs: if they are too high, companies simply do not participate. In addition, one of the interests of running an offset scheme is to reveal information on abatement opportunities, monitoring techniques and costs (Bellassen and Alberola, 2014; Shishlov et al., 2012). In this context, there is a rationale for leaning towards higher MRV costs in order to obtain better information. This is likely why offset schemes tend to exhibit higher MRV costs than cap-and-trade schemes (Table 15.4).

MRV costs decrease with size

Even within the same scheme, MRV costs vary widely. A major factor explaining this variation is the size of entities (Figure 15.1). Indeed, fixed costs or costs that increase only slowly with entity size are numerous within MRV costs. Most monitoring and reporting costs are insensitive to size: a single monitoring report, methodology, project design document, national inventory report, etc. is needed per entity, no matter the amount it emits or reduces. In monitoring, the costs of a meter do not necessarily increase with the amount of material – electricity, fuel, gas, etc. – that it measures. Similarly, sampling costs only increase in proportion to the square root of the sampled population. The same goes for verification: a large part of the workload is proportional to the amount of documentation provided, which is largely independent of the amount of emissions at stake.

Table 15.4 MRV costs across carbon pricing mechanisms and management schemes

For details on acronyms, please refer to Table 15.1. The costs presented are averages of sometimes very wide ranges, most often obtained from company surveys or calculations by the regulator in the impact assessment of its regulation. See the relevant chapters for details.

		Standard or regulation	Cost per entity (€ yr⁻¹)	Cost per emission (€ tCO₂e⁻¹)	Share of verification in total MRV costs
Jurisdiction	National inventories	UNFCCC	800,000	0.02	22%
	Subnational inventories	GHG Protocol/Covenant of Mayors/Bilan Carbone Territorial	18,500	0.003	0%
	Jurisdictional REDD+	VCS	145,000	0.40	24%
Site/company	EU ETS	MRR	22,000	0.07	40%
	Landfills in the Australian CPM	NGER	4,862 (M&R only)	0.22	64%
	Imported electricity in the Californian ETS	MRR	73,000	0.14	not available
	Shenzhen ETS	SZDB/Z 69	no data	no data	no data

Table 15.4 (cont.)

		77,000[a]	no data
Company-level footprint	CDP/Grenelle II Article 225 & 75		
Offset project Projects	CDM	55,000	0.57	32%
Agricultural N$_2$O projects	CAR ACR/JI	no data no data	no data no data	
Reforestation projects	CDM	17,000	0.80	48%
Forest management projects VCS	Likely similar to CDM reforestation projects	Likely similar to CDM reforestation projects	Likely similar to CDM reforestation projects
Fugitive projects	CDM	167,000	0.22	15%

[a] Includes the costs of all MRV frameworks used by the surveyed UK quoted companies which in some cases report under the CDP, the EU ETS and the CRC at the same time.

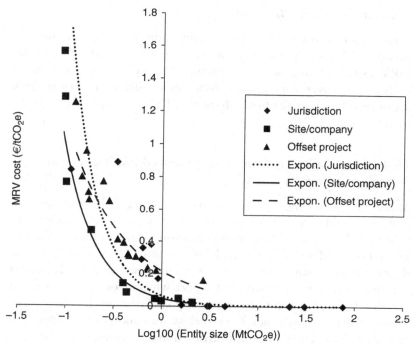

Figure 15.1 Economies of scale in MRV

Note: Each point corresponds to one of the (cost, size) pairs retained in the previous chapters of this book. It can be either an average for a given size range (e.g., EU ETS, CDM), or the estimated value for a specific entity (e.g., Germany's national GHG inventory, a specific jurisdictional REDD project, etc.). As a result, all points do not have the same representativeness.

After entity size, entity and sector complexity also plays into MRV costs (King et al., 2010). A large refinery with hundreds of pipes, connections and gas streams is more difficult to MRV than a simple power plant with a couple of boilers. Across schemes such as the EU ETS, the US EPA GHG Reporting Rule or the Californian ETS, refineries and cement factories face high MRV costs: although cement factories are large and benefit from the aforementioned economies of scale, their monitoring costs under the US EPA GHG Reporting Rule are two times higher than the overall average on a *per tCO₂e* basis (US EPA, 2009). Other types of industries are also impacted by their complexity, such as electricity importers.

The share of verification costs

Contrary to conventional wisdom, verification is usually not the main part of MRV costs. On average, it varies between 0 and 50% of total MRV costs, with most schemes around 25% (Table 15.4). Verification costs are, however, mostly fixed costs. For smaller sources or entities, it can therefore take the lion's share of MRV costs, up to 80% of the total (King et al., 2010).

15.4 "Materiality" is commonly practiced but it does not outweigh economies of scale

Materiality is a concept which comes from the audit industry: an auditor should focus on the riskiest parts of what is being audited. In other words, one should pay more attention to larger numbers than to smaller ones. Materiality has made its way into the verification procedures of most existing carbon pricing mechanisms: accredited auditors can only invalidate a monitoring report when errors exceed a given threshold (e.g., 5 percent of total facility emissions in the Californian Emissions Trading Scheme). Nevertheless, the concept of materiality is not taken into account in most jurisdictional schemes, either because verification does not take place – as is the case for most subnational inventories; or because the guidelines do not contain materiality provisions – which is the case for national GHG inventories (Table 15.5).

The concept of materiality could be extended beyond verification to monitoring and reporting: fewer resources should be spent on smaller sources than on larger sources, or on smaller facilities than on larger facilities. Many provisions exist in carbon markets and carbon taxes to balance stringency with the amount of emissions at stake: smaller facilities are usually not covered by the scheme, and even within the scheme, the uncertainty requirements or the reporting frequency is more lenient for these installations (Table 15.5). Yet, these provisions do not result in a level playing field. Economies of scale have the upper hand and larger facilities and offset projects end up with lower MRV costs per tCO_2e (see Section 15.3). And national GHG inventories ignore the concept: the requirements are almost as stringent for Slovenia as they are for Germany.

This is not to say that the existing "monitoring materiality" provisions are not useful: inclusion thresholds in particular are fundamental

Table 15.5 *"Materiality" across carbon pricing mechanisms and management schemes*

Legend for the fourth column caracterizing the type of materiality provisions.

More stringent requirements for smaller sources	No rules to adapt requirements stringency	Qualitative rules	Quantitative thresholds reducing stringency for smaller sources

For details on acronyms, please refer to Table 15.1.

	Standard or regulation	Rules to adapt requirements stringency to the amount of emissions at stake
Jurisdiction		
National inventories	UNFCCC	None beyond the key category analysis.[a]
Subnational inventories	GHG Protocol/Covenant of Mayors/Bilan Carbone Territorial	None.
Jurisdictional REDD+	VCS	Pools which are not expected to become sources compared to the baseline need not be accounted. Small source can be considered *de minimis* up to an overall 10% of emissions. Frequency of reporting and verification is flexible up to the minimum five year return. Materiality between 1% (large projects) and 5% (small projects) during verification.

Table 15.5 (cont.)

Site/company		
EU ETS	MRR	Inclusion threshold based on various criteria (e.g., thermal input > 20 MW) which can be quite low in terms of emissions (64% of installations below 25 ktCO₂e/yr and 30% below 5 ktCO₂e/yr). Simplified requirements for installations below 25 ktCO₂e/yr. Possibility to reduce stringency based on a cost/benefit analysis where benefit is a function of the amount of emissions at stake. Materiality between 2% (large installations) and 5% (small installations) during verification. Frequency of improvement report depends on installation size.
Waste sector in the Australian CPM	NGER	Inclusion threshold of 25 ktCO₂e/yr (or 10 ktCO₂e/yr in the vicinity of an already included landfill). Verification is only systematic for facilities above 125 ktCO₂e/yr. Smaller installations are verified on an arbitrary basis, at the expense of the regulator.
Imported electricity in the Californian ETS	MRR	No inclusion threshold for electricity importers: all have to report and verify their emissions, no matter how small they are. Materiality set at 5% of facility-level emissions during verification.

Shenzhen ETS	SZDB/Z 69	None.
Company-level footprint	Grenelle II Article 75	Inclusion thresholds (e.g., private companies with more than 500 employees).
	Grenelle II – Article 225	Inclusion thresholds (e.g., private companies with more than 500 employees and an annual income or assets worth more than €100 million).
	CDP	None.
Offset project	CDM	Reporting and verification frequency is up to the project developer. A minimal monitoring frequency is imposed based on reporting frequency. A higher monitoring frequency is therefore mandatory for larger projects which tend to opt for a high reporting frequency. Simplified requirements for small-scale and micro-scale projects. Materiality threshold during verification more gradual than EU ETS: from 10% (<20 ktCO$_2$e/yr) to 0.5% (> 500 ktCO$_2$e/yr).
Agricultural N$_2$O projects	CAR	For monitoring, it is the contrary: an uncertainty adjustment factor makes requirements more stringent for projects with fewer fields. Reporting must be done yearly or every two years for single-field projects. For site visit, it is the contrary: the percentage of fields that must be visited by the auditor is inversely proportional to project size. Materiality threshold of 5% during verification.

Table 15.5 (cont.)

	ACR/VCS/JI	Reporting and Verification frequency is up to the project developer. Materiality threshold between 1% and 5% for VCS during verification.
Reforestation projects	CDM	Emissions from forestry operations are considered *de minimis*. Pools which are not a source need not be accounted (in practice, only living biomass is accounted). MRV frequency is up to the project proponent. Materiality threshold between 0.5% and 10% during verification.
Forest management projects	VCS	Depending on the methodology, several sources may be considered *de minimis* (forestry operations, CH_4 and N_2O emissions from biomass burning, etc.). Depending on the methodology, some pools need not be accounted. In any case, pools which are not a source need not be accounted. MRV frequency is up to the project proponent. Materiality threshold between 1% and 5% during verification.
Fugitive projects	CDM	No specific rules beyond what applies to all CDM projects (see above).

[a] A materiality provision has recently been inserted in the revised reporting guidelines which will be implemented in 2015. Sources simultaneously below 0.05% of the national total and below 500 ktCO2e need not be estimated (decision 15/CP.17). Materiality is still absent from the verification of national GHG inventories.

in limiting costs. The US EPA (2009) assessed the effectiveness of a minimum threshold for inclusion in the perimeter of the regulation. Compared to the 25,000 tCO_2e/yr threshold retained in the US, a 10,000 tCO_2e/yr threshold would increase costs by 35% and cover only 1% more emissions. Conversely, decreasing the inclusion threshold to 100,000 tCO_2e/yr would save 23% of the costs and cover 2.5% fewer emissions.

15.5 Comparability often trumps information relevance

Comparability between entities reporting within the same carbon pricing mechanism is usually a top priority. Most mechanisms offer little leeway in terms of scope, level of source disaggregation and even monitoring method.

Schemes and management systems with limited constraints or financial stakes such as subnational inventories and company-level footprint are the notable exceptions. These entities are usually undertaking their MRV as a means to assess the effectiveness of their internal mitigation strategy. They therefore extensively use the large leeway offered by the relevant MRV guidelines to adapt the MRV procedures so that it suits their specific needs. Cochran (2010) illustrates this phenomenon with the GHG inventories of cities. For company-level footprint, however, the trade-off is a little more balanced: the possibility for outsiders to compare companies between one another and the repeated use of the same consultants within a sector to put together company-level footprints tend to foster comparability on Scope 1 – site-level emissions – and Scope 2 – electricity use. For Scope 3 – upstream and downstream emissions – however, company-level footprints remain very heterogeneous.

National greenhouse gas inventories under the UNFCCC lie somewhat in the middle. Countries must use a very strict reporting format which makes comparison easy. But the choice of monitoring methods is almost unlimited: countries are always offered the possibility to use a "Tier 3" method. "Tier 3" tends to be whatever model the country proposes as long as some general criteria – e.g., the model has been validated and published in the peer-reviewed literature – are met. Use of Tier 3 is fairly uncommon given that even the lower tiers offer significant leeway concerning acceptable activity data and emission factors. As a result, reported figures are not strictly comparable between countries, although verification, and in particular the use of comparison tools provided by the UNFCCC Secretariat, keeps heterogeneity within acceptable limits.

15.6 Staggering MRV vs. carbon pricing implementation

One last cross-cutting point may be noted: existing carbon pricing mechanisms do not all follow the same timing between the implementation of MRV rules and the introduction of formal carbon pricing. The EU ETS and all carbon offset schemes implemented these two simultaneously. While simultaneousness is probably unavoidable in offsetting, it has potentially large financial consequences when MRV rules are partly faulty: some projects have time to obtain windfall profits before the loophole in the MRV framework can be fixed. A similar argument can be put forward for the EU ETS: the over-allocation which took place over 2005–2007 was primarily due to the lack of reliable, MRVed, historical emissions data when the regulator set the cap.

To the contrary, the Kyoto Protocol, the Australian Carbon Pricing Mechanism and the Californian ETS all began with a few years of "MRV only" before the actual carbon pricing came into force. Although this interaction has not been directly addressed in the book, adopting this kind of stepwise approach seems sensible.

15.7 Conclusion

Through the chapters of this book, the reader has come across many more issues and lessons regarding MRV and its economic stakes than the aforementioned five cross-cutting issues. To name but a few:

- The general tendency of putting little **confidentiality** on the reported data is tremendously helpful to policy-makers, researchers and the general public. But this transparency may be used to obtain commercially sensitive information on the reporting companies. This is why reported data are confidential in Shenzhen where the problem is particularly acute as companies are asked to report their added value as well as their emissions.
- The notion of **legacy emissions** for emissions from waste that was deposited in a landfill before a new owner/manager takes charge. In Australia, the new person in charge takes responsibility for them.

The same concept could apply to other emission sources such as forestry or soil carbon.

• The MRV of emissions which occur **outside the regulator's jurisdiction** such as emissions from imported electricity in California. The dilemma here is how much a regulator can mandate within the boundaries of inter-state or international commerce regulation. All regulators considering a border carbon adjustment will face this issue.

Although these issues and many others are worthy of discussion and illustration with real examples, they are somewhat specific to a few sources and carbon pricing mechanisms, and as such they are not addressed in this synthesis chapter.

Regarding our five cross-cutting questions, however, one can conclude that conventional wisdom on MRV is not often promoted in existing carbon pricing mechanisms. One would intuitively encourage quantitative requirements on emissions uncertainty, together with an incentive to improve precision. Most often, this is only partially applied, if at all. Further, the time and resources spent on small sources of emissions would be expected to be limited. While this kind of "materiality" is widespread, the softened rules for smaller sources are largely outweighed by economies of scale: in all schemes, MRV costs are primarily driven by the size of the source. The larger the source, the lower the cost.

This is not to say that existing MRV rules are ill-devised. First, conventional wisdom may be wrong. Economic models indeed struggle to justify the usefulness of incentives to reduce monitoring uncertainty when dealing with many, small sources. Second, some phenomena, such as economies of scale, may be beyond the control of the regulator. MRV rules which create no market distortion are likely an unreachable grail.

Another cross-cutting conclusion to this study is that MRV rules significantly differ not only between "scales," but also within them: the EU, Australia, California and Shenzhen have set different MRV rules in their respective site-level carbon pricing mechanisms. Five thousand sites with emissions lower than 25,000 tCO_2e per year are MRVed under the EU ETS while verification is only mandatory for sites emitting over 125,000 tCO_2e in Australia. The scope of the EU ETS is limited to heat and power generation and some industrial processes while the transportation sector, imported electricity and waste are included in some of the other schemes. Shenzhen even double-counts emissions from electricity.

This is a logical consequence of a world rapidly evolving from a "Kyoto top-down" approach to mitigating climate change towards a multiplicity of bottom-up carbon pricing initiatives. Will these MRV differences lock the world into incompatible frameworks with different carbon prices? Not necessarily. When considering whether to link two carbon pricing mechanisms, mutual confidence in their respective level of ambition will likely be pivotal for the regulators involved. And this confidence can be obtained with reliable MRV procedures on both sides even if they are not strictly equivalent. Only time will tell.

Bibliography

Bellassen, V. and Alberola, E., 2014. *European Offset Projects: A tool to rally Poland towards the 2030 Energy Climate Package*. Tendances Carbone 1.

Cochran, I., 2010. A use-based analysis of local-scale GHG inventories (No. 2010–7), Working paper. CDC Climat Research, Paris.

Cormier, A. and Bellassen, V., 2013. The risks of CDM projects: how did only 30% of expected credits come through? *Energy Policy* 54: 173–183.

Cosbey, A., Droege, S., Fischer, C., Reinaud, J., Stephenson, J., Weischer, L. and Wooders, P., 2012. A Guide for the Concerned: Guidance on the elaboration and implementation of border carbon adjustment (No. 03), Policy Report. Entwined, Stockholm.

European Commission, 2006. Inclusion of additional activities and gases into the EU-emissions trading scheme, Review of the EU emissions trading scheme. European Commission, Directorate General for Environment, Brussels.

King, K., Pye, S. and Davison, S., 2010. *Assessing the Cost to UK Operators of Compliance with the EU Emissions Trading System*. Aether, Abingdon, UK.

Kokoni, S. and Skea, J., 2014. Input–output and life-cycle emissions accounting: applications in the real world. *Climate Policy* 14: 372–396.

Millard-Ball, A., 2013. The trouble with voluntary emissions trading: uncertainty and adverse selection in sectoral crediting programs. *Journal of Environmental Economics and Management* 65: 40–55.

Shishlov, I. and Bellassen, V., 2014. Review of monitoring uncertainty requirements in the CDM (No. 16), Working paper. CDC Climat, Paris, 33pp.

Shishlov, I., Bellassen, V. and Leguet, B., 2012. Joint Implementation: a fron-
tier mechanism within the borders of an emissions cap (Climate Report
No. 33). CDC Climat Research, Paris.

UNFCCC, 2008. Tool to calculate project or leakage CO_2 emissions from
fossil fuel combustion.

US EPA, 2009. *Regulatory Impact Analysis for the Mandatory Reporting of
Greenhouse Gas Emissions Final Rule (GHG Reporting)*. United States
Environmental Protection Agency, Washington, DC.

Warnecke, C., 2014. Can CDM monitoring requirements be reduced while
maintaining environmental integrity? *Climate Policy* 14(4): 443–466.

Index

Printed in the United States
by Baker & Taylor Publisher Services